Mao and the Chinese Revolution

Man and the Coming Era

Mao and the Chinese Revolution

by JEROME CH'ÊN
Lecturer in Asian History in the University of Leeds

with Thirty-seven Poems by Mao Tse-tung
translated from the Chinese by
MICHAEL BULLOCK and JEROME CH'ÊN

London
OXFORD UNIVERSITY PRESS
NEW YORK · KUALA LUMPUR
1965

Oxford University Press, Amen House, London E.C.4
GLASGOW NEW YORK TORONTO MELBOURNE WELLINGTON
BOMBAY CALCUTTA MADRAS KARACHI LAHORE DACCA
CAPE TOWN SALISBURY NAIROBI IBADAN ACCRA
KUALA LUMPUR HONG KONG

Frontispiece © Brian Brake—Magnum

Printed in Great Britain by
Hazell Watson & Viney Ltd
Aylesbury, Bucks

for Victor

臨川羨洪波

同趾憂赤源

Contents

PART TWO

Thirty-seven Poems by Mao Tse-tung
translated from the Chinese by
MICHAEL BULLOCK AND JEROME CH'ÊN

List of Maps

Abbreviations

CCP   The Chinese Communist Party
KMT   The Kuomintang
PLA   The People's Liberation Army
SW   *The Selected Works* of Mao Tse-tung

NOTE: The numbers in the footnotes refer to the Selected Bibliography on pages 392–410.

Part One

Mao and the Chinese Revolution

by JEROME CH'ÊN

Foreword

THE term 'Maoism' is a handy coinage of Western, or more precisely, of Harvard scholars, which has now gained wide circulation. Its meaning has been defined in the writings of Professors B. Schwartz, C. Brandt, and J. K. Fairbank. Professor K. A. Wittfogel, however, thinks that it is no more than a myth, a legend lacking the attributions made by his Harvard colleagues. Useful as they are, Wittfogel's views are not entirely fair and his researches are punctiliously textual rather than factual. It would not be justifiable to lose sight of, say, Professor Schwartz's interest in 'Mao's groping toward the [Maoist] strategy'.

Hitherto, Western scholars have tended to consider Mao's chief innovation to be his reliance on the peasantry while leaving out of account 'the establishment of rural bases and the build-up of a peasant-based Red Army'. The Chinese communist leaders and historians, on the other hand, regard Mao's works on the strategic problems of the Chinese revolutionary wars as the essence of his writings. Indeed, both Hu Ch'iao-mu and Ho Kan-chih[1] go so far as to say that 'to start the revolution first in the countryside by means of armed struggle, establishing bases and increasing their number and size, and then to encircle and subsequently seize the cities' is the 'law' of the Chinese revolution. They and other Chinese writers have refrained from describing Mao's theories as 'Maoism'. Instead, they call them *Mao Tse-tung ssu-hsiang*, suggesting that the honour of suffixing *ism* (*chu-i*) to a personal name should be reserved for more original and more systematic doctrines such as Marxism and Leninism.

1. [14] 196 and [179] 92.

Up to now, the study of Maoism has not been related to Mao's personal experiences, the nature of Chinese society in the twenties and the thirties, and the Chinese revolutionary wars. Yet the close connexion between all of them cannot be denied, and I have been particularly concerned to give full weight to them. I do not claim to have made more than a beginning in this respect, for the limitations of my knowledge and the unavailability of some source materials prevent the book from becoming, in any sense, definitive.

Unanswered Questions

The book attempts to show, among other things, Mao's penetrating understanding and adroit handling of problems and the brilliance of both his words and his actions. The way he has held the CCP together through its changing fortunes, and the poems he has dedicated to his memories of Ch'angsha, Liu Ya-tzu, and the 'Immortals', indicate that he can be a good friend, but his ruthless struggles against opponents and foes demonstrate his formidable qualities as an enemy. In the later stages of the civil war he repeatedly instructed his troops to 'finally and completely wipe out the reactionary forces'[2] and to 'annihilate resolutely, thoroughly, wholly and completely all the Kuomintang reactionaries'.[3] He warned his comrades that 'the enemy will not perish of himself',[4] and that 'the Chinese people will never take pity on snake-like scoundrels'.[5] To his enemies he offered no mercy but sarcasm such as:

the 'ten-year Communist-annihilation campaign' failed to bring about anything resembling a capitalist society under bourgeois dictatorship—is it possible that there are still people wanting to have another try? It is true that the 'ten-year Communist-annihilation campaign' has brought about a 'one-party dictatorship', but it remains only a semi-colonial and semi-feudal dictatorship. As a result of the four years' 'Communist-annihilation' (from 1927 to the Incident of September 18, 1931), a 'Manchukuo' came into being and after another six years of it, in 1937, the Japanese imperialists were able to invade China proper. If anyone were to try today to start an 'annihilation' campaign for another

2. [46] IV, 1364 or *SW* IV (Peking), 288.
3. [46] IV, 1452 or *SW* IV (Peking), 388.
4. [46] IV, 1379 or *SW* IV (Peking), 301.
5. [46] IV, 1382 or *SW* IV (Peking), 304.

ten years, it would have to be a new type of 'Communist-annihilation', somewhat different from the old one. Yet is not there already one who, light of foot, has out-stripped all others and boldly undertaken its new enterprise of 'Communist-annihilation'? That one is Wang Ching-wei, who has already become a 'celebrated' new-style anti-Communist figure.[6]

The simplicity of Mao's life and his fatherly kindness to those working under him conform to the Chinese traditional ideals of leadership or kingship; yet there are habits and styles of work he dislikes intensely. He has no taste for 'cumbersome formalities and ceremonies',[7] nor for boastfulness.[8] In *Combat Liberalism* he denounces these idiosyncrasies:

To indulge in irresponsible criticism in private, without making positive suggestions to the organization. To say nothing to people's faces, but to gossip behind their backs; or to say nothing at a meeting, but gossip after it. Not to care for the principle of collective life but only for un-restrained self-indulgence.

Things of no personal concern are put on the shelf; the less said the better about things that are clearly known to be wrong; to be cautious in order to save one's own skin, and anxious only to avoid reprimands.[9]

Since 1927 he has never allowed himself to sink into such muddle-headedness as 'devoting 70 per cent. effort to expansion, 20 per cent. to coping with the KMT Government, and 10 per cent. to fighting the Japanese'.[10] And about those who have studied abroad but failed to acquire the ability to think critically, he says:

They play the role of a talking-machine and forget their duty of under-taking and creating new things.[11]

On the subject of studies, Mao is definitely utilitarian, having no patience with learning that has no practical value. Comparing knowledge with arrows, he mocks at those who 'with the arrows in their hands, are only caressing them, exclaiming ecstatically, "What a fine arrow! What a fine arrow!" but will never let it fly.'[12] There can be no doubt that Mao knows how to use his

6. [46] II, 675 or *SW* III, 126.   7. [46] I, 67 or *SW* I, 83.
8. *Vide infra*, p. 80.   9. [46] II, 347 or *SW* III, 74.
10. Chang Kuo-t'ao's interview with R. North [164] and Chow Ching-wen, *Ten Years of Storm*, tr. by Lai Ming, N.Y., 1960, 8–9 and 33.
11. [46] III, 818 or *SW* IV, 15.   12. [46] III, 842 or *SW* IV, 36.

knowledge. His analytical power, astute judgement, and pugnacious tenacity are responsible for his political eminence.[13]

Although he embraced Marxism as early as 1919 when he was twenty-six, he did not take up arms against the authorities until 1927. For twenty-two years he fought relentlessly, through the defeat in 1934–5, the Long March, the United Front, and the civil war, to his final victory. The sustaining power is partly due to the malevolence of the KMT persecution and partly to the hatred which is so essential a part of Mao's personality.

Some attribute the intensity of Mao's hatred to the harsh treatment he suffered at the hands of his father, others suggest that it was aroused by his early reading of such novels as *The Water Margin* (*Shui Hu*). I think rather that its origin is to be found in his reading of Darwin, Rousseau, J. S. Mill, and F. Paulsen, which broadened his vision and encouraged him to break away from obsolete tradition. Revolutionary literature by anarchists and Marxists later suggested how the emancipation of his nation could be achieved. His own experience and observation of injustice, poverty, and incessant civil war further increased his indignation. There can be no other rational explanation of his persistent hatred. No one can sustain such hatred without continually seeking a way to end it. Thus Mao's hatred sharpened his vision and enabled him to see beyond the thing he hated so much a new China, the China he wanted to create, which would be independent, free, peaceful, united, and above all, strong and prosperous.

The Chinese people will see that, once China's destiny is in the hands of the people, China, like the sun rising in the east, will illuminate every corner of the land with a brilliant flame, swiftly clean up the mire left by the reactionary government, heal the wounds of war and build a new, powerful and prosperous people's republic worthy of the name.[14]

Or:

once the cock has crowed and all beneath the sky is bright.[15]

This was nothing new. The demand for a powerful and prosperous China had been voiced in the 1860s and throughout the ensuing decades. The difference lay in the means whereby strength and

13. [164].   14. [46] IV, 1470 or *SW* (Peking), 408.
15. *Vide infra*, p. 344.

prosperity were to be achieved. The earliest leaders of the self-strengthening movement[16] prescribed the modernization of China's defence—'strong warships and efficient guns'; the second generation[17] added economic wealth to the recipe. Then came the Sino-Japanese War of 1894–5 and China's ignominious defeat which utterly discredited the self-strengthening policies. What remained unchanged, however, were the ultimate aims of these policies. The third generation[18] gave priority to an administrative reform, aiming at the transformation of China's autocracy into a constitutional monarchy; this, too, failed. Representing the fourth generation, Dr. Sun Yat-sen and Chiang Kai-shek led their revolutions in 1911 and 1926–8 by which they hoped to establish a republic which would at the same time be democratic and conform to the Confucian tradition. Coming to power after the Russian Revolution and at the time of the world economic depression, Chiang's policies were constantly interrupted by civil wars, the communist challenge, and the Japanese aggression. The defeat of Japan with the help of the Allies in 1945 meant that China, for the first time in fifty years, was free from the haunting shadow of her aggressive neighbour, but by that time the 'spectre of communism' had grown to such a menacing size that neither Chiang's military strength nor his will power was enough to exorcise it. Chiang's departure and Mao's inauguration did not mean a change in the immediate aims of China's policies, for what Mao wanted in 1949, as he still does now, was a powerful and prosperous country. In this sense Mao represents a new generation of the century-long self-strengthening movement.

Parallel to the development of the self-strengthening movement was the under-current of China's peasant movement, beginning in the recent past with the T'aip'ing Rebellion, which ravaged the southern half of China for fourteen years, and continuing with the Nien Rebels and the Boxers in the closing decades of the nineteenth century. All these rebels[19] distrusted the Government's ability to fulfil its promise of a strong and prosperous China. The

16. Lin Tse-hsu, Tseng Kuo-fan, and Tso Tsung-t'ang, etc.
17. Li Hung-chang, Chang Chih-tung, Liu K'un-yi, and others.
18. K'ang Yu-wei and Liang Ch'i-ch'ao, for example.
19. The Boxers were initially anti-dynastic.

T'aip'ings and the Niens wanted to overthrow the Manchu régime and replace it with one of their own, in order to end social injustice and put the country on a more solid basis; the Boxers, believing in magic powers, tried to oust foreign influence in China. These rebels followed the traditional pattern of the peasant revolt, a protracted military struggle from one or several base areas with the poor peasants as their main supporters.[20] Mao also relied on the poor peasants in waging a protracted war against the authorities from one or several revolutionary bases. In this sense, Mao was the leader of a new generation of insurgent peasants.

Mao differs, however, from both the self-strengthening leaders and peasant insurgents of the past in that he is a Marxist-Leninist seeking to strengthen his country by the application of Marxist-Leninist doctrines to Chinese conditions. In his view, China could not become powerful and wealthy until she was freed from imperialist and feudal bondage.[21] He believed that the only force strong enough to bring about her emancipation was a Marxist party supported, in theory, by urban workers and rural peasants, but, in practice, mainly by peasants, especially armed peasants. By relying on the peasantry, he is said to have Sinicized Marxism. However, as I shall show, it is by the adoption of the Chinese traditional pattern of the peasant revolt, and by developing a system of strategy and tactics around it in order to realize Marxist-Leninist aims, that he has made his greatest contribution to Marxist thinking and Sinicized communism.

Here I must admit that the question of the precise relationship between the traditional peasant revolt and the Maoist pattern of revolution remains unanswered. Further researches into this are badly needed, and I am conscious of being unable to supply a complete answer.

Because he is a Marxist, Mao differs from other Chinese revolutionaries in yet another sense. His revolution, essentially a military one, also has far-reaching cultural implications. The reforms prior to the 1911 Revolution started with firearms, spread to industries and railways, and finally raised the demand for a constitution. The revolutions of 1911 and 1926–8, aiming at

20. See [46] II, 619 or *SW* III, 75–6.
21. The KMT agreed with this.

democratic republicanism, were accomplished much too quickly. They absorbed so many opportunistic elements into the ranks of the revolutionaries that both the revolutions lost their social meaning. From another point of view, one may see how in the process of reform and revolution China borrowed from the West. The borrowing began with weapons, then extended to machinery and means of transport, and finally to political and legal institutions. Even the pattern of revolution was borrowed from France and Russia. Both the reformers and the revolutionaries felt the need for talented and trained people (*jen-ts'ai*), but, apart from sending students to study abroad, they seemed to be unaware of the importance of an adequate policy of training cadres. Without well-trained and incorruptible cadres to form the middle and lower echelons of the civil service, all the high-minded objectives of a revolution would be lost. Here Mao borrowed from Stalin and the Russian Party the policy of training cadres. Moreover, because of his reliance on politically backward peasants, Mao had to find ways to arouse them, such as the reduction of rent and interest rates and the redistribution of land. So he attacked the vested interests of the land-owning class and has in fact dismantled the traditional structure of Chinese society.

Mao's social revolution does not stop here. He is a feminist, treating women as the equals of men and expecting them to live up to such treatment.[22] He is fully aware of the value of science, though without much understanding of it himself. Literature and the arts he believes should serve the people, the labouring people, and the Chinese should in learning from other nations be selective, discarding the 'undesirable', bourgeois elements. He advocates borrowing from abroad, but is opposed to 'wholesale Westernization'.[23] What is borrowed must be 'integrated with the characteristics of the nation and given a definite national form before it can be useful.'[24] He himself has given the Marxist revolution in China a national form and expects others to do the same to sciences, literature, and the arts.

Before Mao's views on human relations and propriety can be fully understood, more must be known of Chinese communist

22. [46] I, 33 or *SW* I, 45.   23. [46] II, 700 or *SW* III, 154-5.
24. [46] II, 700 or *SW* III, 154.

law, and this is the second problem that I shall not attempt to solve in this book.

The national form of the Marxist revolution in China cannot fail to have international implications and Mao himself is fully conscious of these. He has said:

Thus the protracted and extensive Anti-Japanese War is a war of jigsaw pattern in the military, political, economic and cultural aspects—a spectacle in the history of war, a splendid feat of the Chinese nation, a *world-shaking* achievement.[25]

The turn of the Chinese People's War of Liberation from the defensive to the offensive cannot but gladden and inspire *these oppressed nations. It is also of assistance to the oppressed people now struggling in many countries in Europe and the Americas.*[26]

And:

This is a victory for the people of all China, and also a victory for *the peoples of the whole world.*[27]

What he has in mind may be the application of the Chinese, and his own form of revolution, to other backward countries. The basis of this form or pattern, according to Mao, is the uneven development of a large and populous country, which is caused by an under-development of industries and communications.[28] Therefore at places where there are transport difficulties and the Government's control is weak the communists can set up base areas from which to wage a protracted war. The Mao pattern is consequently an extension of the Leninist theory of the weakest link. Lenin justified the outbreak of a revolution in Russia, rather than in an industrially advanced country, by saying that it was in Russia that the bourgeois control was weakest. Mao likewise justified his reliance on the poor peasants when waging a protracted war from revolutionary bases by saying that it is at places where the control of the Government is the weakest that the sparks of revolution can be lit.

The weakest link alone is not enough; there must also be a large group of pauperized and discontented peasants. The plethora of poor peasants in China in recent years was, in all probability, the

25. [46] II, 463 or *SW* II, 196. My italics.
26. [46] IV, 1244 or *SW* IV (Peking), 158. My italics.
27. [46] IV, 1468 or *SW* IV (Peking), 406. My italics.
28. [46] I, 181–2 or *SW* I, 193–4.

result of the extortions and civil wars of the warlords and the dislocations and upheavals caused by the Resistance War and the hyper-inflation. That Chinese society underwent drastic changes between 1911 and 1949 is beyond question. Mao himself studied these changes and drew his conclusions, and his success may justify his views. Nevertheless, his studies are not comprehensive and his arguments crude. A fuller understanding of this question can come only from a thorough study of Chinese society, and especially of the changes in the villages, during this period. This question is the third that I have not attempted to answer fully.

What are Mao's merits and demerits as a ruler? is the fourth question which remains unanswered for the simple reason that the *terminus ad quem* of the book is fixed at 1949. History shows that an able revolutionary is not always an able ruler. I may, however, draw the reader's attention to the following pointers. On 15 April 1947, Mao's directive to P'eng Te-huai regarding the north-west campaign ended with this sentence: 'Please reply whether you consider the above views sound.'[29] About his plan for the Man-churian campaign in September 1948, he asked Lin Piao: 'Please consider the above and telegraph your reply.'[30] Before the Hsü-chow campaign he gave 'a few points' for Liu Po-ch'eng and Ch'en Yi to 'consider'.[31] Having explained his strategy for the Peking-Tientsin campaign, he asked Lin Piao and Nieh Jung-chen: 'What are your views on this plan? What are its short-comings? Are there any difficulties in its execution? Please consider all this and reply by telegraph.'[32] Despite the personality cult that makes him awe-inspiring, he was not peremptory.

Mao's Classical Training

Born a year before the Sino-Japanese War and brought up through the 1898 Reform, the 1900 Boxer Uprising, the 1911 Revolution, innumerable civil wars,[33] and the 1919 May 4th Movement, Mao could not but be influenced by the trials and failures of those years. He himself has described the process thus:

29. [46] IV, 1222 or *SW* IV (Peking), 134.
30. [46] IV, 1339 or *SW* IV (Peking), 264.
31. [46] IV, 1355 or *SW* IV (Peking), 279.
32. [46] IV, 1370 or *SW* IV (Peking), 292.
33. From 1912 to 1928 Hunan had only three years of peace.

From the time of China's defeat in the Opium War of 1840, Chinese progressives went through untold hardships in their quest for truth from the Western countries. . . . Chinese who then sought progress would read any book containing the new knowledge from the West. . . . In my youth, I too engaged in such studies.[34]

But 'imperialist aggression shattered the fond dreams of the Chinese about learning from the West. It was very odd—why were the teachers always committing aggression against their pupil?'[35] After 1917, 'the salvoes of the October Revolution brought us Marxism-Leninism. The October Revolution helped progressives in China, as throughout the world, to adopt the proletarian world outlook as the instrument for studying a nation's destiny and considering anew their own problems.'[36]

Being a Hunanese, Mao was in his youth under the influence of the patriotic and pragmatic school of Wang Fu-chih. As a man of action, Wang once led a contingent to resist the Manchu Army in 1648 and, as a scholar, he had a keen sense of history. He was against the restoration of ancient institutions[37] and went as far as to say that even human nature had to adapt itself to the constantly changing environment.[38] 'What is not yet completed,' according to Wang, 'can be completed; what is already completed can be reformed.' Much of his knowledge came not only from reading but also from observation.[39] Mao has inherited these views of Wang Fu-chih perhaps indirectly through Yang Ch'ang-chi.[40] His *Selected Works* also quote from the Confucian classics such as *The Book of Rites*, *The Analects*, *The Golden Mean*, and *Mencius*, from Taoist tracts such as *The Tao-te Ching* and *Lieh-Tzu*, from the Han dynasty works such as Prince Liu An's *Huai-nan Tzu* and Tung Chung-shu's *Discussions on the Spring and Autumn Annals*, and frequently from the great work on strategy, *Sun Tzu*. Mao's knowledge of Chinese history comes chiefly from Tso Ch'iu-

34. [46] IV, 1474 or *SW* IV (Peking), 412.
35. [46] IV, 1475 or *SW* (Peking), 413.
36. [46] IV, 1475 or *SW* IV, 413.
37. Wang Fu-chih, *Chou-i Wai-chuan*, 5.
38. Wang Fu-chih, *Shang-shu Yin-i*, ch. 3, 'T''ai-chia', 2.
39. Wang Fu-chih, *Wen-ssu-lu Wai-p'ien*, 'T''an T'ien P'ien' and 'Shuo Jih P'ien'.
40. About Mao's early schooling, see also Stuart R. Schram, *Mao Ze-dong, une étude de L'éducation physique*, Paris 1962.

ming's *Commentary on the Spring and Autumn Annals*, Ssu-ma Ch'ien's *Chronicles*, Liu Hsiang's *Dialectics of the Warring States*, Pan Ku's *History of the Han Dynasty*, and Ssu-ma Kuang's general history, *Tzu-chih T'ung-chien*. He is also well-versed in the essays of Han Yü and Liu Tsung-yüan of the T'ang dynasty, poems by Sadul of the Yüan dynasty, and the *Precepts for Household Management* by Chu Po-lu of the Ming dynasty. Though not a reader of European novels, he refers to *Aesop's Fables* and F. Fadeyev's *Destruction*, and among popular Chinese novels he quotes often from *The Water Margin*, *The Monkey*, *The Red-chamber Dream*, and *The Romance of the Three Kingdoms*. He is particularly fond of Lu Hsün's satirical essays and stories and is full of praise for them.

These books could hardly have failed to affect his way of thinking. From them he acquired his knowledge of other peasant revolts, his ideals of leadership, and his concept of friendship. The last of these may have accounted for his treatment of opponents in the CCP like Li Li-san, Ch'in Pang-hsien, Wang Ming, and Chang Kuo-t'ao, and perhaps also for the absence of bloody purges, except for the Fut'ien Incident of 1930, in the history of the CCP.

Source Materials

In writing this book, I have relied heavily on Edgar Snow's *Red Star over China* and Professor B. Schwartz's *Chinese Communism and the Rise of Mao*, the former, written in 1936–7 when the world had just begun to take notice of Mao, being the embodiment of an able journalist's sensitivity and objectivity and the latter the fruit of a scholar's painstaking research and penetrating judgement. Robert Payne's *Mao Tse-tung, ruler of Red China* was published shortly after Mao came to power, and is a work of uneven quality.

There are two recent books on Mao published in England: one calls him a red barbarian and the other the Emperor of blue ants, as if in the exotic East even barbarians compose poetry and prose and ants have emperors instead of queens. About them a quotation from Goethe seems appropriate:

> *Ach Gott! die Kunst ist lang,*
> *Und kurz ist unser Leben.*

There are however several extremely useful works on Mao in Chinese. Li Jui's *Mao Tse-tung T'ung-chih ti Ch'u-ch'i Ke-ming Huo-tung* (Comrade Mao's early revolutionary activities), although admittedly written from the Marxist point of view, is nevertheless a well-documented book with several items of previously unpublished material. This is an indispensable work for any student of this subject, and should be translated into English. Hsiao San's *Mao Tse-tung T'ung-chih ti Ch'ing-shao-nien Shih-tai* (Comrade Mao's boyhood and youth) is an account of Mao by a schoolfellow and close friend and is much better than Siao Yu's *Mao Tse-tung and I Were Beggars*.

The frequent appearance of [46] in the footnotes shows my dependence on Mao's *Selected Works*. I have collated the Chinese version with its English translations and found no glaring discrepancies. However, I must hasten to add that I am in no position to compare the essays in the *Selected Works* with their earlier versions. I have incorporated Professor R. C. North's and Professor K. A. Wittfogel's textual studies of the report on the Hunan peasant movement, but would not go so far as to say that *The Selected Writings of Mao Tse-tung* has been revised to show that Mao was farsighted and to make what he said correspond with what later developed.[41] A recent work by Professor Hsiao Tso-liang—*Power Relations within the Chinese Communist Movement 1930–1934*—throws considerable light on the period it covers, and itself is a textual study. Stuart R. Schram's monograph, which has already been referred to, C. Johnson's book on Chinese peasant nationalism and communist power, and H. L. Boorman's article on Mao in the January issue of the *China Quarterly* are works of importance, but, alas! published too late for me to make full use of them in this study.

The publication of many reminiscences in the *Hung-ch'i P'iao-p'iao* and *Hsing-huo Liao-yüan* by commanders like Liu Po-ch'eng and Yang Ch'eng-wu and Mao's doctor and bodyguards fills many gaps in the understanding of Mao's personal and political life. These have been selected, collated, and used with care in this book. A list of books and articles by and about Mao is given in the bibliography. I am fully aware of its deficiencies but

41. Chow Ching-wen, *Ten Years of Storm*, 51.

can only hope that in the near future other scholars will remedy them.

Acknowledgements

Many friends have given me encouragement and guidance in the writing of this book, for which I am deeply grateful. I would like to mention, in particular, Mr. E. Grinstead of the Department of Oriental Manuscripts and Printed Books of the British Museum and Mr. J. Lust of the Chinese Library of the School of Oriental and African Studies, whose kind assistance in arranging books and microfilms made my task so much easier. Mr. A. C. Adie of St. Antony's College, Oxford, Mr. H. L. Boorman of Columbia University, Mr. J. Gray of the School of Oriental and African Studies, Mr. R. Harris of *The Times*, and Dr. Victor Purcell (to whom this book is dedicated) of Cambridge read the manuscript and made numerous detailed and helpful criticism.

I must also thank Mr. R. C. Halfhide, F.R.G.S., for drafting the maps for me, and my wife for typing and checking the manuscript. Her companionship, care, and patience have been for years an indispensable part of my life and work.

Method of Writing

Finally, I would like to say a few words about the writing of this book. It is not, I hope, a 'political' book, although it deals with politics and military affairs. It is intended to be a dispassionate analysis of Mao's life and times; it is not a straightforward biography, for it is impossible to separate Mao from the intricacies of Chinese politics and warfare. It does not aim at praising or belittling Mao's achievements, either. As his career is far from ended, it seems premature to judge him, his contributions, or his place in history. I am merely concerned to ascertain and set in order the facts about his childhood, his brothers and sister, his marriages, the kind of books he reads, and the mysterious and little-known period of his life from 1923 to 1927. The last mentioned leads me to examine the entire question of the first united front, particularly the Stalin-Trotsky controversy, the Left Wing KMT, and the beginning of so-called Maoism. The schism between the KMT and the CCP from 1927 to 1937 completely changed the course of the communist movement in China, and it is in the chapters on this period that I come to the central theme of this book—the Maoist pattern of revolution. It is my opinion that the controversies between Mao on one side and Li Li-san, Wang Ming, Ch'in Pang-hsien, and Chang Wen-t'ien on the other centred on this question and Mao's final victory at the Tsunyi Conference was an occasion of historic importance. I am glad to read in Professor Schwartz's article, 'On the "Originality" of Mao Tse-tung' (*Foreign Affairs*, October 1955), that he also has accepted the importance of this conference.

The Long March has already become a saga, and the facts are confused by legend. In the chapter on this subject I have tried to get to the root of the matter and to show that as the March was not planned beforehand, at each stage there was a different destination in view. My interpretation is made possible by the memoirs of those who took the journey and by the Russian translation of the *Chung-kuo Kung-nung Hung-chün Ti-i-fang-mien-chün Ch'ang-ch'eng Chi, Veliki pokhod*, Moskva, 1959, which has perhaps the most detailed itinerary of the March available. The itineraries at the back of this book (Appendix C) are considerably shorter and simpler than the Russian one and, unlike the latter, they show the wanderings of Chang Kuo-t'ao's army after crossing the Yellow River at Chinyüan in Kansu.

Before the publication of Chang Kuo-t'ao's own memoirs, there is little one can say about the disputes between Chang and Mao; but I have tentatively suggested the reasons for Chang's defeat. In dealing with the Resistance War period, I have concentrated on the stalemate after 1939, regarding it as the turning-point in the KMT's fortunes, and my comparative study of Mao's *New Democracy* and *Coalition Government* and Chiang's *Destiny* will, I hope, throw some light on the difficulties after 1945. The final chapter on the civil war begins with a lengthy comparison between the two major parties, which, at the same time, explains the astonishing defeat of the KMT. The choice of the *terminus ad quem* of 1949 is made for two reasons: it is obviously the end of an era and it is also the limit of my knowledge and experience of the subject.   J.C.

March 1963

Chapter I

The Impressionable Age

THE village of Shaoshanch'ung is about twenty-eight miles to the west of the riverine market town of Hsiangt'an in Hunan. Most of the townsmen made their living from trade, with the Hsiang River as the artery through which not only merchandise but also new ideas flowed.[1] Although the province was (and still is) rich in both agricultural and mineral resources, its inhabitants were impoverished, as well as toughened, by the intermittent wars, unrest, and natural catastrophes in the 1850s and 1860s during the T'aip'ing Rebellion and before and after the 1911 Revolution. The province was strategically important too, for any army attempting to unify China had to drive through the Hsiang River valley either northward to Wuhan or southward to Canton—a fact that had contributed much to the trials and tribulations of the Hunanese. The T'aip'ing rebels in 1850s, the troops of the warlords in 1915–25, and Chiang Kai-shek's expeditionary army in 1926 all fought through this valley in their pursuit of conquest. It was in such an environment that Mao Tse-tung was born on 26 December 1893.[2]

His father, Mao Shun-sheng, was a tall, strong peasant, but poor and heavily in debt, and he joined the army in order to escape his creditors. A year later he returned home to become a dealer in pigs and rice, and, managing to save a little money, he bought two and a half acres of land. From this modest beginning, aided by a strong character, industry, thrift, and astute management, he improved his fortunes. He married Wen Ch'i-mei from the neighbouring town of Hsianghsiang, who gave him three sons,

1. [43] 5.   2. [43] 5.

Hunan

HUPEI

Yangtze R.

Yüehchow

Ch'angsha

Shaoshan ✕

Hsiangt'an

Hsianghsiang

Anyüan

P'inghsiang

Hengshan

Hengyang

Hsiang R.

Lingling

HUNAN

KIANGSI

KWANGSI

KWANGTUNG

PEARL R.

0   50   100   150   200
MILES

Tse-tung, Tse-t'an, and Tse-min, and a daughter, Tse-hung.[3] The family consumed some 84 bushels of rice each year, leaving a surplus of 65 bushels as their savings, with which Mao Shun-sheng bought an additional acre. This enabled the family's income to increase to nearly 224 bushels and their savings to 140 bushels a year. The father did not re-invest his increased savings in more land; instead, he lent them to others at usurious rates of interest. Soon his monetary capital reached the impressive sum of 2,000 or 3,000 *yuan* (£200 or £300).[4]

Mao's mother, a woman of medium height with a square face, kind eyes and a kind heart, was marked out by strong moral feelings, a readiness to help the less fortunate, and a deep-rooted faith in the gods. She was a hardy woman, spending her day in cooking, weaving, mending and darning, washing, and gathering fire-wood.[5] In contrast to her love and kindness, the father was stern, despotic, and high-handed. Mao Tse-tung felt a filial loyalty to them both, but was more closely attached to his mother.

This sharp contrast in their characters was, however, nothing unusual in Chinese family life: the father expected to be the strict master of the house and the mother the loving mistress. In this way they complemented each other in handling awkward situations. And it was in such an interplay of contrasts that Mao Tse-tung and his brothers grew up.[6]

3. Robert Payne ([50] 25) and Edgar Snow ([258] 173) say that Tse-hung was the name of a son and Payne also says that the *hung* is the *hung* for 'red'. If so, it is a curious name for a boy. Snow also names Tse-ming [*sic*] as a brother ([258] 360), thus making four brothers in all. Payne, however, does not mention Tse-min at all, in spite of the fact that Tse-min was an important communist. Hsiao San ([39] 3) states that Mao Tse-tung's brothers were Tse-min and Tse-t'an. He does not mention Tse-hung. Here I follow Hsiao and attribute the name Tse-hung to the sister who was killed in 1930.

4. [39] 3, [43] 5–7, and [258] 127.

5. [39] 7–8 and 18, [43] 8, and [258] 126.

6. In his own accounts to Snow, Mao made play with this contrast as an illustration of the working of Hegelian dialectics ([258] 125–9). More recently his European biographers tended to use it for their 'psychoanalysis' of Mao. In fact, the contrast existed in almost every Chinese family. It was quite an ordinary thing for a child to be thrashed by his father and then comforted by his mother. Propriety was learnt in this way; few were brought up differently. At school and at play, the children knew how their companions were treated at home. A sore backside was nothing to be ashamed of, and was not likely to cause abnormal mental development. To attribute Mao's later rebelliousness to the

From his early childhood, Mao had shown a tendency to be thorough. His father once sent him and one of his younger brothers to pick beans. The younger and cheekier of the two chose to work on the plot where beans were planted sparsely. A little while later when their father came and saw that the younger one had finished picking the beans over a much larger area than Mao Tse-tung, he said that he was pleased with him. But on looking closer and finding out that there were in fact more beans in the elder son's basket, he made no further remark.[7]

Mao began to work on his father's land at the age of five.[8] Two years later he was sent to a tutor (such tutors were generally scholars incapable of achieving a more successful career) to be taught how to read and write, so that he might be able to keep accounts and write letters. But reading opened a new world to the child, who now discovered that popular novels such as *The Monkey*, *The Water Margin*, and *The Romance of the Three Kingdoms* were far more enthralling than the arid volumes of the classics.[9] He soon developed an interest in books. But in the mornings and evenings he continued to lend a hand in the fields.[10]

At about ten years of age, Mao began to fight back in his own way whenever he felt that he was being unjustly treated by his father. Such disobedience was a quality that was lacking in an ordinary Chinese boy of his age. Once his father criticized him in the presence of several guests, saying that he was 'lazy and gluttonous'. Angered by this, Mao argued with his father and swore to leave home there and then. He set out along the path between the two ponds in front of his house while his mother chased after him, calling him to come back. He told her that he would jump into the water if his father carried out his threat to beat him. That evening when tempers had cooled down, his mother began her work of mediation and the violent quarrel was finally patched up by Mao apologizing to his father.[11] At about the same time his tutor also administered corporal punishment to

severe punishment given by his father in childhood is to make a very superficial application of the theories of psychology.

In this study both the Hegelian and the 'psychoanalytical' approaches are rejected.

7. [39] 9.   8. Six, according to the Chinese calculation.

9. [39] 10–11 and [43] 5.   10. [258] 128.   11. [39] 20–1.

him, causing him to run away from the school. Fearing that worse punishment might be waiting for him if he returned home, he decided to go to Hsiangt'an. But he lost his way and walked in circles in the hills for three days before his father's men found him. After this 'strike', as Mao himself called it, both his father and tutor became milder in their attitudes. About the same time, too, modern schools were being built at temple sites by more progressive educationists, as a result of which the clay or wood images were destroyed or boarded up. This left an ineradicable impression on Mao's young mind,[12] which had earlier received religious indoctrination from his mother. The destruction of the idols unsettled Mao and made him sceptical.[13]

Two serious famines occurred in Hunan at the beginning of this century.[14] The first, in 1906, was caused by a flood. Mao was then thirteen years of age, still being taught by the same tutor. One day he and other boys heard from rice merchants returning from the provincial capital, Ch'angsha, that rice riots had taken place and that the government offices had been stormed by the rioters. The new governor[15] ordered the execution of those who had participated in the disturbances. Mao, his mind filled with romantic admiration for rebels as described in *The Water Margin*, sympathized with the rioters.[16]

Soon afterwards he left his tutor to work full time on his father's farm. He weeded the fields, looked after cattle and pigs, and kept the books, as he was now the scholar of the family.[17] Since he was working as an adult, he was eligible to receive eggs, fish, and a little meat for his food on the first and the fifteenth day of every month while his mother and brothers were not. On other days there were only rice and vegetables.[18] By now he had grown as tall and as strong as his father.[19]

Now that Mao was physically well-developed, his parents, as was customary, found him a wife and Mao was married in 1907 to a girl four years his senior. According to Mao himself, the

12. [39] 18 and [258] 128.   13. [43] 7 and [258] 130–1.
14. [74] ch. 82, 8413b.
15. Ts'en Ch'un-ming, who took office on 4 September 1906 and was dismissed on 17 April 1910, when the second famine occurred. [67] 217–22.
16. [39] 16–17, [43] 7, and [258] 133.   17. [39] 6–7 and [43] 6.
18. [39] 6–7.   19. [54] 6.

marriage was never consummated, and so he later repudiated it.[20]

After the 'marriage', Mao continued to work on his father's land for another three years. One autumn, during the harvest, rain came and there was a rush to collect the thrashed rice into the granary. Mao, instead of helping his father, assisted his tenants. This angered his father and an argument ensued.[21] But Mao's contention was that the tenants were poorer and needed more help. Another argument between them concerned Mao's studies. Though nearly seventeen years of age, Mao wanted to go to a primary school in his mother's home town, Hsiang-hsiang; his father, however, was opposed to it, for he would lose an able-bodied worker on his farm. Eventually Mao's wishes prevailed.

This was in the spring of 1910 when the second famine, caused by a drought, came. It was so grave that it had attracted nation-wide attention.[22] Once again, there were rice riots and the Manchu Government in Peking, in addition to dismissing the governor of Hunan, took emergency relief measures to check the rapidly worsening situation. In spite of these steps, the poverty endured by the peasants was not eased as the year passed, and groups of paupers were still to be seen when Mao went round to collect debts for his father during his winter holiday. On his way back from one of these errands, he met some tramps and gave them the money he had just collected.[23] After the holiday, when he was on his way to the school, he met a young man in thin and shabby clothes shivering in the snow. Mao engaged him in conversation and ended by giving the young man a thick gown.[24]

The Tung-shan Primary School of Hsianghsiang, was a modern-style school of some repute and it was a county school for which only the children of residents were eligible. Mao was admitted there on the strength of his mother's being a native of the county. He impressed his teachers by his literary gifts and learnt from them the classics as well as history, geography, and natural sciences. He was considered an outstanding boy because of his well-written essays; but, as in the private school of his tutor

20. [258] 144–5.   21. [39] 8 and [258] 129.
22. [26] April and May 1910. This important periodical published two long reports on the famine.
23. [39] 9 and [44].
24. [39] 8.

where he had studied earlier, his interest was concentrated more on extra-curriculum reading. He relished an anthology of biographies of the heroes of the West such as Washington, Napoleon, Peter the Great, Wellington, and Gladstone, as he did also the writings of the reformers such as Cheng Kuan-ying, K'ang Yu-wei, and Liang Ch'i-ch'ao,[25] which aroused his patriotism. It was at this school that he met the Hsiao brothers—Siao Yu and Hsiao San—who became his close friends and later his biographers.[26]

His year at the primary school drew to its end in the summer of 1911 and in that summer Mao sat for the entrance examination of the Hsianghsiang Middle School in Ch'angsha. He was selected and made his way to the capital city, where he was to witness and take part in the first revolution in China in this century.[27]

He was then eighteen.

25. [43] 6–7. Cheng Kuan-ying, though a reformer, did not take part in the famous Hundred Days Reform in 1898. In that year, however, he published his widely read book, *Sheng-shih wei-yen*, which advocated reforms in many aspects of Chinese life, including the election of a parliament, the adoption of European methods of education, the publication of newspapers, the development of industries, and so on ([69] I, 39–129). K'ang Yu-wei and Liang Ch'i-ch'ao were the leaders of the Hundred Days Reform. The tremendous fame they enjoyed during their life-time and after their deaths renders comment upon them unnecessary. It will suffice for me to mention only that students of Mao's generation were nearly all influenced by the brilliance of Liang's books and essays.

According to Li Jui ([43] 6–7), Mao was particularly fond of the *Sheng-shih wei-yen* and the *Hsin-min ts'ung-pao*. He also read some pamphlets on the ways and means to save the Chinese nation and to restore China's past glory. He was then a patriot, also a constitutional monarchist. This tallies with Snow's report ([258] 134–5).

26. Siao Yu is the author of [54] and Hsiao San (Emil Hsiao) of [39]. See also [258] 134. Hsü T'e-li, their teacher, has also mentioned the Hsiao brothers in his reminiscences of Wang Jo-fei ([280] 209).

27. [43] 9.

Chapter II
'The Turbulent Years'

CH'ANGSHA was the place where the province and the empire met; it was also the place where a young scholar could broaden his outlook.

A generation earlier, at the end of the T'aip'ing Rebellion in 1864, the political and intellectual life of the empire as a whole was dominated by such eminent Hunanese as Marquis Tseng Kuo-fan, Marquis Tso Tsung-t'ang and General Hu Lin-i. In 1865 five out of the eight viceroys were Hunanese,[1] and young and talented people of the province were posted all over the country to form the middle and lower echelons of the civil as well as the military services. Marquis Tseng himself an outstanding scholar, together with Kuo Sung-t'ao, Wang Hsien-ch'ien and others, carried on the tradition of patriotism and the pragmatic scholarship of Wang Fu-chih (1619–92) and made it the predominant trend of contemporary Chinese thought. That was in the 1860s and 1870s. In the closing decades of the nineteenth century the foremost figure in central China was Viceroy Chang Chih-tung, who, while upholding traditional values, adopted Western technology in a continued endeavour to strengthen China. But Chang was a northerner. His ascendancy symbolized only the waning influence of the Hunanese. Indeed, in the 1890s the Hunanese influence in national politics was confined more or less to the imperial capital. In 1907 Chang Chih-tung was recalled to Peking to become a Grand Councillor while his viceroyalty was

1. These were Liu Ch'ang-yu (Chihli), Tseng Kuo-fan (Liangchiang), Yang Yüeh-pin (Shenkan), Tso Tsung-t'ang (Minche), and Mao Hung-pin (Yün-kwei). See [67] 135.

given to a Han-Chinese of little importance, as a caretaker, and finally to a Manchu.

When the leaders' influence waned, the followers' discontent waxed. The policies pursued by Tseng Kuo-fan, Tso Tsung-t'ang, Li Hung-chang, and Chang Chih-tung[2] were discredited by the shattering defeat China suffered at the hands of the Japanese in 1895. Thereafter China entered into a period of political chaos which lasted until 1928, or, in other words, from the time when Mao Tse-tung was two to the time when he was thirty years of age. To understand him it is necessary to understand this period.

The war and peace of 1895 put an end to China's suzerainty over Korea and her sovereignty over Taiwan (Formosa) and Penghu (the Pescadores). In addition, she agreed to pay an indemnity of 200 million taels of silver in eight instalments, which virtually rendered her maritime customs to a debt-collecting house for Japan, and to allow the Japanese, or by applying the most-favoured-nation clause, many other nations as well, to build factories on her soil, thus inaugurating a period which Lord Salisbury termed the 'Battle of Concessions'. However, the war's more profound effects were the sense of panic that now seized upon the Chinese mind and the absolute bankruptcy of the policy known to historians as the 'Self-strengthening Movement' or the 'T'ung-chih Revival'.[3]

Therefore new approaches to national strength and prosperity had to be sought. The peasants, relying on black magic, promoted an anti-foreign movement, the Boxer Uprising of 1898–1900, which ended in disaster.[4] The gentry and scholars advocated an administrative reform, culminating in the Hundred Days Reform of 1898 which also ended disastrously. The conservatives, led by the ageing Dowager Empress and many of her courtiers, sought to stem the tide by adopting foreign technology while preserving China's own traditions, pinning their hopes on the creation of a modern army under the command of one Yuan Shih-k'ai. But seven years after the abortive reform the Russo-Japanese War

2. The Self-strengthening Policies. See M. C. Wright, *The Last Stand of Chinese Conservatism*, Stanford, 1957.
3. [84] 45–6. The account of the events before 1916 in this chapter is based on this book.
4. See [64] and [76].

thoroughly convinced the Chinese Government of the necessity of a constitution, for, in Chinese eyes, Japan's victory was the victory of a constitutional monarchy over an autocracy. From 1906, therefore, the Manchu Court embarked on an attempt to draft and adopt a constitution which, it was hoped, would serve to pacify the growing demand for revolution and increase Manchu control over the provinces. Powerful Han-Chinese viceroys, such as Chang Chih-tung and Yuan Shih-k'ai, were recalled and replaced by men of lesser stature.

Two years later the Dowager Empress died, having outlived the young emperor Kuang-hsü by less than twelve hours. Enthroned immediately after was a minor of two years of age whose father, Prince Ch'un, was proclaimed the Regent and continued to consolidate the powers of the Manchu Cabal, first by sending the most powerful of the Han-Chinese ministers, Yuan Shih-k'ai, home to convalesce after 'an affection of the foot', and next by trying to nationalize the railways. One of the reasons why the nationalization programme was conceived was to find securities for foreign loans which were needed to meet the Government's financial demands, particularly its defence budget. In this endeavour, the Regent had the support of Chang Chih-tung and Sheng Hsüan-huai.

The dismissal of Yuan Shih-k'ai epitomized the Regent's striving to gain firm control over the modern troops. In addition, he also brought home a large number of Chinese army cadets trained in Japan. His plan was to use the railways as security against borrowing from abroad and the loans to finance army expansion, so as to strengthen his régime. In fact, both policies hastened its fall.

At this point we must consider a contemporaneous development —the revolutionary movement under the leadership of Dr. Sun Yat-sen. Its origin was again to be found in the 1894–5 war. If the birth of a new China needed a midwife, Japan seemed to have been always willing to act in this capacity. Not once, but twice she played that role, since one of the major results of the 1895 war was the 1911 revolution and of the 1937–45 war the 1949 revolution.

At the height of the 1894–5 war Dr. Sun Yat-sen visited

Tientsin where the redoubtable viceroy, Li Hung-chang, kept his state and directed the war. Sun presented to Li a letter advocating reform measures which were not very different from those of K'ang Yu-wei and Liang Ch'i-ch'ao. Li, being preoccupied by the war, understandably shelved the letter. Having thus been coldly received by the administration, Sun went to Hawaii and formed his first revolutionary organization, the China Revival Society, consisting mostly of members of secret societies. When the Hong Kong branch of the society was established in 1895 its constitution included the political aim of 'Driving out the Tartars'. Thus its reliance on the secret societies, which had always been anti-Manchu, was made abundantly clear and, from the Manchu Government's point of view, it was subversive. An order for Dr. Sun's arrest was thereupon issued and Sun was compelled to live abroad for several years. His headquarters were in Tokyo, the place where political refugees from China congregated. Among the latter were the Hunanese T'ang Ts'ai-ch'ang, Huang Hsing, Sung Chiao-jen, and Ch'en T'ien-hua.

In 1900 T'ang Ts'ai-ch'ang went back to Hupei and Hunan to enlist the help of local secret societies for an uprising in Wuch'ang. The secret of his plan was betrayed and T'ang was captured and executed by the Government.[5] About three years later Huang Hsing returned to Hunan, and, with the help of one T'an Yen-k'ai,[6] founded the Ming-te School in Ch'angsha which, like many other modern schools in Hunan at that period, was a centre of revolutionary activities. Both Sung Chiao-jen and Ch'en T'ien-hua were Huang's followers. The revolutionaries in Hunan were 400 or 500 strong and they formed the Hua-hsing Society for scholars and the T'ung-ch'ou Society which acted as a liaison with the secret societies. Their plan was to stage an armed uprising on the Dowager Empress's birthday in November 1904. Two of the members who took part in the preparations for this plan were

5. [62] I, 253 *et seq.* About the anti-Manchu activities in Hunan, see [71] chapters II and V.

6. (1876–1930), son of T'an Chung-lin (Viceroy of Shenkan from 1881 to 1888), *chin-shih* 1904, Hanlin compiler for a short period, speaker of the Hunan provincial council, Chief of Military Affairs 1911, Governor of Hunan 1912–13, and in later years twice more Governor of Hunan. See [7] 1923, 855 and [27] 1925, 703–3.

arrested in Hsiangt'an and so the uprising had to be cancelled. Huang Hsing himself, with the help of an Anglican clergyman, escaped to Japan.[7]

In 1905 another uprising was attempted, this time by Li Hsieh-ho and his Huang-han Society at Paoch'ing. Once again the secret of the plan leaked out and the attempt was forestalled.[8] In the wake of these failures came the 1906 famine. Fishing in troubled waters, the miners of P'inghsiang in Kiangsi and the garrison of Liling, supported by the secret societies of Liuyang in Hunan, rose up against the provincial authorities, but were soon put down by government troops.[9]

Dr. Sun, in the meantime, took steps to unify the revolutionary groups by establishing in Tokyo in 1905 the Alliance Society which was the direct forerunner of the KMT. As most of the members of the new society were also members of secret societies, a major policy of Dr. Sun's was to strengthen its ties with such societies in China. Another was to develop its membership and propaganda among the ranks of the modern troops, particularly among the Japanese-trained officers. Five underground headquarters of the society were set up on the Chinese mainland; one of these, at Hankow, was the revolutionary nerve-centre of central China including Hunan. This centre of operations made spectacular progress among the lower-ranking officers in the 8th Division under Chang Piao and in the 21st Mixed Brigade under Li Yüan-hung. This was the situation in 1906 and 1907 when Mao Tse-tung was still studying under his tutor in Shaoshan and Viceroy Chang Chih-tung had just been recalled to Peking.

As the viceroy of Hupei and Hunan, Chang Chih-tung initiated but left unfinished the construction of the Hankow–Canton railway which was to provoke violent disagreements between the Ministry of Communications in Peking and the gentry in Hunan. This projected railway was, according to its original plan, to have been built with the capital of the shareholders of Hupei, Hunan, and Kwangtung. The Hunan section of the line was the longest, cutting right across the province from north to south; but Hunan was in comparison the poorest of the three provinces. The financing of

7. [62] I, 503–4 and [70] 85–6.
8. [62] I, 530.   9. [62] II, 464.

this section was therefore a really difficult problem which, in Chang's view, could only be solved by foreign loans. Chang Chih-tung died in 1909. Two years later, when the first Cabinet in Chinese history was formed, Sheng Hsüan-huai became the Minister of Communications with the avowed policy of nationalizing all the railway trunk lines of the empire. This unpopular decision antagonized the gentry class of Hunan (also of Szechwan) whose most vocal spokesman was T'an Yen-k'ai.

Thus in 1911, when Mao Tse-tung walked to Hsiangt'an to take a steamer down the Hsiang River to Ch'angsha,[10] a revolutionary united front between the higher and lower classes of the province was in process of formation. The gentry and scholars had organized a society in aid of the Hunan railway, an institute for the study of self-government, a 1911 club, and a society of physical culture, and had founded several modern-style primary, middle, and teachers' training schools.[11] The lower classes and soldiers grouped themselves into numerous anti-Manchu societies, most of them now under the banner of Dr. Sun's Alliance Society.

With the changes in political reality, the intellectual climate in Ch'angsha also changed. The political thought of the conservative Hunanese[12] and of the northerner, Chang Chih-tung, was openly admitted to be obsolete by the issue of the 1906 edict in favour of a constitutional monarchy. Thereafter the once subversive theories of K'ang Yu-wei and Liang Ch'i-ch'ao, and particularly those of the Hunanese philosopher T'an Ssu-t'ung, became the fashion of the period. Liang had been to Hunan and taught at the School of Current Affairs in Ch'angsha in 1897,[13] and T'an, the martyred reformer of 1898, was among the most influential political thinkers of modern China. The essence of their teaching was that dynastic rule must be preserved while drastic reforms were introduced.

But the trend of events in the opening decade of the present century tended to invalidate even the theories of K'ang, Liang, and T'an. The Regent's pronouncements in favour of a constitution had a ring of falsity in them, the appointment of a Manchu as the viceroy of Hupei and Hunan was regarded with strong

10. [39] 34–5.   11. [62] IV, 551–2.
12. Such as Wei Yüan, Tseng Kuo-fan, Tso Tsung-t'ang, Kuo Sung-t'ao, and Hu Lin-i.   13. [69] IV, 173.

suspicion, and the decision to nationalize the railways was received with resentment. So in Hunan, as in other provinces, a new
generation of intellectuals emerged; among them were the
Hunanese Sung Chiao-jen and Ch'en T'ien-hua. They were
revolutionaries, violently anti-Manchu and ardently supporting
Dr. Sun's political ideas. In their eyes, the erstwhile leaders
Tseng, Tso, Hu, Chang, K'ang, and Liang were traitors to the
Han-Chinese interests and worthy targets of abuse. The days for
reform had gone; the preponderant demand at the end of the
decade was for a revolution with the overthrow of the Manchu
Government as its final objective.

This new trend of thought may not have penetrated into the less
enlightened corners of Hunan; but when Mao arrived at Ch'angsha,
one of the first publications he read was the *People's Strength*, an
organ of the Alliance Society.[14] In great excitement, he wrote an
essay and stuck it on a wall of the Hsianghsiang Middle School.
The essay was a compromise between his old belief in K'ang and
Liang and his new adherence to Sun's prototype Three Principles
of the People, and it proposed that the monarchy should not be
preserved any longer but that a republic be established with Sun
as the president, K'ang the premier, and Liang the foreign
minister. The naïvety of this proposal was obvious, and understandably it was the last time that its author spoke in favour of
K'ang and Liang.[15]

Soon after this, on 22 October, the revolution broke out in
Ch'angsha, twelve days after the Wuch'ang Uprising of the modern
troops of the 21st Mixed Brigade and the 8th Division under the
leadership of General Li Yüan-hung. In Hunan, the revolutionary
leaders were Chiao Ta-feng and Ch'en Tso-hsin, prominent
members of the local secret societies.[16] Three days later, the
provincial revolutionary government was set up with Chiao as the
governor and Ch'en as his deputy. The only modern brigade in
Hunan joined forces with the revolutionaries.[17] Chiao and Ch'en,
being men of humble origins, commanded little respect among the
gentry. Hence, when the military phase of the uprising was over,
dissension began to appear within the new ruling circles. The

14. [39] 34.   15. [39] 35.
16. [62] IV, 553.   17. [63] 437 and 439.

general situation was confused, aggravated by the refusal of the people to accept the paper currency issued by Chiao's government.[18] On 31 October there was a mutiny during which Chiao and Ch'en were killed and after which T'an Yen-k'ai was elected to succeed Chiao as the governor. With financial and other support from the gentry, T'an managed to stabilize the situation. In this he was also helped by the development of the revolutionary war in other provinces. The indications were that the Manchu régime was crumbling and T'an was able to take the opportunity to consolidate his government through the reorganization of his military forces. In this he was aided by General Chao Heng-t'i, a Kwangsi soldier who had earlier led a brigade to the assistance of his comrades in Hupei and was now transferred to Hunan,[19] and in a few days some fifty thousand men were recruited. The original strength of one brigade had by now grown to four divisions.[20] Mao shaved off his queue and joined these forces.[21]

Mao was a private and remained so until 15 February 1912,[22] when Dr. Sun Yat-sen agreed to concede the presidency of the newly founded Republic to Yuan Shih-k'ai. His pay amounted to 7 *yuan* (or 14*s*.) a month, most of which he spent on newspapers. His normal duties included taking part in the daily drill, cooking, and carrying buckets of water. He also wrote letters for his messmates.[23]

Now that the dynasty had fallen, Yuan Shih-k'ai had begun his incumbency as the President of China, and the revolution was over, Mao found no reason to remain in the army. Upon his demobilization, he was at once faced with the problem of choosing a career. He thought of learning a trade, such as soap-making, or of joining the police force, but neither appeared to him a good way of strengthening his country. He searched for opportunities in the classified columns of newspapers and was attracted by the advertisement of a new school of commerce. He sat for and passed the entrance examination, but after a month he gave up his studies in economics because too many textbooks in English were assigned to students to read.[24] Next, he was admitted into the

18. [62] VI, 138-9.
19. [63] 441-2.   20. [62] VI, 142 and [63].
21. [39] 41-2, [43] 9-10, and [258] 137-9.   22. [39] 46 and [84] 134.
23. [39] 41-2.   24. [39] 50, [43] 10, and [258] 140.

Hunan First Middle School—he was the first on the list of the candidates—only to discover that he did not like either the school or the lessons. He left after only six months.[25]

It was then the summer of 1912 and Mao was nineteen years of age and a nobody, neither a student nor a soldier. He was, however, free to read whatever and whenever he liked, in spite of his father's strenuous objection to his aimless drifting. He moved into cheap lodgings in the hostel for Hsianghsiang students in Ch'angsha, lived on 'bread and water', and spent his day in the Provincial Library.[26] In his own words, the library was to him as a vegetable garden to an ox.[27] There he devoured the Chinese translations of the *Wealth of Nations*, *On the Origin of Species*, Huxley's *Evolution and Ethics*, Mill's *Logic*, Spencer's *Study of Sociology*, Montesquieu's *Esprit des lois*, Rousseau's *Du Contrat social*, Greek mythology, world history and geography, and, most important of all, newspapers.[28]

Early in 1913 Mao was admitted into the Fourth Teachers' Training School, which was merged into the First Teachers' Training School in that autumn. Both schools were for scholarship students only who, upon graduation, would become primary school teachers. Humanism was the guiding principle of their training, with emphasis on moral conduct, physical culture, and social activities.[29] The First Teachers' Training School was the only Western-style building of Ch'angsha, towering above the others and surrounded by iron railings in place of the usual wall. 'I have never been to a university,' Mao recalled, 'nor have I studied abroad. The groundwork of my knowledge and scholarship was laid at the First Teachers' Training School, which was a good school.'[30] Mao stayed there from the autumn of 1913 to the summer of 1918.[31]

Before his entry into the First Teachers' Training School there had been another drastic change in the political life of China. The provinces after the revolution were in the hands of warlords,[32] who refused to remit taxes to the Central Government, with the

25. [39] 51 and [43] 10.   26. [43] 10–11.   27. [39] 52.
28. [39] 52–3, [43] 10–11, and [258] 140–2.
29. [43] 15–18.   30. [31].   31. [43] 12.
32. Out of twenty-two military governors, only seven were not warlords. This is based on my statistics in [85], table xiii.

result that Yuan Shih-k'ai's administration was in dire need of money. As the country had no adequate financial system for selling government bonds, the money could only come from abroad. But foreign loans had to be discussed and approved by the newly elected National Assembly. In the bi-cameral Assembly, the KMT had an absolute majority, and its relationship with the President had been strained for several months over the question of the location of the capital, the illegal killing of a revolutionary leader, General Chang Chen-wu, and other matters. The Party's fear was that Yuan might conceivably use any money borrowed from abroad to finance army expansion in order to enhance his personal powers. In fact, Yuan's plan at the time was to borrow £25 million from the consortium of British, Japanese, Russian, French, and German bankers, in the name of governmental reorganization. But China's stock in the international money market was so low that the bankers were unwilling to lend unless proper guarantees could be agreed upon. The arduous negotiations for this Reorganization Loan began almost as soon as Yuan's Government was established, yet their end was slow to come. Eventually, after many vicissitudes, the loan agreement was signed clandestinely in the small hours of 27 April 1913[33] without the approval of the National Assembly. The KMT had been vigorously opposed to the loan and Yuan's reply to this was the assassination of its Hunanese chairman, Sung Chiao-jen, on 20 March. Upon learning the sad news of the assassination, Dr. Sun Yat-sen and his lieutenant, General Huang Hsing, returned to Shanghai from Japan to organize what was known as 'the Second Revolution'.

The KMT's strongholds were Kiangsi, Anhwei, and Kwangtung. Dr. Sun and General Huang reckoned that they also had the sympathies of Chekiang, Kiangsu, Fukien, Yunnan, Hunan, and parts of Szechwan.[34] With nine provinces which might throw their weight behind them, Sun and Huang and their comrades decided to challenge Yuan in a resort to arms. On 12 July 1913 the guns roared, but the KMT soon found that its military strength

33. [84] 158.
34. These provinces were controlled by Chu Jui, Ch'eng Te-ch'üan, Sun Tao-jen, Ts'ai O, T'an Yen-k'ai, and Hsiung K'e-wu respectively.

fell far short of its leaders' expectations. The ill-planned and
hastily started Second Revolution was crushed by the might of
Yuan Shih-k'ai in less than two months. The KMT was thereafter
outlawed; the National Assembly without its major party was
indefinitely adjourned; the dictatorial rule of Yuan Shih-k'ai was
firmly established.[35]

T'an Yen-k'ai, the governor of Hunan, who had shown sympathies with the KMT, was replaced by Yuan's henchman, Admiral
T'ang Hsiang-ming. Realizing that the situation in central China
was still fluid, Yuan dispatched his loyal 3rd Division to Yüehchow[36]—a significant move with far-reaching effects, for the division was commanded by General Ts'ao K'un and under him was
the able strategist Wu P'ei-fu.[37] The fact that they were stationed
in Hunan laid the foundations for the domination of central China
by the Chihli Clique of the northern warlords in later years.
Unfortunately for the warlords themselves, this move also sowed
the seeds of dissension among them. Ts'ao's other duty was to
keep an eye on T'ang Hsiang-ming.

However, on the whole, the defeat of the Second Revolution
greatly enhanced Yuan Shih-k'ai's power, as a result of which the
situation in central China was gradually stabilized. Hunan
breathed peace. Its own forces remained unimpaired. Ch'eng
Ch'ien and Lin Hsiu-mei, whose sympathies were with the KMT
and Yuan's opponents in Kwangsi, Kwangtung, and Yunnan,
could now do nothing but await their chance; Chao Heng-t'i,
commander of the 1st Hunan Division, who favoured the policy
of self-government, adopted an equivocal attitude towards the
northern troops; Ch'en Chia-yu and Chu Tse-huang, commanders of the 3rd and 4th Brigades of the 2nd Hunan Division,
resolutely supported Yuan's policy of unification by force.[38] The
only person who could command the respect of these divergent
forces was T'an Yen-k'ai, but he was now in the wilderness. Right
in the heart of Hunan was Ts'ao K'un's 3rd Division and nearby
were Li Ch'un's 6th Division in Kiangsi and Wang Ju-hsien's
8th Division in Hupei—all were the cream of the northern troops.
Waiting in the south and south-west were Lu Jung-t'ing's Kwangsi

35. [84] ch. IX.
36. [84] 169.   37. [93] 211.   38. [2] 12.11.1916 and [91] 32.

army and T'ang Chi-yao's Yunnan contingents. They checked each other because they served conflicting purposes; they also enhanced each other's importance by their very existence and their situation in or round the periphery of central China. They formed a delicate balance of power which could be preserved as long as Yuan Shih-k'ai was safely in the saddle.

Yuan's fortune began to decline in 1915 because of his weak-kneed policy towards Japan in accepting the notorious Twenty-one Demands and because of his decision to found a dynasty of his own. Both worked to antagonize public opinion and to alienate his political and military following. The proclamation of the empire in December wrought havoc, and because of this, in January 1916, the south-west openly rebelled against him. His European friends, Britain in particular, were engaged in a struggle for life and death and so were unable to assist him; Japan was at first undecided but later expressed disapproval of his imperial adventure. Among his loyal lieutenants, General Feng Kuo-chang at Nanking declared himself neutral and General Tuan Ch'i-jui was 'ill'. The Treasury was empty; the soldiers were battle-shy; the end of Yuan Shih-k'ai was clearly in sight. Before May ended, Szechwan and Hunan declared their independence from Yuan. This acted like Brutus's dagger, and on 6 June 1916 the death of Yuan ushered in the period of warring warlords.

The declaration of independence, however, did not save T'ang Hsiang-ming's position in Hunan. Earlier, the 'ironsides' of the northern army, the 3rd Division, had been sent to Szechwan to quell the insurrection, leaving T'ang to face the discontented local forces who demanded his replacement by T'an Yen-k'ai.[39] These forces, supported by the troops in Kwangtung and Kwangsi, drove out Admiral T'ang Hsiang-ming on 5 July 1916, and welcomed back T'an Yen-k'ai on 3 August.[40] The question now confronting the newly reconstituted Central Government was whether to recognize the *fait accompli*.

In Peking, the nominal head of the Government was President Li Yüan-hung, but at the helm was General Tuan Ch'i-jui, the leader of the Anhwei Clique of the northern warlords. Tuan's ambition was to carry out the policy of unification of the nation

39. [91] 31.   40. [26] 10.1916, 19–20.

by force and over this he and President Li were constantly at loggerheads,[41] Li being in favour of a peaceful settlement with the south. Li also opposed Tuan on the issue of China's participation in the European war. These differences, exacerbated by other, less important disputes, eventually led to Li's dismissal of Tuan on 22 May 1917[42] and his reliance on the pig-tailed General Chang Hsün. Chang came to Peking in June for his own motives. On 1 July he, together with K'ang Yu-wei and others, put the last emperor of the Manchu dynasty back on the throne again.[43] Thus the man who had appeared to Li as an ally turned out to be an enemy of the Republic. Before taking refuge in the Japanese Legation in Peking, Li managed to have his seal of office and two orders smuggled out of Peking just in time. The seal and one of the orders were sent to the Vice-President, General Feng Kuo-chang, at Nanking, delegating all the presidential powers to him; the other order was issued to Tuan Ch'i-jui, re-appointing him premier and charging him with the duty of restoring the Republic.[44] In less than ten days Tuan captured Peking while Chang Hsün begged for sanctuary in the Dutch Legation and K'ang Yu-wei fled in disguise.[45] Another eminent casualty in this tragi-comedy was Li Yüan-hung, who announced his retirement.

The confusion in Peking was the reflection and, at the same time, the cause of the chaos in Hunan. Tuan's original intention before his dismissal had been to transfer Ch'en I[46] from Szechwan to Hunan. This project was abandoned in the face of strenuous local opposition.[47] The empty gubernatorial seat was taken over on his own initiative by General Ch'eng Ch'ien, who styled himself the 'acting governor' pending the arrival of T'an Yen-k'ai.[48] In this adventure, Ch'eng was supported by his Kwangsi allies. Apart from Ch'eng's, there were three other divisions in the province, commanded by Generals Ch'en Fu-ch'u, Chao Heng-t'i, and T'ao Chung-hsün. There were also northern troops under Generals Ni Ssu-ch'ung, Chou Wen-ping, Fan Kuo-chang, and others,[49] but these were soon pulled out of Hunan. Eventually, on 3 August,

41. [90] III, 21–2.
42. [20] 44.   43. [79] IV, 1–34.   44. [79] IV, 5–6 and [88] 401
45. [2] 13.7.1917, [72] 139, and [90] III, 222.
46. He was widely but erroneously known as Ch'en Huan.
47. [91] 31.   48. [91] 31.   49. [26] 10.1916, 19–20.

T'an Yen-k'ai assumed the governorship. As a *quid pro quo* for his approval, Tuan obtained from the Hunanese the agreement to station two brigades at Yüehchow under his trusted General Wu Kuang-hsin in order to counteract the preponderance of the local forces. Yet with the south-west now very much in ascendancy, the balance of power in Hunan was even harder to maintain. Fortunately for Tuan, T'an's mother died on 6 November 1916, and, according to tradition, the governor had to retire from his office. This T'an duly did. Tuan thereupon appointed Wu Kuang-hsin to supersede him, with the result that three garrison commanders in Hunan immediately declared their independence.[50] With the plan of controlling Hunan through a henchman thus thwarted, Tuan asked General Lu Yung-hsiang, an Anhwei Clique warlord, whether he would like to assume the governorship, but Lu declined the honour. At the same time, the Kwangsi warlord General Lu Jung-t'ing proposed that T'an should continue to act as the governor and that the Peking Government should promise not to replace him for the next three years.[51]

The bargaining and the uncertainty went on through the period of Tuan's dismissal and Chang Hsün's attempt at the Imperial Restoration. The situation farther south was also undergoing rapid changes. Dr. Sun Yat-sen had set up his headquarters at Canton and was elected by the members of the National Assembly then in Canton as the generalissimo.[52] Under his nominal leadership, the warlords of the south and south-west formed a temporary alliance with the declared aim of safeguarding the Constitution of 1912. So, at the end of July 1917, the co-existence of two governments in China, with Tuan Ch'i-jui once again the premier in Peking and Dr. Sun the generalissimo in Canton, became an undeniable fact, and consequently the struggle for the domination of Hunan grew fiercer.

Victorious in his campaign against Chang Hsün and convinced of the merits of his efforts to save the Republic, Tuan Ch'i-jui was now more confident in pursuing his policy of unification by force, his first move being the appointment of General Fu Liang-tso, Vice-Minister for the Army, as the Hunan governor on 6

50. [26] and [91] 33 and 140.   51. [90] IV, 13-14.
52. [115] I, 226 and [130] II, 426.

M.C.R.—4

August.[53] Accompanying the new governor were troops from the north dispatched thither by train and by steam-boats. Lacking such modern means of transport, the southern troops could not move as fast to T'an Yen-k'ai's aid and so T'an had to play for time by accepting Tuan's order. However, T'an also took steps to preserve his own and local interests by sending two columns of the Hunan army south to Hengyang and Lingling to arrange a link-up with the Kwangsi troops.[54] Aware of the strategic importance of Lingling in the struggle for hegemony of Hunan, Fu Liang-tso dismissed T'an's garrison commander there immediately on his arrival on 9 September 1917. The order of dismissal left the commander at Lingling with no choice but to flout it, and so he and his neighbouring commander at Hengyang announced their independence. Hunan was at war.[55]

The new governor's mistake at the beginning of the war lay in his gross underestimate of the fighting capabilities of the Hunan troops. He sent no more than the 1st Brigade of the 1st Hunan Division under General Li Yu-wen to Hengyang which went over *in toto* to the insurgents as soon as it engaged them on 1 October. General Li fled back to Ch'angsha alone.[56] After this initial reversal, the northern troops were rushed to Hunan, with General Wang Ju-hsien of the 8th Division as the Commander-in-Chief and General Fan Kuo-chang of the 20th Division as the Deputy Commander-in-Chief. The appointment of these two generals of the Chihli Clique tacitly implied Tuan's concession of central China to his rivals.[57] These two divisions were to launch a frontal attack on Hengyang while the 4th Brigade of the 2nd Hunan Division and Ni Ssu-ch'ung's An-wu Army were to attack the left and right flanks respectively, with Paoch'ing and Hsiang-hsiang and Yuhsien and Liling as their final goals. Action began on 10 October and the northern troops took Hengshan and Paoch'ing in quick succession.[58] Suddenly the Commander-in-Chief and his deputy halted their advancing army without the sanction of the Government.

This mysterious change in the strategy of the northern army

53. [90] IV, 15.   54. [88] 413 and [91] 139–40.
55. [88] 413 and [90] IV, 43.   56. [91] IV, 43–4.
57. [91] IV, 44.   58. [91] IV, 44 and 115.

can only be understood in the light of the political bickerings in Peking. The new President, General Feng Kuo-chang, who was also the leader of the Chihli Clique, was, like his predecessor, in favour of a peaceful settlement and his influence along the Yangtze River was second to none.[59] Supporting his lead, nine brigadiers including Wu P'ei-fu and Feng Yü-hsiang, who were then stationed in central China, made a joint statement against any prolongation of the civil war.[60] The commanders in Hunan responded to these developments by ceasing their attack on the Hunanese troops. The southern troops, however, thought differently. They seized the chance and pushed their northern enemies back. Only then did General Lu Jung-t'ing of Kwangsi, who had maintained a cordial relationship with President Feng Kuo-chang since the later stages of the anti-Yuan Shih-k'ai Campaign in 1916, order his own troops in Hunan to cease fire and, at the same time, urged Feng to co-operate with him in seeking a settlement of the Hunan question. By then Fu Liang-tso had been ejected from Ch'angsha and the northern troops were withdrawn from Hunan. General Wang Chan-yüan of Hupei at once recommended that T'an Yen-k'ai be appointed governor for the third time. With this President Feng complied.

Tuan Ch'i-jui's ill-starred policy of unification by force was once more undermined, but not yet abandoned. At the Tientsin conference of the military governors in December 1917, Tuan obtained strong support from the northern warlords who by threat forced the President to abandon his policy of peaceful settlement. On 16 December President Feng was compelled to dispatch an expeditionary army to Hupei and Hunan[61] under the supreme command of General Chang Huai-chih, for many years the military governor of Shantung. The army was divided into two columns—the first, 50,000 strong, was under the able command of General Wu P'ei-fu with the 3rd Division as its backbone, and the second was commanded by General Shih Ts'ung-pin of Shantung.[62] Bitterly opposed to sending this huge army were the

59. [2] 5.2.1918. 60. [126] II, 59 and 62. 61. [91] IV, 61.
62. The first column consisted of the 3rd Division (with the 5th Brigade under Chang Hsüeh-yen and the 6th Brigade under Chang Fu-lai), the 1st Mixed Brigade under Wang Ch'eng-pin, the 2nd Mixed Brigade under Yen Hsiang-wen, and the 3rd Mixed Brigade under Hsiao Yao-nan. The second

three military governors of Kiangsu, Kiangsi, and Hupei.[63] They succeeded in inducing the President to declare a truce on 26 December, but failed to dissuade him from sending the army.[64]

The battle of Hunan flared up in March 1918. The spearhead of Wu P'ei-fu's troops thrust into the province on the 10th and in just over a fortnight the 3rd Division entered Ch'angsha. The first round of the battle went to the northern troops. On 23 March Peking announced a group of new appointments, including Chang Ching-yao to the new governorship. The selection of Chang, a corrupt and inept warlord of Tuan Ch'i-jui's Anhwei Clique, despite the fact that the battle had been won solely by the brilliance of his command, disappointed Wu P'ei-fu.

At this time Tuan Ch'i-jui had constituted his third Cabinet which, in view of the successes in Hupei and Hunan, confidently resolved to pursue the policy of unification by force to the end.[65] In Hunan itself, there were no less than four divisions, eight brigades, and twenty corps of northern troops,[66] which were ordered to drive farther south by three routes—the central to Hengyang and Hengshan, the left to Liling and Yuhsien, and the right to Hsianghsiang and Paoch'ing. The brunt of the frontal attack in the centre was borne by Wu P'ei-fu's 3rd Division. Ch'eng Ch'ien and the Kwangsi and Hunan armies under him purposely avoided a positional engagement with Wu's crack troops. Instead, they concentrated their counter-attack on the flanks, routing Chang Ching-yao's 7th Division at Liling. Wu's flanks were now exposed.[67]

At the same time a stalemate was reached in Szechwan, Hupei, Fukien, and Kwangtung, along an arc of 700 miles, and some of

column consisted of the 1st Shantung Division under Shih himself, the 6th Kiangsu Mixed Brigade under Chang Tsung-ch'ang, and a part of the An-wu Army under Li Ch'uan-yeh. ([91] 172–3 and [93] 214–15.)

63. Li Ch'un, Ch'en Kuang-yüan, and Wang Chan-yüan respectively. [90] IV, 64.

64. [90] IV, 64.   65. [90] IV, 109–10.

66. [91] 193. These were, apart from Wu P'ei-fu's and Chang Tsung-ch'ang's units, Chang Ching-yao's 7th Division, Sun Lieh-ch'en's two divisions of Manchurian troops, Ma Lien-chia's 20 corps of the An-wu Army, Feng Yü-hsiang's 16th Mixed Brigade, the remnants of the Shantung troops, and Ch'en Fu-ch'u's and Chu Tse-huang's Hunan units fighting on the side of the north.

67. [90] IV, 115–18.

the armies fighting in Hunan—such as the remnants of the Shantung troops, Ts'ao K'un's three mixed brigades, and the two
Manchurian divisions—were recalled.[68] Furthermore, the military
governors of Chihli, Manchuria, Hupei, Honan, and Kiangsi,[69]
in a joint statement, appealed for a cease-fire in Hunan. General
Wu P'ei-fu, disappointed at not being selected for the governorship, threatened by the southern troops on his left flank and
weary of war, felt the time was opportune for a *rapprochement* with
the south. On 15 June 1918, he concluded a truce with his opponents and the battle of Hunan was over.[70]

The turmoil from 1913 to 1918 naturally affected Mao in many
ways but did not involve him personally. He joined Class 5 of the
Teachers' Training School[71] in the autumn of 1913 and at once
impressed his teachers and thirty class-mates by the lucidity of his
essays, some of which were stuck on the walls or exhibited on open
days for others to see. But he had a habit of putting the date of
completion at the end of an essay—a habit which for some reason
irritated his bearded master of Chinese, Mr. Yüan Liu-chi, who
once told him to copy out the last page but leave out the date. Mao
failed to see the reason for this objection and therefore refused to
obey. In a rage, the teacher rushed towards him and tore the last
page of his composition to pieces. Having successfully dealt with
his bad-tempered father and tutor, Mao knew how to handle an
angry man. He dragged Mr. Yüan by the arm, wanting to go to
the headmaster and have the whole case argued out in his presence.
Eventually a compromise was reached, with Mao agreeing to
copy out the page and the master allowing him to insert the date
at the end of it.[72] Afterwards all was forgiven and forgotten. In
later years Mao recalled how Mr. Yüan disliked his style which was
modelled on Liang Ch'i-ch'ao and advised him to read Han Yü.[73]

68. [90] IV, 130–1.
69. They were Ts'ao K'un, Chang Tso-lin, Wang Chan-yüan, Chao Ti, and
Ch'en Kuang-yüan respectively. [85] table viii.   70. [90] IV, 139.
71. [39] 55. Li Jui says that Mao joined Class 8 ([43] 12). This does not
appear to me to be correct. Assuming that only one class was selected each year,
Class 5 which joined the school in 1913 should have completed its five-year
course in 1918, and it did. If this were Class 8 it should have graduated, not in
1918, but in 1921. Li must therefore be mistaken.
72. [39] 55 and 58 and [43] 29 and 47.
73. (768–824), a great essayist and classicist.

'Thanks to the bearded Mr. Yüan for a passable classical style, I
can still write today when the need arises.'[74] Apart from Chinese,
Mao was fond of history, geography, and philosophy; but in
natural history, mathematics, and languages he was a poor
scholar.[75]

He was a fast reader with an extraordinary power of concentration. The hubbub that went on around him never seemed to
disturb him. He was often seen reading in the classroom late at
night.[76]

The school issued him, and also other students, with a black
tunic suit which he wore for several years until it was tattered and
its colour faded. He wore no socks in summer, only a pair of old
slippers, and his winter wardrobe consisted of a cotton-padded
gown, an old lined gown, and a pair of white pyjama trousers.[77]
Emil Hsiao compared him to Bazarov of *Fathers and Sons*[78]—a
comparison applicable to Mao's shabbiness, but not to his physical
features which have never been striking.[79]

He was a man of few words who preferred listening to talking.[80]
While listening, he would make intermittent sounds of 'Eh, eh'.
He was not given to joking, least of all to jokes of a suggestive
nature.[81] This quiet and mild young man was elected one of
thirty-four model students by some 400 schoolmates in June
1917, for he excelled in ethical conduct, self-control, literature,
speech, ability, and courage.[82] Despite a quiet exterior, his boldness
was noticed by his masters and friends. He once helped a school-
mate to free himself from an arranged marriage. The would-be
bride was the niece of the headmaster of a middle school. Mao took
the fiancé to see the headmaster, argued on his behalf, and obtained
the headmaster's agreement to cancel the wedding.[83] In 1915 the

74. [39] 58. In Mao's *Hsüan Chi* [46], two items are written in the classical
style—the *Ten Demands to the Kuomintang* and the *Order of the Revolutionary
Commission of the Central Committee of the Chinese Communist Party* ([46] II,
715–19 and 769. See *SW*, III, 167–74 and 225), and they confirm Mao's
statement.   75. [39] 56, [54] 32, and [258] 142.

76. [39] 55 and 57, [43] 26, and [50] 36.   77. [43] 45.

78. [50] 36.

79. [54] 31. Siao Yu says that Mao's features are quite ordinary.

80. [56] 'He prefers listening to talking. When he speaks, his eyes are fixed
on the ground.' (p. 134.)

81. [31], [39] 72, [43] 26 and 46.   82. [31] and [43] 54.

83. [43] 48.

Teachers' Training School decided to collect 10 *yuan* (about £1) from every student to cover miscellaneous expenses. This provoked a wave of protest from the boys who organized a campaign against the headmaster. The original draft of the students' manifesto attacked the headmaster's private life. Mao objected to it and drafted another to replace it, in which he dealt only with the headmaster's mismanagement. Mao's draft was adopted and printed for distribution. The school's reply to this was its decision to send Mao and fifteen others home, accusing them of leading the other boys astray. Mao would have been expelled had Mr. Yüan, Yang Ch'ang-chi, Hsü T'e-li, and Fang Wei-hsia not intervened.[84] Soon after this, Mao was again at his mischievous tricks by bringing to the school pamphlets written by Liang Ch'i-ch'ao and others against Yuan Shih-k'ai's imperial attempt. T'ang Hsiang-ming, then the governor of Hunan, heard this and sent his police to the school to search for them, but nothing was found.[85] The most daring of his exploits occurred after the fall of Yuan Shih-k'ai when the local forces, including one Lin Tsu-han, under the leadership of T'an Yen-k'ai, worked to oust T'ang Hsiang-ming. T'ang went but Fu Liang-tso came. Soon Fu's northern troops were defeated, retreating northward with the Kwangsi army chasing after them. The retreating units, not knowing the actual situation in Ch'angsha, were wary of entering it, while the city itself was a temporary vacuum. Scattered bands of Fu's troops wanted to take over the school building as their headquarters. The school had broken up and the building was then occupied by a handful of students who had nowhere else to go. Mao was one of these students who went to a nearby police-station and obtained a few real and dummy rifles there. Thus armed, they hid themselves on a hill and in the night rushed down, shouting: 'Fu Liang-tso has fled; Kwangsi troops have entered the city! Surrender, surrender!' The troops in the school surrendered![86]

From 1913 to 1918 Hunan had only one year of peace—the year 1914.[87] Each time when there was war, the school had to

84. [39] 58 and [43] 48.   85. [43] 52.
86. [39] 79–80 and [43] 52.
87. [43] 49–50 and [85], table x. Hunan was at war in thirteen out of the sixteen years from 1912 to 1928.

close down until tranquillity returned. Under such circumstances, it was small wonder that Mao took an interest in military
affairs and, according to Siao Yu, formed the opinion that 'If
people are weak, what is the use of perfecting their virtues? The
most important thing is to be strong. With strength, one can
conquer others and to conquer others gives one virtue.' This
also explains his admiration for Bismarck and Wilhelm II which
Siao Yu recounts.[88]

A book that influenced Mao deeply in this period was Friedrich
Paulsen's *A System of Ethics*.[89] The copy Mao used is still extant
and in its margins there are his notes running to no less than
12,000 characters. These notes show that he was gradually moving
towards radicalism. Paulsen was a disciplinarian, placing great
emphasis on self-control and will power. He defined virtue as
'habits of the will and modes of conduct which tend to promote
the welfare of individual and collective life', and vice as a lack of
will power to harmonize the impulses. He thought that the
fundamental form of individualistic virtue was self-control.[90]
Mao seems to have disagreed with this view, as one of his notes
says: 'No crime is greater than the repression of man's nature,
either by oneself or by someone else.' Another note has this to say
about tradition, particularly Chinese tradition:

Tradition can stifle what is new; the old can overwhelm what is new.
When this happens, man will lose his ability to adapt himself to a new
age and in the end this organic body in history [China?] will perish.
China is now in such a state.

Yet another, to Book III, on *Virtues and Vices*, says:

In the past I worried over the coming destruction of our country, but
now I know that fear was unnecessary. I have no doubt that the political
system, the characteristics of our people, and the society will change;
what I am not yet clear on are the ways in which the changes can be
successfully brought about. I incline to believe that a [complete]
reconstruction is needed. Let destruction play the role of a mother in
giving birth to a new country. The great revolutions of other countries
in the past centuries swept away the old and brought forth the new.

88. [54] 69–70. Hsiao Yü (or Siao Yu) says that Mao 'adored' Bismarck
and the Kaiser.
89. 1899 and its Chinese translation by Ts'ai Yüan-p'ei, Shanghai, 1913.
90. Book III, ch. I, 475–82 and ch. II.

They were the great changes which resurrected the dead and reconstructed the decayed.[91]

This embryonic revolutionary thought can also be found in Chang K'un-ti's diary. On 22 September 1917, after a swim in the Hsiang River, Chang and Mao went to see Ts'ai Ho-sen:

September 23, 1917: . . . It was dusk and we decided to stay there [at Ts'ai's home] overnight. Our conversation went on for a long time. Mao Jun-chih [Mao's courtesy name] said: 'The scope of our people's view being so narrow, it is impossible to produce among them a great man like Tolstoy of Russia to revolutionize our philosophical and ethical outlook and to sweep away our archaic ideas in order to pave the way for new thoughts to emerge.' . . . Mr. Mao also talked about revolutions against the old family system and the master–disciple relations. He added that revolutions do not always entail a clash of arms, but always the replacement of the old by the new.[92]

Not all his revolutionary ideas were stimulated by Paulsen; from 1915 he was a regular reader of the *Hsin-ch'ing-nien* (*La Jeunesse*)—a radical paper edited by Ch'en Tu-hsiu.[93] He read newspapers methodically, and so was always clear about the development of current affairs, and he was also very fond of such classical works as the *Complete Works of Han Yü*, the *Tzu-chih T'ung-chien*, and the *Tu-shih Fang-yü Chi-yao*.[94] He fostered the habit of taking notes from almost everything he read. The result was a basket full of such notes, a volume of which survived the 21 May Massacre of 1927.[95] Running to some 10,000 characters, this volume contains the following fragments:

Understanding must precede decision. Success comes from decisions based on thorough understanding.
  One of the most difficult things in life is to be careful and precise. If one can be so in both great and small matters, one would find that

91. [43] 42–3 and 79.   92. [43] 78.
  93. [43] 27–8. The April 1917 issue of this journal carries an article by Mao, signed Erh-shih Pa-hua sheng. See Stuart R. Schram, *Mao Ze-dong une Étude de L'éducation Physique*, Paris, 1962.
  94. Mao told Snow, 'I had acquired the newspaper-reading habit, and from 1911 to 1927, when I climbed up Chingkan[g]shan, I never stopped reading the daily papers of Peiping, Shanghai, and Hunan.' ([258)] 147. See also [39] 67–9.)
  The *Tzu-chih T'ung-chien* [77] was compiled by Ssu-ma Kuang (1019–86) and the *Tu-shih Fang-yü Chi-yao*, a treatise on historical geography, by Ku Tsu-yü (1631–92). See also [31].   95. [43] 37 and *vide infra*, p. 116.

even sainthood is not hard to achieve. On the other hand, a moment's carelessness can lead to a great disaster.

One should set one's aims in life beyond the bare necessities. This is correct as far as one's ambitions are concerned. But, as a policy of the state, the goal of a kingly rule [in the words of Mencius] is precisely to clothe the common people with silk and to feed them with grain, so that they may not be frozen or starved. [In that sense] the bare necessities do require our special attention.[96]

Mao, however, was not as consistently revolutionary and pragmatic as these quotations suggest. In a more idealistic moment, he wrote this among his notes:

Myself is my smallest being; the universe, my greatest being. The former is my physical being; the latter, my spiritual being.[97]

Since he was interested in 'the nature of men, of human society, of China, [of] the world, and [of] the universe',[98] and had 'not a penny on him [but] every concern to the world',[99] it would be safe to assume that he preferred the amelioration of his spiritual being to that of his physical existence. Hence he was at once untidy and ambitious. On what he considered as 'great matters', he was exceedingly practical and utilitarian with a bent towards revolution. For instance, he wrote to a scholar in Peking in August 1917, criticizing the unrealistic aspects of the oriental civilization and, at the same time, showing his dissatisfaction with the occidental civilization as he knew it. What he groped for was a better civilization, better able to serve man's manifold needs.[1] With regard to himself, he strove to fulfil his ambitions through the study of philosophy and ethics. He again wrote to a scholar in Peking in August 1917:

Ambition must be formed through studies of philosophy and ethics. Only by such studies can one understand the truth and regard it as the precept of one's conduct. One should not stop one's pursuit of the truth until the aim is achieved and only then can one have an ambition. Ten years without an understanding of the truth are ten years without ambition; a whole life without such an understanding is a life without an ambition.[2]

96. [43] 39–40.   97. [43] 38.   98. [258] 145.   99. [54].
1. [43] 79.   2. [43] 79.

In his pursuit of the truth, the fulfilment of his life's ambition, and the solution to China's many problems, Mao had a great number of comrades among his contemporaries, though unknown to each other personally. At a time when agriculture, medicine, and handicrafts were separated from scholarship, when modern industries were not yet developed, and when scientific researches were hampered by a total lack of facilities, the intelligence and energy of the younger generation could only be channelled into enigmatic and speculative studies on China. Speculation is a fascinating exercise and there were many vital and urgent problems facing China to attract the attention of her youth. Mao, like so many of his generation, was not particularly good at chemistry, mathematics, or physics, and therefore found the search for a solution to China's problems the mission of his life.

Yet to find the root of China's weakness and the key to national strength was beyond the intellectual power of a young man in his early twenties. His dedication to this search resulted in what Mao himself described as 'an amusing mixture of liberal, democratic reformist, and utopian socialist ideas'.[3] This self-portrait bore some resemblance to the subject, but was only a sketch. His outbursts against the repression of human feelings and sentiments and against tradition, his fights against arranged marriages (including his own) and the inefficiency of his headmaster, and his clashes with the irrationality of the bearded Mr. Yüan and the timidity of the warlord's soldiers qualified him as a democratic reformer. His praise of destruction betrayed his 'utopian socialist' tendencies. But it would be difficult to prove that he was also a liberal. Furthermore, the description certainly omitted the traditional doctrines he had inherited as shown through his quotations from Mencius and his references to the kingly rule and to the greatest and smallest beings that compose oneself. Even the European terms used to represent his ideas should be accepted with reserve. Mao has never mastered any European language and the European books he read were all Chinese translations. One knows how much can be lost in translation, and in Mao's case, much was Sinicized. Take the *Wealth of Nations* as an example: the translation Mao read was entitled *Yüan Fu* (the Origin of

3. [39] 87.

Wealth) and a later translation was called *Kuo Fu Lun* (On the Wealth of *a* Nation). What was lost here was Smith's plural and with it the international significance. What was originally a book on international wealth became a book on national wealth. Other works, such as Huxley's essays on evolution, Mill's treatise on liberty, and Montesquieu's *Esprit*, introduced at a time when Chinese nationalism was growing, were all used to serve the nationalist aspirations. It was precisely for the fulfilment of such aspirations, or 'ambitions' as he called them, that Mao read these European works and was initiated into European ideas. He chose what would be useful for his purposes and discarded what would not. He, like many other Chinese, was intensely patriotic and in patriotism he found his ambition. He was in this sense thoroughly Chinese.

Not only books and periodicals but teachers and friends also influenced him. He disliked Yi P'ei-chi who was his headmaster.[4] Fang Wei-hsia taught him natural history from 1914 and Hsü T'e-li civics and educational theory from 1913; both were to become communists. But the teacher who influenced him most was Mr. Yang Ch'ang-chi, a dedicated student of philosophy. Having spent six years in Japan and four years in Britain, he returned to Ch'angsha to teach ethics, logic, psychology, educational theory, and philosophy. He was well-versed in Neo-Confucianism, especially in the pragmatism of Wang Fu-chih. Among Western scholars, Kant, Spencer, and Rousseau attracted his interest. He attacked the Confucian concept of human relations, the prevalent attitude of regarding a degree or diploma as a stepping-stone to a civil service career, and the vulgarity of having no philosophical view of life. He exhorted his pupils to take both life and studies seriously and to destroy the conformist self in order to make room for the development of the ideal self. Several of his pupils whom he particularly liked were often seen at his home. Among them were Ts'ai Ho-sen, Ch'en Ch'ang, Chang K'un-ti, Siao Yu, Hsiao San, and Mao Tse-tung.[5] It was through his recommendation that Hsiao San read Rousseau's *Émile* and called himself Emile Hsiao. It was also through his recommendation that Mao read Paulsen.

4. [258] 144.
5. [39] 58–9 and [43] 19–24.

Mao's ideas of 'greatest and smallest beings' may have derived from Yang's 'conformist and ideal selves'; so may also his antagonism to Confucian ethics. Having been trained in Britain and studied Wang Fu-chih, Yang may have adopted a pragmatic and utilitarian attitude towards knowledge which influenced Mao Tse-tung. In his instructions to his sons and grandsons, Wang Fu-chih advised against taking up a civil service career. 'Be a scholar, if you can. Otherwise, be a physician, a farmer, a businessman, or an artisan, according to your own abilities.' These words of Wang may have led Mao to 'value marquisates as dust'. But it was through Yang Chang-chi's introduction that Mao began to correspond with such eminent but not overbearing scholars as Ch'en Tu-hsiu and Li Ta-chao.[6]

The place where Mao and his friends frequently met was the Students Society (Hsüeh Yu Hui) which had been called the Aptitude Development Society (Chi Neng Hui) in 1913 when it was founded, but became the Self-Cultivation Society (Tzu Chin Hui) in 1914. The more pedestrian name of Students Society was adopted in 1915 when Mao was elected to its executive committee as the secretary. He served it in that capacity for four semesters from 1915 to 1917 and then as its chairman and concurrently head of research from the autumn of 1917 to the spring of 1918, when he graduated and left for Peking.[7]

In the summer of 1917 Mao, under the name of 'Mr. Twenty-eight Strokes'[8] (erh-shih-pa-hua sheng), inserted a small advertisement in a Ch'angsha newspaper, saying that he would like to meet young people 'who are interested in patriotic activities . . . and . . . prepared to work and make sacrifices for our country'. Among the five or six replies received, one came from a student at the Ch'angsha Union Middle School by the name of Li Li-san, who subsequently met Mao, listened to what he had to say, and went away without making any definite proposal. He and Mao never struck up a friendship.[9] Ch'en Ch'ang and Lo Chang-lung were among the others who responded.[10] Mao's aim in advertising was to gather a group of people to form a society of their own. Later Mao

6. [43] 30.   7. [43] 55 and 58–9.
8. The three characters for *Mao Tse-tung* have twenty-eight strokes.
9. [39] 81–2, [43] 71, and [258] 144.   10. [43] 71–2 and [258] 144.

and his close friends, including Siao Yu, Hsiao San, Ts'ai Ho-sen, and Chang K'un-ti, met at Ts'ai's home and agreed to form a 'New Citizens Society'.[11]

The New Citizens Society came into being on 18 April 1918 with thirteen founder members.[12] Its principal aims were, according to its constitution, to work for the interests of the country and to train its members to become new citizens. Its regular programmes included weekly or fortnightly meetings to discuss specific problems or current affairs. After the May 4th Movement in 1919 the membership of the Society increased to nearly eighty. Most of these members later went to study in France.[13]

Mao also took a deep interest in the work of an evening class for workers and shop-assistants. According to a day-book kept by Mao, the class was created for the senior students of the Teachers' Training School to practise what they had learnt. About 120 students attended it to learn reading, writing, arithmetic, and general knowledge such as history, geography, hygiene, and current problems. Mao taught history to those who attended.[14] By his contacts with the working men in the evening class he realized that the style of his writing was too abstruse for the ordinary people to understand.[15]

Mao is well known to have led a Spartan life at the Teachers' Training School. He had a cold bath every day in summer and in winter.[16] He was very fond of swimming—a sport he has never grown tired of even today[17]—mountaineering, sun-bathing, and walking shirtless in rain and sleet.[18] In the summer of 1916 he and Siao Yu tramped over a large area in Hunan, living on beans and water or sometimes on nothing.[19] In exchange for a meal or money Mao wrote scrolls for farmers whom he met on the long

11. The *Hsin-min Hsüeh-hui*. Siao Yu says ([54] 59–60) that the Society was established in 1914. He may have confused it with the Students Society. See also [39] 82–4 and [43] 72.

12. The names which can be traced are: Ts'ai Ho-sen, Ho Shu-heng, Ch'en Ch'ang, Chang K'un-ti, Lo Hsüeh-tsan, Kuo Liang, Miss Hsiang Chin-yü, Hsia Hsi, Li Wei-han, Hsiao San, Miss Ts'ai Ch'ang, and Mao. All of them, except Siao Yu, were to become members of the CCP.

13. [39] 82–4 and [43] 73–4.

14. [43] 60.   15. [43] 61–2.   16. [39] 61 and [43] 33.

17. He swam across the Yangtze three times in 1956. *Vide infra*, p. 346.

18. [39] 61, [43] 34, and [258] 145.

19. [54] chs. 18–33. Snow's date of 1913 is wrong. See [258] 86 and 144.

hike. At that time he wrote a good hand in the calligraphic style of
Emperor Hui-tsung (reigned 1011–1125),[20] which was very different from the scribbles he often writes now.

The physical toughening was to prove very useful when he led
the First Front Army on the Long March in 1934 and 1935.[21]

The years at the Teachers' Training School drew to an end in
April 1918. The reason why the school advanced the date of
graduation from summer to spring was that the local forces of
Hunan, having withdrawn from Ch'angsha, the governor, Chang
Ching-yao's troops wanted the school building as their head-
quarters. Apart from graduation, another circumstance affected
Mao personally at this time. Many of the members of the New
Citizens Society were planning to go to France as Work-study
students. His very close friend, Ts'ai Ho-sen, had already gone to
Peking and wrote to urge Mao to join him there.[22] Mao replied
telling him about the work of the newly founded New Citizens
Society:

Our quest in any field is entirely free from restriction or inhibition and
many of our members are planning to study in *Russia*, France, or
Peking. The ultimate aim of our studies, in either specialized subjects
or in current affairs, is to benefit our country.[23]

On 29 May 1918 Mao handed over the chairmanship of the
Students Society to his successor and left the Teachers' Training
School. In September he was on his way to Peking.[24]

20. [39] 64–5 and [43] 92. Li Jui reproduced a postcard from Mao to Lo
Hsüeh-tsan.   21. [50] 156. See also, Stuart R. Schram, *op. cit.*
22. [43] 84.
23. [43] 94. My italics, showing that the word (*O*) may be a later addition.
24. [43] 84.

Chapter III

The Widening Horizon

THE Work-study Scheme, sponsored by a group of leading scholars for those who wished to study in France, was published in the famous periodical, *La Jeunesse*, in 1917.[1] At once it caught the imagination of young people in all parts of China. The scheme required the candidates to provide only the fare to France; once there they would earn their living by working in factories and studying in their spare time. Many of the members of the New Citizens Society took a great interest in it and among the first batch of them to arrive at Peking to prepare for the trip was Ts'ai Ho-sen, who wrote to Mao in June 1918 asking him to come up to the capital and to maintain the liaison between those who would soon be in France and those who were planning to go.[2] Still undecided on what to do after graduation, Mao welcomed this idea and was excited by the prospect of seeing Peking. He may have hoped that he, too, could make the trip to France. So Mao, Lo Hsüeh-tsan, and about twenty others began their journey to Peking in September.[3]

In Peking there were, among those Mao knew personally, Professor Li Ta-chao, the librarian and professor of political economy, Ch'en Tu-hsiu, the editor of *La Jeunesse* and dean of the faculty of letters, Yang Ch'ang-chi, Mao's erstwhile teacher and now lecturer in ethics, and Teng Chung-hsia (Teng K'ang), a student, at the University of Peking.[4] At Yang Ch'ang-chi's suggestion, Li Ta-chao found a job for Mao as an assistant in his

1. [99] vol. III, no. 2. The sponsors were Wang Ching-wei, Wu Chih-hui, Ts'ai Yüan-p'ei, Li Shih-tseng, Chang Chi, and Wu Yü-chang.
2. [43] 85. 3. [43] 84–5. 4. [43] 89 and [258] 148.

library. The duties were to register the names of the library users, and the salary was 8 *yuan* (16s.) a month.[5] Obviously it was not so much a job as a temporary arrangement for him to earn a living. As Mao recalled later: 'My office was so low that people avoided me.'[6] But it was at the library that he met the future leaders of the May 4th Movement of 1919 as well as a student by the name of Chang Kuo-t'ao.

He shared a bedroom with seven friends,[7] worked during the day and studied during the evening. He realized fully that between him and France stood the barriers of language and of money, and so he made an attempt to learn French and English.[8] Languages, however, are seldom easy for a man interested mainly in speculative subjects such as world and national politics, and Mao has never been able to master them any more than he has the natural sciences. Mao did not go to France and later he told Edgar Snow: 'I felt that I did not know enough about my own country, and that my time could be more profitably spent in China.' He also said that he did not study French since he had other plans.[9] With or without regret, Mao offered this as an explanation, perhaps also as an apology, for not having gone. His decision to stay behind helped to shape his outlook on life.

He continued to read and now his books were those by Kropotkin, Bakhunin, and Tolstoy. In his own words, 'my interest in politics increased and I myself became more radical.'[10] He had then a very strong anarchist tendency, corresponded with other anarchists, and even thought for a while of founding an anarchist society.[11] In this he was perhaps influenced by a lecturer in the Journalism Society, Shao P'iao-p'ing,[12] Mao being a member of the society.

The anarchistic development was, however, interrupted by a love affair with Yang K'ai-hui, Yang Ch'ang-chi's daughter,[13]

---

5. [39] 93. The room where Mao worked is in the south-east wing of the Red Building (*Hung Lou*) and now Li Ta-chao Memorial Room. See [38].
6. [258] 148.
7. [54] 170–1.   8. [50] 60.   9. [258] 148.
10. [43] 91, [50] 55–6, and [258] 149.
11. [50] 56.
12. [258] 149. Shao was killed by Marshal Chang Tso-lin in 1926.
13. Yang Ch'ang-chi and family moved to Peking in 1918 and Yang himself died in 1920. See [39] 94, [43] 19–20, and [258] 149.

whose beauty, serenity, and intelligence were an oasis in Mao's otherwise arid existence in Peking.[14]

Early in 1919 Mao went to Shanghai to see Ts'ai Ho-sen and two others sail for France.[15] He visited, *en route*, the Confucian country in Ch'üfou and climbed T'ai Shan in Shantung.[16] After the departure of his friends he returned to Ch'angsha in March, taking up a teaching post at the Hsiu-yeh Primary School.[17] With his views now considerably broadened by the visit to Peking, and armed with 'Victory of the Common People' and 'The Triumph of Bolshevism'—two recent articles by Li Ta-chao on the October Revolution—Mao gave a public lecture in Ch'angsha on Marxism and the Revolution.[18] But his return may have been prompted by a more personal consideration—his mother was seriously ill and soon afterwards died. Saddened by the occasion, he wrote an essay in memory of her, saying that 'love and kindness were my mother's greatest virtues. . . .'[19]

The coming of May found China in convulsion. The May 4th Movement, says Dr. Chow Tse-tsung,

was actually a combined intellectual and sociopolitical movement to achieve national independence, the emancipation of the individual, and a just society by the modernization of China. Essentially it was an intellectual revolution in the broad sense—intellectual because it was based on the assumption that intellectual changes were a prerequisite for such a task of modernization, because it precipitated a mainly intellectual awakening and transformation, and because it was led by intellectuals.[20]

The intellectual awakening manifested itself in the demands for democracy and science, an easily comprehensible style of writing, and an understanding of the individual himself, so that China could be transformed into a modern state. Previous attempts at this transformation had been limited to defence, economy, and politics, and through their failures the Chinese intellectuals be-

14. [39] 94.
15. [43] 91 and [105] 2. The first group of three sailed in March 1919 and the second group, of over 90, on 11 May 1919.
16. [258] 150.   17. [43] 91.
18. Li's articles were published on 5 October 1918 in *La Jeunesse*, V, 5. See [43] 91.
19. The essay has been preserved by Mao's private tutor. [43] 8.
20. [96] 358-9.

came aware that, unless many of her old traditions could be up-rooted, the modernization of China would remain an impossibility. Science could not be reconciled with superstitution; nor could democracy with despotism. Neither could flourish when the grip of Confucianism was still strong on man's mind and on society. For the modernization of China, many archaic ideas and institutions had to be obliterated and this, in turn, called for a critical attitude[21] and a new style of writing in order to express and introduce new concepts.

Up to, and indeed for many years after the May 4th Movement, superstition was still rampant among both the higher and lower classes of the people. For instance, in 1918 the construction of a road in Peking was stopped by the fear of spoiling the geomantic features of the locality. The date for beginning the repair of a pagoda in Anch'ing, Anhwei, had to be decided according to the horoscope of the provincial governor. The presidential election in 1918 had to have the blessings of a fortune-teller before it was announced. A teacher at the Nank'ai Middle School in Tientsin told his class in earnest that Marquis Tseng Kuo-fan had been a python in his previous incarnation. The governor of Hunan, Chang Ching-yao, ordered his soldiers to write the character *te* (to win) on their left and the character *sheng* (victory) on their right hands before a battle and he built a temple for the worship of the Goddess of the Ninth Heaven after it. Ma Lien-chia, the garrison commander of south Anhwei, invited a Taoist priest and his 'celestial officers and soldiers' to exorcize the spirits troubling the mind of his niece.[22] In Shantung there was the *San-yang* Sect, the followers of which claimed to be invulnerable, and throughout the whole country, spiritualist seances, at which famous poets and generals who had died many centuries ago were said to have reappeared, were the fashion of the time.[23] Chiang Monlin told a delightful little story in his *Tides from the West:*

My uncle told me that people had used chemical fertilizers for cabbages the year before, and these grew to such enormous size that they thought

---

21. 'According to my view, the essence of the new thoughts is no more than a new attitude which can be called a "critical attitude".' [100] IV, 152–3. This was written in November 1919.
22. [94] II, 356–7.   23. [94] II, 355 and 357 and IV, 282–4.

the abnormal growth must contain poison. So they pulled them up
and threw them up [away].[24]

That was in 1916. In the following year Chiang observed that
among the young people at least ideas were beginning to change:

They called the worship of gods a superstition. They said that the
burning of paper money before our ancestors was silly. To them there
were no kitchen gods. . . . They thought these images ought to be flung
into the river, so as to banish superstition along with them.[25]

But in other circles, the roots of superstition clutched deep and
firm in people's minds.

Another more sophisticated and perhaps even more powerful
factor in Chinese thought may conveniently be called Confucianism, meaning specifically the Confucian conception of human
relations in particular. The Ruler, according to the Master and his
disciples, should be benevolent and his subjects loyal; the father
should be kind and his children filial; the teacher should give
guidance while his pupils received it; the husband should provide
for his wife while the wife should be faithful and obedient; brothers
and friends should give assistance to each other. The lubricants for
all these relationships were rites and propriety.

The preservation of these doctrines was precisely what Yuan
Shih-k'ai, Chang Hsün, and many other warlords wanted. Some
of them advocated in 1916 and 1917 the establishment of Confucianism as the State religion,[26] and the members of parliament
who belonged to the notorious but influential An-fu Club[27]
tabled a motion in the Senate on 2 October 1919, suggesting that
the new President, Hsü Shih-ch'ang, should worship Confucius.[28]
The motive behind these gestures was to strengthen the domination of Confucian ethics, and thereby to consolidate the traditional
social order. But it was ironical that the guardianship of Confucian
ethics should be left to such depraved people as these and to
discredited scholars like K'ang Yu-wei and Lin Shu.[29]

24. [95] 101.   25. [95] 100.
26. [2] 9.9.1916, 5.12.1916, 9.12.1916, 15.2.1917, and 23.2.1917.
27. The Club was formed in 1918 by a group of pro-Japanese politicians and
military leaders. See [7] 1925, 1121; [26] 21st Anniversary Issue D.10; and [81]
279.   28. [100] I, 226.
29. K'ang's view is well known; so is his part in the 1917 Restoration. Lin
Shu once wrote to Ts'ai Yüan-p'ei, the Chancellor of Peking University,

Neither Confucius himself nor his disciples had ever discussed the ways and means of preventing the Ruler, Father, Teacher, and Husband from abusing their rights and of guaranteeing their compliance with the Confucian rules. This is hardly surprising, for the Confucian ethic was designed for an autocratic society, and it would be an anachronism to try to preserve such ethical doctrines when democracy and republicanism had been introduced into China.

Because of the lack of restrictive guarantees against the excesses of the ruling class, the Confucian moral doctrines were held responsible for corruption and abuse of power and for widespread apathy, indifference, and gullibility, and their destruction was deemed necessary by their critics. Ch'en Tu-hsiu wrote in 1916:

All the [Confucian] moral standards and political doctrines are derived from the theory of three human bonds. The ruler's bondsmen are his subjects . . ., father's bondsmen are his children . . ., and husbands' bondsmaids are their wives. . . . From these relations spring such unalterable moral ideas as loyalty, filial piety, and chastity, all of which are not . . . for the masters, only for the slaves.[30]

And in 1917 he developed this theme thus:

The menial moral standards of the Confucian clan society err in the distinction between the respected and the respectful classes, charging the latter with unilateral obligations. The results of this are that the ruler maltreats his subjects, fathers maltreat their children, parents-in-law maltreat their daughters-in-law, husbands maltreat their wives, masters maltreat their servants, and seniors maltreat their juniors. These unethical and evil deeds are done by those people in the belief that it is their prerogative to do so, and are suffered by the others who comfort themselves in terms of the same servile moral doctrines. No one dares to challenge them. The meek die in grief; the rebellious resort to violence. To guide a modern society and to win people's support with these doctrines with a view to elevating the general moral standard is trying to stop water from boiling merely by stirring it.[31]

Ch'en also wrote to Wu Yü, an anti-Confucian scholar, doubting the pontifical role of Confucius[32] in these words: 'No school of

charging the University with the guilt of 'liquidating Confucian ethics'. See Shu Hsin-ch'eng, *Chin-tai Chung-kuo Chiao-yü-shih*, III, 113 and also Hu Shih, *Chi-nien Wu-ssu*, [68] I, 8, 116.   30. [94] I, 45.

31. [94] IV, 52.   32. [94] IV, 30.

thought should be described as "supreme", for such a description can only inhibit the development of other schools.' Wu agreed with him and added:

I regard Confucius as a great man of *his time*. However, I am compelled to attack those who try to use his doctrines to silence present and future generations, to retard the progress of our culture, and to rekindle the dying flame of despotism.[33]

To Wu, the adherence to Confucian doctrines had been 'the cause of the scourge of despotism'.[34] Ch'en's and Wu's arguments were accepted and translated into more picturesque language by the most sardonic writer of modern China, Lu Hsün, who in his *Madman's Diary* described these doctrines as having 'the ferocity of a lion, the timidity of a rabbit, and the slyness of a fox'[35] and as being 'cannibalistic'.[36] He wanted the Chinese 'to cry out either like an oriole or like an owl. But they must not cry out in the same tone as those who, having just left a brothel, say quite unbashfully: "Chinese moral standards are the best in the world!"' [37]

From the attack on Confucius and his moral doctrines, the critics went farther to doubt the values of what was called the 'quintessence of the Chinese learning' (*Kuo-ts'ui*). Here the critics were divided among themselves. Dr. Hu Shih questioned the competence of those who claimed to be the guardians of the 'quintessence' and proposed to re-examine the entirety of it by using scientific and critical methods.[38] Ch'en Tu-hsiu, however, disagreed with this view from a pragmatic standpoint. 'If the application of this "quintessence" to our society today does only harm, then we should resolutely stop it.'[39] Yet, on this question, the most uncompromising was perhaps Lu Hsün, who argued:

If the quintessence of the Chinese learning is extraordinarily good, why is it that the present conditions of China are so extraordinarily bad?

A friend of mine put it most adequately: 'The quintessence should be able to preserve us before we can preserve it.' [40]

He despised those who had studied abroad and yet wanted to preserve the so-called 'quintessence'. He prescribed for them 'to

33. [94] IV, 29.   34. [99] III, 4.   35. [104] I, 284.
36. [104] 281 and 291.   37. [104] II, 41.
38. [100] IV, 162–3.   39. [99] III, 2.   40. [104] II, 24–5.

bow with both hands in front in the morning and to shake hands in the evening; to discuss physics and chemistry before lunch and chant the *Analects* and the *Odes* after supper.'[41]

The attack on Confucianism, either as a moral doctrine or as the 'quintessence of the Chinese learning', was inevitably bound up with the contemporary problems of China. Yuan Shih-k'ai, K'ang Yu-wei, and Chang Hsün were supporters of Confucius and, at the same time, monarchists, and therefore Ch'en Tu-hsiu saw the incompatibility between Confucianism and republicanism.[42] Many warlords wanted the Constitution to carry a specific article showing reverence to the great Master, and this, for Li Ta-chao, emphasized the contradictions between Confucianism and a republican constitution.[43] Ch'en, Li, and Lu Hsün also cursed the 'devilry' of the people such as robbery, ruthless killing, slave trade, spiritualism, polygamy, opium smoking, foot-binding, and so on.[44] Ch'en regarded it as no less dangerous to the nation than the warlords and foreign enemies[45]; hence he urged not only political but also ethical reform—the former necessitated the latter, for republicanism and democracy required the denunciation of Confucian traditions.[46]

In order to support . . . democracy we are obliged to oppose Confucianism, the code of ritual, chastity, traditional ethics, old politics; and in order to support . . . science, we are compelled to oppose traditional arts and traditional religion; and in order to support . . . democracy and science, we are forced to oppose the so-called national heritage and old literature.[47]

Dr. Hu Shih wholeheartedly supported this attitude.[48]

The introduction of science and democracy formed the more constructive aspect of the May 4th Movement. By democracy the new thinkers hoped to restrict the powers hitherto abused, and by science they hoped to rationalize the attitude to knowledge and to many of the problems which were confronting them. With their introduction the scholars hoped that the prospect of China's

41. [104] II, 57.   42. [99] III, 6.   43. [102] 77–8.
44. [94] III, 603–4, [102] 156, and [104] II, 47.
45. [94] I, 85–6.   46. [94] I, 53–6.
47. [99] VI, 1.   48. [99] VII, 1.

future could be improved. They believed in the omnipotence of democracy and science; so did the young people, including Mao Tse-tung, under their influence.

The movement was also a patriotic and political one, directed against the Japanese occupation of the German possessions in Shantung. The occupation took effect in September 1914 and in May 1915 Japan forced Yuan Shih-k'ai to accept the Twenty-one Demands, the first group of which gave her *de jure* recognition of her rights to inherit what had been Germany's special interests in that province.[49] In order further to secure her gains, Japan reached secret understandings with Britain, France, Italy, and Russia in February and March 1917,[50] and in order to prejudice China's claims at the peace conference after the European War, she lent great sums of money to Tuan Ch'i-jui's pro-Japanese Government, notably the loan on 28 September 1918 for the construction of two railways in Shantung.[51] China declared war against the Central Powers on 14 August 1917.[52] As an allied power, she had every reason to claim the restoration of her sovereign rights in Shantung. President Wilson's Fourteen Articles also greatly encouraged her and gave fresh hopes. As Liang Ch'i-ch'ao put it:

The announcement of the American President's Fourteen Articles caught the imagination of the whole world. All the nations which had had injustice done to them wanted to make an appeal to the President.[53]

Hu Shih, Chiang Monlin, and even Ch'en Tu-hsiu[54] expressed the same feeling. It was with precisely such feelings that the Chinese Delegation went to Paris, but only to be disappointed.

The Paris Peace Conference saw China taking part for the first time in an international meeting. China's as well as Japan's case on the Shantung question was presented and President Wilson gave his support to China. But at the Council of Ten on 27 January 1919, when Lloyd George revealed the contents of the five-power

49. [84] 184–7.
50. [21] III, 1167–9, [224] VII, 85, 87, and 239. See also R. H. Akagi, *Japan's Foreign Relations*, 320–1.
51. [26] July 1919, 169–70 and [109] 618.   52. [25] 15.8.1917.
53. [73] Essays, 35, p. 26.
54. [68] I, 8, p. 117; [95] 110; [94] III, 583.

understanding, there was great consternation.[55] All the major powers of the world, except for America, sided with Japan, who, for her part, threatened to boycott the Conference if her demands were not satisfied.

The dismal news of China's diplomatic failure reached Peking by the end of April, as Dr. Hu Shih recalled:

The ideals of President Wilson were defeated! The power politics of Clemenceau and Makino triumphed! Japan's demand for a free hand in Shantung was satisfied! These heavy blows were too much for the young people of China to bear. . . . They organized and led the heroic and patriotic movement which succeeded in defending their country's rights. Without the May 4th Movement, our delegates [at the Peace Conference] might have signed the Peace Treaty and these rights might have been lost.[56]

The reaction to the news was sharp. Ch'en Tu-hsiu at once described the Conference as a 'sharing-out' of the spoils[57] and he and Li Ta-chao indignantly said: 'This is still a world of robbers!'[58] The students of Peking responded not only with words, but with a gigantic demonstration on 4 May.[59] The movement spread out quickly to other parts of China and, at the same time, gained support from workers and businessmen. But the Peking Government, in the name of maintaining order, was hostile to it. President Hsü Shih-ch'ang issued no less than six decrees banning all demonstrations and his example was followed by the warlords in the provinces.[60] Eventually the Government yielded by allowing the pro-Japanese diplomats to resign and by refusing to sign the Peace Treaty.[61]

The movement succeeded in its patriotic objectives; it also succeeded in propagating new ideas throughout the whole country. 'Enthusiastic' and 'widespread' were the words Liang Ch'i-ch'ao

55. The *New York Times*, 22.4.1919 and also Sir Maurice A. P. Hankey's minutes of the Council of Four, quoted in Ge-zay Wood, *The Shantung Question*, 113.   56. [68] I, 8, p. 120.   57. [94] II, 27.
58. [94] III, 629 and [102], 213–14.   59. [109] 40–1 and [25] 10.5.1919.
60. [2] 7.5, 10.5, 15.5, and 26.5, 1919 and [109] 41, 166–8, 171–3, and 262–3. The warlords who banned students' demonstrations were Chang Tso-lin of Manchuria, Lu Yung-hsiang of Shanghai, Ni Ssu-ch'ung of Anhwei, Ch'en Shu-fan of Shensi, Chao Ti of Honan, Yang Shan-te of Chekiang, Wang Chan-yüan of Hupei, Ma Liang of Shantung, Li Hou-chi of Fukien, and Chang Ching-yao of Hunan.
61. [2] 11.6, and 11.7, 1919.

used to describe it.[62] Yet, like the Reform of 1898 and the Revolution of 1911, it was a movement led by progressive scholars who marched a long way ahead of the ordinary people, even of their fellow scholars. Therefore it lacked breadth in popular support. It also lacked depth in both its destructive and constructive aspects, for neither the effacement of Confucianism nor the introduction of democracy and science could be accomplished quickly. 'Civilization,' said Dr. Hu Shih, 'is built brick by brick.'[63] He believed that the problems facing China should be studied and solved one by one. For the less patient such as Li Ta-chao this was to put the cart before the horse. In Li's view, Chinese society lacked organization and vitality and its organs had ceased to function. 'Under such circumstances, any hope of solving individual problems must be preceded by a solution to the basic question of the society.'[64] While Hu searched for empirical solutions, Li was looking for 'some cosmic act of liberation', and B. Schwartz was not surprised that Li was the first to accept the messianic message of the October Revolution.[65]

The news of the students' movement from Peking stimulated Mao to action, and he and other members of the New Citizens Society issued broadsheets calling for a strike as well as the establishment of a students' union of Hunan. The union came into being on 3 June and on the next day, in response to its call, the students of Ch'angsha went on strike. Following their lead, the students of other towns of Hunan also struck and boycotted Japanese goods.[66] But soon the summer holiday came, the students went home and Chang Ching-yao, the governor, took the opportunity to disband the students' union.[67]

A further development of these organizational activities was the setting up of 'Groups of Ten'. By the middle of July there were more than 400 such groups which formed themselves into an association in October and Mao was elected to its executive committee.[68]

The anti-Confucianism, the demand for democracy and science, and the praise for Marxism which characterized the May 4th

62 [73] Essays, 37, p. 51.
63. [100] IV, 164.   64. Li Ta-chao's letter to Hu, [100] II, 175–6.
65. [52] 12.   66. [43] 95.   67. [43] 115.   68. [43] 98.

Movement were all uncritically and perhaps over-zealously accepted by Mao Tse-tung, as he himself said: '. . . every effort was made to learn from the West. In my youth, I too engaged in such studies.'[69] His writings published in the *Hsiang River Weekly Review* (*Hsiang-chiang P'ing-lun*) gave this its fullest expression. Incidentally, he began at this point to write in the new, easily comprehensible style, *pai-hua*.[70]

The *Hsiang River Weekly Review*, edited by Mao, made its first appearance on 14 July 1919 and was suppressed by Chang Ching-yao in August after only five issues.[71] Its circulation was between four and five thousand copies and each issue contained some 12,000 characters, mostly written by Mao. 'He often worked for the paper into the small hours of the morning and then, after a short nap, went straight to his class unwashed and unbreakfasted.'[72] On world affairs, he severely criticized the policies of Clemenceau, Lloyd George, and Woodrow Wilson at the Peace Conference and advocated a 'union of communist republics' as the only solution to the problems of central Europe. On domestic affairs, he attacked warlords and the civil wars they waged, spoke in favour of democracy and science, and urged young people to take advantage of the Work-study Scheme for going to France. In June Ch'en Tu-hsiu was arrested and Mao wrote in his paper demanding Ch'en's release.[73] But the most important single work by Mao in this period was 'The Great Union of the People' published in Nos. 2, 3, and 4 of the *Review*.

'The contending sides of a reform or a revolt in history, be it a religious, ideological, social, or political struggle,' he wrote, 'must each have its unity, for victory depends on the resilience of the unity. The triumph of the October Revolution was the triumph of the unity of the Russian people.' Having thus set the theme of his article, Mao went on to say that organization was the key to unity. People must be organized according to their social

69. [46] IV, 1475 or *SW*, IV (Peking), 412.
70. This is based on the quotation from Mao's writings in Li Jui's book. It would be of interest to compare Mao with other writers of the same period. Li Ta-chao wrote his first essay in *pai-hua* on 15 April 1918—'The Present' [99] IV, 4, 93–6; Liang Ch'i-ch'ao's first *pai-hua* essay was published on 10 October 1921; Tung Pi-wu taught his students at the Wuhan Middle School to write in *pai-hua* in 1920. [190] 39.
71. [34]. 72. [31] and [43] 99–100. 73. [43] 101–2.

status and classes and he paid special attention to the organization
of peasants and workers.[74] The article drew the notice of both the
left-wing intellectuals as well as the government of Hunan which
branded Mao as a 'radical'. Mao retorted:

What is a radical? . . .
He is no more than a patriot who fights for the interests of his country
and for liberation from a despotic rule.[75]

The article 'The Great Union' and another 'On Radicalism'
impressed a young student of Ch'angsha, Jen Pi-shih,[76] but not
unexpectedly infuriated General Chang Ching-yao, who banned
the paper.

However, Mao was soon able to find an outlet for his views. It
so happened that the students union of 'Yale in China' was in
difficulty over finding contributors to its weekly, the *Hsin Hunan*
(the New Hunan), and so Mao was asked to take over its editor-
ship from the seventh issue.[77] In that issue Mao announced a
set of new objectives for the paper—social criticism, thought
reorientation, introduction of new knowledge, and discussion of
current problems. Three issues later this journal, too, was suppressed by Chang Ching-yao.[78]

Mao also organized a discussion group, the *Wen-t'i Yen-chiu
Hui* (Problems Discussion Group), probably as a result of reading
the famous controversy of 'problems *versus* isms' between Dr.
Hu Shih and Li Ta-chao.[79] Unable to decide which one of these
two should come first, Mao proposed to have problems and isms
discussed simultaneously by the group, but to lay emphasis on
investigation before a problem or an ism came up for discussion.
Copies of the constitution of the group was sent to Mao's friend
at Peking University, Teng Chung-hsia, who published it in
No. 467 (23.10.1919) of the students' monthly of the University.[80]
Very little else about the group is known for it may not have been
a success. One problem, however, is known to have provoked a
great deal of discussion. On 14 November 1919 a bride cut her
throat behind the embroidered curtains of her bridal sedan-chair.

74. [18] 31 and [43] 103–5.   75. [43] 102–3.
76. Hsiao Ching-kuang, 'Tao Pi-shih' (In memoriam of Pi-shih), the *People's
Daily*, 31.10.1950.   77. [43] 108.
78. [43] 109.   79. *Vide supra*, p. 62.   80. [43] 108.

The event was widely reported and Mao published nine articles in the *Ta-kung Pao* of Ch'angsha from 16 to 28 November in which he described the bridal sedan-chair as a symbol of reaction and accused the existing evil social conditions of being responsible for this tragedy. Many people responded to Mao's view and wrote in his support.[81]

The suppression of the *Hsiang River Weekly Review* and the *New Hunan* deepened Mao's hatred of the governor Chang Ching-yao. Chang, being a leader of the Anhwei Clique of warlords and of the pro-Japanese An-fu Club, fared very badly in the anti-Japanese campaigns. The last straw for both Chang and the anti-Japanese was when Chang sent his brother with troops to disperse a mass rally for burning Japanese goods on 2 December. The students of technical and middle schools protested against this action by staging a strike on 6 December, and a week later 13,000 Hunan students signed a manifesto against the governor. Mao was active in this anti-Chang Ching-yao campaign whose leaders decided in January 1920 to send Mao to Peking and Ho Shu-heng and Hsia Hsi to Hengyang. Mao's mission was to gain the support of the Hunanese in the capital and that of Ho and Hsia was to solicit the co-operation of the powerful General Wu P'ei-fu in a joint effort to oust Chang Ching-yao.[82]

Mao went to Peking via Hankow where he issued an anti-Chang statement. Arriving at Peking in February, he rented a small room in a house south of the Lama Temple in Peich'ang Chieh (the North Avenue) whither Teng Chung-hsia often went to discuss Marxism and current problems with him.[83] From Yang Ch'ang-chi he obtained a copy of Kirkupp's *History of Socialism* (translated into Chinese by Chiang K'ang-hu) which filled him with wild excitement.[84] He also read the *Communist Manifesto* (translated into Chinese by Ch'en Wang-tao) as well as the Chinese translations of K. Kautsky's *Class Struggle* and F. Engels' *Socialism: Utopian and Scientific*.[85] Previously Mao's knowledge of Marxism had come indirectly from Li Ta-chao's articles in *La Jeunesse* and

81. [43] 109–11.　　82. [43] 114–18. *Vide infra*, p. 68.

83. Ma Fei-pai, 'Teng Chung-hsia T'ung-chih tsai Pei-ta' (Comrade Teng Chung-hsia at Peking University) [247] I, 90.

84. According to Hsiao San. See [50] 46 and [258] 153.

85. [18] 32 and [258] 153.

from other radical papers founded after the May 4th Movement[86];
now the works by Marx, Engels, and Kautsky put the finishing
touch to his conversion to communism.[87] He wrote to the members
of the New Citizens Society in Ch'angsha, advising them to organize into small groups for the collective study of Marxism.[88]
While he made great strides in his Marxian researches he failed
in his official mission. His life in Peking was as poor and as
miserable as during his first visit in 1918, but once again Yang
K'ai-hui gave him comfort.

In April Mao sold his fur coat for the fare to Shanghai[89] where
he met Ch'en Tu-hsiu again. This encounter under extremely
difficult circumstances was, according to Mao himself, 'probably a
critical period in my life'.[90] Ch'en was the man who influenced
him 'perhaps more than anyone else',[91] even his literary style was
affected by Ch'en.[92] In Shanghai, Mao worked as a laundryman,
tasting for the first time the life of an urban worker. He wrote
to the headmaster of the Ch'u-i Primary School in Ch'angsha:

I am working as a laundryman. The difficult part of my job is not
washing but delivery, as most of my earnings from washing has to be
spent on tram tickets which are so expensive.[93]

He stayed in Shanghai until July.

His return to Ch'angsha in July was hastened by the political
and military changes that had taken place. The peace negotiations
between the north and the south which President Hsü Shih-
ch'ang initiated soon after his investiture at the end of 1918 and
which had continued into the middle of 1919 now finally broke
down.[94] Pleased by this, Tuan Ch'i-jui at once resumed his policy
of unification by force and the army he had been training in the
guise of participating in the European War was now of considerable strength. The cease-fire in Europe did not interrupt his army
expansion programme, except that the three divisions and three

86. [99] VI, 5 and VII, 2. The other radical papers were the *Hsing-ch'i
P'ing-lun* (Weekly Review) of Shanghai, the *Chekiang P'ing-lun* (Chekiang
Review) of Hangchow, and the *Hsing-ch'i Jih* (Sunday) of Ch'engtu.
   87. [258] 153.   88. [43] 120.
   89. Ma Fei-pai, *ibid.* [247] I, 90.   90. [258] 154.
   91. [258] 151.   92. [50] 58–9.   93. [29] and [43] 120.
   94. [2] 10.10.1918, 19.1, 10.3, 22.5, 1919 and [89] I, 436, 441–2 and II, 42.
See also [123] 74.

brigades of the War Participation Army were now renamed the Northwest Frontier Defence Army.[95] Loyal to him were also the 9th, 15th, and 16th Divisions[96] and his friends in Japan. With these forces as his capital, he gambled on a unification by conquest. Tuan's rapid ascendancy alarmed Marshal Ts'ao K'un and his Chihli Clique and Marshal Chang Tso-lin and his Mukden Clique, and, furthermore, the Chihli Clique had so far been in favour of unification by appeasement. In the autumn of 1919 the alignment among the warlords became clear—Chihli, Honan, Kiangsu, Hupei, Kiangsi, and Manchuria reached an understanding among themselves to contain and check the expansion of the Anhwei Clique.[97] In doing so, the warlords reckoned that a war might not be avoidable, and if it broke out Wu P'ei-fu's 3rd Division stationed at Hengyang in Hunan would be indispensable to them.

As long as Wu P'ei-fu held Hengyang, Chang Ching-yao was safe in Ch'angsha. But by the autumn of 1919 Wu's troops had not been paid for *eight months*,[98] and there was little wonder that they wanted to go back to the north. Twice Wu asked for transfer; twice Tuan Ch'i-jui ignored him.[99] Consequently in January 1920 Wu and the southern troops reached an agreement on Wu's evacuation from Hunan at a cost of 600,000 *yuan* paid to him by the south.[1] On 20 May the evacuation began; five days later the 3rd Division was completely withdrawn from Hunan; another two days later the battle of Hunan started.

On paper the northern troops remaining in the province were still quite formidable, a total of some 70,000 including Chang Ching-yao's 7th Division, Li K'uei-yüan's 11th Division, Fan Kuo-chang's 20th Division, and Feng Yü-hsiang's enormous 16th Mixed Brigade. In addition, there were also the temporary 1st and 2nd Divisions under Chang Tsung-ch'ang and T'ien Shu-hsün respectively. But the 11th and 20th Divisions and the 16th Mixed Brigade were units of the Chihli Clique, hence non-participants in the battle, and the 7th, the temporary 1st and 2nd Divisions were fight-shy rabbles.[2]

95. [90] V, 15–16.   96. [26] 6.1919, 165.
97. [88] 443, [90] V, 130, and [93] 344–5.   98. [91] 246.
99. [90] V, 130.   1. [90] V, 131 and [93] 337.
2. [90] V, 142–6 and [91] 253–4.

As a governor, Chang Ching-yao's ineptitude and corruption surpassed most of his fellow warlords. During the European War copper was a scarce metal and Japan was buying it heavily and supplying it to her European allies. Chang assisted her in this enterprise by issuing irredeemable notes in exchange for copper cash which he sold to Japan as metal at a handsome profit.[3] This transaction completely disrupted the monetary system of Hunan; a shortage of the metallic currency and a depreciation of the paper notes ensued. Prices of daily necessities rose sharply and rapidly.[4] In addition, Chang made all his brothers commanding officers who plagued the people of Hunan by extortionate taxation, bullying, and threats of murder. Their ruthless suppression of the students' movement in 1919 antagonized the more articulate sector of the society. Therefore, as soon as Wu P'ei-fu left Hunan, the local forces under T'an Yen-k'ai, Chao Heng-t'i, Ch'eng Ch'ien, and others made a concerted effort to drive Chang Ching-yao out of the province.[5]

From 29 May to 6 June the Hunan troops under Chao and Ch'eng took Hengyang, Hsianghsiang, and Paoch'ing without much fighting and forced the northern troops to retire into Chuchow, Hsiangt'an, and Ch'angsha. On 11 June Chang Ching-yao set fire to Ch'angsha and fled in the resulting confusion.[6] Now, seeing the military situation in Hunan to be hopeless, Marshal Tuan Ch'i-jui, the Premier, deprived Chang Ching-yao of both his governorship and his command of the 7th Division. He tried to reach a *rapprochement* with the Chihli Clique (at the same time sowing seeds of dissension among its leaders) by offering the governor of Hupei, General Wang Chan-yüan, the post of the Inspector-General of Hupei and Hunan while appointing his henchman, Wu Kuang-hsin, Inspector of Hunan. Both Wang and Wu declined the offer. Meanwhile in Hunan itself, General Chao Heng-t'i entered Ch'angsha on 12 June and a few days later T'an Yen-k'ai arrived there to assume the civil governorship.[7]

The battle of Hunan was merely the prelude to the final test of strength between the Anhwei and Chihli Cliques of the northern

3. [43] 112 and 114, quoted: rom an appeal made by the Hunanese in Shanghai.   4. [43] 112.   5. [88] 443.
6. [90] V, 144-5.   7. [90] V, 149 and [91] 256.

warlords—history knows this as the Anhwei-Chihli War of 1920. General Wu P'ei-fu's 3rd Division took up its positions along the Paoting front on 15 June, and after an unsuccessful attempt at mediation by Chang Tso-lin, the war broke out on 14 July. Four days were all that were needed for it to end in Tuan's total defeat. Tuan resigned all his offices on 29 July and the An-fu Club was declared illegal on 4 August.[8] The Chihli Clique now became the masters of Peking.

The war in the north necessitated the withdrawal of the northern contingents in the south and with the departure of Feng Yü-hsiang's brigade on 6 July there was not a single northern soldier left in Hunan—a state of affairs dreamt of by the Hunanese for years. Now their problem was how to prevent the province from being used again as an outpost for either the north or the south. Other provinces which had been in a similar plight were consider-ing the same problem, and consequently between 1919 and 1924 scholars like Liang Ch'i-ch'ao, Hsiung Hsi-ling, Chang T'ai-yen, and Li Ta-chao, and warlords like T'ang Chi-yao of Yunnan, Lu Jung-t'ing of Kwangsi, Liu Hsien-shih of Kweichow, T'an Yen-k'ai of Hunan, and the miscellaneous forces in Szechwan all demanded autonomy and a federation of autonomous provinces.[9] But for Hunan with its strategic position this was a particularly urgent demand.

On the day when Feng Yü-hsiang's troops left, the respectable citizens, including Mao Tse-tung and Ho Shu-heng, published a declaration in the name of the Hunan Reconstruction Association which advocated the abolition of the post of military governor, disarmament, and the establishment of a democratic and self-determining government for Hunan.[10] This was followed by a petition to T'an Yen-k'ai signed by 377 people, including Mao, Chu Chien-fan, and Ho Shu-heng, calling for a provincial con-stitution and democratic elections.[11] T'an reacted quickly by hold-ing a self-government conference on 14 September, while Mao published no less than ten articles in the *Ta-kung Pao* of Ch'angsha in September and October supporting T'an and urging people to take part in politics.[12] Mao's views on this question may have been

8. [2] 29.7, and 4.8, 1920.   9. [81] 287–8, [87] 61, and [149] II, 1032.
10. [43] 124.   11. [43] 127.   12. [43] 125.

influenced by three factors—the years of instability in Hunan, Li Ta-chao's opinion on federalism, and the feeling that T'an Yen-k'ai would be the least of the evils.

After the expulsion of Chang Ching-yao, Hunan had been for a short while under the dual rule of T'an Yen-k'ai and Ch'eng Ch'ien, each controlling six out of the twelve defence areas.[13] T'an had the support of both Kwangsi and Kwangtung, while Ch'eng had that of the KMT. By the end of June T'an succeeded in forcing Ch'eng to leave the province, only to realize that his own power was gradually being undermined by his subordinate, General Chao Heng-t'i, who had very close connexion with the warlords of the neighbouring province of Kwangsi.[14] He was therefore in dire need of popular support in order to secure his own position and in his bid for it he was prepared to make liberal concessions to the people. This was, at least partly, the reason why Mao gave him his support. Furthermore, Li Ta-chao wrote on 1 February 1919 saying that federalism was the only feasible way for the creation of new China and the stepping-stone to the formation of a world union.[15] Mao evidently agreed with this. However, the federal movement was interrupted by several mutinies occurring in October and November, which were unmistakable signs of T'an's lack of control over his military following. Indeed, he was forced to resign his governorship on 23 November and the province was taken over by General Chao Heng-t'i, who styled himself the Commander-in-Chief of the Hunan Armies.[16]

Since his return in July Mao had been the director of the Primary School Section of the First Teachers' Training School, which post he continued to hold until the winter of 1922.[17] Teaching, however, was merely a job which offered him a measure of financial security; his interest was more in political studies and activities. At the same time in France a controversy developed between his friends, particularly between Ts'ai Ho-sen and Siao Yu: the former was in favour of the Russian type of socialism as the way to strengthen China, whereas the latter thought a gradual approach through education, trade unionism, and co-operatives was more suitable

13. [90] V, 108–9 and [91] 260.   14. [90] V, 108.
15. [102] 132 and 134.   16. [43] 130, [90] V, 221, and [81] 287–8.
17. [43] 142 and [54] 175.

for Chinese conditions.[18] Both sides appealed to Mao. Ts'ai wrote in August 1920 saying that, having steeped himself in socialist literature, he had come to the conclusion:

Socialism is certainly the cure for the ills of the world and also suitable for the future reconstruction of China. I think that the first thing we must do is to organize a party—the communist party which will be the promoter, propagandist, vanguard, and commander of the revolution. Unless it is organized, the revolutionary and labour movements in China cannot have a nerve-centre.

He wrote again in September, criticizing Kautsky, praising Bolshevism, and exhorting Mao

to choose carefully reliable people as candidates for the membership of the communist party and to plant them in trade organizations, factories, villages, and government councils. This done, we must formally set up a communist party.[19]

These letters reached Mao in November, and in his reply of 1 December 1920 he expressed his complete agreement with Ts'ai. He also said that the choice between the Russian and the gradual method had been put to the New Citizens Society and that he himself was opposed to the latter method. Education in his view needed money, qualified personnel, and schools, all of which were controlled by the ruling class. Newspapers, too, were in their hands. They dominated the parliament and government, made the law, owned banks and factories, and had the army and police on their side. They used all these to fight against workers and peasants. Therefore, according to Mao, it was impossible for the socialists to utilize education for their purposes unless they were in power. As long as they were not, it was wrong for them to rely on education for the transition to socialism.[20]

In the same reply, Mao criticized Bertrand Russell's speech made in Ch'angsha in October. Russell's opinion was that the communist objectives could be achieved without resorting to war, violence, proletarian dictatorship, or any other method which would destroy the liberties of the individual.[21]

Mao heeded Ts'ai Ho-sen's suggestion of organizing a communist party[22] and proceeded to search for comrades and funds.

18. [43] 134–5.   19. [43] 134–6.   20. [43] 135–6.
21. [43] 135 and [96] 249.   22. *Vide infra*, pp. 78 and 81-2.

His first step was to set up a bookstall; the plan for this was published in the *Ta-kung Pao* of Ch'angsha on 31 July and the meeting of more than 160 shareholders was held at the Ch'u-i Primary School the next day. At first he collected some 400 *yuan* (about £40) and this was increased to 1,000 *yuan* later. The Medical College of the 'Yale in China' agreed to let three rooms in Ch'ao-tsung Chieh to him as the premises of the stall, which was named 'Culture Bookshop' since the popularization of the new culture was its main purpose. Business began on 9 September, and a few months later seven branches were established in other towns in Hunan. The trade was good as the shops dealt with no less than 200 books, including *An Introduction to Marx's Capital*, *A History of Socialism*, *A Study of the New Russia*, and *The Soviet System and China* (all in Chinese) and some 40 periodicals such as 5,000 copies of the *Lao-tung Chieh* (the Workers) and 2,000 copies of *La Jeunesse*. The profits were later used to finance the socialist youth corps and later still the communist party.[23]

In August 1920 Mao and others founded a small Russian affairs study group as well as sponsoring a Work-study Scheme for students to go to Russia. Amongst the younger members who made use of this scheme there were Jen Pi-shih, Hsiao Ching-kuang, and Liu Shao-ch'i.[24] About the same time or slightly later Mao, with Ho Shu-heng, Ch'en Ch'ang, Hsia Hsi, Kuo Liang, and Hsiao Shu-fan, formed a Marxism study group in Ch'angsha which often met at the Primary School or in the office of the Alumni Society of the First Teachers' Training School, Mao being the director of the former and the chairman of the latter.[25] Similar groups had earlier been formed at other places[26] such as Peking and Shanghai, and the Shanghai group began the publication of its official organ, the *Communist Party Monthly* (Kung-ch'an-tang Yüeh-k'an), in November. This number carried articles on the history of the Bolshevik Party, the life of Lenin, systems of employment, Lenin's theory of state and revolution,

23. [43] 137–40. The bookstall in Ch'angsha was destroyed by soldiers during the so-called 'Horse-day Incident' or 21 May 1927 Massacre.
24. [43] 144–5 and 'Shih-yüeh-ke-ming ying-hsiang chi Chung-su kuan-hsi wen-hsien' (Documents concerning the influence of the October Revolution and Sino-Soviet relations), [3] 1957, no. 5, 128.
25. [43] 142–3.   26. *Vide supra*, p. 70.

and the latest activities of the Third International. In November and December Mao wrote articles recommending the paper to the readers of the *Ta-kung Pao* of Ch'angsha. In Shanghai, too, the first cell of the communist party, under the name of 'the communist group', came into existence in May and this was followed by a similar group in Peking and another in Ch'angsha under Mao's leadership.[27] Towards the end of 1920 Mao was busily occupied by the preparations for forming a socialist youth corps in Ch'angsha. The diary of Chang Wen-liang, a student of the First Teachers' Training School, had these entries:

17.11.1920   Received a letter from Tse-tung and the attached ten copies of the constitution of the Youth Corps, the aim of which was to study and carry out social reconstruction. He asks me to meet him on next Sunday morning and to look for true comrades.

21.11.1920   Met Tse-tung at the Popular Education Galleries, who told me that he would go to Liling to inspect schools. He again advised me to look for true comrades and said that this must be regarded as the principal objective of the Youth Corps at this stage. He thinks that we should proceed slowly but steadily.

2.12.1920   Tse-tung came and said that the foundation meeting of the Youth Corps would be held when Chung-fu [Ch'en Tu-hsiu] arrived. The work [of the Corps] would be concentrated on both study and practice. He asked me once again to look for more true comrades.

26.12.1920   Tse-tung came again and told me that the foundation meeting of the Youth Corps would be held in the next week.

27.12.1920   Tse-tung sent me nine copies of the *Communist Party Monthly*.[28]

The socialist youth corps of Ch'angsha was established at the end of 1920. Its members, comprising socialists of various schools, met on Sundays for discussions on political doctrine or current affairs while they were having an outing, a picnic, or rowing boats on the river.

The socialist and Marxist development in Ch'angsha was by no means an isolated phenomenon; parallel developments were taking place in other parts of China. Their confluence was the Chinese communist party founded on 1 July 1921. Among those who

27. [43] 149.
28. The diary was discovered in Ho Erh-k'ang's home. Chang, however, had never taken part in any revolutionary activity and, according to Li Jui, he eventually lost his sanity. [43] 147–8.

attended the foundation meeting were Mao Tse-tung and Ho Shu-heng, both representing Hunan. Hsieh Chüeh-tsai, an old friend and comrade of Mao, recalled:

One night when the sky was laden with dark clouds and it was about to rain, I was told that Mao Tse-tung and Ho Shu-heng were to go to Shanghai. The news was unexpected. Even more unexpected was that our offer to see them off was declined. Later it transpired that they were in fact on their way to attend the first congress of the communist party of China. . . .[29]

29. [40]. Siao Yu tells an entirely different story. According to him, he and Mao shared the same cabin and sailed in the *spring* of 1921. 'I took the upper berth and he the lower. Many friends came down to see *me* off, as they knew I would soon be returning to France; so we were very busy talking with them all afternoon.' [54] 197. (My italics.)

Chapter IV

The Marxist

T HE ten years (1911–21) of 'democratic republicanism' in China had caused three nation-wide civil wars[1] and many local ones, created a thousand warlords, brought about two imperial restorations,[2] and entailed huge domestic and foreign debts, but it had brought neither political nor economic stability, let alone progress. The system of the 'Great West' had been proved, it seemed, totally ineffectual in solving China's problems and the political parties, including the KMT, were shown to be completely impotent. The holocaust of 1914–18 only helped to confirm the defects of Western civilization and of the Peace Conference in particular, and to disappoint the Chinese still more. Moreover, three hundred thousand White Russians, many of them in penury, flooded such cities as Harbin, Tientsin, and Shanghai, bringing to an end the myth of European superiority.[3] The repercussions on the Chinese people of this changed and still changing situation were divided—some went back to what they called 'the quintessence of the Chinese learning'; others, unconvinced of the futility of Western learning, continued to be its advocates; others, again, saw a gleam of light through the October Revolution in Russia.

As has been pointed out before,[4] the first Chinese scholar to receive the message of the Russian Revolution was Li Ta-chao, who, writing in 1917,[5] had hoped for co-operation between

1. These took place in 1913, 1916, and 1920.
2. Yuan Shih-k'ai's restoration in 1915–16 and Chang Hsün's in 1917.
3. [75] 614 and [222] 159.   4. *Vide supra*, p. 62.
5. [99] III, 2.

nobility and commoners, capitalists and workers, and landlords
and tenants, but in 1918 welcomed the Russian Revolution as the
harbinger of a change in the public opinion not only of Russia
herself but also of the world as a whole.[6] He foresaw the replacement of theocracy and autocracy by humanitarianism and freedom
through the influences of the Russian Revolution and the creation
by the Russians of an entirely new civilization on the Eurasian
continent. He knew very little of what had been happening in
Russia, least of all what Marxism really implied. His zeal, partly
romantic and partly metaphysical, was essentially a manifestation
of his sanguine hopes for China's emancipation in a desperate
situation. With the translation of the works by Marx, Engels,
Kautsky, the introduction of Lenin's theories on revolution and
imperialism, and the publication of the Bolshevik party programmes
in Chinese,[7] a more precise assessment of the significance of the
October Revolution became possible. Thus Ch'en Tu-hsiu
recognized the need to found a country for the working class
which would outlaw the exploitation of men by political or legal
means,[8] while Dr. Sun Yat-sen became convinced of the necessity
of adopting the Russian method of revolution.[9] The causes of
China's new orientation were not so much the success of the Soviet
system as the shrewdness of Bolshevik propaganda and China's
own desperation.[10]

Aware of the value of friendly China in the face of the Japanese
invasion of the Maritime Province[11] as well as in her effort to
eliminate Western influence in Asia, Russia made her first overture
to China in 1918. Chicherin's statement in July at the 5th Congress
of Soviets indicated clearly a desire for normal diplomatic relations
with the Government in Peking,[12] but in less than a month the
same Chicherin wrote to Dr. Sun Yat-sen, stressing the common
aims of their countries and saying that 'our success is your
success; our ruin is your ruin'. He went as far as to describe the

6. [102] 104. This was written in July.
7. The programmes were translated by Chang Hsi-man [163] 86–7.
8. [94] III, 556, 1.9.1920.   9. [139] II, 468, 480–1, and 484.
10. The KMT delegates at the Congress of the Toilers of the Far East in
Moscow, February 1922, were disappointed by the poverty and chaos in Russia.
[210] 60–2.
11. J. M. Morley, *The Japanese Thrust into Siberia 1918*, N.Y., 1957.
12. [210] 45 and *Izvestia*, 5.7.1918.

Peking Government as 'a creature of foreign bankers'.[13] At that time Dr. Sun was in Shanghai: his government in Canton had collapsed nearly a year before.[14] Chicherin's two-pronged approach showed that the Bolsheviks were not only revolutionaries but also Russians.

The Russians also made contacts with Chinese warlords—with Wu P'ei-fu in central China and with Ch'en Chiung-ming in Canton.[15] This was the third ingredient of their China policy and the fourth was their contact with the left-wing intellectuals who were to become the founders of the CCP. Thus in February 1920 two agents of the Third International—Gregory Voitinsky and an overseas Chinese Yang Ming-chai[16]—went to Peking to meet and 'exchange views' with Li Ta-chao and then, through Li's introduction, approached Ch'en Tu-hsiu and Dr. Sun Yat-sen, in Shanghai.[17] The problem of organizing a party was discussed.[18]

The foundation of the CCP did have Russian assistance, but this is not to say that the party was a Russian creation. As early as the spring of 1918 Li Ta-chao and Ch'en Tu-hsiu set up a society for the study of Marxism[19] and after the May 4th Movement there were the Enlightenment Society (Chüeh-wu She) in Tientsin led by Chou En-lai and Teng Yin-ch'ao and the Benefit Book Club (Li-chung Shu-she) in Hupei organized by Yün Tai-ying.[20] These societies were not purely Marxist. The Socialism Study Group in Peking, 1919, Chang Hsi-man recalled,[21] was sponsored by Chang himself, Ts'ai Yüan-p'ei, and Li Ta-chao, of whom only Li could be described as a Marxist. An organization created later, the Social Science Study Group, more than a hundred strong, included guild socialists, anarchists, and syndicalists.[22] These were the groups Voitinsky and Yang Ming-chai found upon their arrival in China.

13. A. S. Whiting, *Soviet Policies in China, 1917–1924*, Columbia, 1954.
14. [90] V, 118–19 and [149] II, 1098.
15. [161] 24–5 and [9] II, 98 and 105.
16. [18] 40, [181] 5, [210] 54.
17. [18] 40, [96] 243–4, and 248, and [210] 54–5.   18. [18] 40.
19. [18] 37, [101] 116, and [210] 53.   20. [18] 37.
21. [163] 3. The other members of the group included Ch'en Tu-hsiu, Mao Tse-tung, Chou En-lai, and Ch'ü Ch'iu-pai. (See [163] 87–8.)
22. [163] 144–5. C. Brandt says in his *Stalin's Failure in China*: 'Actually Ch'en [Tu-hsiu] accepted, until well in 1921, the support of a motley crowd of

With the assistance of these two Comintern agents, the communist groups were brought into existence in Shanghai in May, in Peking and Ch'angsha in September, and in Canton at the end of 1920. Their epoch-making significance was that by their formation the Marxist movement in China was shown to have graduated from theoretical studies and entered upon practical action.[23] Before long Chinan, Hangchow, Wuhan, Tokyo, and Paris had their Chinese communist groups.[24] In addition, Ch'en Tu-hsiu initiated the socialist youth corps in August and his example was followed by Mao Tse-tung in Ch'angsha.[25]

Lack of homogeneity among the members of the groups and the corps was still evident. The Shanghai group, for instance, had seven members, but later four left it; the Peking group had, in addition to Li Ta-chao and Chang Kuo-t'ao, eight anarchists, three of whom left the group and were later compensated for by the gain of three new members—Teng Chung-hsia, Lo Chang-lung, and Liu Jen-ching; the Canton group, organized by Ch'en Tu-hsiu during his visit, included T'an P'ing-shan, Ch'en Kung-po, T'an Chieh-t'ang, and several anarchists, and later all the anarchists withdrew.[26] Consequently Ch'en Tu-hsiu began a cleaning-up operation by dissolving the socialist youth corps in May 1921 and reorganizing it in November.[27] Needless to say, this front organization had a larger membership than that of the groups. According to Chang Kuo-t'ao's report on 30 March 1921, the socialist youth corps at Peking University had 55 members in contrast to only about 10 in the communist group.[28]

The Peking group with the Peking–Hankow Railway as the centre of its activities ran workers' evening classes and published *Labour's Voice*; the Shanghai group also ran evening classes and foreign language schools, organized trade unions, and published a workers' tabloid, *Labour World*; the Canton group followed the same pattern by setting up workers' schools and publishing *Labour's Echo*.[29]

malcontents, ranging from anarchists to anti-militarists and anti-Confucianists.' ([161] 21.)   23. [14] 33 and [18] 40.   24 [43] 144.

25. Hu Hua says that the Ch'angsha group was established in October. This was not so. *Vide supra*, p. 73.   26. [43] 148, [193] 48–51, and [161] 21.

27. [43] 148 and [161] 21.   28. [3] 1957, no. 5, 106–8.

29. [14] 34–5 and [210] 55.

The gradual transfer of the emphasis of the communist movement from the intellectuals to the workers inevitably raised this question: with only an embryonic capitalism and a weak proletariat, could China miss out the capitalist stage and arrive directly at socialism? For the impulsive Li Ta-chao the answer was simple and easy:

Although there have not been serious disputes between the Chinese capitalists and workers, the nation is living at a time of growing labour movement throughout the whole world. It is therefore both illogical and impracticable for China to develop her capitalism. Let us examine her position in the world. Other nations have progressed from free competition to socialist enterprise. If we begin now from where the others started and follow their steps, it would be tantamount to starting life from the very beginning while the others have already reached their maturity. . . . As it is, we can only survive and adapt ourselves to the world community by exerting our utmost in the development of socialist enterprises.[30]

With this conviction, the twelve[31] delegates to the first congress of the CCP assembled at the Po-ai Girls' School in the French Concession of Shanghai on 1 July 1921.[32] Later, to avoid police harassment, the congress was moved to the South Lake of Chia-

30. Written on 20.3.1921. See [103] 189.
31. Ho Kan-chih ([14] 44), Hu Hua ([18] 53), Hsiao San ([39] 107–8), Ku Kuan-chiao ([181] 7) and Edgar Snow ([258] 154) all agree that the number was 12, but Tung Pi-wu, talking to Nym Wales ([190] 40), gave 13 names which were accepted by R. North ([210] 56). Ho and Hu name only four—Mao, Ho, Tung, and Ch'en T'an-ch'iu; Snow apparently gives six, including three wrong ones—Ch'en Tu-hsiu, Li Ta-chao, and Pao Hui-a[s]heng; Hsiao San leaves out all he dislikes—Ch'en Kung-po, Chang Kuo-t'ao, Liu Jen-ching, and Chou Fo-hai; Ku Kuan-chiao also leaves out the one he does not like—namely Mao Tse-tung—and replaces him with Ch'en Tu-hsiu who did not attend; Tung Pi-wu's list becomes correct when Pao Hui-sheng's name is deleted. The clue to a correct list is, however, provided by Hu Hua who says that there were two representatives from Hunan (Mao and Ho), two from Hupei (Tung and Ch'en T'an-ch'iu), two from Shantung (Wang Ching-mei and Teng En-ming), two from Shanghai (Li Ta and Li Han-chün), two from Peking (Chang Kuo-t'ao and Liu Jen-ching), one from Canton (Ch'en Kung-po), and one from Tokyo (Chou Fo-hai). See Appendix A.
32. Edgar Snow says that the date was May 1921, but all the others give the date 1 July. About the places, see [39] 107 and Ch'en T'an-ch'iu, 'Reminiscences of the First Congress of the Chinese Communist Party', the *Communist International*, October 1936, 1361–4, quoted by R. North in his notes to [54] 250–3. Li Ta says that the congress was held at 3, Shu-te Li, Wang-chih Lu, Shanghai ([8] 1961, nos. 13–14, 16).

hsing. Apart from the twelve delegates—Chang Kuo-t'ao, Ch'en Kung-po, Ch'en T'an-ch'iu, Chou Fo-hai, Ho Shu-heng, Li Han-chün, Li Ta, Liu Jen-ching, Mao Tse-tung, Teng En-ming, Tung Pi-wu, and Wang Ching-mei, there were also G. Maring and a Russian representing the Comintern.[33] Mao was elected the secretary of the congress.[34]

According to Tung Pi-wu, the records of this congress have long since been lost,[35] but from what can still be pieced together it seems that the delegates adopted the party's constitution and elected the Central Committee, which consisted of Ch'en Tu-hsiu as the party secretary, Chang Kuo-t'ao as the head of the organization department, and Li Ta as the head of the propaganda department, the three alternate members being Chou Fo-hai, Li Han-chün, and Liu Jen-ching.[36] On the basic question of a political philosophy, the delegates were far from unanimous. Ch'en Kung-po and Li Han-chün, the 'democratic minority', proposed a postponement of a decision on this question, pending an inquiry into the merits of Western social democracy as compared with Russian communism.[37] However, judging by the organizational principles followed by Mao in Hunan in the autumn of 1921, the majority must have supported the adoption of the Bolshevik rules and regulations such as its iron discipline, compulsory subscriptions, obligatory attendance at party meetings, and the practice of self-criticism.[38] Another basic question concerned the political activities of the party: Ch'en Kung-po and Li Han-chün considered that in the light of the political situation at the time the party should pursue only such legitimate activities as research and propaganda, whereas Liu Jen-ching, Chang Kuo-t'ao, and Mao

33. [190] 39.
34. [39] 107.
35. [8] 1961, nos. 13–14, 11 and [190] 40.
36. [193] 80 and [258] 155. Snow has a different list which includes Ch'en, Chang, Li as well as Ch'en Kung-po, Shih Tseng-tung [Ts'un-t'ung], Sun Yuan-lu [Shen Hsüan-lu or Shen Ting-i], Li Han-tsen [chün], and Li Sun [Sen]. Tung Pi-wu ([8] nos. 13–14, 11) surprises us all by saying that Mao was also elected to the Central Committee!
37. [137] 23 and [161] 22. Ch'en Kung-po resigned from the CCP shortly afterwards (23–4).
38. [18] 53, [43] 152, and [161] 22. It should be safe to say that Mao followed the resolutions of the congress rather than did something on his own initiative.

advocated that the party should lead the workers in class struggle.[39] Again, the more radical wing was victorious, hence the decision to set up the Secretariat of the All-China Labour League.[40] The third question deliberated upon was the party's attitude towards other political forces in China, particularly Sun Yat-sen's KMT which had established itself once more in the province of Kwangtung.[41] This, however, was not as important as the other two, since the CCP was so small and insignificant, having only some fifty members.[42] Nevertheless, in view of Ch'en Chiung-ming's flirtations with Russia, his invitation to Ch'en Tu-hsiu to organize education and propaganda in Kwangtung, and his appointment of P'eng Pai and Ch'en Kung-po to government posts, above all on account of the preponderance of his military power, the Cantonese delegate to the congress, Ch'en Kung-po,[43] favoured an alliance with General Ch'en instead of with Sun Yat-sen—a view contradictory to the policy of the Comintern.[44] In the end, the congress resolved on a vaguely phrased policy of adopting a critical attitude towards the teachings of Dr. Sun while giving support to his various practical and progressive actions in the form of *non-party* collaboration.[45]

After the congress Mao went back home as the secretary of the Hunan branch of the CCP, his immediate tasks being the absorption of the students and workers in the socialist youth corps into the party and the establishment of a party cell among the miners in Anyüan.[46] Since he was preoccupied by party and other political activities, the New Citizens Society received little of his attention.[47]

For the fulfilment of the first task, Mao and Ho Shu-heng established a training centre, the Self-education College, in Ch'angsha in August 1921, which was, according to an advertise-

39. [18] 53, [43] 150, and [181] 7. Hu Hua refers to 'the struggle for the proletarian dictatorship', Li Jui to the 'struggle of the workers and peasants', and Ku Kuan-chiao to 'class struggle'. I think that it would be premature to talk about 'proletarian dictatorship' with reference to 1921 and the question of peasants received no attention at all at the first congress. Therefore Ku Kuan-chiao's vague expression of 'class struggle' is perhaps the most appropriate.
40. [18] 53.   41. [130] II, 501–2.   42. Appendix A.
43. [193] 50–2. See also [9] II, 101 and [82] 27 and 31, and [161] 23.
44. [161] 23. The reference to T'an P'ing-shan here is wrong, for he did not attend the congress.
45. [18] 53 and [54] 250–3.   46. [43] 151 and [258] 155.
47. [54] 188.

ment which appeared on 16 August, 'for students who wish to study but either lack financial ability or are dissatisfied with the present school system'. It had two departments—arts and political economy—and, apart from foreign languages, there were no classes, only discussions in which the students were asked to take part. The admission of a student was decided on his answers to a questionnaire and two entrance examinations. Six questions were set in the questionnaire: 1. scholastic and other experiences, family and financial background; 2. subjects already studied; 3. subjects proposed to study and why; 4. proposed duration of study and plans after graduation; 5. views on life; and 6. views on social problems. Once admitted, a student was allowed to pursue his studies free of any charge. In April 1923 there were twenty-four students at the college.[48]

In September 1922 a preparatory class was added to the college for students of junior middle school level,[49] the emphasis being on lessons rather than the students' own research. Ho Shu-heng, Li Wei-han, Hsia Hsi, Chiang Meng-chou, Lo Hsüeh-tsan, and Hsia Ming-han were some of the teachers who taught Chinese, English, mathematics, history, and geography to the students who, at the peak of the class, numbered more than two hundred including workers from the factories in Ch'angsha.[50]

On 15 April 1923 the college began the publication of its monthly, the *Hsin Shih-tai* (The Modern Age), whose first issue contained an article on imperialism, a *résumé* of Marx's *Critique of the Gotha Programme*, and Mao's 'Foreign Influence, Warlords, and Revolution' (*Wai-li Chün-fa yü Ke-ming*) advocating co-operation with the KMT against imperialism and warlords as the only way to China's liberation. Mao predicted that the warlords would never be able to achieve a measure of unity among themselves and the increasing misery the people suffered would turn more and more of them to revolution.[51] In the ensuing issues, the monthly carried such articles as 'Marxism and China', 'A Criticism of Idealism', and 'Communism and Economic Progress'.[52]

48. Based on a report published in the Ch'angsha newspapers in April 1923. See [43] 153–4.
49. Equivalent to the first three years of an English secondary school.
50. [43] 156–7.   51. [43] 156.   52. [43] 156.

'The heresy' taught at the college (said a decree issued by the governor of Hunan, General Chao Heng-t'i) 'may endanger law and order.' The college was therefore dissolved in November 1923.[53] But a few weeks later, on 24 November, it reappeared under the innocuous name of the Hsiang-chiang Middle School. While he was a student at the school, Hsia Erh-k'ang wrote in his diary:

1924	a subject for composition: 'Why do not all people believe in communism?'
28.4.1924	two hours of civics devoted to Lenin's thesis on national revolution; prepare for May Day speeches.
5.5.1924	celebrate 107th birthday anniversary of Marx.
7.5.1924	a demonstration against the Japanese, British, and American imperialists and against the Twenty-one Demands.[54]

Although the work among students continued to be an important task for some members of the CCP in Hunan, Mao, according to available records, took a very small part in it. His own time and energy were devoted more to the party itself and to organizing workers. Hunan was industrially underdeveloped, with only antimony mines at Hsik'uangshan, tin and zinc at Shuik'oushan, and the textile factories, mint, and electric power-station in Ch'angsha, all of which employed only a small number of workers. Mao and his comrades consequently had to turn their main attention to the coal mines at Anyüan in west Kiangsi.[55] At the beginning Mao and Li Li-san met with a great deal of resistance from the 2,000 miners who were sceptical of the educated men's motives. In order to win their trust, day classes for their children were established[56] and on 1 May 1922 the Anyüan Workmen's Club was formally opened by Mao.[57] Li Li-san was appointed the director and Chu Shao-lien the deputy director of the Club. Later Mao sent another man to help them when the membership had swelled from the initial 300 to nearly 7,000.[58] He also appointed Kuo Liang to take charge of a larger club of the workers on the Hankow–Canton Railway.

53. [43] 157.
54. [43] 158–9.   55. [17] 60–3.   56. [43] 166.
57. [190] 84, Ts'ai Shu-fan's statement.
58. [43] 183.

The Anyüan Mining Company had been opened in 1898 by Chang Chih-tung with German technical and financial assistance; the working conditions were miserable and the German staff supercilious.[59] The development of the workers' clubs had no effect in alleviating working conditions or improving the attitude of the management. The situation was ripe for a strike.

At the beginning of September 1922, Mao and Liu Shao-ch'i, who was dispatched thither by the Secretariat of the All-China Labour League, went to P'inghsiang and Anyüan to direct the scheduled strike.[60] Liu's terms for the improvement of the workers' lot were refused by the management which, for its part, threatened to dissolve the clubs if the strike took place. But the strike *did* take place on 13 September and the railwaymen's had already begun on 9 September. In both cases the troops intervened, killing six and wounding more than 70 strikers. The violent suppression only provoked more workers to strike action, but eventually through the mediation of the local chamber of commerce the strikes were brought to an end. Wages were raised, pay arrears cleared, the clubs allowed to function, and a trade union was formed.[61] But in 1925 the mines went bankrupt, so the labour movement in Anyüan died out in spite of Liu Shao-ch'i's effort to revive it.[62] Some of the trade unionists joined Mao at Ching-kangshan in 1927.[63]

According to Mao himself, the labour movement in China began in earnest after the first congress of the CCP,[64] and the strikes in September and October 1922 were certainly landmarks in the history of the labour movement in Hunan. Now, realizing the efficacy of this new weapon, the workers of other trades called strikes. By and large they were successful, and at the beginning of November more than twenty unions formed themselves into an association with Mao as its chairman and Kuo Liang, Lo Hsüeh-tsan, and others as his assistants.[65] This association claimed to have 40,000 or 50,000 members, but this figure was a gross exaggeration as the total number of workers in Hunan did not

59. [190] 84.   60 [43] 183-4.
61. [43] 186-7 and [190] 86.   62. [43] 187 and [190] 86.
63. [43] 163.   64. [46] II, 690 or *SW* III, 143-4.
65. [43] 162-3 and 230-1.

exceed 30,000.[66] The political consciousness of the workers was still very low; they were willing to struggle for their own economic benefit or against imperialism, but were scarcely able to grasp the meaning of any other political objective.[67]

By 1923 Mao had Liu Shao-ch'i, Li Li-san, Kuo-Liang, Lo Hsüeh-tsan, and his brothers, Mao Tse-t'an and Tse-min, helping him in the labour movement, while in the work of the party he had the assistance of Hsia Hsi and Hsiang Ching-yü, and in the work of the Communist Youth Corps, that of Hsiao Shu-fan and Li Yao-jung.[68] The Hunan branch of the Youth Corps, nearly 2,000 strong, was the largest in China, but the peasants' association under Liu Chih-hsün,[69] who was killed in 1933, did not receive much attention.[70]

In a wider field, the much discussed question in 1922 and 1923 was the formation of a revolutionary united front. The problem was considered at a congress of communist parties in Moscow in January 1922 and then at a meeting of the Central Committee of the CCP on 18 June. Ch'en Tu-hsiu, the secretary of the CCP, did not favour the proposal that the party should make an alliance with the KMT as a 'bloc within' it, for he 'wanted the CCP to act as an independent party, to expand its energies in the area of mass "education" and mass organization until the time came for the seizure of power by the "proletariat".'[71] His view was supported by Chang Kuo-t'ao, Kao Yü-han, and Ts'ai Ho-sen.[72] Li Ta-chao, too, agreed with him, as he was in favour of an alliance with Wu P'ei-fu.[73] The meeting of the Central Committee in June decided to regard the KMT as an ally, but did not say whether the alliance was to take the form of a 'bloc within'.

On 1 July, the second congress of the CCP was held in Shanghai, with twelve delegates, including Teng Chung-hsia, Ts'ai Ho-sen, and his wife, Hsiang Ching-yü, who represented 123 members.[74] Mao told Edgar Snow that he was sent to Shanghai to help

66. All Li Jui's figures, [43] 161–2.
67. As Teng Chung-hsia remarked: 'Generally speaking, the trade unions of that period had only an organized upper echelon.' ([43] 173 n.)
68. [43] 168–9 and notes on 17, 87, 98, 142, and 157.
69. *Vide infra*, p. 123.   70. [43] 98n., [52] 74, and [258] 160.
71. [52] 83.   72. [14] 71 and [161] 30–1. See also [167] and [137] 25.
73. [161] 25.   74. [14] 49–51 and [18] 66–7.

organize the movement against Chao Heng-t'i in the *winter of* 1922. 'I intended to attend [the second congress]. However, I forgot the name of the place where it was to be held, could not find any comrades, and missed it.'[75] He must have been confusing it with the fourth congress held in the winter (January) of 1925.[76]

The manifesto of the second congress said: 'The alliance with the petty bourgeoisie served the sole purpose of securing the flanks of the proletariat while it laid the groundwork for soviets.'[77] But by 'petty bourgeoisie' the party meant the poor peasants, shop-keepers, and artisans, not the KMT. The congress was also known to have agreed to 'eliminate civil strife, overthrow the warlords, and establish internal peace', and to 'cast off the yoke of international imperialism and achieve the complete independence of the Chinese people'[78]; the method for achieving such aims of a democratic revolution was, however, no more than the formation of a democratic united front[79] with the Soviet Union and the oppressed peoples of the world. The debate over a 'bloc within or without' went on; for the time being no conclusion was reached.

Mao married Miss Yang K'ai-hui in the winter of 1921[80] and there were a boy and a girl of this marriage. In 1930 Yang K'ai-hui, the boy, and Mao's sister, Tse-hung, were all arrested by Ho Chien, then the governor of Hunan.[81] General Ho insisted that Yang should renounce her marriage to Mao, but she refused and so was killed. In 1957 Mao dedicated his poem, 'The Immortals', to her memory:

'My proud poplar is lost to me . . .'[82]

---

75. [258] 156. 76. *Vide infra*, pp. 98-9. 77. [161] 29.
78. [14] 51. 79. [18] 67.
80. [43] 25. Snow says that Mao's second marriage was in 1920 ([258] 153); but this is highly unlikely. Mao returned to Ch'angsha in July 1920 and was penniless after a long spell as a laundryman in Shanghai. At that time Yang Ch'ang-chi, K'ai-hui's father, was either very ill or dying, indeed he died that .year (*vide supra*, p. 53). It would be quite improper for a daughter to marry in such circumstances. A supplementary piece of evidence in ascertaining the date of Mao's second marriage is Hsieh Chüeh-tsai's report of Mao moving house in the winter of 1921. It was probable that he moved to a new house prior to his marriage. See [40].
81. [39] 94, [43] 25, [258] 173, and [54] 44. Snow mentions the arrest of Mao Tse-hung, but Siao Yu is the only one to say that Yang K'ai-hui was killed in 1927.
82. *Vide infra*, p. 347.

Mao Tse-hung was killed too. At the time the whereabouts of the boy was unknown, and later Mao sent people to Hunan to look for him without success.[83] But in a Chinese publication in 1947[84] there was an entry on Mao An-ying, saying that he was the son of Mao and Yang K'ai-hui and had been to Moscow for his education. The report also said that he returned to Yenan in the spring of 1946.

The governor of Hunan in 1923 was General Chao Heng-t'i who became fearful of the growing labour movement in his domain and took steps to suppress it. His action led Mao, as the chairman of the Hunan Association of Trade Unions, and twenty-one other labour representatives to sound the provincial authorities on the question of the government's attitude towards labour. On 11 and 12 December 1922 they saw some municipal officials and on the 13th they were received by General Chao himself. Mao proposed to Chao that the government should announce its labour policy and reaffirm its pledge of freedom of association as embodied in Article 12 of the provincial constitution. He also suggested that there should be constant contacts between the government and the labour unions in order to eliminate misunderstanding and an official mediator should be appointed to help settle disputes.[85] Chao did not commit himself at this meeting, merely saying that his intention was to protect rather than oppress the working man.[86] Afterwards Chao told others: 'So long as Mao Tse-tung is in Hunan there can be no room for me.'

In April 1923 Chao issued an order for Mao's arrest, for Mao was a 'radical' and by 'radical' Chao meant 'either an anarchist, a Marxist, or a communist'.[87] A fortnight later Mao left Hunan for Shanghai.[88]

83. [50] 143.
84. [24] 121. Siao Yu uses the verb 'is' when describing Mao's son on [50] 43.
85. [43] 233–4.   86. [43] 234.
87. [43] 236–7. Three years earlier Mao had been branded a radical by Chang Ching-yao. *Vide supra*, p. 64.
88. [18] 138 and [43] 236.

Chapter V

The First United Front

THE momentous decision to form a united front between the KMT and the CCP was taken in 1923; the match-maker was Russia.

Russia was willing to play this part because a friendly China was of great value to her. Furthermore, as H. Isaacs points out, 'the colonial powers were being challenged in the years after 1918 in almost all the countries of Asia. . . . But circumstances of geography and time fixed China as the main theatre of active Russian intervention.'[1] The intervention by the Soviet Government began with Chicherin's statement of 1918 repudiating the encroachments on China's sovereign rights by Czarist Russia,[2] and this was followed by an even more definitive pronouncement known as the Karakhan Declaration of 1919.[3] These promises to renounce all the secret treaties with the Czarist Government and the conquests made by it greatly heightened the hopes of the Chinese intellectuals.

Nevertheless, the more intensive, also more important, intervention was carried out by the Comintern and the Bolshevik Party. At the second congress of the Comintern in 1920, Lenin came out with a thesis on the alliance with bourgeois democracy in backward countries, proposing that '. . . the Communist International must enter into a temporary alliance with bourgeois democracy in colonial and backward countries, but must not

1. [205] 43.
2. A. S. Whiting, *Soviet Policies in China, 1917–1924*, 30 and [210] 45.
3. [174] I, 159–60 and Whiting, *ibid.*, 30. Compare with *The Times*, 1 April 1920.

merge with it, and must unconditionally preserve the independence of the proletarian movement even in its most rudimentary form.'[4] Subsequently the Comintern resolved on the national and colonial question in these words: 'All communist parties must support by action the revolutionary liberation movements in these [backward] countries.' And 'it is particularly important to support the peasant movement in the backward countries'.[5]

As regards this, Brandt, Schwartz, and Fairbank point out 'the basic ambiguity' of 'Lenin's thesis in its failure to specify the nature and duration of "temporary . . . alliance".'[6] One answer to this may be that the duration could only be determined by the specific conditions in which an alliance was made. But a more serious ambiguity springs from the lack of a clear definition of either 'bourgeois democracy' or 'the revolutionary liberation movement'. When these terms were applied to China, did they mean that the KMT of 1920 was a bourgeois democratic party leading the revolutionary liberation movement in China or was it the movement itself? Trotsky said unequivocally that it was a bourgeois party[7] while Stalin disagreed, putting forward the view that it was a coalition of different classes, not a pure bourgeois party.[8]

At the fourth congress of the Comintern in November 1922, Lenin again urged the communist parties of backward countries to co-operate with bourgeois nationalist groups but at the same time to preserve their political independence. Speaking at the same congress, Karl Radek admonished the Chinese Party: 'Many of our comrades out there locked themselves up in their rooms and studied Marx and Lenin as they had once studied Confucius.'[9] The Chinese representatives at the congress were Ch'en Tu-hsiu and Liu Jen-ching and it was Liu who spoke for the CCP:

If we do not join this party [the KMT] we shall remain isolated; we shall preach a communism which is certainly a great ideal but which

4. Whiting, *ibid.*, 50.
5. [173] I, 143–4. The resolutions were taken on 28 July 1920.
6. [162] 68. 7. [202] 219. 8. [202] 219–30.
9. Lenin's thesis was drafted by M. N. Roy. See [205] 48–9. See also [162] 53 and Whiting, *ibid.*, 96.

the masses cannot follow. If we do join the party . . . we can rally the
masses around us and split the KMT.[10]

The party's earlier reluctance seemed to have given way to a new
attitude.

In China itself, the conditions were not as easy as the Comintern
visualized. When G. Voitinsky called on Dr. Sun Yat-sen at the
latter's refuge in Shanghai, the question of an alliance may not
have been raised.[11] In 1921 G. Maring, having seen Ch'en Chiung-
ming in Canton, called upon Dr. Sun Yat-sen at Kweilin in
Kwangsi where he stayed from 23 to 26 December.[12] At their first
meeting he put forward three proposals: 1. the reorganization of
the KMT into a coalition of classes, particularly of workers and
peasants; 2. the foundation of a military academy; and 3. co-
operation with the CCP. He asked Sun: 'What [in your opinion]
is the basis of [the Chinese] revolutionary movement?' Sun
replied: 'The unbroken heritage from the Great Yao, Shun, Yü,
T'ang, King Wen, King Wu, Duke of Chou, and Confucius to the
present day is the basic principle of my political thought.' Maring
was bewildered and asked the same question again. Sun again
gave him the same reply.[13]

During their second conversation, Maring once more raised the
question of co-operation. Dr. Sun refused it on the ground that
China, being different from Russia, should not adopt Russian
methods. Furthermore, he said that since he was planning a
northern campaign against Wu P'ei-fu in the Yangtze Valley, the
British sphere of influence, his alliance with Russia might induce
Wu to seek British assistance. Co-operation in his view should
be postponed until after the campaign but, for the time being, he
would welcome any moral support from Russia.[14]

The *impasse* at Kweilin did not daunt Maring, who turned round
to the CCP and tried to cajole it into accepting an alliance with the
KMT. The second congress of the CCP agreed in principle to
entering into an alliance but shelved the suggestion of a 'bloc

10. Whiting, *ibid.*, 95, and a similar report can be found in [190] 7.
11. [193] 138–9.
12. [18] 78, [130] II, 519–20, [135] VIb, 100b.
13. [130] II, 518–19, quoting from the *Ssu-min Pao* of Kweilin, 28 December
1921.
14. [130] 519–20.

within'. The question came up again at the Central Committee of the CCP in August 1922 when Maring's recommendation was that the communists should join the KMT as individual members but should not give up their CCP membership. His ulterior motive was 'to make use of the KMT organizational structure as a means for developing their [the communists'] own propaganda and contact among the masses'.[15] The majority of the Central Committee was opposed to this and Maring was compelled to invoke the authority of the Comintern in order to coerce the Chinese into acquiescence.[16]

Russia made another attempt to weld the alliance between the KMT and CCP. V. Dalin, the delegate of the Russian Communist Youth League, presented to Sun a plan of co-operation which Sun rejected, but Sun agreed to admit communists into the KMT as individuals provided that they would obey the KMT discipline.[17] Thus the ground was prepared and the time ripe for Adolf Joffe to meet Sun at Shanghai. Before Christmas 1922 the Far Eastern Bureau of the Comintern issued its first formal instruction to the CCP 'to co-ordinate the activities of the KMT and the young CCP'. According to P. Mif, by then the communists had already entered the KMT as individuals; according to Wang Ching-wei, Li Ta-chao was the first to have done so.[18] Sun met Joffe at a time when he had been ejected from Canton by Ch'en Chiung-ming[19] and his political career was on the verge of ruin. An *entente* of four points was therefore speedily concluded; the policy of a 'bloc within', favoured by Stalin, was formally inaugurated.[20]

While the negotiations between the parties went on, the warlords indulged in another civil war. The arena was Chihli (now Hopei), the time was the end of April and the beginning of May 1922, and the belligerents were Wu P'ei-fu and his Chihli Clique and Chang Tso-lin and his Mukden Clique.[21] From this war Wu emerged the victor. On becoming hegemonic, Wu endeavoured

15. [205] 58 and [210] 64.   16. [162] 52, [167], and [173] II, 5.

17. [161] 31 and [193] 140–1. D. J. Dallin ([202] 210) errs in saying that Dalin approached Sun before Maring.

18. [184] 21–2 and [193] 84 respectively. Li's declaration made on his entry into the KMT is reprinted in [130] IX, 41–8.   19. [88] 485 and [120] X, 3.

20. Stalin was not convinced of the workability of the policy of a 'bloc without' until the second united front in 1935. See [162] 53.

21. [88] 474–7, [93] 379–80, [25] May 1922, and [7] 1923, 575.

to unify the country by force. The Yellow River was his; the Yangtze Valley was under his henchmen, Generals Ch'i Hsieh-yüan and Hsiao Yao-nan; Fukien was invaded by General Sun Ch'uan-fang, and Kwangtung was controlled through Ch'en Chiung-ming and Shen Hung-ying.[22] But Kwangtung, like Szechwan, Shensi, and Hunan, was an exceedingly complex province, supporting some 270,000 troops of different origins and allegiances,[23] which preferred particularism to unity. Ch'en Chiung-ming's supremacy and his a'liance with Wu P'ei-fu there-fore scared these miscellaneous forces. Exploiting this situation, Dr. Sun's troops with their co-operation fought and took Canton in January 1923. Thereafter the fortunes of the belligerents fluctuated as the seesaw battle went on throughout the year.[24]

This was the national political scene Mao found upon his arrival at Shanghai, where he remained until the end of 1923.[25] He assisted in the work of the Central Committee of the CCP for a short time and in June he took part in the third national congress of the party at Canton.

Thirty delegates, representing 432 members, attended the congress which had the problem of the united front with the KMT as the main item on its agenda. Although Chang Kuo-t'ao con-tinued to resist the 'bloc within' policy, Ch'en Tu-hsiu had given up his initial stand in favour of the Comintern attitude. He argued that 'without the help of the bourgeoisie the democratic revolution would lose all its class significance and social basis'. Therefore it was necessary for the revolutionary bourgeoisie and the revolutionary proletariat to come to a compromise and fight shoulder to shoulder against the warlord class. 'The task of the KMT at the moment,' declared Ch'en, 'is to lead the revolutionary bourgeoisie and co-operate with the revolutionary proletariat in the bourgeois democratic revolution.'[26] He was quite willing to concede the leadership of the revolution to the bourgeoisie and only when this stage of the revolution had been won, 'the bourgeois

22. [86] III, 485.
23. [151] II, 92.
24. [130] II, 590–628 and [135] VId, passim, in particular 70b.
25. [43] 237 and [258] 156.
26. Ch'en Tu-hsiu, 'Tzu-ch'an-chieh-chi ti ke-ming yü ke-ming ti tzu-ch'an-chieh-chi' (Bourgeois revolution and revolutionary bourgeoisie) [166].

republic could be overthrown and replaced by the dictatorship of the proletariat'.[27]

Having lost on this basic question, Chang Kuo-t'ao fought a rearguard action by trying to keep the trade unions out of the control of either party while Ch'en Tu-hsiu, perhaps also Maring, advocated KMT-CCP joint control of the unions. A vote was taken and Ch'en had a majority of only one vote.[28] According to Chang Kuo-t'ao, Mao supported him first and changed his vote afterwards to increase Ch'en's majority to two. Li Li-san, however, supported Chang throughout the debate.[29]

Chang Kuo-ta'o's objection to the joint control was of very little practical significance, for the KMT was then a loosely organized party with neither politically conscious cadres nor a solid popular basis, and its control over the unions was not, and was not likely to be, firm. Once inside the KMT, the communists with their usual zeal for work would outstrip the Nationalists in winning popular support and would put the unions under their wing. This must have been the view forming in the minds of Ch'en and Maring and later expressed in the seventh issue of the official organ of the Chinese socialist youth corps on 16 April 1924:

Upon joining the KMT, we must concentrate our attention on the work among the rank and file and avoid unnecessary competition for high posts which may produce harmful effects [on the alliance] and provoke unfavourable reactions [outside the alliance]. We must not, however, restrict the activities of the members of our corps. While adopting a conciliatory attitude, we should direct our attention to the development of our work in the district and city branches of the KMT.[30]

And it may have been this attitude which eventually persuaded Mao to change his vote.

One result of this *volte face* was perhaps his election to the Central Committee.[31] In his own words, his main task was 'co-ordinating the measures of the CCP and the KMT'.[32] It was therefore likely that Mao had joined and won the goodwill of the KMT; otherwise it would have been inconceivable that such a

27. [14] 70–1.
28. Only 27 delegates had the right to vote. ([14] 67 and [18] 74.)
29. [161] 36–7.   30. [113] 92.   31. [179] 10 and [258] 156.
32. [258] 159.

task could be his. Nevertheless, he was ill qualified for it. His experience outside communist circles was confined to a short period as a library assistant at Peking University, a post so humble that people had avoided him, several months as a laundryman in Shanghai, and a few years as a primary school teacher in Ch'angsha. However able and respected he might be among his comrades, he could scarcely be esteemed by Wang Ching-wei, Hu Han-min, Tai Chi-t'ao, Ts'ai Yüan-p'ei, Tsou Lu, and other eminent members of the KMT.

The entry *en masse* of the communists into the KMT began what was known as the left-wing of the party. The students who had become more politically conscious after the May 4th Movement and the Work-study students who had just returned from France or Russia were now the new cadres of the KMT.[33] Above them there was a small group of leaders such as Liao Chung-k'ai and Wang Ching-wei who were convinced of the need to learn from Russia the techniques of party organization, political agitation, and revolution, as they were fully aware of the defects of the KMT organizational structure and the lack of discipline among its members.[34] Their, and especially Dr. Sun Yat-sen's, contacts with Russia and Russian representatives resulted in the appointment of Mikhail Marcovich Borodin, seconded by the Politburo of the Bolshevik Party,[35] as an adviser to the KMT to reorganize and infuse new life into it.[36] After Borodin's preliminary talks with Dr. Sun and his lieutenants, the decision was taken to call the first national congress of the KMT. Mao was one of the delegates from Hunan who, after the December meeting of the Central Committee of the CCP which resolved on the absorption of competent Nationalists into the CCP, sailed to Canton for the opening of the national congress on New Year's Day 1924.[37]

The presidium of the congress, nominated by Liao Chung-k'ai and approved by Dr. Sun, consisted of three rightists, Hu Han-min, Lin Sen, and Hsieh Ch'ih, one leftist, Wang Ching-wei, and one communist, Li Ta-chao[38]; the manifesto of the congress,

33. [7] 1928, 1315 and [116].   34. [214] 160.
35. Maxim Litvinov, according to G. Besedovsky ([194] 127), described Borodin as a 'suspicious character', 'a crook who sprang from the depths of the Chicago Stock Exchange, where he was known as Gruzenberg'.
36. [205] 63.   37. [18] 138 and [181] 21.   38. [130] II, 645.

according to Dr. Sun, was drafted in English by Borodin, approved by Sun himself, and translated into classical Chinese by Liao Chung-k'ai.[39] The congress elected 24 members to the Central Executive Committee—16 rightists, 5 leftists, and 3 communists, who were Li Ta-chao, T'an P'ing-shan, and Yü Shu-te,[40] and 16 alternate members to the Central Executive Committee, including 6 communists—Ch'ü Ch'iu-pai, Shen Ting-i, Lin Tsu-han, Han Fu-lin, Yü Fang-chou, and Mao Tse-tung.[41] These facts and figures show that although the leftists and the communists had made considerable inroads into the centre of the KMT they were not yet in the majority. However, in the execution of policy decisions, the leftists and the communists were clearly more influential than the rightists. On the powerful Standing Committee of eight there were five rightists, two leftists, and one communist (T'an P'ing-shan),[42] but the authority of this body was shared by the Political Council created in July 1924, which was presided over by Dr. Sun with the adviser, Borodin, at his elbow having the right to vote when Sun was absent. The six members of the Council were Hu Han-min, Wu Ch'ao-shu, Shao Yüan-ch'ung (the rightists), Wang Ching-wei, Liao Chung-k'ai, and T'an P'ing-shan (the leftists and the communist). T'an resigned later to be superseded by Ch'ü Ch'iu-pai.[43] Thus with Dr. Sun, Borodin, and three leftists, the left-wing dominated the Council. Furthermore, the important departments of the Central Executive Committee were all in the hands of either the leftists or the communists. The organization department was headed by T'an P'ing-shan; labour by Liao Chung-k'ai with Feng Chü-p'o, a communist, as the secretary; peasant, by Lin Tsu-han, with P'eng Pai, another communist, as the secretary; women, by Madame Liao Chung-k'ai; and industry, by Wang Ching-wei. The propaganda department was first headed by Tai Chi-t'ao, but later by Wang Ching-wei, with Mao Tse-tung as the secretary. Only the youth department under Tsou Lu, overseas Chinese

39. [131] 347–60 and [152] 36.   40. [116].
41. [43] 248, n.1, [131] 246, and [151] I, 148. Tsou Lu and Ku Kuan-chiao ([181] 22) say that Chang Kuo-t'ao was also elected an alternate member. But this is a mistake.
42. [131] 278.   43. [130] II, 676.

under Lin Sen, commerce under Wu Ch'ao-shu, and military affairs under Hsü Ch'ung-chih were free from communist infiltration.[44]

The importance of the first national congress of the KMT, which can hardly be exaggerated, has been discussed fully in several authoritative works. Some of these emphasize how the KMT was equipped with a new vigour, with effective revolutionary techniques of organization and agitation, and with reliable military support; some stress the creation of a real unity among the members and the enforcement of a strict discipline; others interpret the congress as the starting point of a 'new rise in the Chinese revolution'.[45] But, for our purpose, the most important result of the reorganization and of the congress was perhaps the formation of the left-wing which was to control the policy-making of the party, to consolidate and prolong the alliance with Russia and the CCP, and to become a major consideration in Russia's China policy—the policy of the 'revolution from above'—thereby contributing to the struggle between Stalin and Trotsky.

After the first national congress of the KMT Mao went back to Shanghai in March 1924 to take up his new post as the secretary of the organization department of the Shanghai branch of the party.[46] The head of the department was Yeh Ch'u-ts'ang and an eminent leader of the party, Hu Han-min, was there too.

Little of Mao's work in Shanghai in this period is known, except that, according to his conversation with E. Snow, his task was to co-ordinate the policies of the KMT and the CCP. It was probably due to his humble social position, having been a mere library assistant at the Peking National University, a laundryman in Shanghai, and a primary school teacher in Ch'angsha, that he was not treated with respect by his KMT colleagues and his relations with them were far from being happy. Co-operation might have been at times difficult, especially in view of the fact that both Hu and Yeh were members of the right-wing of the KMT. Therefore he did not discharge his task in a satisfactory manner.

44. [131] 278, [130] II, 657 and 677. See also [116].
45. [123] 115, [144] 183, [152] 39–40, and [14] 83 respectively.
46. [50] 78–9 and [258] 156. Mao stayed in Canton for another fourteen days after the congress before sailing for Shanghai to take up the secretaryship. [16] IV, part 3, 342.

Cracks began to appear in the united front as early as 19 November 1923 when eleven members of the Kwangtung branch of the KMT protested against the use of the KMT organization by the communists for their own purposes.[47] This could hardly be considered a credit to Mao's work of co-ordinating the measures of the two parties, and, together with his modest social position, might have been responsible for his failure in not being elected to a full membership of the Central Executive Committee of the KMT.

The ominous protest grew until, in April 1924, a motion of censure was signed by three out of the five members of the Central Supervisory Committee, Teng Tse-ju, Chang Chi, and Hsieh Ch'ih, charging the CCP with creating a 'bloc within' the KMT, which was stopped only on the admonition of the awe-inspiring Dr. Sun.[48] The matter did not, however, rest there. After Sun's death in March 1925, the cleavage between the right and the left widened and deepened simultaneously. The Sun Yat-senism Society was organized by Ch'en Ch'eng and others in April[49]; Tai Chi-t'ao began his attack on communism in July[50]; the members of the Central Executive Committee and the Central Supervisory Committee who remained in Peking after Dr. Sun's death held twenty-two meetings on the Western Hills from 23 November to the beginning of December 1925. The meetings resolved to abolish the Political Council, expel the communists from the KMT, dismiss Borodin as the adviser to the KMT, and transfer the Central Executive Committee from Canton to Shanghai.[51] The dispute went on, culminating in the assassination of Liao Chung-k'ai on 20 August 1925 and the famous Canton *Coup* of 20 March 1926.[52]

In spite of these vicissitudes the united front remained unshaken with the left-wing predominant, but this was due more to Borodin and other communists than to Mao Tse-tung whose 'co-operation'

47. [130] II, 629–30 and [193] 149.

48. [130] II, 670–2 and 674 and [193] 151.

49. This was a society among the cadets of the Whampoa Military Academy. [135] VIIe, 32b.

50. Tai's article, *Kuo-min Ke-ming yü Chung-kuo KMT* (The national revolution and the KMT), was published in July 1925. See [143] III.

51. [118] 43, [129] 115, and [150] I, 181–3.

52. [127] and [135] VIIf, 65a–b. For the Canton *Coup*, *vide infra*, p. 102.

with Wang Ching-wei and Hu Han-min in Shanghai did not seem
to have elicited much respect from either of them. Some say that
he worked as Hu's secretary; others mockingly imply that he was
scarcely more than Hu's orderly.[53] Towards the end of 1924, not
surprisingly, he fell ill, went back to Hunan to convalesce and
stayed there until the summer of 1925, leading a surprisingly
active life.[54] During this spell of illness he organized the nucleus
of a peasant movement and also studied peasant problems.[55]
But he was out of the Central Committee of the CCP. Shortly
before or after June 1925 he switched his interest to the peasant
aspect of the Chinese revolution, for his early experience in the
united front work had probably taught him that he could not
command the respect of the intellectuals and his lack of experience
in urban life and trade unions made him unsuitable for working
among the proletariat. Few at that time seemed to understand the
importance and the potentialities of the Chinese peasants, and
certainly few regarded it as a fashionable or progressive under-
taking to work among such 'bumpkins'. Mao's new interest in the
peasants seemed to be a 'retreat'[56] from more important work.

Mao's illness compelled him to miss two very important events—
the fourth congress of the CCP and the strikes of 30 May 1925.
The fourth congress was held after the formation of the united
front and in the wake of the second Chihli-Mukden War. The war
began on 19 September and ended on 25 October 1924, resulting
in the defeat of General Wu P'ei-fu and the Chihli Clique of
warlords[57] mainly because of the defection of General Feng
Yü-hsiang, the commander of the left wing of the Chihli Army,

53. [50] 78–9, [161] 37.
54. [43] 237 and 248 and [258] 156. Chang Kuo-t'ao says that Mao was sent
back to Hunan because of his rightist tendencies [164]. [16] (IV, part 3, 342
and also I, part 2, 135) says that Mao quarrelled with the KMT head of the
organization department of the Shanghai branch, Yeh Ch'u-ts'ang.
55. [43] 237 and [258] 156.
56. C. Brandt says that Mao's return to Hunan was 'a retreat' ([161] 49 n.)
and there is good reason to believe in this, as his and my descriptions have
shown. I use this word with a slight twist in its meaning.
   Admittedly he had worked among the miners of Anyüan and P'inghsiang, but
his experience in trade union work, compared with that of Chang Kuo-t'ao,
Teng Chung-hsia, Li Li-san, and others, was meagre.
57. [2] 18.9, and 25.10, 1924 and [7] 1925, 837–9 for an excellent description
of the war.

who suddenly pulled his troops back from Jehol and marched on Peking, thus throwing the rear of Wu's army into chaos. Wu P'ei-fu then fled south to try to rally some of his old subordinates and restore his authority, while in the north neither the Christian General nor the Mukden Warlord was strong enough to become the undisputed master of Peking. A new situation developed in 1925 as the country was virtually divided into five parts under the rule of five power groups: General Chang Tso-lin controlled Manchuria, parts of Chihli, and Shantung; General Feng Yü-hsiang, parts of Chihli and the north-west; General Wu P'ei-fu, central China; General Sun Ch'uan-fang, the east and south-east of China; and the KMT, the south of China. Never before had a lack of unity among the warlords become so conspicuous and it was in this sense that the 1924 war was decisive.

The fourth congress of the CCP, held in Shanghai in January 1925, fully realized that the rule of the warlords was rapidly collapsing[58] and that the situation was favourable for the further development of the bourgeois democratic revolution. The party itself had grown from 432 members in June 1923 to nearly a thousand[59] and the twenty delegates who represented it decided to redouble its efforts in the trade union movement. The peasantry, though it received some attention, was not adjudged important enough to merit a special agrarian programme.

The party's policy of concentrating on the trade union movement was given a unique opportunity for success in May and June 1925 when the Japanese and British guns shot and killed the Chinese strikers in Shanghai and Canton with the result that the whole nation rose up 'into a single body of protest'.[60] The determination and indignation were eloquently demonstrated not only by the strikes that spread from city to city but also by the year-long boycott of Canton–Hong Kong trade.[61] The fervour the Chinese

58. [14] 88.
59. [14] 88, [18] 102–6, and [181] 22. Ku Kuan-chiao is wrong to say that the CCP was then 1,500 strong and that there were 70 delegates at the congress.
60. *Christian Century*, 18 June 1925. This is a leading religious journal in the U.S.A.
61. [7] 1926 gives detailed accounts of the strikes and boycotts in Shanghai, Canton, and other places (919–71). See also [200] 100–22, [204] II, 82–99, and a special supplement of [26].

showed in the May 30th Movement surpassed that of the May 4th
Movement of 1919 and was to be equalled only by the bitterness
against Japan in 1931 and 1937. The CCP was greatly helped by
these strikes as its membership leapt from about 1,000 in May to
10,000 six months later[62] and that of the communist youth corps
from 2,000 to 9,000 in September 1925. The Shanghai strikes
were organized by Ch'ü Ch'iu-pai, Ts'ai Ho-sen, Liu Shao-ch'i,
and, in particular, Li Li-san.[63] Teng Chung-hsia (Mao's friend)
and Chang Kuo-t'ao (Mao's foe) were also known to be leading
the workers' movement at this time. But Mao himself played no
part at all in this great event. He was quietly convalescing and
unspectacularly agitating among the peasants of Hunan. Once
again General Chao Heng-t'i, the governor, issued an order for his
arrest[64] and thereupon he fled to Canton 'at the time the Whampoa
students had defeated Yang Hsi-ming (min)' in June 1925.[65]

In Canton Mao was put in charge of a training college of
organizers for the peasant movement.[66] This was only to be
expected, because he had by now some experience in such work
and also in teaching, and the peasant question attracted the luke-
warm attention of the KMT and the CCP. By accepting this
post he was placed directly under Lin Tsu-han, the head, and
P'eng Pai, the secretary, of the peasant department of the KMT,
hence below both of them in rank. He was, however, on friendly
terms with Lin, also with Liao Chung-k'ai and Chou En-lai, the
political commissar of the 1st Army of the KMT.[67] The class
Mao trained was the sixth, consisting of 327 students from 19
provinces, who, in a four-month course, were required to attend
252 lectures. The arrangement of the curriculum was interesting:
the Three Principles of the People and the History of the KMT
took up 6 hours each while Conditions in Russia and Imperialism
were allotted 18 and 14 hours respectively. Among the lecturers
there were Chou En-lai on Peasant Movement and Military

62. [193] 74. Ku Kuan-chiao's estimate of 58,000 members at the end of
1925 is not accepted here ([181] 24 and 26).
    63. [7] 1928, 1326–7 and [18] 113.   64. [43] 237.
    65. Yang Hsi-min was defeated and he fled to Hong Kong on 14 June 1925.
[135] VIIe, 89a–90a. But [16] (IV, part 3, 343) says that Mao arrived at Canton
in November.
    66. [258] 157.   67. [135] VIIg, 23a and [190] 30.

Campaigns (6 hours), Li Li-san on the Trade Union Movement in China (17 hours), Hsiao Ch'u-nü on Imperialism, History of the Chinese Revolutionary Movements (5 hours), and Social Problems and Socialism (9 hours), P'eng Pai on the Peasant Movement in Haifeng and the East River Area in Kwangtung (4 hours), Yün Tai-ying on Chinese History (16 hours), and Mao himself on the Problems of the Chinese Peasants (23 hours) and Village Education (9 hours).[68] Li Fu-ch'un, whose wife was Ts'ai Ch'ang, a close friend of Mao, was in charge of the Political Training Centre and invited Mao to lecture to his students on the peasant problems.[69] Shortly after his arrival at Canton, Mao was invited to become the secretary of the propaganda department headed by Wang Ching-wei, and perhaps it was in this capacity that he edited the *Political Weekly* of the KMT. Later, in October 1925, he deputized for Wang as the head of the department and was assisted by Shen Yen-ping (Mao Tun) as his secretary.[70]

Mao's stay in Canton was brought to an abrupt end when the news of Chao Heng-t'i's brutal suppression of the miners at Anyüan reached him. A regiment of troops was sent to Anyüan by Chao and others and ordered to shoot to kill the miners on strike. Huang Ai-yüan, the communist director of the workers' club, and a dozen miners fell victims to these ruthless killings while many communist cadres migrated to Canton for refuge.[71] Mao left for Shanghai at the end of 1925 to organize a campaign against Chao, and so he did not attend the second national congress of the KMT from 4 to 19 January 1926.[72] It is not clear whether his trip to Shanghai was absolutely necessary, but it was certainly unfortunate for him to have missed two national congresses in one year.

The second congress marked the complete domination of the KMT by the left-wing. Its manifesto spoke of the national revolution of China as a part of an international movement, emphasizing the need of an alliance with Russia and the colonies and semi-colonies of the world. Among the 250 delegates, more than 100

68. [201] 21–2 and 23n. See also [43] 237–8. All the lecturers mentioned here are communists.   69. [43] 249.
70. [16] I, part 2, 136 and IV, part 3, 344–5; [258] 157; [272].
71. [43] 189.   72. [43] 177 and [258] 158.

held two party cards each; there was, therefore, no doubt that the left and the communists in the KMT were in the majority.[73] This majority was reflected in the composition of the Central Executive Committee of 1926. Of the 36 members (including the absent Tai Chi-t'ao), 13 were leftists and 7 communists, making the ratio between the left and right 20 to 16 (or 15 if we exclude the absent Tai).[74] The Standing Committee was enlarged from eight to nine members, including six leftists and only three rightists.[75] Even the exclusively rightist territory of the Central Supervisory Committee was invaded by both leftists and communists as its enlarged membership of 12 had now 3 leftists and 1 communist.[76] Mao Tse-tung retained his alternate membership of the Central Executive Committee, whose 22 members were made up by 11 rightists, 4 leftists, and 7 communists. However, no communists of consequence were in Mao's company.[77]

Mao seems to have paid another short visit to Canton at the beginning of 1926 before sailing again to Shanghai 'about the time Chiang Kai-shek attempted his first *coup d'état*' on 20 March 1926.[78] About the *coup* a great deal has been written, but one of Chiang's most trusted lieutenants said, 'the entire story could never be told until his [Chiang's] own diary revealed the facts after his [Chiang's] death'.[79] As Chiang is still alive and his diary not yet published, the whole story is still not known. However, Chiang's book of 1957 revealed that he had taken action to forestall a plan of kidnapping him and sending him 'as a prisoner to Russia via Vladivostok'.[80] For readers of Chang Ch'i-yün's history of the KMT and Hollington Tong's biography of Chiang, this is not a new story.[81] If one may hazard a guess, the heart of the

---

73. For the full text of the manifesto, see [131] 325–39. See also [1] II, 232, [16] I, part 1, 95, and [181] 24.

74. [131] 322–3 and [193] 214.   75. [20] 199.

76. [131] 323 and [20] 198.

77. [131] 323. Apart from Mao, the other communist alternate members were Hsü Su-hun, Han Fu-lin, Ch'ü Wu, Tung Yung-wei, Teng Yin-ch'ao (Madame Chou En-lai), and Mao's friend Hsia Hsi. See also [16] I, part 1, 96.

78. [258] 158. See also [16] I, part 2, 136 and IV, part 3, 346.

79. This is General Wang Po-ling's recollection, published in [157], 164–8. See also Ch'en Po-ta [117] 17.

80. [169] 39.

81. [115] II, 508 and [153] II, 317.

matter lay most probably in Chiang's succinct remark to Wang
Ching-wei on 8 March 1926: 'The actual power of controlling the
revolution must not fall into the hands of outsiders.'[82]

The timing of the *coup* was excellent. Hu Han-min, a powerful
leader of the right-wing, was in eclipse and away in Moscow[83];
Wang Ching-wei, the supreme leader of the left, was indisposed[84];
Borodin was in the north parleying with General Feng Yü-
hsiang.[85] In their absence, Chiang swiftly put the Russian advisers
in Canton under surveillance and arrested many communists.
The Canton branch of the CCP also reacted swiftly by voting for
immediate action against Chiang.[86] Moscow, however, was reticent
and hence the Central Committee of the CCP vetoed the resolution
of the Canton branch.[87]

Not a word about the incident appeared in the official organs
in Moscow, while the Comintern even went as far as to condemn
Reuter and Hong Kong reports about the *coup* as lies.[88] Trotsky
thought differently. He demanded 'the liberation of the CCP from
the strait-jacket of the KMT' and the adoption of a policy of
agrarian revolt.[89] Bukharin attacked this idea in *Pravda*, arguing
that the withdrawal of the communists from the KMT would
mean a loss of contact with the masses and the surrender of the
banner of revolution to the Chinese bourgeoisie. To this Trotsky
retorted: 'In preparing himself for the role of an executioner,
Chiang Kai-shek wanted to have the cover of world communism—
and he got it.'[90]

Why did not Russia assist the CCP to seize power at that
juncture? Borodin explained: 'We could have seized power in
Canton, but we could not have held it. We should have gone
down in a sea of blood. We would have tried it if we had had a
25 per cent. chance of surviving the *coup* for one year.'[91]

On the ground of defending the interests of his party alone
Chiang could justify his action, the results of which were the
departure of Wang Ching-wei for France on 11 May 1926, the

82. [135] VIIIa, 72b.   83 .[210] 85.   84. [153] I, 71–2.
85. [176] II, 649.   86. [173] II, 276 and 337.
87. [173] II, 276 and [193] 227.   88. [173] II, 276 and [205] 97.
89. [205] 103.   90. [173] II, 277 and [215] 271.
91. [176] II, 647.

restriction of the communists' activities in the KMT, and Borodin's support for launching the Northern Expedition.[92]

The Standing Committee of the KMT, meeting at the beginning of June 1926, approved Chiang Kai-shek's plan for the Northern Expedition and appointed Chiang the commander-in-chief.[93] It also made a few changes in the organization of the Central Executive Committee: in the department of organization Ch'en Kuo-fu (one of the CC leaders in later years) replaced T'an P'ing-shan, in the peasant department Kan Nai-kuang replaced Lin Tsu-han, in the secretariat Yeh Ch'u-ts'ang replaced Liu Fen, and in the department of propaganda Ku Meng-yü replaced Mao Tse-tung.[94] Chiang ordered the mobilization of his troops on 1 July 1926.[95]

In Shanghai, Mao took up the newly created post of the head of the peasant department of the CCP, and, with the swift advance of Chiang's expeditionary army which disposed of Chao Heng-t'i and took control of Hunan by the end of July, he was able to go back to his native province and work among the peasants.[96] Of his old friends and comrades only Hsia Hsi, Kuo Liang, and some others remained there[97] in charge of the work of both the KMT and the CCP. Judging by Hsia's later differences with him,[98] he may not have received as cordial co-operation from Hsia as he had expected. None the less, the nine months from August 1926 to May 1927 spent among the peasants of Hunan were to be of great importance not only to Mao and his country but also to the world communist movement. It was also in this period, more precisely late in the autumn of 1926, that he composed his first poem, 'Ch'angsha' (officially dated 1925).

A few basic data must be introduced at this stage before we analyse the problems of the peasant movement in the 1920s. The average (median) size of a farm throughout China was as small

92. [135] VIIIb, 61a and [193] 228.
93. The approval has been attributed erroneously to the second plenum of the Central Executive Committee held in May 1926 ([193] 230). See [135] VIIIb, 78a and VIIIc, 13a–14b.
94. [193] 229.   95. [135] VIIIc, 1a.
96. [135] VIIIc, 105b–112b and [196].   97. [43] 17, n. 25.
98. [239] and *vide infra*, p. 174. General Wang Chen makes it abundantly clear that Hsia was following, in his view, an erroneous policy.

as 3·31 acres,[99] and what made things worse was the steady decline in the total area under cultivation.[1] From this small farm an adult male could earn, on the average, 65·51 *yuan* per annum,[2] out of which he required the astonishingly small sum of 38·44 *yuan* for his and his family's livelihood.[3] His total productivity in terms of grain amounted to 446 kilograms,[4] but his landlord usually took 50 per cent. of this.[5] Most peasants had to borrow money in order to tide over the period between sowing and harvesting and the interest they paid was usually as high as 30 per cent. or more.[6] Land being so scarce and capital so hard to come by, it followed that the majority of the farming population were tenants. The rule of warlords brought to them three additional burdens—inflation through the issues of irredeemable paper notes, taxation in advance, and military *corvée*. About the paper notes, E. Kann wrote:

All the provinces of China, with the possible exception of Kiangsu and Chekiang, are suffering in a similar way, being saddled with paper money for which there is no metallic reserve and for the redemption of which no one seems to assume liability.[7]

And all the provinces, too, were suffering from the scourge of taxation in advance. The northern provinces paid taxes one or two years in advance; the central provinces, four or five years in advance; Hunan in 1924 paid up to 1930; Fukien in 1926 paid up to 1933; Szechwan in 1926 paid up to 1957.[8] Moreover, in 1924 and 1925 there were 17 provinces at war.[9]

The result of all this was the pauperization of the peasants. In 1918 50 per cent. of them were occupying owners and 30 per cent. tenants; but in 1926–7 the former were reduced to only 25 per cent. while the latter had increased to 55 per cent.[10] This trend of development was particularly serious in the south. According to the late Professor Tawney's figures, the percentage of tenants in the rural population of Fukien was 65, of Kwangtung 66, and of

99. [111] 40.   1. [26] 1930, no. 8.
2. [110] 85. See also Colin Clark, *Conditions of Economic Progress*, London, 1940, 244.
3. [110] 386–7.   4. [111] 284.   5. [145] 66.
6. [110] 159.   7. *Chinese Economic Journal*, March 1928, 273 *et seq.*
8. [83] 23.   9. [85] table x.
10. 1918 figures, see [145] 34 and 1926–7 figures; see [124] II, 67 and 491 as well as [201] 3–5.

Hunan 80.[11] Under the crushing burden of heavy taxes, *corvée*, interest, and rent, many landless peasants were forced to leave their homes and become unemployed and this abundance of unemployed labour made the warlords' task of recruiting soldiers an easy one. The larger the number of new recruits, the more frequent the civil wars became. Thus one condition became the cause of the other, with the result that China was helpless in the grip of this vicious circle. On the eve of the Northern Expedition, the situation in rural China was explosive.

Brief as it is, this short description should be sufficient to indicate that China's agrarian problems were in urgent need of immediate relief as well as of long-term improvement in productivity. The former depended to a great extent on the reduction in usurious rates of interest and rent and the elimination of both the extortionate taxation and *corvée*; the latter required the industry to become more capital- but less labour-intensive. For immediate relief a change in the credit and tenure systems was needed and, above all, an end to the rule of the warlords; the long-term improvement required a great number of factors working together in a peaceful context. This was a view generally accepted by economists and politicians alike, with differences only in emphasis— economists tended to insist on a thorough-going solution which was bound to take some time, whereas politicians urged expedience to obtain immediate political aims.

In the eyes of the policy-makers of the Comintern, the clamours of the landless peasantry in China and other backward countries provided 'the mass basis for communist activities',[12] and the instruments for satisfying such demands were 'soviets of peasants' or 'the dictatorship of the poor peasants'.[13] But these policy-makers were also aware of the deficiencies and incapacity of the peasants; so the thesis on the agrarian question adopted by the second Comintern congress on 4 August 1920 read:

Only [the] urban industrial proletariat led by the Communist Party can liberate the working masses of the countryside from the yoke of capital and large landownership.

11. [145] 64.   12. M. N. Roy's thesis of 28 July 1920. [173] I, 139.
13. Lenin's and Bela Kun's thesis. [173] I, 138 and 105 respectively.

Two years later, at the fourth Comintern congress, the thesis on the Eastern question had this passage:

The revolutionary movement in the backward countries of the East cannot be successful unless it relies on the action of the broad peasant masses. Therefore the revolutionary parties of all Oriental countries must formulate a clear agrarian programme, putting forward the demand for the complete abolition of the feudal system and survivals of it in the form of large landownership and tax farming.[14]

But when Borodin arrived in China in September 1923 there was 'not a single pamphlet on the agrarian question', not to speak of a 'clear agrarian programme'—'the character of the Chinese economy was neither known nor understood'.[15] Borodin proceeded to discuss the peasant question with Dr. Sun Yat-sen on 16 November 1923, proposing the confiscation of landlords' holdings and the collection of rent for distribution according to the peasants' own discretion.[16] Sun objected strongly. His own policy of 'land to the tillers' was a long-term one to be realized only by stages and he had never said that it should be used to lure peasants into taking an active part in the national revolution. Moreover, confiscation of land or other private property ran counter to his political principles, and for him to agree to it would have been tantamount to the KMT's resignation from the revolution in favour of the communists.[17] Sun and Borodin eventually compromised on the reduction of rent by 25 per cent. and the establishment of peasant associations.[18] This was in November 1923.

The Chinese communists for their part had from time to time paid some attention to the peasant question but only as a romantic ideal. Li Ta-chao wrote in the *Ch'en Pao* of Peking on 20 February 1919, exhorting young people to find opportunities for development in rural areas where their service was badly needed,[19] and in a letter to Mao Tse-tung in August 1920, Ts'ai Ho-sen argued:

Some say that China has no class distinctions—a view with which I totally disagree. Chinese workers and peasants are ignorant, believing poverty and misery to be their fate. Once they become class conscious, they will, however, exert as much influence as their counterparts in Western and Eastern Europe.[20]

14. [173] I, 387.   15. [176] II, 647.   16. [176] II, 637.
17. [176] II, 647.   18. [176] II, 638.   19. [102] 149.
20. [43] 134.

There was also P'eng Pai who began his work at Haifeng in Kwang-tung from May 1921, ironically, under the auspices of the warlord Ch'en Chiung-ming who happened to be the biggest land-owner in Haifeng and Lufeng.[21] The peasant association P'eng established in 1922 grew to be a considerable force (said to be 100,000 strong) on the eve of the 1924 reorganization of the KMT.[22] In Hengshan, Hunan, Liu Tung-hsüan and Hsieh Huan-te, both communists, started to organize the peasants in 1923.[23] But these beginnings received scant attention from the leaders of the communist movement. P'eng Pai, for instance, was not even among the delegates to the first congress of the CCP although he was the only communist of any practical influence in any part of China. Subsequently P'eng became the leader of some 100,000 peasants, yet he was selected to attend neither the 1922 nor the 1923 congress of the CCP. No one, in fact, represented the interests of the peasants in the Central Committee of the party until Mao's appointment as the head of the peasant department in 1926 or in the congress until his presence at the fifth congress in 1927.[24]

Indeed, the party secretary, Ch'en Tu-hsiu, saw the im-practicability of organizing peasants into the ranks of the revolu-tion. He wrote in 1923:

The peasants are widely scattered, therefore it is not easy to organize them into an effective force. Their cultural standards being low and needs being simple, their outlook is therefore conservative. China being a big country, making it easy for them to migrate, they therefore tend to shy away from difficulty and become complacent. These are the three factors preventing them from participating in the revolution.[25]

Ch'en's may have been the predominant view among the members of the Central Committee before 30 May 1925, as then all the provinces except for Kwangtung were controlled by warlords whose suppression of what they considered rebellious was brutal, and the peasant movement, again except for that in Kwangtung, remained in the traditional secret-society stage as under the Red Spears in Honan.[26]

21. [18] 63, [82] 31, and [124] II, 22.
22. [18] 63 and [190] 199–201.   23. [18] 63.
24. [52] 77.   25. [18] 135.   26. [19] II b 75.

After the May 30th Movement, however, a serious attempt was made to organize the peasants in Hunan while in Kwangtung the peasant association continued to expand.[27] In 1926 Wei Pa-ch'ün, himself a Chuang tribal leader, led a band of peasants of the Chuang tribes in an attack on Tunglan in Kwangsi. This uprising, still in the traditional manner, was soon quelled. Years later it was again Wei Pa-ch'ün who set up the first peasant soviet in that province.[28]

Meanwhile, in Moscow, the sixth plenum of the Executive Committee of the Comintern, meeting on 13 March 1926, adopted this resolution:

The most important question of the Chinese national liberation movement is the peasant question. The victory of the revolutionary democratic tendency . . . depends on the degree to which the 400 million Chinese peasants take part in the decisive revolutionary struggle together with the Chinese workers and under their leadership.[29]

This was on the eve of Chiang's Canton *Coup* and the launching of the Northern Expedition. In the ensuing battle of Hunan in July, Chiang's forces were assisted by local peasants acting as their spies and porters,[30] thereby contributing to the victories of P'ingchiang,[31] Yüehyang,[32] and, most important of all, the Tingssu Bridge where one of the fiercest engagements of the Expedition was fought.[33] The peasant movement expanded *pari passu* with the enlargement of the areas under the KMT control. At the beginning of June 1926 there were nearly one million organized peasants in all China and this was increased to nearly 10 million a year later.[34] Some of the peasants were armed with the rifles and Mausers abandoned by the defeated soldiers.[35]

Although after the meeting of the Standing Committee of the KMT in June the peasant department was no longer headed by Lin Tsu-han, the lower ranks of the peasant movement were still

27. [159] 208–9.   28. [265] I, 171–2 and 181.
29. [173] II, 279.   30. [18] 79 and [153] I, 78–9.
31. [19] II, b 147 and [286] 73.   32. [19] II, b 148.
33. The *Hua-ch'iao Jih-pao*, Hong Kong, September 7, 1926.
34. Figures given by the Central Executive Committee of the KMT, 1 August 1926, and the ministry for the peasants of the Wuhan Government. See [201] 17–19.
35. [201] 6.

manned by communists[36] who led the peasants in fighting for the reduction of rent and interest[37] and for the modification in the terms of their leases.[38] But towards the end of 1926 the association, now over one million strong under the leadership of Mao Tse-tung, began to confiscate land.[39]

The growth of the peasant movement in Hunan, according to Mao himself, could be divided into two distinct periods, with September 1926 as the watershed. Before that was the period of organization when the association emerged from underground to open activities with a strength of below 400,000; after that point it entered into the period of revolutionary action with its membership jumping to nearly two million at the beginning of 1927.[40] Its activities included auditing the accounts of various government offices headed by local bullies and bad gentry who were often found guilty of embezzlement. The culprits were either fined or imprisoned, and in more serious cases banished or shot.[41] The peasants also held demonstrations or engaged in economic struggles against them.

This may be a convenient place to introduce Mao's views on the revolutionary peasant movement. His first important essay, *Analysis of the Classes in Chinese Society*,[42] written in March 1926, concluded with these words:

The industrial proletariat is the leading force in our revolution. All sections of the semi-proletariat and the petty bourgeoisie are our closest friends.[43]

The semi-proletariat, according to Mao, consisted of the overwhelming majority of the semi-tenant peasants, poor peasants, handicraftsmen, shop assistants, and pedlars, while the petty bourgeoisie included owner-peasants, master handicraftsmen, and the petty intellectuals. The success of the national revolution depended on the alliance between the industrial proletariat as the leaders and the semi-proletariat and petty bourgeoisie as its

36. [150] I, 166.   37. [18] 63 and [201] 274.
38. [201] 37 and 274.   39. [19] II, b 211 and [201] 274.
40. [46] I, 14–15 or *SW* I, 22–3.   41. [46] I, 26–8 or *SW* I, 35–9.
42. [46] I, 3–11 or *SW* I, 13–20.
43. [46] I, 9 or *SW* I, 20. Mao's views on the composition of the Chinese society remained unchanged in 1933 ([46] I, 121–2) and 1939 ([46] II, 633–41).

closest friends. In no way was this conclusion different from the orthodox communist position, yet, said Mao, Ch'en Tu-hsiu refused to publish this essay in the party organ *Hsiang-tao* (Guide Weekly) on account of its 'radical land policy'.[44]

Mao's second article—'Report of an Investigation into the Peasant Movement in Hunan'—was the result of his tour of inspection in Hunan from 4 January to 5 February 1927 and was published in the *Chung-yang Fu-k'an* (a supplement of the *Central Weekly*), a KMT journal,[45] on 15 March 1927. What is particularly interesting is its last section which, being an account of the peasant movement in Hunan from July 1926 to February 1927, corresponded almost point by point with the twelve instructions to the CCP from the Comintern on 16 December 1926.[46]

This last section defines 'Fourteen Deeds'. The first, organizing the peasants into the peasant association, tallies with instruction (i)—maximum support by the [Canton] Government for all peasant organizations, including the peasant unions [associations]; the second, dealing political blows against the landlords (or 'to smash the political prestige and power of the landlord class . . . and to foster the growth of the power of the peasants'), tallies with instruction (f)—all-round support by the Canton Government of peasant interests, in particular, protection of the peasants against oppression and persecution by landlords, gentry, and usurers; the third, dealing economic blows against the landlords, tallies partly with instructions (e) and (f) and partly with instruction (a)—maximum reduction of rents; the fourth, overthrowing the feudal rule of the local bullies and bad gentry (the *Tu* and *T'uan*, militia forces), tallies with instruction (g)—disarming the *Min Yuan* [militia] and all the landlord forces; the fifth, overthrowing the landlords' armed forces and building up the peasants' armed forces, tallies partly with instruction (g) and partly with instruction (h)—arming the poor and middle peasants and subordinating all armed forces in the village to the local agencies of the revolu-

44. [258] 157.
45. K. Wittfogel says that the 1st section of the Report was published on 12 March in the CCP Weekly (*Hsiang-tao?*) and a condensed version including details from the last section appeared on 15 March in *Chinese Correspondence*—a KMT weekly organ. [57] II, 17.
46. [46] I, 23–44 or *SW* I, 33–59 and [173] II, 344.

tionary government; the sixth, overthrowing the political power of His Excellency the county magistrate and his bailiffs, tallies roughly with instruction (f); the seventh, overthrowing the clan authority of the elders and ancestral temples, the theocratic authority of the city gods and local deities, and the masculine authority of the husband, has some resemblance to instruction (d)— confiscation of church and monastery lands, and of land belonging to reactionary militarists and compradores, and those landlords and gentry who are waging civil war against the KMT National Government; the eighth, extending political agitation, the ninth, the peasants' prohibitions, and the tenth, eliminating banditry, have no corresponding instructions; the eleventh, abolishing exorbitant levies, tallies with instruction (b)—abolition of the various forms of taxes weighing on the peasantry and their replacement by a single progressive agricultural tax; the twelfth, cultural movement, has no corresponding instruction; the thirteenth, the co-operative movement, tallies with instruction (j)—provisions of cheap government credits, fight against the usurers, support of peasant mutual-aid associations, and also with instruction (k)— government help for co-operatives and mutual-aid associations; and finally, the fourteenth, building roads and embankments, has no corresponding instruction.

If anything, Mao's 'Fourteen Deeds' were less drastic than the Comintern instructions, for they did not advocate the confiscation of land. But on one important point Mao's Report and the Comintern resolutions differed. While both realized the urgency of the peasant problem and the insufficient attention given to it by the CCP, the Comintern stated: 'the class which decisively tackles this basic question and is able to give a radical answer will become the leader of the revolution . . . in the given situation in China the proletariat is the only class able to pursue a radical agrarian policy'[47]; but Mao described the broad peasant masses as having 'risen to fulfil their historic mission . . . to overthrow the rural feudal power', and said: 'The main force in the countryside which has always put up the bitterest fight is the poor peasants. Throughout both the period of underground organization and that of open

47. [173] II, 343, being a quotation from the resolution on China at the seventh plenum.

organization, the poor peasants have fought militantly all along.'[48] The section on 'An Awful Mess!' and 'Very Good Indeed!' of his Report leaves an unmistakable impression that he regarded the poor peasants as the main force, 'the vanguard of revolution'.[49] The expressions such as 'the hegemony of the proletariat' and 'the leadership of the communist party'[50] did not appear in his Report at all.

Mao's Report attracted the attention and unqualified praise of the chairman of the Comintern, Bukharin, who was then Stalin's close ally. Speaking at the eighth plenum of the Executive Committee of the Comintern, he described it as 'excellent and interesting'. A Russian translation of the first section appeared in the *Revolutsionnyi Vostok* in 1927 and an English translation appeared in the *Communist International* on 15 June 1927.[51]

In recent years the Report has become the focal point of the Maoism controversy between B. Schwartz and K. Wittfogel. Schwartz sees in the Hunan Report 'a unique trend within the Chinese Communist movement',[52] for 'it looks to the village as the key center of revolutionary action', and 'it judges the worth of any revolutionary party by its willingness to place itself at the head of the peasantry'.[53] He goes farther to say that the Report 'is an implicit attack on the whole Comintern line'.[54] The *Documentary History* compiled by C. Brandt, B. Schwartz, and J. K. Fairbank contrasts the Marxist–Leninist view that the 'revolutionary vanguard' was the urban proletariat with Mao's view that it was the poor peasantry.[55] In his *Stalin's Failure in China*, C. Brandt remarks that over the question of revolutionary means Mao differed from Stalin in his emphasis on 'revolution by the peasants' rather than 'revolution for the peasants' and regards this as Mao's contribution to Marxism.[56] Fairbank, too, interprets the Report to mean that the application of the communist theory to rural China's

---

48. [46] I, 17 and 21–2 or *SW* I, 25 and 31.
49. [46] I, 19 or *SW* I, 29.
50. [52] 76. Mao does mention the leadership of the CCP in the post-1949 editions of the *SW*, but K. Wittfogel points out, after a careful textual study, that in earlier editions there was no such reference. See [57] II, 19. See also [310], 11.
51. [57] II, 21–2.   52. [52] 73.   53. [52] 75.
54. [52] 77.   55. [162] 79.   56. [161] 109.

concrete realities meant that the peasantry would be the class on which revolution was founded and that 'this became the basis of "Maoism" which was the final Sinification of communism in China'.[57]

These attributions puzzle Wittfogel,[58] who does not agree that the Report can be described as doctrinally original; nor does he accept that it laid emphasis on the peasantry as the main force of the Chinese revolution.[59] Therefore he calls 'Maoism' a 'legend'.

But it is essential to understand that in his notable monograph of 1951, Schwartz is interested more in analysing the Maoist strategy than in judging Mao's doctrinal 'originality'[60] or in considering his assessment of the decisive role of the peasantry in the Chinese revolution.[61] Of the strategy, Schwartz points out, Mao is the chief but by no means the only exponent.[62] He defines the strategy thus:

Essentially, the Maoist strategy involves the imposition of a political party organized in accordance with Leninist principles and animated by faith in certain basic tenets of Marxism–Leninism on to a purely peasant mass basis.[63]

The instruments for carrying out such a strategy successfully are a strong mass basis, a strong party, and a strong red army waging a revolutionary war from a border area.[64] In 1955 Schwartz's definition of the strategy remained unchanged:

concentration on the peasantry, the establishment of rural bases, and the build-up of a peasant based Red Army.[65]

But, with regard to the Hunan Report, Schwartz said in 1960:

The Maoist strategy only took full form at the end of 1927 and the Hunan Report and the Autumn Harvest Uprisings are treated in my book only as landmarks in Mao's groping toward the strategy.[66]

The strategy did not, in fact, take full form until 1936[67] and was far more complicated than hitherto realized. It was the marriage

---

57. [12] 240.   58. [57] I, 75.   59. [57] II, 18.
60. Schwartz's own quotation marks. See 'On the "Originality" of Mao Tse-tung', *Foreign Affairs*, XXXIV, no. 1, October 1955.
61. [53] 36.   62. [52] 173.   63. [52] 189.
64. [52] 189–90.
65. 'On the "Originality" of Mao Tse-tung', *Foreign Affairs*, XXXIV, no. 10, 70.   66. [53] 40.   67. *Vide infra*, pp. 214-24.

of Marxism–Lenism to the traditional pattern of the Chinese peasant revolt by which Mao has changed the entire concept of revolution in China—perhaps also in other backward countries. As to the Hunan Report itself, Schwartz is quite right to point out that 'it does not contain the whole of the Maoist strategy since parts of the strategy represent a response to a situation which did not exist at the time'.[68]

Wittfogel is right too when he says that Mao did not touch on the question of land confiscation in his Report. But, in actual fact, Hunan peasants began to redistribute the land they had taken over from landlords immediately after the Conference of the Peasants' Delegates in Ch'angsha in December 1926.[69] In the countryside the peasant association became the sole organ of authority[70]—a state of affairs hardly tolerable for the landowners and their military friends. Suppression of the association's activities began as early as in September 1926 and was intensified from March 1927.[71]

A wave of anti-communism swept across the country at the same time. Beginning in Kiangsi on 16 March when the communist-dominated headquarters of the KMT was smashed by a mob,[72] it spread to Anch'ing in Anhwei a week later.[73] In the north, Marshal Chang Tso-lin ordered his police and *gendarmerie* to search the Russian official buildings in Peking, except for the embassy itself, and they arrested more than sixty people including Li Ta-chao who was subsequently executed on 28 April.[74] Yet the peasant association of Hunan chose precisely this time to issue a message to all of its members, calling for the confiscation of the land belonging to big owners[75]—a move that only intensified the hatred of the owners. General T'ang Sheng-chih, the pillar of the Wuhan military force, at once asked his Government to order the arrest of Mao Tse-tung, the secretary of the Hunan CP.[76] Fortunately Mao, also Kuo Liang, Hsia Hsi, and T'eng Tai-yüan, got

68. [53] 40.   69. [197] 74–5 and [201] 274. Also [19] II, b 211 and [43] 259.   70. [14] 132.   71. [43] 265 and 273–5.
72. [207] VIII, 133–5.   73. [207] VIII, 137–8.
74. [26] 25.6.1927, 119 [102] 11, [178] 3, and [193] 408.
75. [Liu] Chih-hsün, 'Ma-jih-shih-pien ti hui-i' (Recollections of the Horse-day Incident), *Pu-erh-shih-wei-k'e*, no. 20, 30 May 1928, quoted from [201] 384.   76. [190] 47.

wind of this beforehand and fled to Kiangsi whence he made his way to Wuhan.[77] The redistribution of land, nevertheless, went on unabated in the Hsianing Village near Ch'angsha,[78] provoking Colonel Hsü K'e-hsiang into attacking the armed pickets in Ch'angsha with the regiment under his command. The machine-guns mowed down several hundred communists, catching them unprepared. This was on 21 May, the 'Horse Day', ten days after Mao's departure. His close friend and comrade, Lo Hsüeh-tsan, died in this massacre. The provincial headquarters of the CCP was in a panic, not knowing what to do, while information from Wuhan was confusing. It was said that the leaders in Wuhan were to send representatives to Hunan to investigate the incident and to iron out misunderstandings between the communists and the military; so the provincial branch of the party thought it unwise to stage an uprising lest the whole situation became untenable. Hesitation and inaction were the order of the day.[79]

The defeat of the much boasted workers' pickets in Shanghai in April and the peasant association in Hunan in May did irreparable damage to the prestige of the CCP. General Chu P'ei-te therefore dared to deport all known communists from Kiangsi at the beginning of June and General Ho Chien to order a purge in Hunan at the end of that month.[80]

It was under these circumstances that the fifth congress, the crucial one of Ch'en Tu-hsiu's incumbency as the secretary of the CCP, was held in Wuhan on 27 April. Eighty delegates, representing nearly 58,000 members, attended it.[81] Earlier, after Chiang's Canton *Coup*, Ch'en had suggested an end of the 'bloc within' policy[82]; now he brought forward the same proposal at the congress, not once, but twice, yet he was overruled.[83] The discon-

77. [16] I, pt. 2, 179 and [190] 47.   78. [Liu] Chih-hsün, *op. cit.* [201] 308.

79. [190] 33, Wang Chen's recollection. See also [181] 33 and [201] 383. Ch'en Tu-hsiu is generally blamed for cancelling the uprising, but Mao himself does not say so ([46] I, 75 or *SW* I, 93). See also [203].

80. Chu's order was issued on 4 June. See [217] 122 and Lei Hsiao-ts'en, *San-shih-nien Tung-luan Chung-kuo* (China in a generation of turmoil), Hong Kong, 1955, I, 80.

81. [14] 159 and [181] 31. See R. C. North and X. J. Eudin, *M. N. Roy's Mission to China*, chapter IV.

82. Ch'en was overruled by both the Politburo of the Russian Party and the Comintern, [173] II, 276–7.

83. Now he was overruled by the congress, [173] II, 391.

tinuation of the policy, in his view, did not necessarily mean the dissolution of the alliance. On the contrary, he sought to co-operate with the KMT as a 'bloc without', thus freeing the party from the KMT restrictions.[84] A corollary to the question of co-operation was the peasant movement. Unless the CCP was willing to curb the overzealous actions of the peasants, continued co-operation was clearly impossible. T'an P'ing-shan had pointed out this dilemma at the seventh plenum of the Executive Committee of the Comintern on 12 December 1926, but his plea for a resolution was unheeded. Underneath this dilemma was the contradiction between the policy of 'revolution from above' as well as a 'bloc within' favoured by Stalin and that of 'revolution from below' as well as a 'bloc without' advocated by Trotsky. In China, the personification of Stalin's policy was Borodin but he and the Comintern representative, M. N. Roy, held divergent views. At the fifth congress the question of restraining the peasants was heatedly debated, with Ch'ü Ch'iu-pai, Mao Tse-tung, Liu Shao-ch'i, and Jen Pi-shih in the minority opposition.[85] According to Mao,

Ch'en Tu-hsiu did not understand the role of the peasantry in the revolution and greatly under-estimated its potentialities at this time. Consequently, the fifth Conference [congress], held on the eve of the crisis of the Great Revolution, failed to pass an adequate land programme. My opinions, which called for rapid intensification of the agrarian struggle, were not even discussed. . . . The Conference [congress] discussed the land problem by defining a landlord as 'a peasant [farmer] who owned over 500 *mou* [approximately 76 acres of land]—a wholly inadequate and unpractical basis on which to develop the class struggle and quite without consideration of the special character of land economy in China'.[86]

Not only were his opinions, which represented the decisions of the conference of the peasants' delegations held in the spring of 1927, ignored, but he himself was held responsible for some of the happenings in Hunan and was deprived of the right to vote at the congress.[87] After a few sessions he stopped attending on the ground

84. [173] II, 276.   85. [18] 189.
86. [258] 159. Bearing in mind that the average size of the Chinese farm was barely over three acres. Also R. C. North and X. J. Eudin, *op. cit.* 82, n. 31.
87. [18] 189.

M.C.R.—9

of illness.[88] Having been thus rebuked, he was nevertheless elected chairman of the All-China Peasants' Union established immediately after the congress.[89]

The theory behind this disciplinary action against Mao lay not with Ch'en Tu-hsiu but with Stalin and his policy of 'revolution from above'. In Stalin's view, the KMT was 'a bloc, a sort of revolutionary parliament, with the Right, Left, and the Communist', and the left and the communists were in the majority, solidly behind the revolution. The right-wing was the minority and useful; hence there was no need to get rid of it. He said in his famous and often quoted speech at a meeting of three thousand functionaries in the Hall of Columns in Moscow on 5 April:

... the people of the Right have relations with the generals of Chang Tso-lin and understand very well how to demoralize them and to induce them to pass over to the side of the revolution, bag and baggage, without striking a blow. Also, they have connections with the rich merchants and can raise money from them. So they have to be utilized to the end, squeezed dry like a lemon, and then flung away.[90]

A week after this speech Chiang's troops shot down the workers' pickets in Shanghai and a rival government was set up in Nanking against the Wuhan Government. Moscow's attitude towards Chiang changed accordingly, and it now denounced him as 'the hangman',[91] and its alliance with the KMT became one with the left-wing only. But what was the left-wing? No one seemed to have any clear idea. In his celebrated article, 'The Question of the Chinese Revolution' (*Pravda*, 21 April 1927), Stalin merely urged the CCP to turn the Wuhan KMT into an organ of the revolutionary-democratic dictatorship of the proletariat and peasantry,[92] but on 1 August he called the Wuhan Government of the left-wing 'a bourgeois revolutionary organization'.[93] Stalin did not say whether in those three and half months, from April to August, the CCP had succeeded or not in its work of transforming the left-wing. The Comintern, too, when speaking about the Wuhan KMT, was uncertain. Its analysis in December 1926 was that the left represented the petty bourgeoisie, working-class, and peasant

88. [18] 189.   89. [258] 159.   90. [205] 162.
91. [173] II, 363 and [202] 229, n. 18.   92. [174] II, 197.
93. [174] II, 240.

masses,[94] and in May 1927 that the Wuhan Government and the leaders of the left-wing represented not only the peasants, workers, and artisans, but also a part of the middle bourgeosie, and was not yet a dictatorship of the proletariat and peasantry.[95] The Chinese communists, Stalin ordered, should remain 'in the KMT, intensifying their work in it'.[96] The withdrawal from it would be a grave mistake, for 'it means [abandoning] the battlefield and [leaving] in the lurch its allies in the KMT, to the joy of the enemies of the revolution. This means [the weakening of] the CP, [the undermining of] the revolutionary [left] KMT, . . . [the delivery of] the flag of the KMT, the most popular flag in China, into the hands of the Right Wing members of the KMT'.[97] The Comintern echoed: 'Remain in the KMT and work to change it into a really mass organization.'[98]

The lone voice in Moscow belonged to Trotsky: 'Hankow is a fiction. Organize Soviets in its territory, even if these Soviets defy the Hankow Central Government. Raise a Red Army. Arm the workers!'[99]

The motive of preserving the alliance was to retain the so-called 'banner of revolution' as a cloak of legitimacy, which, according to the resolution of the seventh plenum of the Executive Committee of the Comintern was extremely useful for approaching the peasantry, and the class which could successfully approach it and solve its manifold problems would become the leader of the revolution.[1] Nevertheless, a new question arises here: before the CCP was strong enough to lead the revolution and coerce the left-wing into doing what the party wanted it to do, clashes might occur and in such an event should the CCP preserve the alliance or protect the interests of the peasants and workers? A clear-cut answer to this question was not easy to find. Stalin's instruction to the CCP in October 1926 was that the peasant movement should be kept in check,[2] and Borodin's opposition to agrarian revolution had the support of both the Comintern and Stalin.[3] Treint, a member of the sub-committee of the Chinese Commission of the

94. [173] II, 338.   95. [173] II, 389.
96. [173] II, 337.   97. [174] II, 198.   98. [173] 387–8.
99. [176] II, 671.
1. [173] II, 343.   2. [173] II, 337.
3. [210] 91, being a resolution adopted by the Comintern.

eighth plenum of the Executive Committee of the Comintern, recorded a discussion held after the Shanghai Massacre.[4] Stalin, according to Treint, referred to Borodin's assertion that the KMT would turn against the CCP had there been an agrarian revolution, and urged that time was needed to enable them 'to manoeuvre'. Treint asked whether the CCP would be expected to support Wuhan in the armed suppression of the peasants, to which Bukharin was said to have replied 'yes', while Stalin was satisfied that the CCP had sufficient authority with the Chinese masses to make them accept the policy of restraint.[5]

This was the background against which the peasant movement was kept in check by Ch'en Tu-hsiu and Li Wei-han, and also by the head of the peasant department, Ch'ü Ch'iu-pai.[6] It was the background as well to the disciplining of Mao Tse-tung.

Down at the village level, the choice between the masses and the KMT was vividly portrayed by Liu Chih-hsün:

What about ourselves? [We] were then in a quandary. On the one hand, we had to fight against the feudal forces of local bullies and bad gentry and the bourgeoisie; on the other, we had to co-operate with the KMT which represented them. We had to make friends and come to terms with the remnants of feudalism, landlords, and capitalists. We had to prevent workers and peasants from solving their problems by themselves. We told them to wait for orders from the headquarters of the KMT. But the wait was as endless as that for the waters of the Yellow River to become clear.[7]

The attitude of Moscow being such, Ch'en Tu-hsiu could hardly be blamed for adopting the policies he did. On the question of burying arms, for instance, in late March 1927 the Comintern telegraphed the Central Committee of the CCP to avoid military conflict between the workers and Chiang's troops at all costs and instructed the Committee to hide all the workers' fire-arms. This order the CCP duly obeyed.[8] Bukharin, indeed, had asked: 'Was it not better to hide the arms, not to accept battle, and thus

4. Chiang's Shanghai *Coup*, 21 April 1927.
5. [173] II, 382.   6. [162] 99–100.
7. [201] 382.
8. [193] 402. Chinese communists to a man condemn Ch'en Tu-hsiu for the order to bury arms. See [217] 128 and Ts'ai Shu-fan's statement in [190] 86.

not permit oneself to be disarmed?'[9] Later, in Hankow, the story repeated itself—arms were again buried in order to avoid an open clash.[10] In various other ways as well efforts were made to fulfil Moscow's instructions for preserving the CCP–KMT *entente*[11]: the ministries of agriculture and labour avoided proclaiming a single policy which might ameliorate the conditions of the peasants and workers[12]; the communist minister of agriculture went on a tour to check peasant excesses[13]; and the CCP agreed to dissolve some front organizations such as the workers' pickets and children's corps.[14]

There was also the famous telegram of 30 May from Stalin to the CCP, and to Borodin and Roy, ordering them: 'Confiscate land, but do not touch the land of the military officers; check the peasants' overzealous action with the power of the Party Head-quarters; destroy the present unreliable generals; arm 20,000 communists and select 50,000 workers and peasant elements in Hupei and Hunan to create a new army; put new workers and peasant elements in the Central Executive Committee of the KMT to take the place of the old members; and organize a revolutionary court with a well-known member of the KMT as its chairman to try reactionary officers.'[15] Was it possible to carry out these self-contradictory measures at one time? Since 'all the land-owners were directly or indirectly protected by the officers',[16] confiscation was bound to lead to a clash of arms with the officers as it had done before. As to arms, Ts'ai Shu-fan at one time stated that the Wuhan workers had ten rifles and six pistols,[17] at another that they had over 1,000 rifles.[18] In either case, the Wuhan workers had much less than the 1,700 rifles their comrades in Shanghai had had in April.[19] Even if, as L. Fischer optimistically estimated, some

9. N. Bukharin, *Les Problèmes de la Révolution Chinoise*, 56, quoted from [205] 163.   10. [190] 128 and [217] 128.

11. 'Pa-ch'i kao t'ung-chih shu' (A circular letter to the comrades, 7 August 1927), quoted from [19] II, b 221.

12. [19] II, b 221 and [173] II, 391.   13. [19] II, b 232.

14. [193] 285.

15. [154] III, 230–1, [169] 50–1, and [212] 520–1, n. 13. Ho Kan-chih praises the telegram as 'a programme for action which would lead to victory' in the Chinese version of his *History of Modern Chinese Revolution* (I, 106), but *not* in its English translation.

16. [167].   17. [190] 86.   18. [190] 87.   19. [217] 109.

10,000 Hankow workers could be armed, the generals had 75,000 men and the stockpile in the Hanyang Arsenal.[20] Moreover, Russia was a long way away and the possible supply route over land was blocked by General Feng Yü-hsiang. Therefore even a radical like Ch'ü Ch'iu-pai had to admit that to arm the workers was 'extremely difficult', 'because to change the class groups in the army meant the capture of the army by the CCP'.[21] The setting-up of a tribunal would mean 'presumably to appoint T'ang Sheng-chih to judge Hsü K'e-hsiang' who was T'ang's trusted lieutenant, and to 'appoint Wang Ching-wei to judge T'ang Sheng-chih' who happened to be the pillar of the military strength of the Wuhan Government.[22] Can one wonder that Borodin deemed it impossible to carry out these measures, and that Ch'en Tu-hsiu described them as 'shameful policies'?[23] M. N. Roy evidently took a different view. Being an advocate of the 'revolution from below', he welcomed Stalin's change to a more radical policy and so showed the telegram to Wang Ching-wei. He 'was prepared for a showdown, thinking that the KMT left-wing had no way out except to follow the lead of the CCP'.[24]

Indeed, the left-wing was no more than a pillow-case stuffed with red feathers. Mao Tse-tung himself, for instance, had been the secretary of the organization department of the Shanghai branch of the KMT and Hsia Hsi the head of the Hunan branch. Ch'ü Ch'iu-pai admitted that 'the local branches of the KMT were in the hands of the communists'[25] and General T'ang Sheng-chih anxiously warned the Wuhan Government that 'the party branch in Hunan is run by the terrorists who are members of both parties'.[26] As early as 20 May 1925 Tsou Lu, a prominent leader of the right-wing of the KMT, wrote to Chiang Kai-shek, asking him:

How many non-communists are dispatched to other provinces from our headquarters in Canton? How many non-communists are sent to other places to organize peasants' associations? How many non-communists are responsible for organizing workers? Need I ask you any more before you are aware of the situation?[27]

20. [176] II, 672.   21. [199] 90.   22. [205] 246.
23. [205] 246.
24. [199] 101. Wang Ching-wei agreed with Ch'ü's view on this matter. [154] III, 232 and [144] 157.   25. [199] 55–6.
26. [217] 122. The telegram is dated 29 May 1927.   27. [151] III,122.

Four days before this letter Chiang himself expressed to Borodin his worries over what he called 'small party's victory over a big party'.[28] Wang Ching-wei twice admitted that the Wuhan Government and party were under communist domination.[29] Workers were under such leaders as Chang Kuo-t'ao, Li Li-san, Liu Shao-ch'i, and Teng Chung-hsia and peasants under Mao Tse-tung, P'eng Pai, Liu Chih-hsün, Wei Pa-ch'ün, and others.[30] Tsou Lu again observed that the peasants' associations and militia were entirely under the control of the communists.[31]

It is clear that the pyramid of the left-wing was formed thus: the prominent leaders of the wing with their relatives, friends, and pupils stood at the top, the communist members of the KMT were the cadres of the middle, and the mass organization of the peasants and workers led by the communists lay at the bottom. The mainstay was in fact the communist cadres. It is also clear that Stalin's policy of alliance with the left-wing of the KMT was no more than linking the two arms of one person—an alliance of communists with communists.

In one department the left-wing of the CCP was conspicuously weak; this department was the army. After the split between Nanking and Wuhan the latter could count on the loyalty of the three armies under T'ang Sheng-chih and three others under Chang Fa-k'uei. Even this force, meagre as it was compared with the military power of Nanking, was at times awkward for the civilians in the Wuhan Government to handle, as was pointed out by Borodin to Anna Louise Strong:

Did you ever see a rabbit before an anaconda ... trembling, knowing it is going to be devoured, yet fascinated? That's the civic power before the military in Wuhan, staring at the military and trembling.[32]

The weakness of the party and government of Wuhan compared with the power of the military seems to suggest that the mass basis was not as strong as has been described by many. A Russian report on 5 March 1927 said: 'The people are rather indifferent

28. [135] VIIIb, 66a–b.   29. [154] III, 169–71 and 229.
30. [7] 1928, 956, [181] 16–17, [190] 84 and 201, [201] 9, 399, and 407–8.
31. [150] I, 166.
32. [213] 38–9. The estimates of the military strength of the Wuhan Government were made by the military intelligence department of Nanking ([130] XV, 748 and XVII, 1019–1025).

toward the Revolution and appear less afraid of the National
Government than they did a month ago.'[33] Mao Tse-tung himself
pointed out the existence of bad elements in the peasant association of Hunan.[34] Indeed, serious shortcomings were common
among the peasants' organizations in Hupei, Kwangtung, and
other places.[35] Exaggeration was another defect. General Feng
Yü-hsiang said that a meeting of less than 10,000 was reported as
one of more than 100,000 or even of 200,000.[36] An eye-witness,
Owen Chapman, said that people were *ordered* to attend mass
rallies.[37] These observations can be corroborated by Lominadze
and Bukharin. The former admitted after the Canton Uprising
he had helped to organize that 'we exaggerated the strength of
peasant revolts and the readiness of the workers and peasants
to come to the aid of the revolutionary Canton'[38]; the latter spoke
at the fifteenth congress of the Bolshevik Party thus: 'We did not
have a sufficiently broad social basis for a victorious insurrection.'[39]
The lack of mass support was also noticed by the fifth congress of
the CCP.[40] The tenacity of the masses was exaggerated too. So,
when challenged by Chiang Kai-shek's bullets and bayonets, the
peasant associations and workers' unions crumbled to pieces. At
the critical time when Wuhan and Nanking were in bitter enmity
the masses disappeared and the left-wing military wavered. Wang
Ching-wei, according to Mif, posed these questions bitterly:

But where are the masses? Where are the highly praised forces of the
Shanghai workers or the Kwangtung or Hunan peasants? There are
no such forces. You see, Chiang Kai-shek maintains himself quite
strongly without the masses. To go with the masses means to go against
the army. No, we had better go without the masses but together with
the army.[41]

These were telling questions, revealing that the heart of the matter
was, in Ch'ü Ch'iu-pai's words, 'the struggle between the military
and the party'.[42] And on this issue Wang Ching-wei had to make
his stand. The way he did it completely upset Roy's expectations;
the first united front between the KMT and the CCP was broken.

33. [193] 435.   34. [46] I, 32–3.   35. [201] 213, 368–9 and 400–1.
36. [86] III, 697.   37. [197] 24–5.   38. [173] II, 414.
39. [174] II, 436.   40. [19] II b, 229.   41. [184] 139.
42. [199] 56.

The communists, clinging to the faintest of hopes, decided to withdraw from the Wuhan Government only, not from the KMT, in order to 'make it clear that the Wuhan Government is a national, not a communist, government'.[43] But the less hesitant Wuhan declared the CCP outlawed on that fateful day of 13 July 1927. The so-called White Terror thus began and chaos ensued. Tung Pi-wu was in Wuhan and he relates:

I had to hide. I kept connection with only one other comrade.[44]

Many of the less stout-hearted simply resigned from the CCP, and so in less than six months the membership fell from over 50,000 to under 25,000.[45] A temporary politburo with Chou En-lai, Chang T'ai-lei, Li Wei-han, Ch'ü Ch'iu-pai, and Li Li-san was formed to deal with the emergency. At a meeting of the temporary body on the same day when the KMT outlawed the communists, a new party line was adopted and Chou En-lai was appointed secretary of the Front Committee and dispatched to Nanch'ang to organize an armed uprising.[46]

'The First Great Revolution' was undeniably a failure from the communist point of view, and, in retrospect, when he talked to Edgar Snow, Mao blamed Borodin and Ch'en Tu-hsiu for it.[47] But in October 1939, when writing in a more coherent manner, he summed up the failure in this way:

But the Party at that time was after all still in its infancy, a party inexperienced in the three basic problems of the united front, the armed struggle and Party building, a party without much knowledge about *China's historical and social conditions*, about *the characteristics and laws of the Chinese revolution*, and a party which had yet no complete understanding of the unity between the theory of Marxism–Leninism and *the practice of the Chinese revolution*. Hence in the last period of this stage, at its critical juncture, those occupying a dominant position in the Party's leading body were unable to lead the whole Party to consolidate the victories of the revolution and, deceived by the bourgeoisie, caused the revolution to suffer defeat.[48]

Trotsky, on the other hand, in a different frame of mind and seeing things differently, uttered bitter words:

43. [173] II, 392.
44. [190] 43.   45. [212] 1570.   46. [217] 131.
47. [258] 161.   48. [46] II, 601 or *SW* III, 61 (my italics).

The cruel massacres of the Chinese proletariat ... and the general weakening of the position of the Comintern and the Soviet Union, the party owes principally and above all to Comrade Stalin.[49]

But from our description and analysis it may be justifiable to say that the root of the failure lay in the mistaken policy of 'revolution from above' and its corollary, the 'bloc within' policy. Both policies were rendered meaningless and should have been abandoned, from the communist point of view, after the Shanghai Massacre of April 1927, for the alliance, as has been pointed out above, had since become one between the two arms of one person. The left-wing was an empty shell. To preserve an alliance with it at the expense of the development of the mass movement was certainly unwise.

49. [173] II, 392.

Chapter VI

The Autumn Harvest

IN 1928 Mao described the situation in China after the dissolution of the first united front in these words:

Having fought in various places in the past year, we are keenly aware that the revolutionary upsurge in the country as a whole is subsiding. ... Wherever the Red Army goes, it finds the masses cold and re-served. ... We have to fight the enemy forces hard whoever they are and scarcely any mutiny or uprising has taken place within the enemy forces. ... We have an acute sense of loneliness and are every moment longing for the end of such a lonely life.[1]

Ho Kan-chih, the communist historian, gives his explanation:

The imperialists, landlords, bureaucrats, compradores, and the Right Wing of the KMT formed a counter-revolutionary alliance whose strength far surpassed that of the revolution. So the revolution reached a low ebb.[2]

But in Moscow Stalin saw the situation in a more sanguine light. The Chinese revolution, according to him, had entered into the second stage in which 'the agrarian movement grew into a mighty revolution embracing tens of millions of peasants'. The tide of revolution was still rising; hence the CCP, said Stalin, should 'push the Wuhan KMT to the left towards the agrarian revolution, ... turn it into a centre of struggle against the counter-revolution and into the kernel of the future revolutionary-democratic dictatorship of the proletariat and the peasantry.'[3] In spite of

1. [46] I, 80 or *SW* I, 99.   2. [14] 179.
3. Stalin's speech to a joint conference of the Central Committee and Central Control Committee of the CPSU on 1 August 1927. [174] II, 238-9.

The Route to Chingkangshan

the fact that the Wuhan KMT had already outlawed the CCP, he counselled that to break away from the Wuhan KMT was to break away from the masses and to deprive the communists of popular support.[4]

While Stalin wanted the non-existent alliance preserved, the Comintern directives to the CCP on 14 July 1927 advised: 'leave the Wuhan Government at once, make public Wuhan's hostility to the agrarian revolution and the workers' movement, but do not leave the KMT.'[5] The CCP duly obeyed and the unilaterally recognized alliance was 'prolonged' until September.

Meanwhile Chou En-lai arrived at Nanch'ang to ignite the uprising there. Stationed in the vicinity was the 2nd Front Army under General Chang Fa-k'uei, which comprised the 4th Army (the 'Ironsides') commanded by General Huang Ch'i-hsiang, the 11th Army newly placed under the command of the communist General Yeh T"ing, and the 20th Army under the pro-communist General Ho Lung.[6] Inside the city there was a regiment of cadets from Yünnan and Kwangsi under a commandant by the name of Chu Te.[7] The total strength Chou En-lai hoped to be able to mobilize amounted to some 20,000, including such officers and political commissars as Lin Tsu-han, Wu Yü-chang, Chang Kuo-t'ao, Li Li-san, Yün Tai-ying, Li Fu-ch'un, Lin Piao, Su Yü, Chou Shih-ti, Liu Po-ch'eng, and Nieh Jung-chen.[8] The garrison of Nanch'ang under General Chu P'ei-te was, however, scarcely more than 5,000.[9]

The superiority of the communist and pro-communist military strength at Nanch'ang explains the choice of the location of the first armed uprising organized by the CCP. It may have been hoped that by taking this important city which lay between the quarrelling Nanking and Wuhan, the communists would be able to turn the whole situation to their favour. Since revolutions in the past—the French, the Russian, and the Chinese of 1911—had all been touched off by an armed uprising, why should not the planned Nanch'ang operation shake the entire area south of the

4. [174] II, 240.   5. [173] II, 395–6.
6. [169] 53, [178] 174, [181] 37–8, and [214] 285.
7. [234] 28–9 and [242] 130.   8. [17] 78, [181] 37–8, [234] 28–9.
9. [19] II, b 234, [234] 45, and [243] 3–4 and 10.

Yangtze and rally together the scattered bands of revolutionaries? Hitherto revolution had known no other pattern.

Early in the morning of 1 August the operation began with the disarming of the garrison followed by the occupation of the city. The 'KMT Revolutionary Committee' was set up by the communists, being intended as the rallying point, but no one else rose to its support. Meanwhile the troops loyal to the KMT were converging on Nanch'ang and in a swift action forced Yeh T'ing, Ho Lung, and Chu Te to evacuate the city on 5 August.[10] The question was, where could they now go?

Generals Chang Fa-k'uei and Huang Ch'i-hsiang led the bulk of the 4th Army along the Kan River back to Canton[11]; Ch'en Ming-shu, Chiang Kuang-nai, and Ts'ai T'ing-k'ai led that of the 11th Army via east Kiangsi to Fukien; what was left of the 2nd Front Army under Yeh T'ing, Ho Lung, and Chu Te took the Juichin-Huich'ang-P'ingyüan route to Ch'aochow in Kwangtung to join forces with P'eng Pai's peasant soviet in Haifeng and Lufeng.[12] The hastily conceived, planned, and executed Nanch'-ang Uprising which had neither a political programme nor popular support thus ended ignominiously. However, it marked the disintegration of the once famous 4th Army and the beginning of the Red Army in China.[13] Another perhaps not insignificant result was that along their route of retreat the communists left behind small bands of guerrillas to roam in south Kiangsi.

In the wake of this defeat the urban intellectuals of the Politburo of the CCP called the celebrated 7 August Conference at Kiukiang which inaugurated the putschist line of Ch'ü Ch'iu-pai.[14] Twelve members of the Central Committee, including Mao, Teng Chunghsia, Wang Jo-fei, and Ch'ü, but excluding Ch'en Tu-hsiu and his supporters who were then in Shanghai, three alternate members of the Central Committee, five members of the Central Committee of the Communist Youth Corps, and two representatives of local branches attended it.[15] The deliberations ended with the conclusion that the tide of the bourgeois revolution was still rising, that the democratic dictatorship should still be the goal of the

10. [14] 186-7.   11. [130] XVII, 1095.
12. [18] 212-13, [130] XVII, 1094, [265] I, 188, and [286] 178.
13. [19] II, b 235.   14. [18] 223.   15. [18] 223-4.

party's struggles, and that the KMT was still the proper political vehicle—but that it should be 'reorganized' by the communists into 'a genuine organization of the working masses of town and country'. The agrarian revolution under the leadership of the urban proletariat was now the crux of the bourgeois democratic revolution.[16] The Conference also censured Mao Tse-tung, who was now the first chairman of the All-China Peasants' Union, for his 'opportunistic' directives to the peasants after May 1927,[17] but he was given the task of planning and directing the Autumn Harvest Uprising in Hunan and Kiangsi.[18]

The reason for staging the Autumn Harvest Uprising was to take advantage of the harvesting period to intensify the class struggle in the villages. The slogan was the transference of political power into the hands of peasant associations, and the land belonging to large and middle landowners was to be confiscated and distributed among the poor peasants.[19] This done, Mao and the Hunan branch of the CCP were to be relied upon by the Politburo to take Ch'angsha and, using it as the new rallying point, to change the whole situation.[20]

Under Mao, the secretary of the Front Committee, and Lu Te-ming, the commander, there was the first Workers' and Peasants' Revolutionary Army of four regiments—the first were mostly deserters from the KMT *gendarmerie* of Wuch'ang who were ordered to approach Ch'angsha via Ch'angshouchieh, the second, a motley collection of Anyüan miners and P'inghsiang and Liuyang peasants gathered together by Mao himself, who were to attack Ch'angsha from the east, the third, the armed peasants of Liuyang organized by Mao himself, who were to take the Tungmenshih route to Ch'angsha, and the fourth, renegades from Hsia Tou-yin's units who were to take P'inghsiang. These detachments, under-strength and inexperienced, were yet expected to set up soviets and confiscate land without seeking the co-operation of the KMT in Hunan.[21] The communist *Central*

---

16. [52] 94–5 and [162] 97–8.   17. [162] 100.
18. Mao told Snow that the Autumn Harvest Uprising in Hunan was not sanctioned by the Central Committee. This must not be understood to mean that it was not sanctioned at all ([258] 165).
19. [162] 122 and [234] 59.   20. [19] II, b 245.
21. [18] 214–15, [234] 60, and [258] 163.

News (Chung-yang T'ung-hsün) carried this report from Hunan on 30 September 1927:

From September 8 to 12, the first few days of the Uprising, we were winning. The amount of arms and ammunition in our hands was more than doubled. At P'inghsiang our peasant army had 700 or 1,300 rifles and at Anyüan, about 2,100. Thousands of peasants came with their spears and swords to join us. All the important towns in east Hunan [*sic*]—P'inghsiang, Liuyang, Liling, and Chuchow—fell into our hands. Therefore Ch'angsha was in the grip of a panic on September 13.[22]

But the expected support from the workers in Ch'angsha did not come.[23] Worse still, the fourth regiment suddenly turned against the first regiment at P'inghsiang and a confused battle resulted; the second regiment was surrounded and annihilated by the KMT troops at Liuyang; the third ran into an ambush at Tungmenshih. The entire operation was thus thrown out of gear and ended in a miserable failure.[24]

One day during the operation, on reaching Wenchiashih in Liuyang, Mao was detained by members of the local militia, but luckily was not recognized and was able to buy his release. As he was making his way towards the northern section of the Lohsiao Ranges the militia who had let him go came after him. Only by hiding among the thick and tall reeds near a pond till sunset did he manage to escape detection. Afterwards he bought a pair of walking sandals, an umbrella, and some food and walked day and night until he made contact with his troops who had by then lost their commander.[25] Mao gathered together the remnants of his four regiments, about 1,000 men, at Sanwan in Yunghsin, Kiangsi, and reorganized them into the 1st Regiment of the 1st Division of the 1st Workers' and Peasants' Revolutionary Army under his direction as the secretary of the Front Committee.[26] In October he and his troops established the first communist base on the middle section of the Lohsiao Ranges, better known as Ching-kangshan.

For his failure in the Autumn Harvest Uprising which was due to a lack of military experience and popular support,[27] Mao was

22. Quoted from [19] II, b 251.   23. [19] II, b 253.
24. [18] 215.   25. [234] 59–60 and [258] 163–4.
26. [18] 214–15.   27. [46] I, 198 or *SW* I, 212 and [52] 101.

severely punished by dismissal from the Politburo[28] while an order for his arrest was issued by the KMT on 10 December 1927.[29] But neither setback affected him much, for he had already firmly entrenched in his mountain fastness.

The uprising in Hunan and Kiangsi under Mao's direction was by no means an isolated event. Similar attempts were made in Haifeng and Lufeng in Kwangtung under P'eng Pai, in north Shensi under Liu Chih-tan, and in several parts of central China under Ho Lung, Chang Kuo-t'ao, Tuan Te-ch'ang, and others, and minor disturbances also occurred in Chihli, Shantung, Kiangsu, and Hainan[30] about the time when the Politburo of the CCP met in an enlarged plenary session in Shanghai in November 1927.[31] At the plenum, Ch'ü Ch'iu-pai's report on 'The Present Situation in China and the Party's Tasks' was adopted as a resolution which refused to admit the defeat of the 1927 revolution. Instead, it adjudged that the revolution in China was a 'continuous upsurge' calling for further uprisings. The setbacks suffered by the communists were attributed to a lack of co-ordination between the workers' and peasants' insurrections, for 'a purely peasant uprising without the leadership and help of the working class cannot achieve conclusive victories'.[32] But in later years Mao was able to pin-point the mistakes of 1927. Writing in 1938, he said: '. . . war was not yet made the centre of gravity of the Party's work.'[33] In 1945 he remarked:

. . . the ultra-revolutionism of the petty bourgeoisie, aggravated by hatred of the Kuomintang's policy of massacre and indignation at Ch'en Tu-hsiu's capitulationism, also found its expression in the Party and led to a rapid rise of 'left' sentiment. . . . Organizationally, it initiated an excessive, sectarian inner-Party struggle, over-stressed the importance of the working-class origin of leading cadres to the exclusion of other considerations, and brought about a serious state of extreme

28. [52] 101, [190] 10, and [258] 165. See also [57] II, 33.
29. [26] 10.2.1928, 129.
30. [18] 216 and 229, [181] 80, [190] 152, [247] V, 108–18, and [258] 67–8 and 211. A word about Ho Lung may be necessary here. In 1925 he commanded the 9th Mixed Brigade under General Hsiung K'e-wu and was stationed in Hunan. In March he went over to General Chao Heng-t'i who appointed him the garrison commander of Linfeng in northwest Hunan. It was in that area he later established a red base. ([135], VIIh, 67a.)
31. [173] II, 414.   32. [18] 220–2 and [52] 104.
33. [46] II, 536 or SW II, 274.

democratization in the Party. At the enlarged meeting of the Central Committee in November 1927, this 'Left' sentiment, which continued to rise after the 7 August meeting, became a 'Left' line of reckless action (adventurism) and for the first time brought the 'Left' line to a dominant position in the Party's central leading body. The advocates of reckless action characterized the Chinese revolution as a 'permanent upsurge' . . . and consequently, heedless of the fact that the enemy was powerful and the people had just suffered defeat in the revolution, they still refused to organize an orderly retreat, but commanded handfuls of Party members and the Party's followers to undertake local insurrections all over the country without the slightest hope of success.[34]

Failure alone was enough to prove that these words of Mao's were correct; apart from emphasizing the panic and obstinacy of the central leadership of the party and charging it with 'adventurism', Mao also pointed out that the tide of revolution was undoubtedly ebbing. Profound as they are, these observations were not made until years after the events. At the time no one was able to see the errors, not even Mao himself.

At this meeting, Ch'en Tu-hsiu and his supporters were severely criticized for their 'capitulationist' mistakes and subsequently they began to show dissentient tendencies by organizing various societies of their own. Ch'en started the Proletarian Society; Liu Jen-ching, the October Society; Huang Yüan-ming, the Struggle Society; but T'an P'ing-shan and Shih Ts'un-t'ung simply resigned from the party and joined the Third Party.[35] Following Ch'en's expulsion in November 1929, the dissidents formed themselves into the Anti-cadres Group (*Fan Kan-pu P'ai*) and published their periodical, the *Spark* (*Huo-hua*) in Shanghai.[36]

Now we must go back to the defeated troops at Nanch'ang, which, moving southward through the difficult terrain in sweltering weather, had to evade the enemies and solve the besetting problem of supplies before reaching Ch'aochow and Swatow on 24 September 1927.[37] They took the towns, but were at once beleaguered and forced to fight, with the result that they had to abandon them on 29 September. Thence they moved on to Haifeng and Lufeng where P'eng Pai had set up a soviet.[38] Hot on their heels were the

34. [46] III, 980 or *SW* IV, 175–6.   35. [181] 67.
36. [14] 199 and [181] 67.
37. [234] 33–4 and 52–3, [265] I, 188, [286] 178.   38. [234] 34–5.

Kwangsi army under Huang Shao-hsiung who cut the communist
column into two and encircled both sections. Ho Lung managed
to pull out most of his men while Yeh T'ing's troops received
crippling blows. Chu Te and Chou Shih-ti were forced to withdraw their 2,000 men towards Ch'aochow and then to the Hunan
border where his old Yünnan colleague, General Fan Shih-sheng,
was stationed.[39] Ho and Yeh, having joined forces with P'eng Pai,
reorganized their detachments into the 1st and 2nd Red Army
of the East River and founded a revolutionary régime which
lasted only a week from 1 to 7 November.[40] Thereafter Yeh
T'ing, Nieh Jung-chen, and Chou En-lai, who was suffering from
malaria, took a small boat and sailed to Hong Kong whence Yeh
was able to smuggle himself back to Canton to direct the uprising
there in December.[41]

In Moscow, the 15th congress of the Russian Party was scheduled for December and Stalin craved for a victory in China that
might redound to his credit.[42] Telegrams like snowflakes flew daily
from Moscow to the CCP, urging the CCP in the most definite
tones to bring about uprisings in Canton and other major cities.[43]
Stalin reported to the congress: 'Only the blind and the faint-
hearted can doubt that the Chinese workers and peasants are
moving forward to a new revolutionary surge.'[44] His agents in
China, no longer Borodin and Roy, but a 29-year-old Georgian
by the name of Besso Lominadze and a 26-year-old German,
Heinz Neumann, were instructed to prepare for the Canton
Uprising.[45]

Why Canton? To begin with, the uprising had to be at a major
city which could become a rallying point. With Peking still under
the control of warlords and Shanghai, Nanking, and Wuhan being
obviously out of the question, Ch'angsha and Nanch'ang had
already been proved too strongly guarded, and Canton became the
only choice. It had been the scene of a recent conflict between the
Kwangtung troops under Chang Fa-k'uei and the Kwangsi troops
under Li Chi-shen[46] which had greatly weakened the defences of

39. [189] 209–13, [234] 34–5, and [265] I, 188–90. See also [203] 33.
40. [234] 53–4 and [235] 199–213.   41. [280] 248. Also [235] 213.
42. [173] II, 414, and [215] 29.   43. [182] 32–4.
44. [174] II, 287.   45. [212] 559.   46. [130] XVII, 1096.

the city. At the time of the planned uprising the city was guarded by a regiment of cadets under none other than Yeh Chien-ying and some security police under Liang Ping-shu, both being pro-communist.[47] The city was far away from Wuhan or Nanking where the KMT military forces were concentrated, but was near Haifeng and Lufeng where P'eng Pai's units, though heavily defeated, were not yet exterminated. The planners of the uprising therefore hoped that, once the signal was given, the workers and peasants who had responded to their calls for action so readily in the past, as the year-long anti-British boycott, for instance, showed, would once again rally under their banners. Later events were to disappoint them.

Indeed, Yeh T'ing was rather pessimistic about the whole adventure, for, according to his estimates, the party could mobilize some 4,000 members in addition to the 1,200 cadets under Yeh Chien-ying, while the KMT had between 6,000 and 7,000 soldiers equipped with 5,000 rifles, a good number of machine-guns, and 35 small trench mortars.[48] The most feared were perhaps the 50,000 troops under Li Chi-shen and Chang Fa-k'uei stationed nearby.[49] The communist's arms and ammunition were limited to 2,000 rifles, 200 grenades, and about 30 automatic rifles.[50]

The operation, however, proceeded swiftly and smoothly. Canton was taken in the small hours of 11 December and at once the Commune was set up with Su Chao-cheng as its chairman,[51] but the KMT troops converged on the city and by the afternoon of 13 December all was over.[52] In those three chaotic days the city was gutted by fire and thousands of people were butchered.[53] Neumann admitted ruefully that the soldiers had ignored the uprising; Lozovsky reported that the workers paid almost no attention at all to it.[54] The uprising, like so many of its predecessors, was abortive.

47. [286] 187.
48. [52] 106 and Teng Chung-hsia, 'The Canton Commune and the Tactics of the CP', 39, quoted from [212] 557–8.
49. [19] II, b 266, [205] 283–4, and [212] 558.   50. [205] 283.
51. Lists of officials, see [26] 10 February 1928, 129 and [19] II, b 262.
52. [19] II, b 262, [130] XVII, 1087–8, and [205] 285–90.
53. [181] 42 and [205] 291.
54. [173] II, 414–15. Hua Kang believes that the uprising was warmly supported by the broad masses ([19] II, b 257 and 264–5).

Nevertheless, it was just enough to give Stalin the required encouragement. So, in spite of everything, on 15 December the Executive Committee of the Comintern were rejoicing: 'In Kwantung [sic] the soviet power is holding out strongly in five areas. New battles are inevitable. The movement is growing, despite partial defeats. The bourgeois counter-revolutionaries will be defeated. The imperialist robbers will be thrown out of Chinese territory. But at the moment the heroic Chinese revolution, the revolution of workers and peasants, stands beneath their axe.'[55]

Trotsky, on the other hand, fumed: 'If these are the methods of the bourgeois revolution, what will the proletarian revolution be like?' To this Mao Tse-tung agreed by charging the party leadership with 'confusing the democratic revolution with the socialist revolution'.[56] But in a more bitter mood, Trotsky wrote:

At the end of 1927, Stalin's faction, frightened by the consequences of its own mistakes, tried to make up at one stroke what it had failed to do over a number of years. Thus the Canton revolt was organized. The leaders continued to labour under the assumption that the revolution was still on the increase. In reality the revolutionary tide had already been replaced by a downward movement. The heroism of the foremost workers of Canton could not prevent the disaster caused by the adventurous spirit of its leaders. The Canton revolt was drowned in blood. The Second Chinese Revolution was definitely crushed. ... Early in 1928, when the Chinese revolution was at a low point, the Ninth Plenary Session of the Executive Committee of the Communist International proclaimed a course toward an armed uprising in China. The result of this lunacy was the further defeat of the workers, the liquidation of the best revolutionaries, the disintegration of the party, and demoralisation in the workers' ranks.[57]

The defeat of the Canton Uprising virtually ended the Ch'ü Ch'iu-pai line, whose fulsome author was rebuked and called to Moscow where he was to remain under the name of Strakhov until 1930.[58] It also marked the end of a phase in Sino-Russian relations.

55. [173] II, 416.   56. [215] 128 and [46] III, 980 or *SW* IV, 176.
57. *Byulleten 'Oppozitzii'*, 1930, no. 15–16, 2–3.
58. [52] 108.

Chapter VII

The Revolutionary Bases

THE precipitous Chingkangshan lies between Kiangsi and Hunan; its fastness is almost impregnable. The mild weather and adequate rainfall enrich its soil on which rice, tea, cotton, beans, and groundnuts grow. The mountains are covered with forests of firs, bamboos, and other trees which supply the inhabitants with timber, with *t'ung*-trees which give them oil, and with camphor, mint, and a variety of herbal plants which provide them with medicine. Coal, iron ore, and gypsum are known to have been under production when Mao and his men occupied this area with a circumference of 250 kilometres.[1] There were five large villages with a population under 2,000 living in a stone-and-wood age and a clan society—all the inhabitants of a village were often members of a single clan. Deep in the woods, however, it was wild life that reigned—wild life consisting of tigers, leopards, boars, jackals, and wolves and the less menacing muskdeer, beavers, and pheasants.[2] The setting was far removed from that of Shanghai, Canton, or Wuhan, even from that of Ch'angsha or Liuyang, and so Mao had to admit that it was exceedingly difficult for Bolshevism to take root.[3]

On his way to Chingkangshan, Mao ran into a former student of his at Ningkang, who introduced him to the commander of a local force, Yüan Wen-ts'ai. The two of them and Yüan's friend, Wang Tso, decided to merge their forces into two regiments— Mao's own was denominated the 31st and Yüan's the 32nd—

---

1. [14] 196–7, [46] I, 58 n. 12 and 76 or *SW* I, 346, ns. 12 and 14, [234] 82, and [241] 1–5.
2. [46] I, 76 or *SW* I, 94 and [241] 7–9.   3. [46] I, 76 or *SW* I, 94.

which took the undefended Chingkangshan in October and Ch'a-
ling in Hunan in November 1927. Subsequently party cells were
set up in the clan villages of Ningkang, Yunghsin, and Suich'uan.[4]

It is understandable that in these vastly different circumstances
Mao would have to adopt policies which might not conform to the
party line. He had no industrial workers to lead the peasants and
it was by relying on the peasants that he obtained new recruits
and supplies for his army. To refuse to utilize the peasants would
mean his own defeat. In order to woo them he adopted the policy
of 'complete confiscation and thorough redistribution' of land
which, however, encountered a great deal of resistance, particularly
from what he called 'the intermediate class'—small landlords and
rich peasants. When Mao's military strength appeared to be on
the increase this class showed itself obedient; when his strength
appeared on the wane it became troublesome. In a clan society
it could make full use of the influence of the family tie for persuasion or dissuasion in order to preserve its own interests and to
divide and isolate the poor peasants. As in the beginning, Mao's
military control was weak, the policy of confiscation and redistribution may not have been carried out thoroughly, nor was the
land redistributed in relation to the ability to work it, as laid down
in the party centre's directive.[5] Soviets were organized, but very
few people understood their meaning and very few of the 'councils
of workers, peasants, and soldiers' were worthy of the name.[6]
For all this, Mao was rebuked by the Central Committee of the
CCP, and for regarding the industrial workers as auxiliaries of
the peasants.[7] And in March 1928 the Hunan special commissar—
in all probability someone Mao knew very well—sent an emissary
to see Mao at Ningkang, criticizing him and his comrades in the
Chingkangshan base 'for leaning to the Right, for having not
done enough burning and killing, and for having failed to carry
out the policy of "turning the petty bourgeois into proletarians
and then forcing them into the revolution"; . . .'[8] The Front

4. [234] 61 and 74–7, [241] 14, and [258] 165.
5. [46] I, 71–3 or SW, I, 87–90. According to Sung Hsin-huai, who was at
the Chingkangshan base at that time, the land reform began in February 1928.
See [233] 48.
6. [46] I, 74–5 or SW I, 91–3.　　　7. [52] 102 and [173] II, 436.
8. [46] I, 80 or SW I, 99–100 and [258] 165.

Committee which Mao headed was therefore abolished and replaced by a party committee for the army headed by Ho T'ingying, while Mao himself became the secretary of the newly created Border Region Special Committee.[9] The change meant that he lost direct control over the troops for the time being.

Skirmishes between Mao's regiments and General Wu Shang's 8th Army occurred almost as soon as the base had been established, and in January 1928 Mao scored a major victory by defeating an enemy battalion at Hsinch'eng in the Ningkang district.[10] About the same time, Chu Te, Ch'en Yi, and Lin Piao led their retreating soldiers to Chenchow where, having made contact with Mao Tse-t'an, they continued to advance towards Chingkangshan, most probably in April.[11] It is not clear how strong the Red Army was after this historic merger. Edgar Snow says that it had 50,000 men and 4,000 rifles, whereas Shih Yüan and Li Wei estimate that there were just over 10,000 men.[12] Whichever may be correct, the enlarged army was now reorganized and denominated the 4th Army,[13] with Chu as the commander and Mao the party representative. The divisions, the 10th, 11th, and 12th, were commanded by Chu, Mao, and Ch'en Yi respectively—each nominally having two regiments but with the actual total strength scarcely exceeding four.[14] The mountain fortress was their rear with Maop'ing, where the headquarters of the army was situated, and Talung as their advanced positions.[15] Around the army there were several satellite organizations such as the red guards, insurrection corps, young

---

9. [46] I, 61 and 80 or *SW* I, 73 and 100.   10. [241] 16.

11. Shih Yüan and Snow say that it was in May ([234] 54–5 and [258] 166), while Liu Hsing, Ho Chung-jen, and Li Wei maintain that it took place in April ([234] 61, 74–6 and [241] 18). Mao himself often refers to 'after April', 'since April', or 'in April when our entire army had arrived in the border area . . .' ([46] I, 53, 61, and 80 or *SW* I, 67, 73, and 100). See also Yang Chih-ch'eng, 'Nanch'ang ch'i-i tao Chingkangshan hui-shih', the *Kuang-ming Jih-pao*, 31 July 1962.

12. [234] 54–5, [241] 19, and [258] 360. Ku Kuan-chiao says that there were under 5,000 rifles and T"ang Leang-li under 3,000 rifles ([181] 45–6 and [244] 99).

13. [181] 45–6 and [234] 74–7. See also Appendix B. The 1st Army was under Hsü Hsiang-ch'ien and Chang Kuo-t'ao, the 2nd under Ho Lung and Chou Yi-ch'ün, the 3rd said to be under either P'eng Te-huai or Lo Ping-hui, but both were then KMT officers.

14. [46] I, 61 or *SW* I, 74, [181] 43, [234] 55, and [241] 19.

15. [241] 19.

vanguards, peasant associations, and children's corps, often armed with Mausers, lances, and swords.[16]

Shortly after the merger, Generals Yang Ch'ih-sheng and Yang Ju-hsüan led two divisions in their first assault on the Chingkangshan base in May. At Ch'ihsiling, a precipitous mountain pass, Chu Te deployed three regiments, lying in wait for the enemy while Mao and Yüan Wen-ts'ai each led a regiment to attack the enemy's left and right flanks from the rear. The KMT troops arrived at Ch'ihsiling hot and tired and were pounced upon by Chu Te's regiments in the front. They fled after a short engagement, only to find Mao and Yüan at their back. The two divisions were thus scattered and the first suppression campaign ended in a complete failure.[17]

In the jubilation of this victory, the first congress of the representatives of the party in the border area[18] was held at Maop'ing in Ningkang on 20 May and elected the First Special Committee of twenty-three members with Mao as its secretary.[19] Between this body and the Provincial Committee of Hunan which directly controlled it, serious differences soon developed over both economic and military policies. At the insistence of the Hunan party, the border area 'quite rigorously confiscated the property of the middle merchants in the cities and assessed contributions from the small landowners and rich peasants in the countryside. The slogan of "All Factories to the Workers" put forward by the Southern Hunan Special Committee [not the border area Special Committee] was also widely propagated.'[20] Mao regarded these measures as 'ultra-left' which only drove the 'petty bourgeois' to the side of the landed gentry. Mao also blankly refused to carry out the 'policy of burning and killing'.[21] However, a more irreconcilable dispute between Mao and the Hunan party occurred in the sphere of military strategy. Mao reported in November 1928:

As regards the plan for our action here, the Hunan Provincial Party Committee changed its mind three times within a few weeks in June

16. [46] I, 68 or *SW* I, 84 and [241] 20.   17. [241] 22 and [234] 49.
18. [46] I, 68 or *SW* I, 84. The area now covered the counties of Ningkang, Yunghsin, Lienhua, Ch'aling, Linghsien, Suich'uan, and Wanan.
19. [46] I, 78 or *SW* I, 97.   20. [46] I, 80 or *SW* I, 100.
21. [46] I, 80 or *SW* I, 100.

and July. At first Yuan Te-sheng came and approved of the plan for establishing our political power in the middle section of the Lohsiao mountain range. Then Tu Hsiu-ching and Yang K'ai-ming arrived and proposed that the Red Army should drive ahead to Southern Hunan, 'without the least hesitation', leaving only a force of two hundred rifles to defend the border area together with the Red guards; they said that this was an 'absolutely correct' policy. The third time, barely ten days later, Yuan Te-sheng came again, bringing us a letter which contained, besides much admonition, a proposal that the Red Army should set out for eastern Hunan; this was again said to be an 'absolutely correct policy' and we were again asked to act 'without the least hesitation'. When we received such rigid directives we indeed found ourselves in a dilemma, because failure to comply with them would be tantamount to disobedience while compliance with them would mean certain defeat. When the second letter came, the Army Committee, the Special Committee, and the Yunghsin County Committee held a joint conference, which considered it dangerous to go to southern Hunan and decided not to carry out the proposals of the Provincial Committee.[22]

The result of this decision was that Yang K'ai-ming replaced Mao as the secretary of the Special Committee of the border area.[23] Thereafter the 28th and 29th Regiments—Chu Te's crack troops— were ordered to attack Chenchow from which most of the soldiers of the regiments came.[24] The KMT took the opportunity afforded by the weakened defences of the border area to launch the second suppression campaign.

In the middle of July Wu Shang, Wang Chün, and Hu Wen-tou with their eighteen regiments invaded Chingkangshan.[25] Wu Shang's 8th Army drove into Ningkang and made a concerted attack on Yunghsin with Wang Chün's 3rd Army and Hu Wen-tou's 6th Army. The communist regiment stationed there waged stubborn guerrilla warfare against great odds for twenty-five days before the town of Yunghsin was abandoned. Soon Lienhua and Ningkang were taken by the KMT troops. As a total defeat

22. [46] I, 82 or *SW* I, 102.
23. [46] I, 78 or *SW* I, 97. Hsiao Tso-liang says: 'As a matter of fact, Mao emerged as the main leader of the Communist Movement in Kiangsi even since his days on Chingkangshan in 1927–28. . . .' This tends to overlook Mao's conflict with the Hunan Committee. See [237] 111.
24. [46] I, 82 or *SW* I, 102.
25. [46] I, 62 or *SW* I, 75, [234] 49, and [241] 22.

threatened the communists at Chingkangshan, a quarrel broke
out between Wang Chün and Hu Wen-tou and grew into a full-
scale war at Changshu. Wu Shang's troops were therefore compelled to withdraw and the second suppression campaign too was
foiled.

Meanwhile the 28th and 29th Regiments under Chu Te engaged
his Yunnanese colleague, General Fan Shih-sheng, at Chenchow.
At a critical time the 29th Regiment, acting on its own, fled towards Ichang with the result that a part of it was annihilated at
Loch'ang by bandits. Only some one hundred men of this regiment could be collected together when Chu Te led his defeated
28th Regiment to Kweitung where on 23 August he made contact
with the reinforcement hurriedly sent to him under the command
of Mao Tse-tung. Mao and Chu decided to retreat to Chingkangshan via Ch'unyi, but as soon as they arrived at Ch'unyi a battalion
of their troops mutinied. The remnants did not reach the border
area until 26 September.[26]

It was small wonder, then, that the bungling secretary of the
Special Committee, Yang K'ai-ming, who had replaced Mao in
July, was 'ill' when Mao and Chu returned to Chingkangshan.[27]
At the second congress of the border area party the 'August De-
feat' was thoroughly reviewed and the mistakes of the Provincial
Committee were mercilessly criticized. Thereafter the Special
Committee was completely dominated by Mao's and Chu's men
as its Standing Committee was now headed by T'an Chen-lin.
On 6 November the Front Committee, headed by Mao himself,
was reconstituted, with the Special Committee and the Army Committee under Chu Te as its subsidiary organization.[28] The result of the review and reorganization was reported in full to the
Central Committee of the CCP by Mao—an act indicating that he
was no longer at the mercy of the imbeciles of the Hunan party.

From Mao's report—'The Struggle in the Chingkang Mountains'—it may be surmised that the Provincial Committee wanted
an enlargement of the border area. This change in policy from ap-
proving to opposing Mao's 'conservatism' coincided with the sixth
national congress of the CCP held in Moscow, which laid the

26. [46] I, 62–4 or *SW* I, 75–9.   27. [46] I, 78 or *SW* I, 97.
28. [46] I, 79 or *SW* I, 98.

foundation for the well-known Li Li-san line.[29] In order to understand Li Li-san's views and his differences with Mao it is necessary for us to give a brief account of the state of the nation.

In the summer of 1927 it became clear that the future leader of China was a man in the prime of his life, Chiang Kai-shek, although in August he was forced to relinquish the supreme command of the National Revolutionary Army to Generals Li Tsung-jen, Pai Ch'ung-hsi, and Ho Ying-ch'in.[30] This temporary retirement afforded him a chance to see to some personal matters, such as his marriage. He paid a visit to Japan in October and November, partly to ask permission from Madame Sung, who was then convalescing there, to marry her daughter, Miss Mayling Soong, and partly to see General Tanaka, the Japanese Prime Minister, with a view to entering into an alliance with Japan.[31] He was received by Tanaka who impressed upon him that Manchuria was a special area, different from China proper. According to Mamoru Shigemitsu,[32] the understanding reached between Chiang and Tanaka was that:

with regard to China proper, ... General Tanaka intended to assist the KMT and Chiang Kai-shek to accomplish their aims [of unification], in return for which aid he hoped to obtain the latter's acquiescence in the proposed relations between Japan and Manchuria.

For the purpose General Tanaka kept in touch with Chiang during his northern campaign ... gave his approval of the northward advance.

After his resumption of command, Chiang made this statement to a group of Japanese journalists on 6 March 1928:

Of the wars in the past only Kuo Sung-ling's insurrection against Chang Tso-lin three years ago was not motivated by personal considerations. But it soon ended in defeat; Kuo lost his life and his troops were destroyed. Although the true reasons of this defeat are still being debated, [I like to submit] two for consideration. (1) Kuo chose Manchuria as the battlefield; (2) he had neither a party, not even a political programme, to rally the people around him nor popular support. ... The Northern Expedition of the Revolutionary Army is entirely different. *Its chosen arena is the Yellow River Valley, not Manchuria.* Its pro-

29. [52] 127–8, [162] 131 and 143, and see also [18] 245.
30. [144] 163 and [263] 5.
31. He sailed for Japan on 28 September ([20] 270). See also [115] II, 564.
32. [221] 47.

gramme is the shining Three Principles of the People. . . . The Chinese National Revolution will eventually succeed and its triumph will mark the beginning of the true friendship and co-operation between China and Japan. [I] hope that our friends in Japan will understand this work for the victory of the [Chinese] National Revolution, and thereby lay the foundation of the co-operation of our two countries.[33]

Later events—Chiang's avoidance of a conflict with the Japanese troops in Chinan in May 1928, Japan's jettisoning of Chang Tso-lin,[34] and the halting of the advancing KMT troops south of the Great Wall—tended to support both Shigemitsu and Chiang.

What kind of man *was* Chiang Kai-shek? Let us see a revealing letter he wrote to Chang Chi in 1926:

My wish is to succeed Ch'en Ch'i-mei, Chu Chih-hsin, and Liao Chung-k'ai. I dare not follow the examples of those who fish for reputation; nor dare I accommodate the slightest notion of complacency. . . . The success of our party is certainly what every member should strive for. But if, against our wish, it cannot be realised, the blame will be entirely mine.[35]

This shows that even in those early days when he was neither the most senior in rank nor the most formidable in power in the KMT he claimed nothing less than the mantle of Dr. Sun Yat-sen and the leadership of the party. But he did not seek mere reputation and he had never at any time been complacent. The support he gave to Dr. Sun at the most difficult times in the latter's career— Ch'en Chiung-ming's attack on Sun in Canton on 16 June 1922[36]— when very few among the 'old comrades' went to Sun's aid, demonstrated that he was a man of rare qualities. The Canton *Coup* of 1926 and the Shanghai *Coup* of 1927 made manifest his ability to decide with speed and astuteness and to act in secrecy and without mercy. He embraced Christianity in 1927 and has since remained faithful to it. At the same time he praised Confucianism, revered such Confucian soldier-statesmen as Marquis Tseng Kuo-fan,[37] and professed to be a faithful follower of the

33. [130] XVIII, 24–5.
34. Marshal Chang Tso-lin was assassinated by Colonel Kawamoto. See the Transcript and Exhibits of the International Tribunal for the Far East, 1818–20 and 1951–3 quoted in [223] 44 and n. 2.
35. [120] VIII, 37–8. 36. [120] X, 3.
37. One of the conquerors of the T'aip'ing Rebellion, see A. W. Hummel, *Eminent Chinese of the Ch'ing Period*, II, 751–5.

Three Principles of the People. He could weep bitterly in public[38] and he helped to perpetuate an archaic tradition by taking the oath of brotherhood.[39] He could also resort to buying over his enemies.[40] These stratagems suggest that he tended to overlook the power of true persuasion in favour of undue reliance on emotional appeal, monetary enticement, and military strength.[41] In later years there were many events to prove that he had strong, often excessive, will-power[42] generated by his deep moral convictions—some he received from Christianity but more from Confucianism. In Confucianism, as we have shown above, human bonds are those of loyalty to the Ruler, parents, tutors, and husbands, who, at their own discretion, reciprocate with favour. When Chiang had become the supreme leader of the nation he expected unconditional loyalty from his followers.

Under the leadership of such a man, the National Revolutionary Army fought the second stage of the Northern Expedition from the beginning to June 1928 and brought it to a triumphant conclusion. There were sanguine hopes for a serious and united effort towards national recovery and reconstruction; yet they were soon dashed. In January 1929 the Demobilization Conference, handling what was obviously the most urgent question, produced some disastrous results. General Feng Yü-hsiang became sceptical of Chiang's good-will and sincerity[43] while Li Chi-shen, an important leader of the Kwangsi Clique, was interned in Nanking.[44] Pai Ch'ung-hsi, another leader of the same clique, who at that time commanded troops in Peking, was replaced by T'ang Sheng-chih and had to escape with the help of a Japanese cargo boat from Tientsin to Hong Kong.[45] A war between Chiang and the Kwangsi Army became inevitable and in May 1929 the latter was defeated.[46]

The swift victory had been ascribed to Chiang's military sagacity, but perhaps he should be given the credit for securing the support of the Kwangtung military leaders such as Ch'en Chi-t'ang

38. In front of Dr. Sun's coffin, Peking, 1928. [86] III, 760 and [126] 9.
39. [126] 7.   40. [302] 92.   41. [12] 224.
42. [123] 123 and [324] 275.
43. [134] 73.   44. [153] I, 144 and [265] I, 197–8.
45. [7] 1929–30, 733, [153] I, 144, [265] I, 198.
46. [7] 1929–30, 732–5 and [153] I, 144–6.

and Ch'en Ming-shu[47] and the neutrality of Feng Yü-hsiang owing
to Chiang's promise to give him the province of Shantung.[48]

But the promise was not kept. Consequently, before the dust of
the war in the south-west had time to settle, Feng appointed himself the Commander-in-Chief of the North-West Army for the
Protection of the Party and Salvation of the Country.[49] On 23 May
Feng was expelled from the KMT. The situation in the north-west
was tense. A war would have broken out then but for Chiang's
deftness in buying over Feng's military supporters like Han
Fu-ch'ü and Shih Yu-san.[50] However, in September Chang Fa-
k'uei and T'ang Sheng-chih made some strange moves in central
China while in the north the delayed conflict between Chiang and
Feng broke loose. The coming of 1930 did not bring with it a
message of peace, as, in spite of the defeat of T'ang Sheng-chih by
Chiang's troops,[51] an anti-Chiang alliance came into being between
Feng and Yen Hsi-shan, the Shensi warlord, in the north and Li
Tsung-jen and Chang Fa-k'uei in the south. The internecine war
continued into September 1930 involving more than a million
troops on both sides.[52] Of the total expenditure of the Nanking
Government in 1929, 48 per cent. was consumed in the flames of
the war, and in 1930 the amount became even larger.[53]

Upon hearing the news of these renewed struggles, Wang
Ching-wei hurried home to convene an enlarged plenum of 'the
KMT' at Peking—the congress of the Reorganization Clique—
and proclaimed another 'National Government'.[54] But Chiang
again played a trump card by successfully procuring the support
of Chang Hsüeh-liang, son of Marshal Chang Tso-lin, whose
Manchurian troops marched on Peking and scattered the unarmed
members of the Reorganization Clique.[55]

Not only did Wang Ching-wei think the opportunity ripe for
action, the Comintern and Li Li-san had the same idea. Bukharin,
for instance, predicted: 'the workers' and peasants' revolution is

47. [7] 1929–30, 733 and [153] I, 144.
48. [7] 1929–30, 734.   49. [7] 1929–30, 736.
50. [7] 1929–30, 736 and [153] I, 148.
51. [7] 1931, 431 and [153] I, 151–2.
52. [7] 1931, 429–30 and [153] I, 153.
53. [260] 112 and also [7] 1938, 471.   54. [153] I, 155.
55. [7] 1931, 565.

approaching a new surge.'[56] The 'new surge' was epitomized by the endless fighting among the new military leaders and the formation of revolutionary bases. The growth of these bases and of the Red Army demanded a new political line. Such was the background of the Li Li-san line.

Let us go back to the sixth national congress of the CCP convened in Moscow in July 1928.[57] The sixteen delegates (among whom Mao was not included) resolved that 'the present stage of the Chinese revolution is [still] bourgeois-democratic', that 'the twin major tasks of the revolution' are by armed insurrection and by setting up a democratic dictatorship of workers' and peasants' soviets under the leadership of the proletariat, and that 'at present there is no revolutionary rising tide'.[58] Nevertheless, the resolutions added, the CCP should prepare for such a rising tide by advocating armed insurrections on a national scale in order to win over the masses and to overthrow the KMT régime when the time was ripe.[59] On the peasant movement, the congress decided that although confiscation of landlords' holdings was necessary, it was wrong to confuse the issue by waging an intensive struggle against the rich peasants. The poor peasants were 'the basic strength of the proletariat in the villages', whose guerrilla units should be supported and enlarged. Furthermore, the party should develop the Red Army and consolidate and expand the soviet bases.[60] Though Mao was elected to the Central Committee, the secretaryship went to the innocuous Hsiang Chung-fa, the organization department to Chou En-lai, the labour department to Liu Shao-ch'i, and the propaganda department to Li Li-san who became the body and soul of the Politburo.[61]

The mistaken hypothesis of these resolutions was that the assumed progressive qualities of the urban proletariat made it the class predestined to lead the revolution, despite the fact that the CCP was becoming less and less of a workers' party. Chou En-lai,

56. Resolution adopted at the 9th plenum of the Executive Committee of the Comintern, 1928, 48, quoted from [52] 110.

57. Neither Ho Kan-chih ([14] 201) nor Hu Ch'iao-mu ([179] 24) refers to the place where the congress took place. B. Schwartz quotes Ypsilon (*Pattern for World Revolution*, 425), who says that Mao and Li Li-san went to Moscow; but Schwartz also warns us that this is not to be relied upon. See [52] 151.

58. [162] 130–1 and 143.   59. [162] 143–4.   60. [162] 151.
61. [14] 201, [179] 26, and [181] 50. See also [162] 34–5.

reporting on the 'Organization Problems of the Party',[62] pointed out that 'at the time of the sixth congress the proletariat still constituted 10 per cent. of the party membership. Now [1929] this proportion has been reduced to 3 per cent.' The *Hung-ch'i* (Red Flag) of 20 March 1930 said that the workers made up 66 per cent. of the party membership in 1926 but only 8 per cent. in 1930.[63] The decline in the proletarian membership was undeniable. Worse still, the proletariat showed no enthusiasm for the party leadership.[64] Therefore, when he returned to China Li Li-san was to experience the loneliness Mao had felt among the peasants and soldiers a year earlier. He tried to organize strikes, but succeeded in rallying only 2,000 workers in Shanghai, 1,000 in Wuhan, and a meagre 500 in Tientsin. In the country as a whole the secret trade unions under communist control had a membership of less than 32,000.[65] Li Li-san also directed P'eng Te-huai, T'eng Tai-yüan, and Huang Kung-lüeh—all officers of General Ho Chien's 1st Division in Hunan—to carry out an insurrection at P'ing-chiang, east Hunan. P'eng obeyed by creating a soviet and an army, the 5th Red Army, in July, but shortly afterwards he was driven away from P'ingchiang to seek sanctuary on Mao's Chingkangshan at the end of 1928.[66] In the wake of P'eng's abortive attempt, Mao and Chu suffered the August Defeat, and upon P'eng's arrival at Chingkangshan the question confronting the 4th and 5th Red Armies was how to avoid annihilation in the imminent third suppression campaign.

The third campaign was launched in December 1928 with eighteen regiments of Kiangsi and Hunan troops under the joint command of Generals Lu Ti-p'ing and Ho Chien. Chu Te and P'eng Te-huai decided to divert their enemies by an attack on southern Kiangsi, leaving P'eng with some 700 men to garrison the mountain fortress. Every effort, including the use of wooden cannon,[67] was made to save the Chingkangshan base, but eventually, in the face of tremendous pressure from the KMT army,

---

62. [229] 2–3 and [177] I, 1930, 4.   The latter says that there were only 5.5 per cent. of proletarian members in the party.

63. [190] 10.   64. [52] 128.   65. [18] 244.

66. [18] 229, [181] 44, [189] 234–5, [234] 157, and [258] 273.

67. [189] 231. The cannon was a log of wood, hollowed out and filled with dynamite. For details and photographs, see [282] 201.

P'eng had to abandon it temporarily and turned his men over to guerrilla warfare in southern Kiangsi. Meanwhile Chu Te, Mao Tse-tung, and Mao's bride, Ho Tzu-chen,[68] roamed from southern Kiangsi to western Fukien where the Red Army took Ch'angting by defeating a regiment of KMT troops commanded by Kuo Feng-ming from his sedan-chair. This was an important victory, for both the morale and supplies of the Red troops were low and the capture of a large town with its garrison commander and huge quantities of munitions was a great encouragement. For Mao himself the booty was a horse which was to be his mount through all the vicissitudes of the Encirclements and the Long March until 1938.[69]

It was at Ch'angting where Mao and Chu heard from P'eng Te-huai. At once they changed course towards Juichin where P'eng joined them and where they received a message from Li Li-san.[70]

In this letter of 9 February 1929,[71] Li Li-san expressed a pessimism which was then common in the ranks of the Red Army and also a fear that the ascendancy of the peasantry in the party might threaten the hegemony of the proletariat, with consequences detrimental to the cause of the revolution.[72] Li advised Chu and Mao to switch to pure guerrilla warfare by dividing up their forces into small units so as to preserve their strength and to arouse the masses.[73] Mao's reply dated 5 April showed strong disagreement with Li:

This [the dispersion of the Red Army into small units] is an unpractical way of thinking. . . . The reasons are: (1) Most of the soldiers in the main force of the Red Army came from the outside and are different from the local Red guardsmen in their origin. (2) With small dispersed units, the leadership will become so weak as to be unable to cope with adverse circumstances, hence we will be liable to suffer defeat. (3) Small units are easy for the enemy to crush separately. (4) The more adverse the circumstances, the greater becomes the need for the forces to be concentrated and for the leadership to conduct a resolute struggle, for only thus can we achieve internal unity against the enemy. Only in

68. [45] 13. Mao married Ho Tzu-chen in 1928. Some say the marriage took place in 1930.
69. [28] 54–5.   70. [18] 229, [181] 49–50, [189] 251–3 and [190] 138.
71. [46] I, 106 or SW I, 121–2.   72. See also [177] I, 4 (1930).
73. [46] I, 106 or SW I, 121.

favourable circumstances can the forces be divided for guerrilla operations, and it is only then that the leaders need not stay with the ranks all
the time, as they must do in adverse circumstances.

Mao went on to explain the essence of *his* guerrilla warfare:

The tactics we have worked out during the last three years in the course
of the struggle are indeed different from any employed in ancient or
modern times, in China or elsewhere. With our tactics, the struggles of
the masses are daily expanding and no enemy, however powerful, can
cope with us. Ours are guerrilla tactics. They consist mainly of the
following points:

Disperse the forces among the masses to arouse them, and concentrate the forces to deal with the enemy.

The enemy advances, we retreat; the enemy halts, we harass;
the enemy tires, we attack; the enemy retreats, we pursue.

In an independent régime with stabilised territory, we adopt the
policy of advancing in a series of waves. When pursued by a powerful
enemy, we adopt the policy of circling around in a whirling motion.

Arouse the largest numbers of the masses in the shortest possible
time and by the best possible methods.

These tactics are just like casting a net; we should be able to cast
the net wide or draw it at any moment. We cast it wide to win over
the masses and draw it in to deal with the enemy. Such are the
tactics we have applied in the past three years.

About Li's fear of the ascendancy of the peasantry, Mao remarked:

... in our opinion it is ... a mistake for any of our Party members to
fear the development of the power of the peasants lest it become stronger
than that of the workers and hence detrimental to the revolution.

Mao conceded that the struggles (not uprisings) in the cities should
be continued and that proletarian leadership was the sole key to the
victory of the revolution, but he refused to predict when a new
upsurge would begin.[74]

Mao was particularly acrimonious about Li Li-san's idea of
'pure guerrilla warfare' which he called 'the idea of the roving
insurgents [bandits—*liu-k'ou*]' arising from the 'vagabond elements' in the Red Army.[75] The road to victory he envisaged in
1929 and 1930 was not the dispersion of the Red troops in order
to preserve their own strength and to arouse and win over the
masses, but the formation and development of the Red military

74. [46] I, 106–7 and 110 or *SW* I, 121–3 and 128.
75. [46] I, 96–7 or *SW* I, 114–15.

forces in order to establish revolutionary bases and thereby to accelerate the nation-wide revolutionary upsurge.[76] Li Li-san's method, with its emphasis on agitation, was intended only to prepare the peasants to accept the signal for action, not to give it, for the signal had to be given by the urban proletariat. The pattern of revolution Li followed, on the one hand, was the classical Franco-Russian pattern and its underlying theory was the orthodox Marxism[77]; the pattern Mao followed, on the other hand, was the classical Chinese peasant war and its theoretical basis was Marxism adapted to suit the Chinese background. Personal experience may have been a factor contributing to these divergent views—Li had always been an agitator among urban workers, whereas Mao was a leader of peasant uprisings. Personal interest may also have played a part—Li, being the leader at the party centre, naturally wanted to strengthen the leadership of the centre, whereas Mao, controlling a large base, would eschew any plan which might weaken the position of the base. So a conflict arose between them which went on until the beginning of 1930.

Mao devoted the year 1929 to the expansion and consolidation of the south Kiangsi base with Juichin as its centre.[78] From February to December he had been to west Fukien three times and had created a satellite soviet there. This was done against the wishes of 'comrades in our party'.[79] He worked very hard, normally beginning his 'office hours' late at night under a small oil lamp. When tired he freshened himself up with a hot face-flannel or a bath.[80] In September he contracted malaria and there was no quinine to cure him. A man was sent to buy the drug in Shanghai; he made two journeys but never returned from the second. However, Mao's life was saved by Dr. Nelson Fu (Fu Lien-chang), a Christian

76. [46] I, 101 or *SW* I, 116.

77. It may be of interest to quote from a speech General Huang Hsing made in 1903: 'One way of starting a revolution is to capture the capital, Peking, so as to command the rest of the nation. The French Revolution broke out in Paris, and the English one in London. . . . But the nature of these revolutions is different from ours. . . . We cannot rely on the ignorant and easy-going Peking populace; nor can we co-operate with the alien palace guards. *Therefore we can only start in one province and hope for simultaneous uprisings in all of the others.*' ([71] 18, my italics).

78. [14] 208.   79. [46] I, 101 or *SW* I, 116.

80. [249] 215–16, reminiscences of Ch'en Ch'ang-feng, Mao's orderly.

convert from the British Baptist Mission in Ch'angting who joined the Red Army and headed its medical corps.[81] It was also reported that Mao suffered at this time from serious tuberculosis, and this led the ill-informed Comintern to publish the obituary notice of 'Comrade Mao Tze-dung' on 20 March 1930.[82] But Mao continued to live and flourish nevertheless.

Other guerrilla bases were being established in central China in the same period. Hsü Hsiang-ch'ien, having escaped from the Haifeng and Lufeng area in the spring of 1928, arrived at the border region of Hupei, Honan, and Anhwei where, with some 200 rifles, he, Chang Kuo-t'ao, and others organized the 1st Red Army and created the O-yü-wan base.[83] Ho Lung was active among the secret societies in Hunan after the Autumn Harvest Uprisings and with Chou Yi-ch'ün and Tuan Te-ch'ang organized the 2nd Red Army and the west Hupei-Hunan base.[84] Fang Chih-min and his guerrillas established a workers' and peasants' democratic government in the border region of Fukien, Chekiang, and Anhwei[85] and their army was denominated the 10th. In Kwangsi, the communist Chuang tribal leader, Wei Pa-ch'ün, set up a soviet in Tunglan and its adjacent counties which was called the Right River base, while other communists under the leadership of Teng Hsiao-p'ing and Chang Yün-yi established a soviet in the Paise-Lung-ch'uan area which was called the Left River base. These local forces—the 8th and 7th Red Armies respectively—were soon defeated by Pai Ch'ung-hsi and ordered by the CCP to retreat to Kiangsi. It is not clear which route they took during their retreat; but what can be ascertained is that Teng Hsiao-p'ing and Chang Yün-yi made their way first to Tunglan where they and Wei Pa-ch'ün decided to leave a guerrilla force—the 21st Division of the Red Army under Wei—to harass the pursuing KMT troops, while Teng and Chang in all probability led the remainder of the communists through the difficult terrain of northern Kwangsi and southern Hunan. When this Red contingent reached Ching-kangshan, it discovered that the mountain base was under the con-

81. [189] 262.
82. *International Press Correspondence*, X, no. 14, quoted from [52] 136.
83. [14] 209, [181] 80–1, [190] 152, Hsü Hsing-ch'ien's recollection.
84. [14] 206–10, [18] 229, [181] 81, [190] 47, and [258] 67–8.
85. [18] 229 and [185] 74–5.

trol of P'eng Te-huai's 5th Red Army which had retaken it in June 1929[86] with the co-operation of the small bands of guerrillas led by Hsiao K'e, Wang Chen, and Jen Pi-shih.[87] The Ching-kangshan base was now renamed the Hunan-Kiangsi base.[88] In all, at the beginning of 1930 there were 15 Red bases, including the north Shensi base under Liu Chih-tan and a small one near Swatow.[89]

Parallel to these local developments, the party centre in Shanghai engaged itself in preparing for a new upsurge. In October 1929 the Comintern in a letter to the CCP gave the signal for action, calling for the shift from peasant struggles to urban insurrections.[90] Li Li-san's response to this was, first of all, a series of articles, all highly polemic, obviously hitting at Mao Tse-tung's report to the Kut'ien Conference in December 1929 and his letter to 'a comrade' written on 5 January 1930.[91]

The Kut'ien Conference was the ninth assembly of the party representatives in the 4th Red Army which adopted Mao's report *On the Rectification of Incorrect Ideas in the Party*. Hitherto Mao had written on social studies, on peasant movement, on military strategy and tactics, but never on party lines. In this first exposition on ideological matters, Mao attacked 'adventurism', calling for its complete elimination from both theory and practice, thoughts and actions. He defined 'adventurism' as (1) to act blindly regardless of subjective and objective conditions; (2) to carry out inadequately and irresolutely the policy for the cities; and (3) slack military discipline, especially in moments of defeat.[92] Who could have been responsible for the implementation of the inadequate and irresolute urban policy but Li Li-san? Again and again in this report Mao stressed the non-combatant work of the soldiers such as political propaganda and the organization of the masses which, according to him, was the *raison d'être* of the Red Army; he also attacked, as we have mentioned, the 'idea of the roaming bandits'—

86. [188] 15–16 and [241] 34.
87. [234] 180–1, T'an Yü-pao's recollection.
88. About the Kwangsi soviets, see [18] 230, [185] 76, and [249] V, 54–61.
89. [18] 230, [247] V, 108–18, [258] 211–14. Also [190] 64.
90. *Hung-ch'i*, no. 16, 15.2.1930, 10, quoted from [52] 29. See also [162] 180 and [190] 11.
91. [46] I and *SW* I, items 5 and 6.   92. [46] I, 98 or *SW* I, 115.

the pure guerrilla tactic.[93] Following up this exposition, he wrote the famous letters of January 1930, 'A Single Spark can Start a Prairie Fire', pointing out for the first time the twin characteristics of Chinese national politics—a semi-colony contended for by many imperialist powers and the prolonged strife within the ruling class. Only by an understanding of them, according to Mao, could one grasp the importance of the peasant problem, gauge the width and depth of the peasant movement, comprehend the meaning of the workers' and peasants' democratic power, fathom the reasons for the survival of the Red Army, guerrilla units, and Red areas, and pay attention to the formation and development of the Red Army, the guerrilla units, and Red areas as the highest form of the peasant struggle. Only thus could one understand that 'the policy of purely mobile guerrilla-like activities cannot accomplish the task of accelerating the nation-wide revolutionary upsurge, while the kind of policies adopted by Chu Te and Mao Tse-tung and Fang Chih-min are undoubtedly correct'. The policies were, in essence, the establishment of base areas, the building up of political power according to plan, the deepening of the agrarian revolution, and the expansion of the people's armed forces from the Red guards to the regular troops. Only by means of the bases and the Red Army could the communists shake the foundations of the reactionary régime, precipitate its disintegration, and win the confidence of the revolutionary masses.[94] Mao went on:

Comrades who suffer from revolutionary impetuosity unduly over-estimate the subjective forces of the revolution and under-estimate the forces of the counter-revolution. Such an appraisal largely stems from subjectivism. In the end, it will doubtless lead to the path of adventurism.[95]

But Li Li-san totally disagreed with this analysis. For him, the cities were the brains and heart of the ruling class whereas the villages were merely their limbs. Lethal blows should be dealt where the brains and heart lay.[96] This was written on 29 March 1930. A week later Li wrote again:

93. [46] I, 87–8 and 97 or *SW* I, 106–7 and 114–15.
94. [46] I, 101–2 or *SW*, I, 116–17.   95. [46] I, 102–3 or *SW* I, 117–18.
96. '*Chun-pei chien-li ke-ming-cheng-ch'üan yü wu-ch'an-chieh-chi ti ling-tao*' (Preparations for the establishment of a revolutionary régime and the leadership of the proletariat), *Hung-ch'i*, 29 March 1930, 2.

All the talk of 'encircling the city with the country' or of relying on the Red Army to take the cities is sheer nonsense.[97]

In Li's view, 'the great struggle of the proletariat is the decisive force in the winning of preliminary successes in one or more provinces. Without an upsurge of strikes of the working class, without armed insurrection in key cities, there can be no successes in one or more provinces.' 'Henceforth,' he laid down, 'the organization of political strikes and their expansion into a general strike, as well as the strengthening of the organization and training of the workers' militia to set up a central force for armed insurrections, are major tactics in preparing for preliminary success in one or more provinces.'[98] He mocked at Mao's revolutionary strategy of a protracted warfare as 'boxing tactics', for he was not willing to wait for a victory until his hair had turned grey.[99] As far as he could see, the masses wanted big actions, not tiny ones,[1] and therefore, brushing aside the idea of creating 'local regions' and 'regional governments', he ordered the provincial party headquarters to prepare diligently for successful insurrections in the light of the development of the general situation.[2]

Li's proposals were accepted by the Politburo in Shanghai[3] and the plan for insurrections was drawn up. As the first step, the Red Army, now nearly 65,000 strong, was reorganized—the 3rd Army under Huang Kung-lüeh, the 4th Army under Lin Piao, and the 12th Army under Lo Ping-hui[4] were grouped together into the 1st Army Corps under the command of Chu Te with Mao as the political commissar and ordered to march on Nanch'ang; the 2nd Army under Ho Lung and the 6th Army under Tuan Te-ch'ang were grouped into the 2nd Army Corps under the command of

97. *Hung-ch'i*, 5.4.1930, quoted from [52] 139.
98. 'The new revolutionary rising tide and preliminary success in one or more provinces', resolutions on 11 June 1930. See [162] 190–1 and [46] III, 982 or *SW* IV, 178.
99. [46] I, 229 or *SW* I, 249.   1. [46] III, 982, or *SW* IV, 178.
2. [162] 191.   3. [18] 241.
4. [42] and [188] 18. Hsiao Tso-liang is wrong to say that Huang Kung-lüeh commanded the 6th Army ([237] 106). General Lo Ping-hui surrendered to his Yunnanese colleague Chu Te at the beginning of 1930, served first under Huang Kung-lüeh, and was appointed the commander of the 12th Army in July 1930. See [189] 270 and [247], V, 180–224. Both Snow ([258] 171) and Ku Kuan-chiao ([181] 45–6) are wrong on this point.

Ho Lung with Yün Tai-ying as the political commissar, and ordered to attack Wuhan in conjunction with the 4th Army Corps, consisting of the 1st and 15th Armies, under the command of Hsü Hsiang-ch'ien with Chang Kuo-t'ao as the political commissar; the 5th Army under P'eng Te-huai and the 8th Army under Chang Yün-yi and Teng Hsiao-p'ing were grouped into the 3rd Army Corps under the command of P'eng Te-huai with T'eng Tai-yüan as the political commissar, and ordered to attack Ch'angsha. The 10th Army under Fang Chih-min with Shao Shih-p'ing as the political commissar was to take Kiukiang.[5] The workers in these target cities were instructed to stage strikes in support of the attacking armies. An interesting point in this reorganization was the changed position of Chang Kuo-t'ao's 1st Army Corps, implying that the forces directly under Chu and Mao were the strongest among all the others.

The orders for action arrived at Ch'angting directed to Chu Te and Mao Tse-tung, apart from whom 'there was very little opposition to the Li Li-San line. We [Mao and Chu] had no choice but to accept it'.[6] This was in June 1930 when General Chang Fa-k'uei, on his way to Canton, had led his troops into Ch'angsha on the 6th and out of it again on the 20th, General Ho Chien offering him no resistance.[7] In the wake of this event, P'eng Te-huai attacked and took the city on 28 July and kept it for ten days[8] before being dislodged by the KMT troops. During those ten days P'eng not only obtained ample supplies of food and ammunition but greatly raised the hopes for an immediate success of the Li Li-san line. The Comintern hailed this victory as 'the commencement of a new chapter of the Chinese revolution'.[9]

The news of P'eng Te-huai's entry into Ch'angsha and the establishment of the General Action Committee and a soviet under Li Li-san also encouraged the weary soldiers under the command of Chu and Mao, who were approaching Nanch'ang, and those under Chang Kuo-t'ao and Ho Lung, who were threatening the

5. [18] 243.   6. [182] 154 and [189] 274.
7. [7] 1931, 431.
8. [16] says that the occupation lasted from 27 July to 11 August (III, 335).
9. Chieh Hua, 'The occupation of Changsha', *International Press Correspondence*, 7 August 1930, quoted from [52] 144.

security of Hankow.[10] If both these cities could have been taken by the communists within three days or a week, Chinese history would have run an entirely different course. But the defence of Nanch'ang was too strong for the inadequately equipped 1st Red Army Corps and the time chosen for the attack, 1 August, with all its romantic connotations,[11] could not be considered militarily wise. The 1st Army Corps fought for twenty-four hours and many of its soldiers died in vain before the onslaught was called off by Chu and Mao. The remainder of the Army Corps was regrouped into three columns and given orders to withdraw westward in the direction of Wuhan. On the way Chu and Mao met P'eng Te-huai who brought with him fresh orders from Li Li-san for another attack on Ch'angsha. The combined strength of the 1st and 3rd Army Corps exceeded 20,000 men, by far the greatest concentration of Red troops hitherto known, on whose preservation or annihilation, success or failure, hung the future of the communist movement in China. Li's new decision to throw them into the second attack on Ch'angsha was therefore a desperate move to rescue the waning prestige of both the party and himself. He must have been fully aware what would be left of the Li Li-san line of thinking and of his own career had he cut his losses by cancelling the attacks on big cities in August. So he was playing for high stakes, with Mao, Chu, and P'eng as his pawns and Mao, Chu, and P'eng disliked his move.[12]

The second attack on Ch'angsha began on 1 September and lasted until the 13th. It was a clash between the small arms of the Red Army and the heavy artillery, aeroplanes, and gunboats of the KMT. That the attack was maintained as long as it was must be attributed to the bravery and discipline of the communist troops, but its outcome was a foregone conclusion. Knowing that this unequal and hopeless struggle was bound to end in a disaster, Mao persuaded his colleagues to retreat along the Hunan-Kiangsi border back to Chian and then to the south Kiangsi base. It was a momentous decision, taken without the sanction of the party

10. [7] 1931, 431 and [189] 277–8.
11. 1 August 1927, the Nanch'ang Uprising. *Vide supra*, p. 129.
12. [46] III, 1020, n. 4 or *SW* IV, 340, n. 5. See also [18] 245, [181] 51-2, [190] 124, [234] 197–8, and particularly [189] 278–9.

centre,[13] and it compelled Li Li-san to abandon his plan for nation-wide insurrections.[14]

Apart from the loss of two or three thousand men and the collapse of the Li Li-san line, the second attack on Ch'angsha, together with the first, yielded other results. It greatly alarmed Chiang Kai-shek and other leaders of the nation who at once patched up their differences in September 1930 so that fuller attention could be given to the communist problem. Thus more intensive search for and arrests of communists were made in big cities while the First Encirclement, launched in December, was being prepared.[15] The defeat in 1930 also alarmed the Comintern which at once sent Ch'ü Ch'iu-pai back to China in September and, at the 3rd plenum at Lushan, he succeeded in obtaining an admission of his mistakes from Li Li-san but was unable to reverse the Li Li-san line, since important members of the Politburo like Chou En-lai were still supporting it.[16] On the one hand, the disunited party centre could not make up its mind on a new line of policy; on the other, the regional leaders remained strong and their strength was growing.[17] It was a topsyturvy situation which required both the Comintern and the CCP centre to take immediate action in order to rectify it. The action was taken by the so-called Twenty-eight Bolsheviks, including Wang Ming, Ch'in Panghsien, Chang Wen-t'ien, Shen Tse-min, and Wang Chia-hsiang under the leadership of their teacher, Pavel Mif, recently returned home from Moscow.[18] For Mao himself, the failure strengthened his belief in 'encircling the cities with the countryside'—a policy he did not reverse until eighteen years later when in September 1948 he ordered Lin Piao to attack Mukden. Patience had its reward!

13. Hu Hua says that Mao had obtained the sanction ([18] 245), but neither Mao's own writing ([46] III, 1020, n. 4 or *SW* IV, 340, n. 5) nor Chu Te's recollection ([189] 278–9) supports this assertion.

14. The word 'persuaded' was Mao's and 'compelled' was Chu's. See also [52] 182, [137] 32–3, and [237] 22.

15. [7] 1931, 431, and [244] 60.   16. [52] 151–2.

17. [46] III, 998 or *SW* IV, 196.

18. [52] 148 and [190] 14. Shen Tse-min was Shen Yen-ping's (Mao Tun) brother ([16] I, part 2, 156).

Chapter VIII

The Five Encirclements

THE reader of Mao's *Selected Works* will notice that from January 1930 when the Li Li-san line was entering into its militant phase to October 1934 when the Long March began, Mao had not written a single word on military strategy or guerrilla tactics. If he goes on to read Agnes Smedley's *The Great Road* based on the story related to her by Chu Te, he will notice that there is a complete blank regarding the south Kiangsi soviet from 1931 to 1934. Is this purely a coincidence? Edgar Snow's celebrated *Red Star* gives Mao's own explanation: '[From 1932] I myself devoted my time almost exclusively to work with the Soviet Government, leaving the military command to Chu Te and others.'[1] This is unconvincing, because these words were uttered by a man who believed in 'political power coming from the barrel of a gun'. All the histories of the CCP and the Red Army of China reveal an extraordinary paucity of available information about Mao during the years when the fierce Encirclement Campaigns were fought. This is a mystery that needs unravelling and in doing so we are fortunate to have the studies made by Schwartz and Hsiao Tso-liang. But, before we attempt it, we must take a closer look at Mao's strategic thought.

To begin with, Mao accepted the directives of the Third International and the party centre that 'the content of China's democratic revolution includes overthrowing the rule in China of imperialism and its tools, the warlords . . . [and the elimination of] the feudal exploitation of the peasants by the landed

1. [258] 178.

gentry'.[2] This decision had been determined by his and the party's observation of Chinese society and its urgent problems. Chinese society was undesirably semi-feudal and semi-colonial and both imperialist and feudal domination must be eradicated. Thus far in the analysis of the Chinese revolution, Mao had made no original contribution. In March 1926 his idea of an alignment in the revolution was still quite conventional—the proletariat being the leading force with 'all sections of the semi-proletariat and the petty bourgeoisie'[3] as its allies. But a year later, after he had worked among the peasants of Hunan, his view began to change:

... the broad peasant masses have risen to fulfil their historic mission; the democratic forces in the rural areas have risen to overthrow the rural feudal power. ... To overthrow this feudal power is the real objective of the national revolution. What Dr. Sun Yat-sen aimed at in the forty years he devoted to the national revolution but failed to accomplish, the peasants have accomplished in a few months. This is a marvellous feat which has never been achieved in the last forty or even in thousands of years.[4]

By relying on both the 'semi-proletarians' and the 'petty bourgeois' of the peasants (the poor peasants and the rich peasants as well as small landowners), Mao was able to establish a guerrilla base at Chingkangshan and this minor success also influenced his views. He saw in such bases a chance of survival and expansion, leading eventually to final success. He analysed the possibilities of the continued existence of the bases in these terms: (1) China was ruled only indirectly by imperialists through their agents, the warlords, whose 'White régime' was split and plagued by prolonged wars; (2) there were in China areas affected by the revolution of 1926 and 1927 and where the militarists' control was weak; (3) while the militarists continued to wage wars against each other, the nationwide revolutionary situation was simultaneously developing; and (4) a regular Red Army was coming into being.[5]

2. [46] I, 50 or SW I, 64. This was written in October 1928. Mao continued to hold this view until 1949, but for our purpose at this stage it suffices to refer also to [46] I, 79 (November 1928) and 101 (January 1930) or SW I, 99 and 116.
3. [46] I, 9 or SW I, 20.   4. [46] I, 17 or SW I, 25.
5. [46] I, 51–2 or SW I, 65–7. This was written in October 1928. On 25 November 1928 he expressed the same view (59 or 71–2 respectively). Mao's reliance on peasantry is fully discussed by Schwartz [52]. In 1955 Schwartz said: 'The proletarian nature of the CP is a function of its possession of correct

Although Mao admitted that the leadership of the CCP was indispensable, he maintained that the struggle at the base 'is exclusively military, both the Party and the masses have to be placed on a war footing'[6] in order to preserve both the base and the Army. Consequently he insisted that the officers and men must have adequate military and political training; that the party branch must be organized on the company basis at a ratio of one party member to three non-party soldiers; that the officers must treat the men in a democratic way by accepting equal pay, allowing the men the freedom of assembly and speech, stopping corporal punishment, and eliminating cumbersome formalities; that the regular troops must be supported by armed volunteers such as the Red guards; that prisoners-of-war must not be treated with brutality and should be released after indoctrination; and that the soldiers must undertake non-combatant duties such as arousing and organizing, and even arming, the masses who would in turn help them to strengthen the revolutionary political power.[7] Since survival and expansion were the foremost tasks at the base, the land policy had to be adapted to the accomplishment of such tasks. Here Mao's attention was concentrated on the 'middle class', the rich peasants and small landowners who should not be unwisely alienated by harsh and excessively radical measures. While at the Chingkangshan base, Mao carried out the party's policy of indiscriminate confiscation of all land, but later, in April 1929, he introduced a milder land policy at Hsingkuo by confiscating only the land belonging to the local government and landlords.[8] He also disagreed with the party centre in regard to the criterion by which land should be redistributed. The party insisted on redistributing according to a person's ability to work, while Mao shared out land according to the size of a family.[9] The party's criterion might ensure more efficient use of land, but Mao's certainly helped to relieve the hardships of the poor peasants, and this showed political astuteness.

doctrine rather than of any tie to an actual proletariat—may still be considered one such innovation.' ('On the "Originality" of Mao Tse-tung', *Foreign Affairs*, October 1955, 74).   6. [46] I, 65 or *SW* I, 79.

   7. [46] I, 66–8, 73, 85 n. 16, and 88 or *SW* I, 79–87, 91, 348, n. 16, and 106.

   8. [46] I, 71–3 and 85, n. 18 or *SW* I, 87–91 and 348, n. 18.

   9. [46] I, 86, n. 21 or *SW* I, 348–9, n. 21.

By using these military, economic, and political tactics, rather than weapons, Mao and his colleagues hoped to strengthen their guerrilla base. When the ruling classes were at war among themselves the Red Army might adopt a strategy of 'comparatively venturesome advance' by dividing itself up to fight in a comparatively large area; but when the ruling classes were at peace, and therefore strong, the Red Army could only pursue a strategy of 'gradual advance' by concentrating its might for the consolidation of the base. From November 1928 to January 1930 Mao in his reports emphasized this point no less than *five* times,[10] and, as has been shown above, this was one of the major issues between him and Li Li-san. It was from this central strategic idea that Mao evolved the tactical theories quoted on p. 151.

It must be noted here that before the Encirclement Campaigns Mao had said nothing explicit about the unevenness of the Chinese revolution or the protracted nature of the Chinese revolutionary wars which characterized Mao's strategic thinking of later years. What may be argued is that the germs of the ideas were there; yet what cannot be said is that he *had developed* such ideas before the Encirclements. His own writings show beyond any doubt that he for the first time fully expounded such ideas and such a strategy, thereby pointing out a distinct possibility of success, not in the early thirties, but in December 1936 when the second united front between the KMT and the CCP was being formed.[11] It must be remembered that by then the feud between Mao and Chang Kuo-t'ao had already worsened beyond possibility of reconciliation and a contributary factor to this may have been the lack of clarity and persuasiveness of Mao's strategic thought in its embryonic form. The Maoist strategy as it was stated in 1930 could hardly be regarded as a serious military theory able to command the attention of the leaders of the soviets other than those in south Kiangsi, not to speak of that of the Twenty-eight Bolsheviks and Moscow.

To quote from Mao without regard to the time when the statement was made does not help the understanding either of the development of his views or of the disputes between him and his

10. 25.11.1928 ([48] I, 59–60 and 68–9 or *SW* I, 71–2 and 85), December 1929 ([46] I, 97 or *SW* I, 114–15), and January 1930 ([46] I, 102 and 107 or *SW* I, 116–17 and 123).   11. [46] I, 163 *et seq.* or *SW* I, 175.

colleagues. Our story is still in 1930; what Mao thought in 1936 does not yet matter.

A sequel to Mao's quarrel with Li Li-san and his retreat from Ch'angsha without Li's sanction was the Fut'ien mutiny in December 1930. The *dramatis personae* included Liu Te-ch'ao,[12] Li Wen-lin, and the 20th Red Army which according to Mao[13] rose in open revolt and arrested the chairman of the Kiangsi soviet and many officers and officials. Regarding their political connexions there have been divergent suggestions. Mao said that they were members of the AB (Anti-Bolshevik) Group, attacking Mao and his followers 'on the basis of Li Li-san line'.[14] The AB Group, in the words of Hu Hua, was 'a motley crowd of political rascals organized by Chiang Kai-shek as his special agents'.[15] Chu Te alleged that these people were proved 'to be connected with the AB Corps and had been among the most determined followers of Li Li-sanism' and by this he 'was convinced that landlordism in Tungku [where the 20th Red Army was stationed], which the Communists had not yet cleared out, was the real cause of the mutiny. . . .'[16] Chu also defined the AB Group as 'a cloak-and-dagger outfit of the Kuomintang secret police which had a network of sabotage and terrorism throughout the Soviet areas'.[17] Other writers such as Kung Ch'u, Li Ang, Ku Kuan-chiao, and Kan Yu–lan[18] all interpret the mutiny as a continuation of the Mao–Li Li-san struggle in a more violent form. Ku, in particular, goes as far as to say it was instigated by Li. Had Li been directly involved in it he would not be where he is today.

The 20th Red Army was said to be a part of the 3rd Army Corps[19] under P'eng Te-huai who, judging by his conduct in 1930, was an ardent supporter of Li Li-san. If this is true, Liu Te-ch'ao may well have been a Li Li-sanite prompted into taking action against Mao by what he considered Mao's betrayal of Li. The mutiny hap-

12. Snow ([258] 175) and Smedley ([189] 286) give the name Liu Ti-tsao; Schwartz gives Liu Ti-ts'ao; Hsiao Tso-liang writes Liu T'ieh-ch'ao (meaning 'iron-excellent'). But Ku Kuan-chiao and Kan Yu-lan ([181] 71 and [41] 176) say the name was Liu Te-ch'ao (meaning 'virtue-excellent').
13. [258] 175–6.
14. [258] 176 and Hsiao Tso-liang agrees with Mao, [237] 98–9.
15. [18] 176.   16. [189] 286–7.   17. [189] 280.
18. See [240] 255 *et seq.*, [82] 152–4, [181] 71–2, and [41] 176–7 respectively.
19. [41] 176.

pened just before the first Encirclement, perhaps on 9 December. Its gravity was obvious and therefore urgent steps had to be taken to deal with it. At once Mao and Chu accused Liu and his followers of being members of the AB Group and sent P'eng Te-huai and Tseng Shan to suppress them. Between two to three thousand officers and men were liquidated in this, the bloodiest purge in the entire history of the CCP.[20] In the spring of 1931 the party centre appointed a man to investigate the incident, and he came to the following conclusion:

No doubt the Fut'ien incident was in fact an act directed against the party and the revolution. Though it has not yet been proved that they [the rebel leaders] organizationally are all members of the AB League and the Liquidationists, their action against the party and against the revolution was objectively in agreement with the reactionary behaviour of the AB League and the Liquidationists.[21]

No one could have liked this vague and evasive verdict, least of all, Mao. The investigator turned out to be none other than Hsiang Ying.[22]

At this time there were three soviets in Kiangsi and its adjacent regions—the central soviet in south Kiangsi led by Mao, Chu, and P'eng Te-huai with its capital at Juichin,[23] the Kiangsi-Chekiang-Anhwei soviet in the east led by Fang Chih-min and Shao Shih-p'ing with Iyang as its centre, and the Kiangsi-Hunan soviet in the west led by Hsiao K'e, Wang Chen, and Mao's erstwhile student, Jen Pi-shih, with Chingkangshan as its centre. Other soviets included the Hupei-Honan-Anhwei under Chang Kuo-t'ao and Hsü Hsiang-ch'ien, the west Hupei-Hunan under Ho Lung, Tuan Te-ch'ang, and Chou Yi-ch'ün, and the north Shensi under Liu Chih-tan and a young student trained by the Russian advisers employed by Feng Yü-hsiang whose name was Kao Kang. It is not known how the liaison among the soviets was conducted. Presumably it was through the party centre in Shanghai. If so, then it would be rash to say that the soviets were under Mao's control.

20. [181] 72 and [45] 33–5.   21. [237] 109 and [45] 43–4.
22. [237] 109, quoting from the Circular no. 2 of the Central Bureau—'Resolution on the Fut'ien Incident', 23.1.1931. See also [45] 43.
23. The major towns in the central soviet were Hsinch'ang, Shihch'eng, Hsingkuo, Yütu, Juichin, Huich'ang, Ningtu, Shanghang, Lungyen, and Yungting. See [181] 52.

But the fact may have been that the soviets enjoyed a high degree of autonomy, acting without much co-ordination between them under the intractable conditions of the Encirclements.

In the winter of 1930 Chiang Kai-shek summoned the governors of Hupei, Hunan, and Kiangsi to Lushan to plan the first campaign against the communists, resulting in a tripartite scheme with General Ho Ch'eng-chün responsible for mopping up the small bands of guerrillas in Hupei, General Ho Chien responsible for eliminating K'ung Ho-ch'ung's contingent in north Hunan, and General Lu Ti-p'ing as the Commander-in-Chief responsible for attacking the central soviet in Kiangsi.[24] Eleven divisions, with a total strength over 100,000 men, were allotted to Lu's command. The fact that none of these units could be called Chiang's own was noticed by both the KMT and the Red Army, giving rise to a suspicion of Chiang's true purposes in launching this campaign.[25] However, Chiang himself promised in November that within three months the 'scourge of communism' in China could be completely wiped out, and his confidence was shared by the commanding and staff officers[26] who knew very little of the terrain around the soviet and almost nothing at all about the conditions and deployment of their enemy.[27] They resorted to brutality in an attempt to extort information and to frighten the peasants, but all they achieved was to be led into traps by them.[28] Their own troops were deployed over a wide area—the 5th, 8th, and 24th Divisions were ordered to drive from Nanfeng and Kwangch'ang to Ningtu and Tungshao, the 56th to wedge into the soviet itself by way of Chienning and Lich'uan, the 77th to lie in wait along the Kan River, and the 60th and 61st to garrison Chian and T'aiho as the reserves. The brunt of the attack was borne by the three divisions—the 18th, 28th, and 50th under the Field Commander Chang Hui-tsan—in a pincer movement to meet the main forces of the Red Army at Huangp'i and Hsiaopu. This wide dispersal unavoidably weakened the force

24. [181] 52.

25. [46] I, 211 or *SW* I, 227 and [155] 41, being Dr. Sun Fo's comment in 1931, which suggests that Chiang actually wanted the Red Army to destroy these troops on his behalf.

26. [181] 53 and [155] 41 say that the KMT officers grossly underestimated the fighting qualities of the communists.

27. [181] 53 and [244] 40.   28. [189] 301.

of the KMT onslaught and made co-ordination among the units arduous. The actual fighting started on 27 December; but five days later it was virtually all over.[29] The communists let Chang Hui-tsan's troops come in and then swooped down upon them, cutting the two divisions under Chang's direct command to pieces and capturing over 10,000 men with nearly 6,000 rifles and the Field Commander himself.[30] Still clad in his smart khaki uniform and knee boots and decorated with his insignia of rank, Chang Hui-tsan was brought to see Chu Te and his first question was reported to be, 'How much will you demand for my release?' Chu simply took him along to watch the operation against the other jaw of the pincer—the 50th Division which was smashed within 24 hours on the last day of 1930 and the first of 1931. Thereafter the KMT troops at Tungku, T'oup'i, and Fut'ien beat a hurried retreat and thus ended the first Encirclement Campaign.[31] Chang Hui-tsan was subsequently tried by the communists and punished by death.[32]

Among those who distinguished themselves in this battle were Lin Piao and Huang Kung-lüeh.[33] The communists suffered a loss of 7,000 men, but this was made good soon afterwards. Their booty included 3,000 prisoners who were willing to fight for the communist cause, about 6,000 rifles and several million rounds of ammunition, and two radio sets which they did not know how to operate, never having seen one before.[34]

Determined not to give the communists a chance to rest, Chiang ordered his trusted lieutenant, General Ho Ying-ch'in, to launch the second Encirclement Campaign in February 1931. According to Chiang's biography,[35] only three divisions were mobilized for this campaign; but Chu Te, Mao Tse-tung, and others all say that the KMT deployed more than 13 divisions with a total strength of nearly 200,000 men.[36] In addition to their numerical superiority, they were equipped with 200 heavy guns and 100 aeroplanes, and

---

29. [181] 54.   30. See Mao's poem on this campaign, *vide infra*, p. 330,
31. [46] I, 211–12 or *SW* I, 227–8, [153] I, 199, [181] 52–3, [189] 287–90,
[234] 198, [244] 40, and [50] 115–16 which is vivid but not all accurate.
32. [189] 290.   33. Huang died in October 1931. See [42] and [189] 288.
34. [50] 116 and [190] 124.
35. [153] I, 199.
36. [46] I, 212–13 or *SW* I, 228–9, [181] 55, [189] 300, and [234] 199.

assisted by German advisers.[37] None the less, they were merely 'miscellaneous' forces, aware of being used as pawns and hence interested chiefly in preserving their own strength.[38] Ho, adopting a strategy of advancing step by step while consolidating his gains, pushed his troops forward in a semi-circle, with their arrow-heads pointing to Hsiaopu and T'oup'i where, it was hoped, the final battle would be fought and Chu Te's main forces would be destroyed.[39] At the extreme west sector of the semi-circle was the 19th Route Army under General Ts'ai T'ing-k'ai and at the extreme east sector the 26th Route Army under General Sun Lien-chung, both seasoned units, so that the communists avoided them. Tucked in between was an agglomeration of northern troops unaccustomed to mountain warfare and it was against this weak link that the might of the communist counter-attack would be brought to bear. At first the advance was made slowly according to plan, although every move was reported to the communists by the peasants.[40] Suddenly in May the Red Army appeared, pounced on Kung Ping-fan's Division, and annihilated it. Then it swept from west to east, covering 230 miles in a fortnight and winning five engagements in quick succession.[41] The results of the second Encirclement were 20,000 prisoners and as many rifles together with more than 10 counties to the communists and a comment of 'not encouraging' for the KMT.[42]

A mere month separated the second and the third Encirclements; Chiang himself assumed the command and five divisions of his own crack troops[43] were thrown into the campaign. The overall strategy was again entirely different, with the troops moving at a great speed and seeking out the enemy for a series of battles of annihilation.[44] Chiang's troops were organized into three 'routes'[45] advancing from Fuchow-Ihuang, Nanfeng-Kuangch'ang, and Chian-Hsingkuo respectively to Ningtu and Yütu, where on the

37. [50] 122.   38. [181] 54–5.
39. [46] I, 212–13 or *SW* I, 228–9, [181] 55–6, and *vide infra*, p. 332.
40. [189] 296.   41. [46] I, 213 or *SW* I, 229, [181] 56, and [234] 199.
42. [7] 1932, 542, [181] 56, and [153] I, 199.
43. Under Ch'en Ch'eng, Lo Cho-ying, Chao Kuan-t'ao, Wei Li-huang, and Chiang Ting-wen. [46] I, 213 or *SW* I, 230 and [181] 56.
44. [46] I, 213 or *SW* I, 230 and [181] 56.
45. The central under Ho Ying-ch'in, the left under Chu Shao-liang, and the right under Ch'en Ming-shu.

right bank of the Kan River the decisive battle was expected to be fought.[46] The communists, *vis-à-vis* such a strong invading army— the odds being ten to one—had no option but to adopt hide-and-seek tactics, relying on speed and secrecy to evade the strong section and to engage the weak in a desperate attempt to disrupt its formation and to tire it out. Twice they managed to slip through a gap between the concentrations of the KMT troops and won three engagements against the less robust divisions. Yet nothing could stop Chiang's main forces from driving towards Juichin, the Red capital. By 13 September Juichin was in jeopardy, although the mainstay of the communist forces remained unharmed.[47]

At this time information about a possible incident in Manchuria reached the Japanese Foreign Ministry and under pressure from both the Emperor and Shidehara, the Foreign Minister, Major-General Tatekawa, was sent to Mukden by the Minister of War to prevent an incident at all costs. On 18 September the envoy arrived there to spend an enjoyable evening with *geisha* girls and turned his attention to completing his mission only when the well-known Mukden Incident had already become a *fait accompli*.[48] The occupation of Manchuria shocked not only China and Japan but the whole world. The third Encirclement was therefore called off.

The Mukden Incident caught China in the throes not only of a war against the communists but also of a furious quarrel between Nanking and Canton. The latter began in February 1931 when, because of a dispute over the convocation of the National People's Convention and the proposals of a Constitutional Compact, Chiang Kai-shek had an eminent leader of the KMT and the President of the Legislative Yüan, Hu Han-min, interned on the outskirts of Nanking.[49] On 5 May the Convention held its opening session, elected Chiang the President of the National Government, and adopted the Constitutional Compact of the Tutelage Period.[50]

46. [7] 1932, 543, [46] I, 213 or *SW* I, 230, and [181] 56.
47. [7] 1932, 543, [46] I, 213–14 or *SW* I, 230–1, [50] 123, [153] I, 199–200, [181] 57, [234] 199–200, and [244] 41.
48. [223] 75 *et seq.*
49. [153] I, 159 says: 'Chiang insisted that Hu must continue to stay in Nanking.' See also [7] 1932, 544, which says that Hu did not leave Nanking until 14 October 1931. See [155] *passim.*
50. [7] 1932, 531–7 and [153] I, 159–62.

Following these personal triumphs, Chiang's troops suffered reverses in Kiangsi at the hands of the communists while his political opponents of varying shades of opinion congregated at Canton to form another 'National Government'. These were the old leftists, members of the Western Hill Group, military leaders of Kwangtung and Kwangsi, elder statesmen, and Dr. Sun Yat-sen's son, Dr. Sun Fo.[51] That these opponents who had all been defeated by Chiang dared challenge him again was partly due to Chiang's inability to quell the communists. In order to foil them again, Chiang had to show some quick results in his suppression of the 'Red Bandits', hence the launching of the third Encirclement and the deployment of his crack troops in it. At the same time his representatives, Chang Chi and Wu T'ieh-ch'eng, were sent to Canton to parley with the 'dissidents' who demanded his resignation and at the same time dispatched their troops to Hunan.[52]

However, the Japanese action at Mukden put an end to both the third Encirclement and the Nanking-Canton discord. The Shanghai Conference between Nanking and Canton in October agreed upon Chiang's retirement and the reorganization of the Government in Nanking. Subsequently Lin Sen was elected President, Chiang, Wang, and Hu were elected as the only three members of the Central Standing Committee, and Ch'en Ming-shu was appointed the acting premier by a plenum of the Central Executive Committee of the KMT; but Chiang withdrew into his hermitage in Fenghua, Chekiang, Wang Ching-wei was having his diabetes treated in Shanghai, and Hu Han-min would not leave Hong Kong. Nanking thus became a big city of small people. Sun Fo assumed the premiership and Eugene Ch'en became Foreign Minister, only to resign before they had warmed their ministerial chairs. It was so evident that China could not do without Chiang or Wang that the Central Political Council at an emergency meeting adopted a resolution urging both these statesmen to resume their leadership. On 17 January 1932 Chiang and Wang met at Hangchow to mark the end of a feud which had lasted four and a

51. [7] 1932, 538–9, [153] I, 162–3, [155] 66. They included Wang Ching-wei, Eugene Ch'en, Tsou Lu, Teng Tse-ju, Li Tsung-jen, Pai Ch'ung-hsi, Ch'en Chi-t'ang, T'ang Shao-i, and Hsü Ch'ung-chih.
52. [153] I, 163–4.

half years and the beginning of a co-operation which was to go on for the next six.[53]

The reconciliation between Chiang and Wang in January 1932, however, marked the beginning of another dissension caused by Hu Han-min's continued stay in Hong Kong: Eugene Ch'en and Feng Yü-hsiang resigned from their government posts, and Chang Hsüeh-liang followed suit in August after a violent quarrel with Wang Ching-wei.[54] The reason behind this was the rise of an opposition to the Chiang-Wang 'weak-kneed policy' towards Japan. These new 'dissidents' were in the years to come to be the strongest advocates of a war of resistance. Having occupied Manchuria, the Japanese invaded Shanghai on 28 January 1932,[55] compelling the Nanking Government to transfer itself to Loyang in Honan. Yet in spite of this blatant aggression, Chiang and Wang refused to break off diplomatic relations with Japan, so that Shigemitsu, the Japanese ambassador, remained in China and recorded the following change in Wang Ching-wei's attitude towards his country:

His [Wang's] main idea was 'liberation of Asia', his avowed policy 'Asia for the Asians'. He hoped that other nations would co-operate and by their united efforts restore the fortunes of Asia. He keenly hoped to find ways and means by which Japan and China might agree on a common policy. . . .

As Foreign Minister he had warmly supported my exertions for a cease-fire after the first battle of Shanghai and thereafter, also, he had spared no effort to bring about an understanding with Japan.[56]

As for Chiang, the urgent tasks after the Mukden Incident and the battle of Shanghai were internal peace and the strengthening of China's defence, without which a war of resistance could only end in greater disasters. So, as soon as the dust of the Japanese crisis had settled, he embarked on further encirclement campaigns against the communists.

The trials and tribulations of the KMT from September 1931 to April 1932 gave the communists a much needed respite. Following in the tracks of their retreating enemy, they expanded the

53. [7] 1932, 546–53 and [153] I, 164–8.
54. [7] 1933, 241–2 and 247–9.   55 [220].
56. [221] 165.

territory of the central soviet to include twenty-one counties[57] with a population just under 2,500,000 and they were able to carry out a directive from the party centre in Shanghai issued in March, instructing them to prepare for the first all-China congress of soviets. The congress took place in Juichin on 7 November and adopted the Constitution of the Soviet Republic, its land and labour laws, and its economic policies. Under the Constitution, the Provisional Soviet Government was elected with Mao as its chairman and Chang Kuo-t'ao and Hsiang Ying its deputy chairmen. The Commander-in-Chief of the Red Army was Chu Te.[58] Since the soviets remained semi-autonomous and a closer military and administrative co-ordination was impossible during the siege, all these posts were more honorary than real. Even the new land law approved by the congress was not very different from the one adopted in March 1930.[59] The reasons for holding the congress therefore appeared difficult to understand. However, as Mao himself admitted:

Comrades upholding the correct line, with Comrade Mao Tse-tung as their representative, totally opposed the third 'Left' line during the period of its dominance. Since they *disapproved* of it and demanded its rectification, *their correct leadership in various districts was removed by the Central Committee reconstituted at the plenary session of January 1931* or by the agencies or representatives sent by it.[60]

This, and the fact that none of the commissars of the Provisional Soviet Government belonged to Mao's central soviet except Mao himself and perhaps Teng Tzu-hui, made manifest the party centre's effort to intensify its control over the soviets. It also set about depriving Mao of military power by appointing Chou En-lai to take charge of the operations against the fourth Encirclement.[61] According to Liu Po-ch'eng who attended the congress and by

57. [46] IV, 1129 or *SW* IV (Peking), 17–18. The names of the counties are given on [46] IV, 1136 n. 12 or *SW* IV (Peking), 25 n. 21.

58. The other officials were People's Commissar for Foreign Affairs, Wang Chia-hsiang; for Finance, Teng Tzu-hui; for Education, Ch'ü Ch'iu-pai; for Justice, Chang Kuo-t'ao; for Labour, Hsiang Ying; for Land, Chang Ting-ch'eng; for Interiors, Chou I-su; and Attorney-General, Ho Shu-heng. ([181] 59).

59. [310] 44–5 and [162] 224–6.

60. [46] III, 991 or *SW* IV, 187–8 (my italics).

61. [258] 179. See also [237] 220–1 and 202 and *vide infra*, p. 176.

then had perhaps already lost one of his eyes,[62] Mao was criticized by the representatives for persistently pursuing the rightist, opportunistic, rich peasant line.[63]

After the departure of Li Li-san the party centre in Shanghai fell into the hands of Wang Ming, Ch'in Pang-hsien, and other young students who had just returned from Moscow with their teacher Pavel Mif.[64] Their relations with Mao were anything but happy, owing, among other things, to Mao's growing influence and perhaps also to his flouting of the party discipline by retreating from Ch'angsha probably without the party's sanction. Their foremost task was therefore the restoration of the centre's authority before the tendency towards decentralization reached an irreversible stage.[65] Rich neither in years nor in experience but only in impetuosity,[66] they commanded little respect from old comrades like Ho Meng-hsiung and Lo Chang-lung at the fourth plenum in January 1931, and these latter subsequently organized another 'Central Committee' against the newly reconstituted provisional centre in Shanghai.[67] In addition to this heavy blow, Hsiang Chung-fa, the party secretary, was arrested and killed and Ku Shun-chang, the chief of the 'special affairs unit' of the CCP, on a visit to Wuhan to obtain money from the soviets for the use of the Central Committee, was arrested and turned traitor with the result that Ho Meng-hsiung and many other leaders of the party were captured and shot by the KMT police.[68] It is reported that Mao's old friend, Ts'ai Ho-sen, was also killed at this time[69] and that, as a reprisal,

62. [24] 137.
63. Schwartz said in 1951: 'By the end of 1931, Mao's position of leadership within the Soviet area was sufficiently strong to win him the position of the chairman of the newly established Soviet Provisional Government' ([52] 178), and in 1955 he modified this position. See 'On the "Originality" of Mao Tse-tung', *Foreign Affairs*, October 1955, 68 and 71. See also Hsiao Tso-liang [237] 151-2 and 171.
64. [52] 148 and [190] 12–13.
65. Chou En-lai, for example, spoke of 'co-ordination of all the soviets and concentration of the leadership over the Red Army', for he felt the party centre's leadership over the Army was not sufficiently strong ([230] III). See also [237] 171.
66. Hsiao San described Ch'in Pang-hsien as 'showy' ([280] 245).
67. [181] 74.
68. [52] 185, [181] 74, [182] 143, [244] 59, and also [46] III, 987 and 1021 ns. 6, 7, and 8 or *SW* IV, 183, 340–1, ns. 7, 8, and 9.
69. [43] 66.

Chou En-lai killed Ku Shun-chang's whole family in Shanghai.[70] The Wang Ming line had thus an ominous start.

Although Wang emphasized the importance of the city work, exaggerated the weight of capitalism in China's economy, over-stressed the significance of 'the factors of socialist revolution', and denied the existence of an intermediate camp or a third group,[71] he established excellent liaison with the principal soviets except for the central one. He sent Hsia Hsi, another friend of Mao's but opposed to him, to the west Hupei-Hunan soviet where Hsia set a branch of the Politburo to take over the control from Chou Yi-ch'ün and Ho Lung[72]; he also managed to convince Chang Kuo-t'ao of the correctness of his strategy which Chang supported at the all-China congress of soviets and later tried to put into practice.[73] The 'victory' of the communists in the third Encirclement, the discord between Nanking and Canton, and the Mukden Incident gave Wang and Ch'in, who was then the secretary of the CCP, fresh heart and led them to believe that a new revolutionary upsurge was coming.[74] They interpreted the Incident as a prelude to an eventual Japanese invasion of the Soviet Union and the successful counterattack of the communists as a manifestation of their military capabilities. Consequently they called for preparations for capturing big cities and scoring victories in one or more provinces—in fact, a revival of the Li Li-san strategy.[75] This, indeed, was still the only pattern of revolution they could conceive.

At this point, two communist commanders, Kuo Ping-sheng and Lung P'u-lin, went over to the KMT. The defection was later blamed on Mao's erroneous leadership.[76] But on 12 December 1931 the 73rd and 74th Brigades of the 26th Route Army at Ningtu under Tung Chen-t'ang and Chi Chen-tung respectively surrendered to Chu Te, bringing with them nearly 20,000 rifles, several hundred heavy and light machine-guns, more than 100 pieces of artillery, and many wireless sets. This was a tremendous stimulus to the communists and Chu at once reorganized them into the 5th Red Army Corps with Chi Chen-tung as the com-

70. [181] 74.
71. [46] III, 958 or SW IV, 181.   72. [237] 193 and [239] 5.
73. [18] 268, [50] 128, and [185] 89–90.
74. [46] III, 988 or SW IV, 184.
75. [185] 87–9.   76. [181] 76.

mander, Hsiao Ching-kuang as the political commissar, and Chao
Po-sheng and Tung Chen-t'ang as the commanding officers of the
13th and 14th Red Armies in this corps.[77] This brought the total
strength of the regular Red Army in the central soviet to three
army corps—the 1st under Lin Piao with Lo Jung-huan as the
political commissar, the 3rd under P'eng Te-huai with T'eng
Tai-yüan as the political commissar, and now the 5th under Chi
Chen-tung with Hsiao Ching-kuang as the political commissar.
Nearby at Chingkangshan there was the 6th Army Corps under
Hsiao K'e with Jen Pi-shih as the party representative and Wang
Chen as the political commissar,[78] at Iyang there was the 10th Red
Army under Fang Chih-min with Shao Shih-p'ing as the political
commissar, and the 7th Army Corps was being formed by Hsün
Huai-chou and Su Yü in Fukien.[79] Elsewhere there were the 4th
Army Corps under Hsü Hsiang-ch'ien with Chang Kuo-t'ao as
the political commissar and the 3rd Army under Ho Lung with
Hsia Hsi as the political commissar.[80] It was estimated that in
January 1932 the total strength of the Red Army in China reached
200,000 with 150,000 rifles.[81] Small wonder that Ch'in Pang-hsien
and Wang Ming came to the conclusion that the guerrilla phase
was over and from now on the Red troops should engage the
enemy in positional warfare in order to attain victories involving
big cities and in one or more provinces.[82]

The new party line was first followed by Ho Lung's troops who,
leaving their soviet base behind, poured out to menace west Hupei
and in the three months between January and March 1932 doubled
the area under their control. Now 30,000 strong, they became a
real threat to the security of Wuhan. The 4th Army Corps under
Hsü Hsiang-ch'ien and Chang Kuo-t'ao was also active around its
base in Hupei-Honan-Anhwei. Alarmed by these developments,
Chiang Kai-shek at once flew to Wuhan to plan another Encirclement Campaign.[83]

77. [46] I, 159 n. 12 or SW I, 355 n. 13, [181] 58–9, [185] 86. See also
[16] III, 309.
78. [18] 268, [234] 319, [244] 100, [247] V, 226, and [258] 109–10.
79. [250] 85 and [274] 185.   80. [185] 89–90 and [239].
81. [244] 75.
82. [46] I, 199–200 or SW I, 213–14 and [237] 161, 167, 202.
83. [7] 1933, 247 and [239].

The fourth Encirclement was in fact not an encirclement as such but three huge concentrations of troops pushing forward all the time and seeking to destroy the communists. Their slogan was: 'Fear no bandits, under-estimate no bandits, seek for them, and destroy them.'[84] This, however, does not mean that the fourth campaign was a short one; in fact it lasted nine months from June 1932 to March 1933.[85] From June to October 1932 the brunt of the attack was borne by the soviets around Hupei and then it was thrown against the central soviet in Kiangsi. In all, Chiang mobilized half a million troops; the greater part of them were placed under the command of a young soldier who had distinguished himself in the third Encirclement, General Ch'en Ch'eng.[86]

The 100,000 troops deployed in Hupei under Chiang's personal command soon scored resounding victories by wiping out the soviet at Lake Hung in south Hupei,[87] driving Ho Lung's troops to the Miao areas on the borders of Hupei, Hunan, Szechwan, and Kweichow, and chasing away Chang Kuo-t'ao's 4th Army Corps to north Szechwan.[88] The scattered bands of guerrillas in Hupei were eventually gathered together and organized into the 25th Army by Hsü Hai-tung.[89]

In preparation against the imminent attack on the central soviet, the Ningtu Conference of the party, army, and government leaders was convened in August. Mao went straight to the conference from a campaign in Fukien where at Changchow he had cut Chang Chen's division to pieces. But again he was severely criticized. After that he fell ill, and whatever military power he had retained was taken over by Chou En-lai as the general political commissar of the Red Army and concurrently of the 1st Front Army.[90] Dr. Nelson Fu examined him and ordered him to stay in the hospital for four months When better he was invited to dinner at Dr. Fu's home. Later Mao told Fu:

The other day you asked me to dine with you and I did. But we are comrades, so there was no need for you to prepare so many dishes or to invite so many other guests. We must not forget that there is a war. We must be very careful not to do things in a lavish way.

84. [181] 60.   85. [18] 267.
86. Now Vice President on Formosa. See [181] 60.
87. [185] 90.   88. [18] 268, [185] 89–90, [234] 9–10.
89. [18] 268.   90. [181] 76 and [237] 220–1.

And Dr. Fu's reaction was:

Suddenly my face went as red as beetroot. Chairman Mao's remark hit right at one of my weaknesses! Although I came from a peasant family, my work as a physician and the head of a hospital affected my way of life. I had acquired unproletarian ideas and become less ascetic. [Chairman Mao's remark made] me really ashamed of myself.[91]

At the Conference, Mao insisted on following the same strategy as the previous three campaigns, but Chou En-lai and Liu Po-ch'eng, backed by the party centre, prevailed with their plan of 'halting the enemy beyond the gate'.[92] The enemy came in three columns,[93] all advancing towards Kuangch'ang to meet the concentration of the communist forces. Having found out the enemy's intentions, the communists switched their main forces from Kuangch'ang to the south of Ihuang where they lay in wait. On 27 February the first column of the KMT troops arrived and was ambushed in the darkness of night; the two divisions of the column were almost completely wiped out with one of their commanders killed in action and the other taken prisoner. Four weeks later, the KMT organized another assault which was smashed in a short encounter by the combined might of the troops under Lin Piao, P'eng Te-huai, Tung Chen-t'ang, and Lo Ping-hui. The commander of the KMT 11th Division died in action. The new strategy was thus proved correct and Mao's over-cautious 'guerrilla-ism' was considered obsolete.[94]

The only man who had been following Mao's strategy in the fourth campaign appeared to be one Lo Ming who was the acting secretary of the Fukien branch of the CCP. Instead of 'halting the enemy beyond the gate,' he evacuated the inhabitants of Shanghang, Yungting, and the adjacent areas and waged a guerrilla warfare inside the soviet territory against invading troops. For this he was criticized as being 'an opportunist-liquidationist' and a 'flightist'. Not only was Lo cashiered, but a 'struggle against the line of Lo Ming' was launched, involving such people as Mao's

91. [36].

92. [46] I, 200 or *SW* I, 214 and [237] 218.

93. Under Ch'en Ch'eng while the first column was led by Lo Cho-ying, the second by Chao Kuan-t'ao, and the third by Wu Ch'i-wei.

94. [181] 60–1 and 75–6 and [234] 200–1.

secretary Ku Po and his brother Mao Tse-t'an, T'an Chen-lin, Teng Hsiao-p'ing, Teng Tzu-hui, and Hsiao Ching-kuang.[95]

This was the height of the Wang Ming-Ch'in Pang-hsien line, although Wang had left for Moscow in 1932 and in January 1933 Ch'in was forced to transfer the party centre from Shanghai to Juichin.[96] Accompanying Ch'in was a German communist whose Chinese name was Li T'e.[97] Little is known about this mysterious man, except for the fact that he directed the communist military operation during the fifth and last Encirclement. His counterpart, the chief military adviser to Chiang Kai-shek, was also a German, General Hans von Seeckt.[98]

In April 1933 the communist troops were within striking distance of Nanch'ang where the retreating KMT forces congregated. Chu Te, K'ung Ho-ch'ung, and Fang Chih-min made an attempt to take the city, but were forestalled by Chiang's swift action in sending fresh divisions to strengthen the defence.[99] Thereafter both sides decided to have a rest in order to prepare for the next round of the fighting. The communists called a conference to review the campaign just ended and to plan the one about to come, and again Mao was criticized though he was absent with a fever.[1] The conference also decided to create two more army corps—the 7th under Hsün Huai-chou stationed in Fukien and the 9th under Lo Ping-hui stationed in the central soviet.[2] Anticipating a long siege and protracted war of attrition, the conference deemed it necessary to consolidate the economic front and the task was given to Chairman Mao who was then also a member of the Politburo.[3] To fulfil this task, Mao placed the emphasis of his economic policy on increased production rather than equality of distribution, with a guarded leniency towards the rich and the middle

95. [46] III, 1022 n. 33 or SW IV, 342 n. 34 and [181] 75–6.

96. The date is variously given as 1931, 1932, and late in 1932. See [18] 280, [52] 187, [46] III, 968 or SW IV, 185, and [237] 162.

97. [50] 136.

98. [134] 93, [153] I, 203, and [258] 186.

99. [153] I, 202–3.   1. [35].

2. [181] 86, [247] V, 180–224, and [274] 185.

3. The four articles Mao wrote in 1933 and 1934 were all dealing with economic problems. See [46] I, 113–36 or SW I, 129–52. His membership of the Politburo, see [18] 280. Hsiao Tso-liang refers to an interview of Mao in which Mao appeared to have toed the Ch'in Pang-hsien line ([237] 241–2).

peasants as distinguished from the landlords.[4] He also divided the soviet economy into three sectors—the nationalized, the co-operative, and the private—and encouraged expansion of all three, particularly the co-operative sector. In this way he hoped to see a rise in production, so that more could be exported for the exchange of badly needed goods, especially salt, and so that the government revenue would increase proportionately.[5] But the KMT blockade was too tight for Mao to achieve much with his policy. Entire villages were resettled elsewhere in order to create a No Man's Land between the 'white' and the 'red' areas, thus reducing the inter-area trade to a trickle and causing serious shortages of food, cooking oil, and clothing in the soviet.[6] Just before the Long March the food ration was as small as 14 ounces per head per day.[7] Chiang also deliberately raised the price of salt. Together with the blockade, this drove the price of salt in the soviet up to over 2 *yuan* a lb. On the assumption of 4 ounces per person per week, salt alone cost a communist nearly 10 cents a day in 1934 whereas at Chingkangshan six years earlier he had had to spend only 5 cents a day on his meals except for the rice.[8] Salt became so scarce that many communists could not afford to have it for weeks on end.[9] In the summer of 1934 Mao organized a special corps to run the blockade, but without avail.[10]

Chiang also organized a special corps consisting of no less than 24,000 men whose duties, beside enforcing the economic blockade, included espionage against the communists and mobilization of the people. The commandant of this corps was K'ang Tse.[11] Following Tseng Kuo-fan's methods against the T'aip'ing rebels, Chiang encouraged and helped the local gentry in organizing and arming militia forces to maintain law and order, particularly in recovered areas.[12] In February 1934 he initiated the well-known New Life Movement and in May the Standing Committee of the KMT resolved to respect and observe the teachings of Confucius,

4. [46] I, 121-4 or *SW* I, 138-40.
5. [46] I, 125-30 or *SW* I, 141-6.
6. [46] I, 127 or *SW* I, 143 and [234] 188.   7. [247] V, 103.
8. [46] I, 67 or *SW* I, 82, [181] 81, and [234] 188 and 257.
9. [234] 188.
10. [234] 202-3. There were more than 300 in this corps.
11. [153] I, 208-9.   12. [153] I, 201 and [244] 43-4.

both being attempts to effect moral renewal of the Chinese people in the face of the challenge of alien doctrines such as Marxism.[13] But the most deadly of Chiang's new measures was the building of a ring of blockhouses round the soviets and the construction of a network of motor-roads to facilitate the transport of his troops. This was a stranglehold that tightened with the progress of the fifth Encirclement Campaign.[14]

With such elaborate preparation on both sides, one can hardly dispute the wisdom of considering the fifth Campaign as 'the decisive fight between the two ways in China'.[15] The communist tactics in the Campaign, however, occasion some surprise. They sought to defend every inch of the soviet territory regardless of loss in lives while Chiang sought to engage and destroy the Red forces. The battle began in August 1933, when Chiang's 75 divisions under his personal command pushed cautiously forward in four columns.[16] On the communist side, the Kiangsi-Chekiang-Fukien soviet had now been merged into the central soviet and Fang Chih-min's 10th Red Army had been incorporated into the 7th Army Corps,[17] bringing the total area of the central soviet to 70 counties and its total strength to 100,000 men.[18] The initial encounter at Hsünk'ou ended in favour of the communists, thereby heightening their morale and confirming their belief in 'halting the enemy beyond the gate'.[19] A period of seesaw battles ensued until November 1933 when a dramatic event took place in Fukien.

The heroic defenders of Shanghai in January 1932 during the Japanese invasion, the 19th Route Army under Ts'ai T'ing-k'ai, had been for some time a group of discontented soldiers cooped up in the remote province of Fukien. They were opposed to Chiang's policy of appeasing the Japanese while fighting the communists. Since the communists proposed a truce and the formation of an anti-Japanese united front with the KMT in the summer of 1933, Ts'ai made contact with them in the hope that they would assist

13. [7] 1935, 91–2 and [153] I, 179–81.
14. [7] 1935, 89, [190] 99, [244] 42–3.
15. [46] III, 999 or *SW* IV, 196.
16. The north under Ku Chu-t'ung, the south under Ch'en Chi-t'ang, the east under Chiang Ting-wen, and the west under Ho Chien, and the rear was commanded by Wei Li-huang. [181] 85.   17. [185] 91.
18. The total strength of the Red Army in China was about 300,000. See [185] 91.   19. [249] 3.

him in his adventure against Chiang Kai-shek.[20] Eventually Ts'ai and the Red troops arrived at a *rapprochement* in October which precipitated the establishment of a 'Chinese Republic'. Its government was known as 'the People's Government'.[21] Chiang dealt with this open rebellion with speed and deftness by sending emissaries to Canton to prevent Ch'en Chi-t'ang from aiding Ts'ai T'ing-k'ai and also to Hong Kong to discuss a reconciliation with Hu Han-min.[22] Meanwhile his troops forged southward along the Kiangsi-Fukien border, endeavouring to separate Ts'ai from the communists.[23] After this, in January 1934, he launched an offensive against Ts'ai whose resistance collapsed in two weeks[24] before the communists had time to make up their minds whether to help him.[25]

At the 5th plenum of the Central Committee of the CCP in January 1934, Mao and Ch'in Pang-hsien engaged in a fierce debate on strategy with Mao favouring an aggressive plan to save the soviet by sending troops to east China, so as to threaten Hangchow, Soochow, Nanking, and Nanch'ang.[26] This, according to Mao, was the way to defeat the blockhouses and to transform 'the strategic defensive into a strategic offensive by menacing the vital positions of the enemy and challenging him to battle in the vast zones that were devoid of blockhouses'.[27] Whether this plan could

20. The result of this was an agreement between Ts'ai and P'eng Te-huai to form an anti-Japanese united front. See [7] 1934, 371 and [147] I, 380–4. The former reports that P'eng agreed to transfer the Red troops to Ts'ai's command. This, however, should be taken with a pinch of salt.

21. Headed by Ch'en Ming-shu with Ts'ai as the chairman of the Military Council, Eugene Ch'en as the Foreign Minister, Chang Po-chün as the Minister of Education, and Huang Ch'i-hsiang as the chief-of-staff. Other members of this insurgent government included Chiang Kuang-nai, Li Chi-shen, and Hsü Ch'ien, but not Madame Sun, who on 23 November, three days after the founding of the government, declared her decision to have nothing to do with it. [7] 1934, 369–72 and [153] I, 174.

22. [7] 1934, 374–8. 23. [153] I, 174.

24. [7] 1934, 378 and [181] 77. See also [147] I, 384.

25. Mao seemed to think that the CCP, instead of the Red Army alone, should have assisted the Fukien insurgents, but he did not blame the party leadership for its nonchalance ([46] I, 231 or *SW* I, 251). Ku Kuan-chiao and Kung Ch'u, on the other hand, make a startling suggestion that Mao was actually opposed to lending support to Ts'ai ([181] 77 and [237] 250–1) and because of this Mao was punished by being kept in the party on probation.

26. [46] I, 230–1 or *SW* I, 251, [190] 14, and [205] 161.

27. [46] I, 230–1 or *SW* I, 251.

have worked is open to question, but it would certainly have meant a return to guerrilla warfare which Ch'in Pang-hsien opposed and described as 'countryside policy' and 'banditry doctrine'.[28] The plan was rejected. It must be remembered that hitherto the Red Army had not suffered serious setbacks to make them doubt the wisdom of the Ch'in Pang-hsien strategy, although the block-houses had caused a good deal of economic embarrassment to Chairman Mao. In fact, the Red Army scored further victories in March 1934 at Shuik'ouyü and T'uants'un, though at heavy loss to themselves.[29]

However, in April the tide began to turn. Following the occupation of Suich'uan on the periphery of the Chingkangshan soviet,[30] Ch'en Ch'eng won a decisive battle at Kuangch'ang, taking the town and opening the gateway to Juichin.[31] The communist strategy of 'halting the enemy beyond the gate' thus collapsed and had to be switched to that of a pure defensive.[32] The fish was now in the net; the question was how to draw it in. In July the KMT troops made further gains in both south and east Kiangsi while in Fukien they threw back a communist offensive which was probably designed to divert them from east Kiangsi so that a break-through could be made by Fang Chih-min. Fang's endeavour to fight his way north from Iyang and Hengfeng was in itself a move to distract the KMT's attention from the central soviet, in spite of the fact that his column was called the 'Anti-Japanese Vanguards'. But as soon as he had wriggled out of the net, he was isolated and his column cut into several sections. Fang himself was taken prisoner while his chief-of-staff, Su Yü, collected the remnants of his troops, regrouped them into a division, and waged guerrilla warfare on the Chekiang-Fukien border until 1938 when the division was incorporated into the New Fourth Army.[33]

Soon after this, in August, another attempt to break through the

28. [190] 14.   29. [46] I, 220 or *SW* I, 239.   30. [153] I, 206.
31. [181] 86–7, [237] 285 and 288, and [247] 3. Chou En'lai fully realized the importance of the battle of Kuangch'ang.   32. [247] 3.
33. [181] 87, [185] 92–3, [187] 16–18, and [234] 256–61. The first reports that Fang was captured in January 1935; the second reports that he was defeated in November 1934; the third reports that he was captured in July 1934 and put to death on 6 August 1935; and the fourth says that he died in action. But there are Fang's writings during the imprisonment to prove that he was captured.

Encirclement was made, this time by Hsiao K'e and Wang Chen, from Chingkangshan to north-east Kweichow, aiming at joining forces with Ho Lung and strengthening his soviet base there. This was unmistakably the prelude to the final break-through of the main forces and it was successful. Hsiao and Ho met in October and at once their forces were merged into the 2nd Front Army with Ho as the commander and Jen Pi-shih as the political commissar. Jen's appointment was of historical importance, for it was Jen who prevented Ho Lung from supporting Chang Kuo-t'ao when the 2nd and 4th Front Armies met in west Szechwan in 1936.[34]

The departure of Fang Chih-min and Hsiao K'e meant the loss of north Fukien and west Kiangsi by the communists, making the central soviet even smaller. Meanwhile the KMT advanced relentlessly, taking Ch'angting in August and Hsingkuo in September.[35] The 70 counties were now reduced to only six![36] But Yütu was still held and there Mao was laid low with malaria. At the time when Hsingkuo fell his temperature touched 105° F. Owing to Dr. Fu's careful treatment, however, he was brought back to health towards the end of September. Fu recalled that one day he stewed a chicken for his patient who insisted on the doctor himself having it:

I was so deeply touched that I lost my power of speech. I felt my eyes grow warm and fill with tears in them.[37]

Mao recovered in time to take part in the momentous decision, the only feasible one at the time, to abandon the central soviet and, following Hsiao K'e's tracks, to withdraw to north-east Kweichow.[38] The decision was made on 2 October; a military council was formed to direct the retreat with Mao, Chu, Chou En-lai, Wang Chia-hsiang, Liu Po-ch'eng, and the German Li-t'e as members[39]; and a week was all the time the communists had for their preparation.[40] P'eng Te-huai was appointed the commander of the van-

34. [18] 268, [181] 87, [185] 93, [187] 17–18, [190] 101 and 139, and [247] V, 226.
35. [7] 1935, 89–90, [153] I, 206–7, and [181] 86–7.
36. [153] I, 207.   37. [35].
38. [181] 87, [190] 65, [249] 4, and [250] 88.   39. [190] 67.
40. [190] 65.

guard of the 1st Front Army and Mao Tse-min took charge of the transport of the gold, silver, documents, and equipment.[41] On 16 October 1934 the journey began. Among the 100,000 who joined it there were 35 women, including Mao's wife who was heavy with child and K'ang K'e-ch'ing whom Chu Te married in January 1929.[42]

Left behind to fight the rearguard action to slow down the pursuing enemy, and to spend long and lonely years until 1938, were bands of guerrillas scattered through some 14 areas.[43] Ch'en Yi and Hsiang Ying had with them the consumptive Ch'ü Ch'iu-pai and Mao's younger brother, Tse-t'an, and 28,000 soldiers including 20,000 wounded ones.[44] While roaming the countryside of the old central soviet, they witnessed the fall of Juichin on 10 November[45] and later, in March 1935, they lost both Ch'ü Ch'iu-pai and Mao Tse-t'an.[46] But Ch'en Yi and Hsiang Ying fought on while T'u Chen-nung and Liu Ying harassed north-east Kiangsi and north Fukien, Su Yü, Chang Ting-ch'eng, and Teng Tzu-hui were active in south Fukien, and Kao Chün-t'ing and his men troubled the Hupei-Honan-Anhwei border. They were all placed under Hsiang Ying's direction.[47]

It was either late in October or early in November that Moscow advised the CCP by radio message to 'pull out' when the historic Long March was already a fortnight old.[48]

41. [247] V, 152–3 and [258] 273.   42. [50] 143 and [190] 211.
43. [46] I, 161 and II, 389–90, also 389 n. or *SW* I, 357 n. 27 and II, 287–8 n. 7.
44. [189] 308–9.   45. [7] 1935, 90 and [153] I, 207.
46. Ch'ü was arrested and Mao Tse-t'an died in action. See [181] 69 and [41] 247.
47. [181] 87 and [274] 43–4. These were the beginnings of the New Fourth Army of 1938. *Vide infra*, p. 234.
48. [190] 14.

Chapter IX

The Long March

ONE may compare the Long March with Hannibal's journey across the Alps and say smugly that the Chinese did better, or with Napoleon's retreat from Moscow and say coldly that the Chinese did worse. But it must be admitted that man has never seen the equal of it before or since. It was a flight in panic; yet it was also an epic of human endurance. In 370 days from 16 October 1934 to 20 October 1935 the 1st Front Army under Mao Tse-tung walked on and on, to cover a distance of 6,000 miles.

The trek fell naturally into two parts with the crossing of the Gold Sand River (Chin-sha Chiang) in May 1935 as the dividing line. Before it the communists had to fight hard against enemies from all directions; after it they had to conquer the most difficult terrain in China. But nothing could stop them reaching the only remaining soviet in north Shensi. It could be said that they were running for their lives, and had they stopped they would have perished. But there was more to it than that. Politically also the trek can be divided into two parts with the Tsunyi Conference of the Politburo in January 1935 as the watershed. Before that, the communists were just roaming without a conscious political purpose; afterwards, the journey acquired a new meaning.

It was force of circumstances rather than deliberate planning which made the journey so immensely long. In 1946 Mao told Robert Payne: 'If you mean, did we have any exact plans, the answer is that we had none.'[1] In fact, the initial plan was no more than a march from Juichin to Sangchih in north-west Hunan to

1. [50] 140–1.

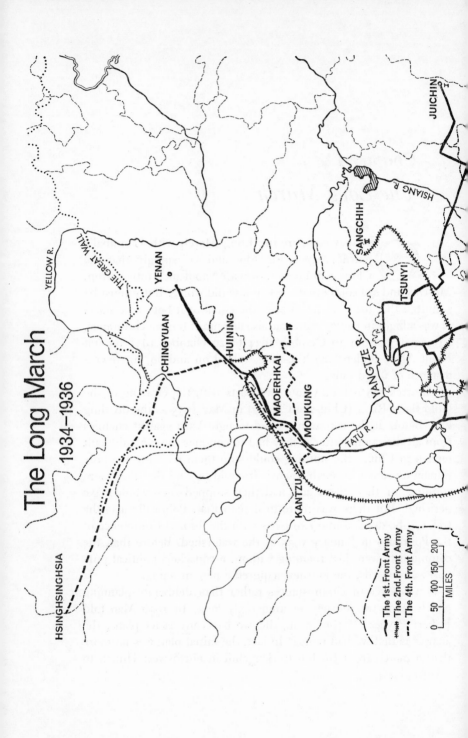

The Long March
1934–1936

YELLOW R.

THE GREAT WALL

HSINGHSINGHSIA

CHINGYUAN

YENAN

HUINING

MAOERHKAI

MOUKUNG

KANTZU

TATU R.

YANGTZE R.

SANGCHIH

TSUNYI

HSIANG R.

JUICHIN

— The 1st. Front Army
╫╫╫ The 2nd.Front Army
╌╌ The 4th. Front Army

0   50   100 150 200

MILES

join forces with the 2nd Front Army under Ho Lung.[2] This explains why the communists brought with them sewing machines,
printing presses, gold and silver, and even soviet banknotes, but
no adequate maps.[3] They took the Juichin-Hsinfeng route, breaking the siege on 21 October and cutting across north Kwangtung
to reach south Hunan in November.[4] During the first week they
marched only at night and then, having dispersed the Kwangtung
troops, changed their schedule to four hours' marching and four
hours' rest throughout day and night. By this new schedule they
journeyed on faster, but not fast enough to shake off the pursuing
army.[5] As soon as they entered Hunan and Ho Lung began to take
the offensive their intention became known to Chiang, who at once
dispatched several divisions to reinforce the line along the west
bank of the Hsiang River in north Kwangsi. The battle of the
Hsiang River ensued and went on for five days during which the
combatants of the communist column fought in two parallel lines
in order to make a lane for the non-combatants to go ahead. It was
a bloody battle which the communists won at a heavy cost.
Though they were now on the south-west bank of the river, they
found that between themselves and Ho Lung's troops there stood
an enemy army of five or six times their own strength.[6] It was impossible to break through; the initial plan had to be cancelled; the
immediate question was where they should go. At that time the
only alternative was to penetrate through the sparsely defended
province of Kweichow and thence to Chang Kuo-t'ao's soviet in
north Szechwan. This may have been exactly what Mao counselled.

The 30,000 communists of the 1st Front Army[7] now turned
west, and took Lip'ing in east Kweichow in December. At
Lip'ing they halted for a short while. The troops were regrouped
and the members of the Politburo conferred. Then it was decided
to march on to Tsunyi via Chenyüan and Meit'an. On New Year's
Day 1935 Lin Piao's 1st Army Corps led the crossing of the 250-

2. [50] 141, [190] 65, Hsü Meng-ch'iu's statement; [249] 4, Liu Po-ch'eng's
statement, and 19, Li T'ien-yu's statement; [250] 88.
3. [190] 72–3 and 76, [234] 169 and 176–7, and [247] 3–4.
4. [190] 65 and [249] 3–4.
5. [190] 65 and [249] 3–4.   6. [249] 4–5 and 19.
7. An agreed figure, see [18] 283 and [187] 23.

metre-wide Wu River[8] and about a week later, literally without firing a shot, captured Tsunyi.[9] There the front army stopped for a rest and reorganization during which the famous and epoch-making Tsunyi Conference of the Politburo took place.

As a result of decisions taken at the Conference, the divisions were abolished and replaced by regiments under the same commanders. Chu Te remained Commander-in-Chief with Liu Po-ch'eng as his chief-of-staff, and under them Lin Piao led the 1st Army Corps with Nieh Jung-chen as the political commissar and Tso Ch'üan as the chief-of-staff, P'eng Te-huai led the 3rd Army Corps with Yang Shang-k'un as the political commissar, Tung Chen-t'ang led the 5th Army Corps and Lo Ping-hui led the 9th Army Corps.[10] The chief of security was Teng Fa and the safety of the leaders was entrusted to a regiment of Red cadres under Ch'en Keng and Sung Jen-ch'ung.[11] By this simplification, the columns which had at times stretched tens of miles long became less unwieldy.[12]

Famous as it is, the Tsunyi Conference is still shrouded in mystery; information about it is scanty. Hu Ch'iao-mu records that even the calling of it was the subject of a fierce struggle.[13] Those who were opposed to it may have advanced the reason that the Lip'ing Conference had been held only a short while earlier, therefore there was no need for another. But Mao Tse-tung considered it necessary and he prevailed; so the Conference sat. According to Mao himself, the members discussed only 'the most urgent military problems of the moment' and 'the organization of the Secretariat and the Revolutionary Military Commission of the Central Committee'.[14] From what happened during and after the Conference, it is possible to deduce that the military problems deliberated upon probably included the reorganization of the 1st Front Army, the reintroduction of Mao's principles of mobile warfare in order to regain some tactical initiative,[15] and the route to be taken to join forces with Chang Kuo-t'ao's 4th Front Army in north Szechwan. It is safe to conjecture that the mistakes of the

8. [249] 30–1. In this operation Keng Piao distinguished himself.
9. [249] 43–7.   10. [249] 23, 29, 31, 38, 54, 71, and 132.
11. [249] 48 and 107.   12. [249] 49–50.   13. [179] 35.
14. [46] I, 138 or *SW* I, 153.
15. [249] 6.

fifth Encirclement period and of the battle of the Hsiang River which cost nearly 50,000 men were thoroughly reviewed and bitterly criticized, resulting not only in the complete bankruptcy of the Wang-Ch'in line, but also in the resignation of Ch'in from the party secretaryship. The new secretary, Chang Wen-t'ien, though one of the 'Twenty-eight Bolsheviks', had considerably less power than his predecessor, for the leadership had now gone to the chairman of the Politburo, Mao Tse-tung. Thus for the first time Mao became the supreme leader of the CCP. Apart from being a personal triumph, his election to such an important post represented a victory of the rural soviet over the urban party centre, of a man who had spent all his life among the peasants and the lower orders of society over those who were well-versed in doctrines, Eastern and Western.[16] In an interview in 1944 when Gunther Stein asked Mao whether he had ever been in the minority, Mao replied:

Yes, I have been in the minority myself. The only thing for me to do at such times was to wait. But there have been very few examples of that in recent years.[17]

The fact behind this understatement is that Mao, on major issues, had seldom had the majority of the party with him before the Tsunyi Conference and has never been in the minority since.

The Conference also adopted 'Go north to fight the Japanese' (*pei-shang k'ang jih*) as a slogan. Earlier the party had expressed its wish to form a united front to fight the Japanese, but the tone was lacking in conviction.[18] The adoption of this slogan at the time gave a sense of direction to the men of the 1st Front Army, who were incessantly asking: 'Where are we going? Where are we going to establish a new soviet?'[19] The new slogan indicated that they would go north, perhaps make a detour along the borders of Szechwan to join the 4th Front Army, and then advance to Shensi to fight the Japanese in Inner Mongolia. The route they took was from Tsunyi north to T'ungtzu and Sungk'an and then west to Hsishui and T'uch'eng where they fought back a contingent of Szechwan

16. [14] 269–70, [181] 77–8 and 89, [190] 14, [234] 225, and [249] 5.
17. [296] 92.
18. The Soviet Republic declared war on Japan on 15 April 1932. See [237] 188 and [249] 48.
19. [249] 49.

troops and crossed the Ch'ihshui River. Upon entering Szechwan they found that the province was strongly defended by both the Central and the local government troops. Therefore they turned back to Tsunyi, pushed on to Jenhuai and Maot'ai where the Red soldiers bathed their tired feet in pools of the vintage wine for which Maot'ai was famous.[20] They made a second attempt to break into Szechwan, but again the way was blocked in front of them.[21]

Meanwhile in north Szechwan the 4th Front Army under heavy pressure of the attacking Szechwan troops decided to abandon the soviet and withdraw to the minority areas in the west of the province. This move cut the ground under Mao's feet, and so it was unlikely to have had his approval. Ever since Chang Kuo't'ao has been labelled a 'flightist'.[22]

It must be remembered that Chang Kuo-t'ao and Hsü Hsiang-ch'ien set up a soviet in Szechwan at an opportune time in 1933 when the warlords of that province were busily fighting one of their many civil wars[23] and Ho Lung was at the same time threatening the south-east corner of Szechwan.[24] In 1934 when the province was at peace again, the warlords launched a joint campaign against the soviet without much success. The seesaw battle between the communists and the warlords went on throughout 1934 till February 1935 when the Szechwan troops pierced right into the heart of the soviet, thus forcing Chang Kuo-t'ao to take to flight.[25] A feature of Chang's evacuation was the existence of an independent regiment of 2,000 women among his columns.[26] On 19 March,

20. [288].   21. [190] 64–5, [249] 6–7 and 58, and Appendix C.

22. [14] 271, [46] III, 990 or SW IV, 187, and [249] 9. In an interview with R. North, Chang Kuo-t'ao said that soviets were entirely unsuitable to conditions in China (see also [190] 14). He held this view at the time of the Tsunyi Conference and North interprets this as the beginning of the dissension between Chang and Mao. But in view of his later attempts to establish soviets in the north-west, this statement of his does not seem to ring true.

23. Chang lost the Oyüwan soviet in October 1932 and wandered to north Szechwan from south Shensi in the spring of 1933. See [153] I, 205, [181] 83, and [190] 159.   24. [181] 83–4.

25. [20] 401, [181] 83–4, and [190] 159. The main forces against the communists were Liu Hsiang's. It is of interest to note that Yang Sen and Wang Ling-chi fought the reds the hardest, T'ien Sung-yao and Teng Hsi-hou less hard, and Liu Wen-hui seldom fought them at all. These facts may help in the understanding of their respective positions after 1949, except for Liu Hsiang who died at the beginning of the Japanese War.   26. [249] 374.

Chang crossed the Chialing River at Ts'anghsi and followed a zig-zag route along the northern border to Moukung where they arrived either in or before June. According to Liu Po-ch'eng, Chang had created a 'government of the north-west confederation' aiming at a union of all the minority areas in the north-west provinces of China.[27]

Chang's evacuation meant that Mao had to adapt his plan to the new, besetting circumstances. Pulling his main forces back to Maot'ai and leaving the 9th Army Corps to ward off Wu Ch'i-wei's pursuing troops, Mao re-crossed the Wu River north of the capital of Kweichow which he threatened to take. Chiang Kai-shek at once flew to that panic-stricken city to arrange for its defence,[28] while Mao diverted his troops towards Lungli in south Kweichow and slipped westward to Yunnan. It was at this time that the death of Chu Te was announced. However, General Chu for ever like a phoenix had managed somehow to rise from his 'ashes' more than a dozen times.[29]

The route Mao took at this time was the only possible one which, being thinly defended, offered the 1st Front Army a chance to penetrate west China in order to reach the only remaining soviet, the north Shensi base. The front army entered Yunnan in three columns,[30] making a gesture of attacking Kunming by driving due west but suddenly turning north towards the Gold Sand River. It took the 1st Front Army eight days and eight nights, from 1 May, to ferry across the river in small boats to Sikang.[31] Having thus left behind the pursuing troops for the time being, the Red troops marched on along the Anning River valley with considerably less trouble until they reached the Tatu River where their epical exploits began.

A part of the 1st Army Corps under Liu Po-ch'eng and Nieh Jung-chen crossed the river in two small boats at Anshunch'ang and went north along the east bank to the Luting Bridge while the

27. [249] 9–10 and Appendix C.   28. [249] 7.   29. [189] 316.
30. The left under Lin Piao, the right under P'eng Te-huai, and the central under Liu Po-ch'eng. See [190] 69.
31. [190] 69 and [249] 105 *et seq.* These eight days and eight nights without serious harassment from Lung Yün's troops suggest that Lung adopted an equivocal attitude to the communists and may also explain his position after 1949.

main body of the 1st Front Army, still on the west bank, was also making a forced march towards it. At Anshunch'ang the river measures 300 metres wide and the rapids flow at a speed of 4 metres per second, but at the bridge it measures only 100 metres wide with the water flowing much faster. The bridge was constructed with no more than thirteen swaying chains with some wood boards thrown on them. When the communists arrived there, the boards had been taken away. Twenty volunteers, carrying with them swords and hand grenades, and covered by machine-gun fire, crawled along the chains to the other side, overawed and overpowered the guards, took the boards out of the warehouse, and placed them back on the bridge. Only three of the twenty died in this heroic operation.[32]

Having completed the crossing, the Red Army made a bee-line for T'iench'üan and Lushan where they met with little resistance and then pushed on to the Great Snow Mountain. They were tired and frozen and Mao, who had walked most of the way hitherto, had to be carried on a stretcher, for he was ill with fever.[33] It was at Chiachinshan south of Moukung that the 1st and 4th Front Armies met on 12 June 1935.[34]

The meeting was charged with tense emotion. There were cheers and tears and endless cross-questioning among the ranks,[35] but the feelings between Mao and Chang Kuo-t'ao were different. The two had made one another's acquaintance first in 1928 at Peking University where Mao worked as a library assistant and Chang was an undergraduate. They met again at the first and third national congresses of the CCP and it was at the latter that their first clash of opinions occurred. According to Chang, Mao changed his vote from supporting him over the question of trade unions to supporting Ch'en Tu-hsiu. It is almost certain that they saw each other at the fifth congress in 1927 and eight years had elapsed between then and their reunion at Moukung. During those eight years they both controlled soviet bases and conducted guerrilla warfare against the KMT troops, but none the less Mao's experience and background were quite different from those of Chang Kuo-t'ao.

32. [190] 71–2, [247] II, 11–13, and [249] 132 *et seq.*
33. [50] 151 and [258] 87.   34. [190] 73 and [249] 165.
35. [249] 165.

Chief among the differences was the fact that Mao had for the greater part of the 1921–35 period worked among peasants while Chang had operated among industrial workers. It was Chang who led the famous strike of the Peking-Hankow railway men in 1923,[36] and it was he who wrote in the *Hsiang-tao* (Guide Weekly), no. 12, December 1922:

The peasants take no interest in politics. This is common throughout the whole world, but is particularly true in China, for most of the Chinese peasants are smallholders. They are not interested in politics. All they care about is having a true Son of Heaven to rule them and a peaceful, bumper year.

Now, at the time of the junction of two front armies, Mao was the leader of the party whom Chang had to obey; yet under Chang there were 50,000 seasoned and well-rested troops compared with 45,000 tired and ragged soldiers led by Mao and Chu Te.[37] In these contrasting conditions, the stormy[38] sessions of the Lianghok'ou conference of the Politburo took place.

Mao and the majority of the Politburo advocated that the Red Army should continue to march northward to join Hsü Hai-tung, Liu Chih-tan, and Kao Kang in north Shensi whence they could drive east to meet the Japanese in battle, hoping that the patriots would rally to their support; but Chang Kuo-t'ao deemed this plan wishful thinking. His contention was that, since the revolution was at a low ebb, the enemy too strong, and the Red Army in flight,[39] it was impossible to create an advanced position in order to carry out an anti-Japanese struggle.[40] The better alternative, according to him, was to remain in Sikang and north-west Szechwan, build a soviet there, and then contact the USSR through Sinkiang.[41] It is not clear whether at this stage the Comintern intervened.[42] A compromise, perhaps suggested by Chu Te,[43] was, however, reached with the two front armies now divided into two columns: the east column, consisting of the 1st and 3rd Army Corps and the 4th and 30th Armies, was to be led by Mao, and the

36. Tung Pi-wu's statement, see [190] 40 and *vide supra*, pp. 93 and 100.
37. [189] 328–9 and [258] 203.   38. [189] 330. Chu Te's adjective.
39. [46] I, 144 or *SW* I, 160.   40. [185] 95.
41. [181] 89, [185] 95, and [190] 221.   42. [190] 221.
43. [181] 89 and [189] 330.

west column, consisting of the 5th and 9th Army Corps and the 31st and 32nd Armies, by Chu Te and Liu Po-ch'eng.[44] In other words, in each column there were two army corps of the 1st Front Army and two armies of the 4th Front Army. In the east column, Mao's strength was the stronger while in the west column, Chang's was. This regrouping and the delicate balance of strength, together with the charge of 'warlordism' against Chang Kuo-t'ao in later years,[45] perhaps reveal what was really at issue—the wranglers had the control over the army in their minds.

Following the Lianghok'ou conference, the Politburo met again at Maoerhkai at the end of July, where it adopted and issued its 'Appeal to Fellow Countrymen Concerning Resistance to Japan and National Salvation' on 1 August, calling for the formation of a united front.[46] Once again the issue between Mao and Chang was brought up and once again Mao prevailed. The two columns were made ready to brave the elements on the Grassland.

The crossing of the Grassland from towards the end of August to early September 1936 was undoubtedly the most difficult episode in the history of logistics. The Grassland is in fact a vast swamp covered by a thick mat of grass and hidden by low-lying mist. Under the grass is stinking, black mud. There is always strong wind, bringing with it either rain or hailstones. When night falls it is unbearably cold.[47] The communists during those days and nights on the Grassland had to sleep standing in pairs or groups of four back to back.[48] Many of them did not live long enough to see the end of the ordeal.[49]

In addition to the natural hazards, Hu Tsung-nan's 49th Division was ready to welcome the communists at Paotso where in a fierce battle they scattered Hu's division.[50] But in the meantime Chang Kuo-t'ao changed his mind, sending radio messages to Mao to demand the return of the east column to Apa. Mao refused and led his troops on to Panyu. Unfortunately for him, he lost Hsü Hsiang-ch'ien's 30th Army which, without the aid of either a map or a compass, walked into a pocket surrounded by an endless

44. [249] 10.
45. [46] III, 990 or *SW* IV, 187.   46. [14] 288 and [190] 16.
47. [249] 174-5.   48. [249] 175.   49. [190] 73.
50. [190] 74 and [249] 385 *et seq.*

swamp and therefore had to turn towards the south to join Chang
Kuo-t'ao's west column.[51] At Latzuk'ou, the east column repeated
its victory over Hu Tsung-nan's army. Afterwards it cut through
two more enemy lines, crossed the Liup'an Mountains, and on 20
October 1935 reached Wuch'ichen where Mao met for the first
time the commander of the 15th Red Army Corps, Hsü Hai-tung.
'Is this Comrade Hai-tung?' Mao inquired, 'Thank you for taking
so much touble to come here to meet us.'[52] Then in the happiness
of the moment both men became silent. For Mao the trials of the
Long March were over.

But for Ho Lung, Hsiao K'e, Jen Pi-shih, and Wang Chen and
the 2nd Front Army the journey was only about to begin. On 19
November 1935 they broke through the encirclement from Sangchih and attacked several towns in central Hunan, partly to divert
the enemy troops thither so that their intended route of evacuation
would be cleared of obstructions, and partly to 'gather' some money
for the long trek.[53] These objectives achieved, they dashed towards
Kweichow border with great speed, feasted on chicken and pork
there on the New Year's Day of 1936, and then embarked on a
hit-and-run campaign across the province of Kweichow from east
to west for two months. By the end of April they were safely in
Sikang, having crossed the Gold Sand River at a point where it
bends like a horse-shoe. Their objective was clearly Chang Kuo-
t'ao's soviet in north-east Sikang.[54]

Returning from the Grassland to Maoerhkai, Chang Kuo-t'ao,
with the acquiescence of Chu Te and Liu Po-ch'eng, established
the 'Special Independent Government of the Minorities' in
K'angting in October 1935.[55] Early in 1936 the Szechwan armies
and the Central Government troops led by Hsüeh Yüeh launched
two relentless assaults on this soviet and succeeded in dislodging
Chang's troops from K'angting. In March, Chang and the 4th
Front Army had to flee from Tanpa to Kantzu, but the country,
being so poor, was quite unable to sustain the heavy burden of
feeding such a large army. By hook or by crook the political com-

51. [190] 74 and [249] 12.   52. Hsü's own account, see [249] 233.
53. [249] 264–5.   54. [249] 263–70. See also [190] 139–40.
55. [190] 231 and [249] 12. Agnes Smedley writes ([189] 332): 'General Chu
Teh never talked with me about the year he spent in Sikang as the virtual
prisoner of Chang Kuo-t'ao.'

missar of the 32nd Army, Li Hsien-nien, managed to conclude a 'trade pact' with the Tibetans and solved to some extent the dire problem of food.[56] In mid-May the 32nd Army drove south to defeat two KMT regiments and thus pave the way for Ho Lung's 35,000 men. Soon the junction of the two front armies took place and the leaders dined, not on butter and millet (the staple diet of Sikang), but on such delicacies as seaslugs and shark's fins recently captured from the KMT regiments.[57] It was at the urging of Ho Lung, Hsiao K'e, Jen Pi-shih, Chu Te, and others that Chang Kuo-t'ao, for the third time, crossed the Grassland together with the 2nd Front Army,[58] but this time it took them forty days during June and July to complete the crossing. When they re-emerged in south Kansu in August, the 1st Front Army sent Nieh Jung-chen and Tso Ch'üan with eight divisions to clear the way for them. At Lint'an Chang and Ho Lung decided to part, with Chang now following a shorter route through T'ungwei and Chingning to Huining and fighting all the way against Hu Tsung-nan's troops, while Ho made a detour along the Kansu-Shensi border in order to distract Hu Tsung-nan's attention, and then turned back to Huining.[59] Meanwhile Nieh Jung-chen and Tso Ch'üan thrust westward also to Huining, taking an American physician, Dr. George Hatem with them.[60] On 8 October 1936 the column led by Chu Te and Chang Kuo-t'ao met Nieh and Tso at Huining and Dr. Hatem recorded:

What a reunion! Men threw their arms around each other, laughing and weeping at the same time, or walking arm-in-arm and pouring out questions about other comrades. Chu Teh was completely swallowed up [in the crowd].

Hatem also noticed that while Chu was 'thin as a ghost', Chang Kuo-t'ao 'is fat, tall and smooth. I wonder how he kept so fat while others lost every ounce of excess weight?'[61] His curiosity could be due to his observations as a physician or his preconceived ideas about Chang Kuo-t'ao. On the 19th and 20th, the column led by Ho Lung and Hsiao K'e arrived, thus bringing the two years' migration to its end.[62] Chang, however, resolved to march on, per-

56. [249] 395.   57. [249] 395.
58. [189] 331–2 and [249] 12–13.   59. [249] 12–13.
60. [189] 344.   61. [189] 344.   62. [189] 344.

haps to prove the practicability of his policy of establishing a soviet in the far north-west and making contact with the Soviet Union, and ordered the 5th Army Corps under Tung Chen-t'ang, the 9th Army Corps under Lo Ping-hui, and the 30th Army under Hsü Hsiang-ch'ien to cross the Yellow River at Chingyüan. Chang crossed the river with them, but later returned to Shensi before the end of the year to appear at his trial on New Year's Day.[63] What followed the crossing was a series of heavy defeats at the hands of Hu Tsung-nan's and the Muslim general, Ma Pu-fang's brigades, first at Kulang, then at Kaot'aich'eng, and finally at Liyüank'ou, before the communists sought protection among the mountains of the Ch'ilien Range. The 5th Army Corps was almost completely wiped out and its commander, Tung Chen-t'ang, was killed in action; the 9th Army Corps also lost heavily. The 30th Army now had about 1,000 men left while the 9th Army Corps had only a pitiful 500. It was not until 1 May 1937 that they met the party representatives, Ch'en Yün and T'eng Tai-yüan, at Hsingh-singhsia on the Kansu-Sinkiang border and were taken to north Shensi in lorries.[64]

The Long March did not seem to have affected Mao's habit of working till late hours at night,[65] though he could not have afforded himself the luxury of lying in bed in the morning as he did in Yenan. Since his election to the chairmanship of the Provisional Soviet Government in November 1931, he had been called, instead of 'Commissioner Mao' (Mao *Wei-yüan*), 'Chairman Mao' (Mao *Chu-hsi*), and the title of 'Chairman' acquired a new meaning after the Tsunyi Conference.[66] Although he had at his disposal a dun-coloured horse which he had captured from the enemy in December 1928, he walked most of the way during the March.[67] He was seen wearing an octagonal cap and a grey cloth tunic.[68] Now, at forty-three years of age, he was 'a gaunt, rather Lincolnesque figure, above average height for a Chinese, somewhat stooping, with a head of thick black hair grown very long, and with large searching eyes, a high-bridged nose and prominent cheek-bones', as well as a black mole under his lower lip. He carried a prize of 250,000 *yuan* (about £17,000) on his head.[69] The hardships and

63. [189] 347.   64. [13] 138 and [249] 437–41.   65. [249] 214–16.
66. [249] 215.   67. [258] 87.   68. [249] 385.   69. [258] 80.

hazards of the journey did not seem to have dulled his wits or his poetic inspirations, as he had composed seven poems in one year. Never before or since has he written so many in so short a period of time. And what is more noteworthy was that the first of the seven was composed a few days after the triumphant Tsunyi Conference.

His wife, Ho Tzu-chen, however, had a trying time during the year of the Long March. She gave birth to a child as well as suffering more than a dozen wounds caused by the splinters from a bomb.[70] In 1937 she bore another child, a girl, and soon afterwards she was sent to Russia for medical treatment.[71] Of Mao's brothers, Tse-min arrived at Shensi and Tse-t'an, as mentioned before, died in March 1935 when Ch'ü Ch'iu-pai was captured.[72]

Most of the communist leaders who took part in the Long March arrived at Shensi safe and sound. Chou En-lai, for example, who was elected the deputy chairman of the Central Committee at the Tsunyi Conference, suffered no more than one spell of illness during the crossing of the Grassland.[73] K'ang K'e-ch'ing, Chu Te's wife, distinguished herself as a tough member of her sex, who carried her own rifle and knapsack and once or twice even carried a wounded soldier on her back.[74] Many new leaders rose during the journey, notably Jen Pi-shih, Ch'en Keng, Tso Ch'üan, Liu Po-ch'eng, and Hsü Hai-tung. Chief among the political casualties were Ch'in Pang-hsien and Chang Kuo-t'ao, Mao's chief opponents, the latter of whom was put on trial in January 1937 and ordered to study until he had rectified his mistakes.[75] Later in April 1937 at the Yenan Conference of the Politburo in which Chang himself took part, the Chang Kuo-t'ao line was criticized in detail and still later, in 1938, Chang went over to the KMT.[76]

The end of the Ch'in Pang-hsien line and the collapse of Chang Kuo-t'ao's opposition to Mao enabled the CCP to achieve a measure of unity never before known. But the party and the Red Army also suffered tremendous losses during the March. At the beginning of the fifth Encirclement Campaign there were at least

70. [50] 143 and [258] 82. For unaccountable reasons, she is called Ho Tzu-nien in Snow's book. 71. [41] 249.

72. [41] 247.   73. [249] 173.   74. [190] 211.

75. [189] 347.   76. [46] LI, 524 n. 4 or SW II, 293 n. 4.

five major soviet bases but these were reduced to only one at the end of the Long March,[77] when the total membership of the party did not exceed 40,000 and the labour and peasant movements, except for those in north Shensi, were practically dead.[78] Upon arrival at Wuch'ichen, the column Mao commanded numbered about 8,000. This and the 15th Army Corps in north Shensi, and the columns led by Chu Te and Ho Lung made up a total strength of 30,000 officers and men,[79] compared with 300,000 a year earlier.[80] Of the 1st Front Army, only the 1st Army Corps under Lin Piao and the 3rd under P'eng Te-huai had any considerable strength left, while that of the 5th and the 9th had been squandered by Chang Kuo-t'ao in Kansu and Sinkiang; of the 4th Front Army, only about 1,000 men had survived; of the 2nd Front Army some 10,000 were left. The disappearance of the 4th Front Army was of course the most significant, being mainly responsible for the down-fall of Chang Kuo-t'ao. Another significant point was the link between the Red Army in 1936 and the formation of the 8th Route Army in 1937. The remnants of the 1st Front Army were used to form the 115th Division under Lin Piao and Nieh Jung-chen; those of the 2nd Front Army became the 120th Division under Ho Lung and Hsiao K'e; and what was left of the 4th Front Army, together with the 15th Army Corps, was denominated the 129th Division under Liu Po-ch'eng and Hsü Hsiang-ch'ien.[81] The guerrilla forces left behind in central China at the beginning of the Long March were to be assembled together in 1938 and re-organized into the New Fourth Army.

Summing up the Long March, Mao said on 27 December 1935:

We say that the Long March is the first of its kind ever recorded in history, that it is a manifesto, an agitation corps, and a seeding-machine. . . . For twelve months we were under daily reconnaissance and bombing from the air by scores of planes; we were encircled, pursued, obstructed and intercepted on the ground by a big force of several hundred thousand men; we encountered untold difficulties and great obstacles on the way, but by keeping our two feet going we swept across a distance of more than 20,000 *li* through the length and breadth of

77. The major soviets were the central, the Oyüwan, the west Hupei-Hunan, the Hunan-Kiangsi, and the north Shensi.
78. [181] 92.   79. [179] 30 (the Chinese edition), [181] 92, [249] 10–11.
80. [179] 30 and [181] 92.   81. [185] 115.

eleven provinces. Well, has there ever been in history a long march like ours? No, never. The Long March is also a manifesto. It proclaims to the world that the Red Army is an army of heroes and that the imperialists and their jackals, Chiang Kai-shek and his like, are perfect nonentities. It announces the bankruptcy of the encirclement, pursuit, obstruction and interception attempted by the imperialists and Chiang Kai-shek. The Long March is also an agitation corps. It declares to the approximately two hundred million people of eleven provinces that only the road of the Red Army leads to their liberation. Without the Long March, how could the broad masses have known so quickly that there are such great ideas in the world as are upheld by the Red Army? The Long March is also a seeding-machine. It has sown many seeds in eleven provinces, which will sprout, grow leaves, blossom into flowers, bear fruit and yield a crop in future. To sum up, the Long March ended with our victory and the enemy's defeat.

Earlier in the same speech, Mao also said:

... the Red Army has failed in one respect (in preserving its original bases), but has achieved victory in another respect (in fulfilling the plan of the Long March). The enemy, on the other hand, has won victory in one respect (in occupying our original bases), but has failed in another respect (in realising his plan of 'encirclement and annihilation' and of 'pursuit and annihilation'). Only this statement is correct— that we have in fact completed the Long March.[82]

82. [46] I, 144–5 or *SW* I, 161–2. It may be of interest to compare the Long March with Shih Ta-k'ai's expedition from 1857 to 1863. The latter not only lasted a longer period, but also covered nearly twice the distance.

Chapter X

The Second United Front

THE idea of a withdrawal to the north-west so as to set various military factions of the country in motion and to set up a Red base in the vicinity of the Soviet Union was mooted by M. Borodin and Ch'en Tu-hsiu at the fifth congress of the CCP in 1927,[1] but was rejected. No one brought it up again until seven years had elapsed and the attempts to penetrate Szechwan were thwarted in March 1935.

The period at north Shensi was preceded by a mystery. A month before Mao arrived there, the 25th Red Army under Hsü Hai-tung, having roamed from west Anhwei to south Shensi,[2] came into contact with Liu Chih-tan's 26th and 27th Armies through Liu's brother and the secretary of a local party branch by the name of Hsi Chung-hsün.[3] The union of the three armies took place on 18 September, resulting in the formation of the 15th Army Corps with Hsü as the commander and Liu as deputy commander.[4] This is Hsü's own account. However, according to Mao, in the autumn of 1935 one Chu Li-chih, claiming to be a representative of the party centre, arrived at the north Shensi soviet and in league with the leftists, imprisoned both Liu Chih-tan and Kao Kang who did not regain their freedom until November.[5] When talking to Edgar Snow in 1936 Mao gave another version of the same story. He named one Chang Ching-fu as the culprit who gaoled Liu and Kao in August.[6] Someone's memory has played a

1. [212] 549 n. 2 and [202] 233.　　2. [187] 18.
3. [247] III, 168–80. Hsi is now a member of the Central Committee.
4. [247] III, 175–6. See also [46] I, 160–1 n. 24 (*SW* I, 357 n. 26 being very different), [185] 96, [189] 341, and [190] 75.
5. [46] I, 160–1 n. 24.　　　　6. [258] 214–15.

trick here. But Mao also reported that the KMT troops began an onslaught on the north Shensi soviet in July and in September the newly formed 15th Army Corps, about 7,000 strong, defeated the 107th and 110th Divisions of Chang Hsüeh-liang's Manchurian Army.[7] The second wave of attack of the Manchurian troops coincided with the arrival of Mao's column which, in a combined effort, drove off the 106th and 109th Divisions in November, thus putting an end to the attack.[8]

The unfortunate Liu Chih-tan, who, if he had been imprisoned at all, may well have been freed by Hsü Hai-tung, now led a contingent of troops to invade Shansi in February 1936. Caught unprepared, the perennial governor of the province, Yen Hsi-shan, was glad to accept Chiang Kai-shek's offer of help in the form of the 2nd and 25th Divisions under Ch'en Ch'eng, which defeated the communists and killed Liu in a battle near Shihhsien.[9] A result of this episode, as of the communist invasion in Szechwan, Kweichow, Yunnan, and Kansu, was the extension of Chiang's authority into a province hitherto ruled by warlords. Another result was the stepping up of the KMT attack on the north Shensi soviet.

Chang Hsüeh-liang's Manchurian troops and Yang Hu-ch'eng's Shensi troops launched another offensive in March which grew in intensity in April,[10] only to be sadly defeated again by the communists. Many prisoners were taken and indoctrinated by the Red Army before being released. These nostalgic Manchurians, having lost their homes in 1931, were particularly susceptible to such propaganda slogans as 'Form an anti-Japanese united front', and 'Fight back to Manchuria'. Therefore when they went back to their own camp they said that the communists were patriotic, wanting to fight the Japanese like themselves, and they thus influenced their officers and men, in particular the commander of the 67th Army, Wang Yi-che. Chou En-lai, at the same time, wrote to Chang Hsüeh-liang, proposing the cessation of hostilities between their armies. Soon contacts were made between them and also between Chou and Yang Hu-ch'eng. Chang went even as far as to invite Yeh Chien-ying, a communist strategist, to Sian where Chang's headquarters were situated, to discuss ways and means of

7. [46] I, 160–1 n. 24.   8. *ibid.*
9. [181] 96.   10. [181] 97.

improving the fighting qualities of the Manchurian troops.[11] These negotiations led to the issue of a decree by Mao to halt all offensives against the Manchurian units from October 1936.[12]

In spite of these developments, the Manchurian troops were ordered by Chiang to make another concerted attack with Hu Tsung-nan's forces in the winter of 1936. In fact, only Hu's units were fighting and were defeated, while the Manchurians merely feinted and watched. Wang Yi-che, for example, was ordered by Chiang to take Wayaopao, the Red capital, and instead of taking it by force, exchanged Yenan for it with his opponents. The Red Army moved into Yenan in December and made it the capital in January 1937. Thus began the well-known Yenan period.[13]

At the height of the latter campaign the history of China entered into a new phase; Chiang Kai-shek was kidnapped by Chang Hsüeh-liang at Sian. Thereafter the KMT and CCP agreed on a truce between them. Through the war and peace, however, the north Shensi soviet expanded from its original six counties in 1935[14] to twenty-three on 6 September 1937 when the Shensi-Kansu-Ninghsia Border Region was established.[15] Its population remained more or less stationary at the level of 1,500,000 throughout the years of the Resistance and the ensuing civil war[16] and, as expected, 90 per cent. of it was peasants.[17] The products on which the livelihood of the inhabitants depended included cotton, grain, livestock, salt, kerosene, coal, and iron.[18] The last named seems to have been of particular importance during the war years, since after 1940 when the old city of Yenan (Fushih), having been badly damaged by Japanese bombing, was abandoned and the new city was built in a somewhat slipshod way, there were as many as fifty blacksmiths' forges among a total of 300 shops in the city.[19]

In the winter of 1939 there was another KMT attack which took five counties from the Border Region[20] and afterwards a ring of

---

11. [181] 98 and [258] 33–4.   12. [189] 345.

13. [162] 239, [181] 98, [189] 345 and 347, [190] 75, and [258] 34 and 407.

14. They were Yench'uan, Ansai, Yench'ang, Paoan, Anting, and Chingpien. See [289] 6.

15. [289] 7.   16. [289] 8 and [318] 194.   17. [318] 194.

18. [289] 8.   19. [273] 56.

20. [46] II, 714 n. 8 or *SW* III, 257, which has no corresponding translation of this footnote.

blockhouses was erected and some 200,000 of Chiang's best troops were stationed round the Region.[21] Opposing this awe-inspiring KMT force was an army of garrison troops under Ho Lung in 1943, which was later replaced by the 359th Brigade under Wang Chen,[22] together with militia units. The blockade of the Border Region from 1939 onward tended to make the communists more 'self-reliant and self-sufficient'[23] and also resulted in a loss of understanding between them and the people in other parts of China. 'Without mutual understanding, there could not be mutual trust, hence there was less frankness one to the other.'[24]

Under the guiding hands of Lin Tsu-han and Mao Tse-min,[25] the economy of the Border Region went from strength to strength,[26] owing mainly to a more moderate land policy. The earlier indiscriminate confiscation, which had either driven away the land-owners or forced them to lay waste their holdings in order to avoid the opprobrious name of a 'landlord', was drastically modified to a restriction on rent. All rates of rent were reduced in 1937 by 25 to 40 per cent. so that in no case did they exceed one-third of the yield of the land. In addition to this, the government also took steps to ensure the renewal of tenancy unless there was a transfer of ownership through purchase, mortgage, gift, or inheritance. On the other hand, the government guaranteed that all landowners would be able to collect their rents in full according to the terms of the contracts. By these new measures, landowners were transformed into rich peasants who worked as well as collected rent for their maintenance, and rural labourers into tenants with small pieces of land to cultivate. For those who had either lost and now regained their land or never had any before, these arrangements stimulated zeal for work and led to an agricultural revival.[27] Furthermore, the government encouraged people to reclaim waste land by granting exemption from the grain tax for the first three years. The blockade since 1939 served to stimulate the government

---

21. [46] II, 776 n. 3 or *SW* III, 258 n. 3.
22. [273] 230–1 and [282] 73–4.   23. [269] 189.
24. [273] 52 and 57.
25. Lin was the chairman of the government and Mao Tse-min in charge of finance until 1938. See [43] 181 n. 22 and [247] X, 122–55.
26. See Appendix D.
27. [273] 190–2. See also [162] 275, [181] 94, and [318] 8–9 and 12.

and people to work even harder so that by 1941 the Border Region had achieved self-sufficiency in food supply.[28] However, the blockade also caused a serious shortage in cotton goods and industrial products. According to Mao Tse-tung's estimates, the people in the Border Region needed some 3 million catties of raw cotton each year, and, under the assumption of 20 catties from each *mou* (1/6 of an acre) of land, a total of 150,000 to 200,000 *mou* of cotton fields must be required for self-sufficiency in cotton.[29] This was not attained until 1943 or 1944. In the meantime the government relied on the export of salt and kerosene to meet the demands of the people living in areas adjacent to the Region,[30] either through the State Trading Bureau or private merchants.[31] In 1941 the KMT blockade of the Border Region went a step farther by suspending the grant-in-aid to its government, which at once threw the public finances of the Region into chaos. Before effective measures to offset this could be taken, the government had to rely on borrowing from the Bank of the Border Region which, in turn, issued irredeemable notes to finance public enterprises as well as to keep the government afloat.[32] The result of this was rapidly worsening inflation as shown in the rates of exchange between the *pienpi* (Border Region currency) and the *fapi* (the government currency). In February 1944 the *pienpi* dived to the low level of 11 to 1 *fapi*, but this rate slightly improved in June when it stood at 8·5 to 1.[33] The inflation, however, helped to discourage the exportation and encouraged the importation of goods, thus making supplies more plentiful. But, on balance, it was harmful to the economy. In order to combat its undesirable results the government resorted to two important measures: taxation in kind and the attainment of economic self-sufficiency by government bodies, party branches, and military units. The former was a progressive

28. The total food consumption was estimated at 1,620,000 piculs and the total production of grain reached 1,630,000 piculs in 1941. See Appendix D and [282] 83.   29. [318] 33.
30. [282] 24 and [296] 146.   31. [258] 235 and [296] 147.
32. [273] 74 and [296] 156–7. See also [318] 123–4. G. Stein's economic figures should be used with care, for the author is not a trained economist. For instance, he could say that the total issue of the *pienpi* up to May 1944 was 1,600,000 *yuan* while the budget of the Border Region government amounted to 7,800,000,000 *yuan*! See [296] 157 and 167.
33. [273] 74 and [296] 158.

tax, ranging from 3 to 35 per cent. of the payer's income[34]; the latter was the famous production drive.

The system whereby soldiers took part in farming and other productive activities had been used many times before and was known as the garrison field system (*t'un-t'ien*). It had had notable success in the past and the communists' production drive was a modern, more elaborate version of it. The Red officials and soldiers not only ran co-operatives, planted vegetables and cereals by opening up hitherto unused land, kept pigs and sheep, made bean-curd, and grew bean-sprouts, but also darned socks, made shoes, and knitted jerseys and gloves. By 1943, in addition to better food and clothing for those who participated in this campaign, the government's budget assumed an unwontedly healthy outlook.[35] Here are some figures:

Revenue	per cent.	Expenditure	per cent.
Productive enterprises		Defence	45
of the government and		Administration	17
the army	62	Education	15
Taxes	20	Health	6
Loans	18	Others	17

And, in 1944, the government ceased to have to depend on borrowing any longer. The inflation was checked.[36]

There were no modern industries in north Shensi when the communist armies arrived, but the sewing-machines, lithographic printing blocks, and lathes they brought with them gave this rural area a modest industrial beginning. A repair shop and a tailoring workshop were immediately set up with a staff of about 100.[37] During the years of the blockade new industries were developed and old ones continued to grow up to 1944 when there were about 90 workshops employing some 20,000 men. None the less, the Border Region remained industrially backward and far from being self-sufficient.[38]

During the production drive some became 'labour heroes', such

34. [273] 217.
35. [273] 214–15, [289] 16–17, [296] 165, and [318] 119–23.
36. [296] 165.   37. [289] 15 and [282] 78.
38. [273] 210 and 216 and [318] 109–10. See also [258] 254–5.

as General Wang Chen and his brigade,[39] and one Wu Man-yu earned the honour of shaking hands with Chairman Mao and drinking with General Chu Te—in his own words, 'We bumpkins are being praised to high heaven!'[40] But others embezzled funds or fiddled their statistics.[41] On the whole, however, the material life of the ordinary folk was quite happy. For a ten-hour day of work a man could get nearly one and half pounds of rice and his meat ration came to two pounds a month. If he was a technician, a soldier, or a leading cadre, his reward was even more.[42] Consequently he looked 'ruddier and healthier' than those who lived in other parts of China.[43] Apart from work, there were many meetings for him to attend—meetings of the poor people's society, of the anti-Japanese society, of the peasant society, and of the young vanguards,[44] leaving very little time for jokes and gossip.[45] There was almost no time for love. Yenan was 'sexless', although most of its inhabitants were young. The soldiers were either married and living apart from their wives or unmarried and did not seem to have the slightest urge to find female companionship. Rape or the insult of peasant women by them was virtually unheard of.[46] The intellectuals had a unanimously agreed ideal of love—an ideal lover should be a model *worker* in his or her chosen field, other considerations being of secondary importance. Marriage itself was made much simpler; so was divorce. All that was needed for either was registration, except for the stipulation that no woman could be divorced when she was pregnant. Legitimacy applied only to sexual relationship, not to any child which, if 'illegitimate', was to be brought up by the father. Women intellectuals dressed like men and when asked why they dressed in this way, their terse reply was: 'Why should we look like women?'[47]

After ten years of the communist rule, there were still over one million illiterates, about two-thirds of the total population, and two thousand Shamans.[48] The primary schools, which numbered 752

39. [273] 199 and [318] 127 and 129–65.
40. [273] 208–9 and [318] 195–200.
41. G. Stein says that there was no embezzlement ([296] 109), but Mao disagrees with him ([318] 202–3 and 213).
42. [273] 76.   43. [269] 213.   44. [258] 224 and [296] 107.
45. [273] 83.   46. [273] 56, 77–8, 90, and 169–70 and [258] 268.
47. [273] 90.
48. [46] III, 1031 or *SW* IV, 225.

with an enrolment of over 3,000 at the end of 1945, taught the
children to write letters and keep accounts while the middle
schools, which numbered only six with an enrolment of 200, concentrated on the training of teachers and government officials.
Only 19 per cent. of the students of middle schools went to the
University of Yenan which in 1944 had an enrolment of 1,300. At
the University a student was expected to follow his own course of
studies and to take part in discussions under a tutor rather than to
attend classes. All the subjects aiming at the refinement of sentiments and tastes were labelled 'bourgeois' and all theoretical
studies were treated with disdain. From elementary to higher
education the emphasis was on practical usefulness.[49] With regard
to extra-mural reading, there were the *Liberation Weekly*, inaugurated in 1937 but changed into a daily in 1941,[50] the *Masses Weekly*
and others, all run by either the government or the party, hence
there was no need of a formal censorship.[51] The paper shortage
which Edgar Snow noticed in 1936 had become a thing of the past
when Robert Payne visited Yenan in 1946.[52]

The nucleus of the life in the Border Region was, of course, the
party—an expanding, united, and well-led party whose members
were the cadres in every aspect of social life. In Mao's own words,
'the success or failure of a work is, apart from the correctness of
the policy, determined by the efficiency of the cadres'.[53] But the
correctness of a policy depended to a great extent on the sagacity
of the leaders. Supreme among them was Mao Tse-tung.

Mao continued to work during the night and rest during the
day.[54] He was a man of extraordinary energy. On 16 July 1936 he
discussed the strategy of the Resistance War with Edgar Snow, who
recorded:

It was past 2 o'clock in the morning and I was exhausted, but I could
see no sign of fatigue on Mao's pale, somewhat jaundiced-looking
face.[55]

49. [273] 79–80, 149–51, and 158–9.
50. [46] II, 390 n. 8 or *SW* II, 288 n. 8, [269] 219, [296] 181 and 183, [273]
138 and 164.
51. [273] 138.   52. [258] 275 and [293] 54–5.   53. [318] 210.
54. [28] 9 and [258] 274.
55. [258] 106.

Eight years later, at the end of an interview from 3 p.m. to 3 a.m., Gunther Stein wrote:

At 3 in the morning, when I finally got up to go, with a bad conscience, aching limbs, and burning eyes, he [Mao] was still as fresh and animated and systematic in his talk as in the afternoon.[56]

Snow heard in 1936 that Mao usually worked '13 or 14 hours a day, often until very late at night, frequently retiring at 2 or 3. He seems to have an iron constitution.'[57] Mao's bodyguard, Chai Tso-chün, tells how the famous essay *On the Protracted War* was written in 1938. For the first two days Mao did not sleep at all, working continuously by the light of a pair of candles and sometimes forgetting his meals. When he was tired he freshened himself up with a hot face-flannel. On the fifth day he was visibly thinner, ate even less, and his eyes were blood-shot, yet he went on writing. On the seventh day he was so engrossed in his work that he did not notice that the fire was burning a hole in his right shoe until his toes felt the pain. He jumped up and burst into laughter while he and his bodyguard looked at his exposed toes. 'How did this happen?' he asked, and then drank some wine and resumed his work. It was not surprising that he had a headache on the eighth day and was unable to eat or sleep. The doctor was sent for and he correctly diagnosed fatigue as the cause of Mao's indisposition. However, the patient went on working until the ninth day when the essay was completed. He checked it through before passing it on to Liu Shao-ch'i, Ch'en Yün, K'ang Sheng, and Chang Wen-t'ien for their criticisms.[58]

He also read like a glutton. Snow recorded:

Once, when I was having nightly interviews with him on Communist history, a visitor brought him several new books on philosophy and Mao asked me to postpone our engagement. He consumed these books in three or four nights of intensive reading during which he seemed oblivious of everything else.[59]

Reading, a habit often acquired in one's youth as in Mao's case, made him well-informed, particularly so in his profound knowledge of China.[60] His deftness in synthesis and sharpness in criti-

56. [296] 83.   57. [258] 86.   58. [28] 10–17.
59. [258] 85–6.   60. [258] 84–5 and [269] 215.

cism were attributed to his knowledge of history,[61] but Mao himself seemed to think that 'knowledge starts with practice, reaches the theoretical plane via practice, and then has to return to practice'. For him, knowledge is valuable not when it is merely rational but when it has leapt from rational theories into revolutionary practice.[62] Therefore Gunther Stein was impressed by the logic of his arguments which 'stood out forcefully against the background of the social and political life I watched every day during my five months in the Border Region'.[63]

His own life in the Border Region was plain and simple. At Paoan in 1935 and 1936 he lived in a cave and slept in a brick-bed which had to be warmed with wood or hay underneath it in the winter months.[64] In 1937 he moved to the northern outskirts of Yenan, still living in a cave which had, to begin with, three chambers; later an additional one was dug. The cave was whitewashed, sparsely furnished with a rickety chair, a low sofa with bad springs, and a shaky miniature table, and was surrounded by an orchard of date-trees.[65] The additional chamber may have been made for his fourth wife, a film actress by the name of Lan-p'ing or better known as Comrade Chiang Ch'ing among the communists,[66] whom Mao married probably in 1939 during Ho Tzu-chen's sojourn in Moscow. Mao's brother Tse-min was with him until 1938 when he went to work in Sinkiang as the head of the finance department. After a transfer to the civilian department, Mao Tse-min was arrested in September 1942 and put to death in 1943 by the governor of Sinkiang.[67]

Since his youth, Mao had never paid much attention to his clothes. The only change was that as a student he wore a black, baggy cotton uniform and now as the Chairman of the Politburo of the CCP he wore a grey, baggy cotton uniform.[68] His food, rice and wild vegetables in 1936 and rice, two dishes, and a soup in 1938, was roughly the same as everybody else's, except that being

61. [273] 66.   62. [46] I, 281 or *SW* I, 292–3.   63. [296] 83.
64. [28] 18–19.   65. [28] 5 and [296] 82.
66. [28] 37–8 and [296] 178.

67. He and Ch'en T'an-ch'iu died at the same time. See [43] 181 n. 22, [247] X, 155, and Chang Tzu-i, 'Tao-nien Li Ho t'ung-chih' (In memoriam of Comrade Li Ho), the *People's Daily*, 17.8.1962.

68. [28] 6 and 18, [258] 84, and [296] 67.

a Hunanese, he was very fond of pepper.[69] He was a chain-smoker, sucking in the smoke with a strange noise quite unpleasant to those who heard it. Perhaps because of this habit of chain-smoking, his teeth were almost completely black, like those of a betel-nut chewing Annamite.[70] Once, on a hot summer's day, he shocked Snow by taking off his trousers in the presence of Lin Piao and Snow, and then 'for 20 minutes carefully studied a military map on the wall'.[71] Retailing this story, Robert Payne added the word 'altogether' after 'taking off his trousers', thus depicting the Chairman as standing in his birthday suit at the age of forty-three.[72] And it is perhaps because of this Mao has been called a 'Red barbarian'. One speaks German while in Germany or does what the Chinese do while in China. It is nothing shocking to take off one's long pants while keeping one's shorter on, even in the presence of other Chinese men. It can be said with certainty that Lin Piao did not share Snow's astonishment, nor would Snow agree with Payne's addition of the word 'altogether'. The Chairman did not stand there studying a map with *nothing* on.

However, these personal habits and idiosyncrasies tend to show that Mao was an informal man. He was often seen moving among crowds of people[73] and no ritual of hero-worship was yet built up around him in 1936.[74] He appeared to be quite free from symptoms of megalomania.[75] Even in 1944 or earlier, when he had become idolized, he was still quite approachable. His portraits were to be seen everywhere and scrolls of his calligraphy were hung in factories and schools. The number of copies of his photographs sold at bookshops in the Border Region was three or four times that of all the other famous people put together.[76] His words, even when intended only as a basis for discussion for the party leaders, were treated as infallible, unquestionable truth among the lower echelons of the party, government, and army.[77] The personality cult of Mao Tse-tung began probably after the sixth plenum of the

---

69. [28] 18–19 and [258] 84.
70. A friend who had met Mao told me this. About his cigarette smoking, see [258] 81 and [296] 82.
71. [258] 87.   72. [293] 84.
73. [28] 7 and [258] 114.   74. [258] 83.
75. [258] 84.
76. [258] 84.   77. [273] 64 and [296] 177.

sixth Central Committee in October 1938 when he had finally smashed Wang Ming's opposition to his united front tactics.[78]

Mao impressed his visitors as honest and sincere, even forthright in his dealings with other people. Edgar Snow observed in him a man of considerable depth of feeling:

I remember that his eyes moistened once or twice when speaking of dead comrades, or recalling incidents in his youth. . . . One soldier told me of seeing Mao give his coat away to a wounded man at the front.[79]

This is corroborated by the lamentations in his poems *Ch'angsha* and *the Immortals* dedicated to the memories of his deceased wife, Yang K'ai-hui, and his old friends like Ts'ai Ho-sen, Ch'en Ch'ang, Chang K'un-ti, and Liu Chih-hsün. His elegant prose is often sprinkled with wit and humour and occasionally betrays a streak of ruthlessness. For instance, he wrote in 1927:

. . . a revolution is not the same as inviting people to dinner, or writing an essay, or painting a picture, or doing fancy needlework; it cannot be anything so refined, so calm and gentle, or so mild, kind, courteous, restrained and magnanimous. A revolution is an uprising, an act of violence whereby one class overthrows another.[80]

The calm of his mind shown through his political and philosophical dissertations and military orders is reminiscent of the way he handled his quick-tempered teacher of the classics, the bearded Mr. Yüan.[81] Edgar Snow writes:

I never saw him angry, but I heard from others that on occasions he has been seen roused to an intense and withering fury. At such times his command of irony and invective is said to be classic and lethal.[82]

But a man can only be lethal in his use of irony while he still retains a measure of coolness of mind. Being a politician, Mao was not incapable of parading his humility. The burnt right shoe we have just mentioned, for instance, was beyond repair, yet Mao insisted that it must be mended. One day he saw his bodyguards eating millet and asked: 'That's fine. Why am I not given the same?' Afterwards he instructed his cook to serve him with millet instead of rice.[83]

Under this learned, resolute, experienced, ruthless, and sensitive

78. [46] II, 526 or *SW* II, 262.   79. [258] 87.
80. [46] I, 18 or *SW* I, 27.   81. *Vide supra*, p. 41.
82. [258] 84.   83. [28] 19 and 22–3.

man, the CCP attained unity, strength, and eventually complete victory. No one else in the entire communist movement in China can claim a greater share of the merit for this success; no other of Mao's policies were more responsible for this success than that of the second united front in the context of the Resistance War.

Coming immediately after the five Encirclement Campaigns and the Long March, the decision to establish yet another united front with the KMT was not taken without misgivings among the members of the CCP. So, at the Wayaopao plenum of the Politburo in December 1935 Mao had to win over his comrades to the idea.[84] Subsequently he summed up the new resolution and his own position in a report to the Activists Conference held on 27 December, and it was then he pointed out that the Japanese encroachments were converting the status of China from that of a semi-colony shared by several powers to that of a colony of Japan alone. As a consequence of this transformation, a line of division between those who advocated a war of resistance and those who preferred continued appeasement became evident, splitting 'the national bourgeoisie and its representative, the KMT', into two. The disagreements among various factions of the KMT, according to Mao, should be 'collected together' and forged into weapons against those who were opposed to the resistance.[85] Mao went on to point out that 'imperialism is still a force to be seriously reckoned with,' and, for the first time, that 'the unevenness in the development of the revolutionary forces is still a serious defect', and therefore 'to defeat our enemies we must be prepared to fight a protracted war'. 'The present situation demands that we boldly give up closed-door sectarianism, form a broad united front and curb adventurism. Before the time is ripe for a decisive battle, or before we have adequate strength for it, we must not rashly fight a full scale battle.'[86] This clearly was the continuation of the policy adopted at the Tsunyi Conference in January and the Maoerhkai Conference in July and August 1935—a policy which had the blessings of the Comintern.[87]

84. [46] I, 138 or *SW* I, 153.
85. [46] I, 137–44 or *SW* I, 153–60.
86. [46] I, 148 or *SW* I, 165.
87. [18] 299–300, [162] 239, and [181] 94–5. Speaking at the seventh congress of the Comintern on 2 August 1935, G. Dimitrov praised 'the initiative taken

But how was the protracted war to be conducted? Edgar Snow put this question to Mao on 16 July 1936, and he answered it in a telling manner. The war, Mao assumed, would be fought on Chinese territory with the Japanese troops entirely surrounded by a hostile Chinese people.[88] The implication of this assumption was that large areas of China would have to be conceded to Japan in the initial stages of the war while Japan, being a small country, would not be able to spare enough personnel for an effective control of the occupied territories. This would create power vacuums behind the enemy lines, giving opportunities for the Chinese guerrillas to carry on mobile warfare against the Japanese. His strategy was 'that of a war of manoeuvre over an extended, shifting and indefinite front: a strategy depending for success on a high degree of mobility in difficult terrain, and featured by swift attack and withdrawal, swift concentration and dispersal. It will be a large-scale war of manoeuvre rather than the simple positional war of extensive trench-work, deep-massed lines and heavy fortifications.'[89] Although the fortified warfare was not completely denied its part in the campaign, pitched battles disputing one or two vital positions on a narrow front must be avoided in the early stages of the war. Gradually, when the guerrillas had gnawed away the enemy's morale and fighting spirit as well as his military efficiency, the time would be ripe for a counter-attack along the entire front and the protracted war of attrition would then be won.[90]

Snow is to be envied for being the first to record this historic exposition, but, at the same time, it is to be regretted that he missed the chance of asking other pertinent questions. How, for instance, should the command system be organized and whose would be the guiding hand in it? Assuming that the guerrillas operating behind the enemy lines were to enjoy a considerable degree of autonomy, how could strategic co-ordination be achieved? Of the KMT and the CCP military forces, which, in Mao's and other people's opinion, was the more proficient in guerrilla tactics? Who would be filling up the vacuums in the occupied terri-

by our courageous brother party of China in the creation of a most extensive anti-imperialism united front against Japanese imperialism and its Chinese agents'. See the *International Press Correspondence*, 20 August 1935, [190] 16, and [18] 298–9.   88. [258] 106.
    89. [258] 104.   90. [258] 105.

tories? When the time of the counter-offensive came, how should the operational duties be apportioned between the regular and the guerrilla forces? When the enemy was pushed back and the regulars and guerrillas came into contact, who was to have the power of control of the recovered territories? In case of disagreement arising between them, how should clashes be avoided? If disagreements could not be resolved, how much of China would be left under the KMT and how much under the CCP? As far as strategy was concerned, what would be in essence the difference between Mao's protracted war of resistance and a protracted war of revolution?

The answers to some of these questions can be found in Mao's later statements and writings. Concerning the command system and strategic co-ordination, he told James Bertram on 25 October 1937: 'The line of operation now adopted by the Eighth Route Army is, as we call it, guerrilla warfare and mobile warfare carried on *independently and on our own initiative*.'[91] Writing on 11 November in the same year, he said:

We have sponsored and resolutely carried out the new strategic principle of 'carrying on *independently and on our own initiative* a guerrilla warfare in the mountain regions', thus basically ensuring the Eighth Route Army's successes in fighting and in carrying out other tasks. *We have rejected the Kuomintang's request to appoint its members as cadres of the Eighth Route Army and have upheld the principle of the Communist Party's absolute leadership of the Eighth Route Army.*[92]

And a year later, on 5 November 1938, he devoted a lengthy part of his report at the sixth plenum of the sixth Central Committee to *The Question of Independence and Autonomy within the United Front* which said even more explicitly:

In the enemy's rear, we can only, in accordance with our agreement with the Kuomintang, do things *independently and on our own initiative*, and we have no means of getting 'everything through'. Or calculating what the Kuomintang would be likely to consent to, we can 'do things first and ask for approval afterwards'. . . . At present there are things for which we should secure the Kuomintang's approval beforehand, such as changing the designations of three divisions into those of three armies—this is asking for permission first and doing things afterwards. There are other things which we should first turn into accomplished

91. [46] II, 369 or *SW* II, 95–6. (My italics.)
92. [46] II, 383 or *SW* II, 111. (My italics.)

facts and then inform the Kuomintang, such as expanding our troops to more than 200,000 strong—this is doing things first and asking for approval afterwards. There are still other things, like convening the Border Region Assembly, which we, believing that the Kuomintang will not give consent to at present, shall for the moment do without asking for approval. But there are also other things which we will for the moment neither do nor ask for permission to do, *e.g.* things which, if done, would jeopardise the whole situation. In short, neither should we break the united front nor should we bind ourselves hand and foot; hence the slogan of 'everything through the united front' should not be put forward. . . . Our policy is for independence and autonomy within the united front, a policy which is at once for unity and independence.[93]

Bertram asked: 'Could the good points of the Eighth Route Army be acquired by the other Chinese armies?'—a question at once admitting the communists' proficiency in guerrilla tactics and doubting the KMT's ability to emulate it. Mao replied: 'Entirely so.'[94] But he did not proceed to substantiate his point beyond digressing on the history of the KMT Army. If the proficiency was inimitable, the vacuum behind the enemy lines could be filled only by the communists who, by the principle of independence and autonomy, would refuse to hand over the power over their occupied areas to the united front or to the KMT. Disagreements or clashes were bound to occur at a time when more than half of China, and the better half at that, would be under communist domination. Therefore Mao said: 'The line of operation [in the Resistance War] is, in essentials, the same as the line we adopted during the civil war. . . .'[95]

The short statement on the protracted war which Mao made to Snow was later developed into a systematic theory of mobile warfare in a series of essays, beginning with the *Strategic Problems of China's Revolutionary War* of December 1936, following up with the *Interview with James Bertram* in October 1937, the *Strategic Problems in the Anti-Japanese Guerrilla War* of May 1938, *On the Protracted War* also of May 1938, and ending with the *Problems of War and Strategy* of November 1938. In just over two years he had written 200 pages on strategy, 165 pages on political matters, and

93. [46] II, 527–8 or *SW* II, 265–6. (My italics.)
94. [46] II, 370 or *SW* II, 97.
95. [46] II, 369 or *SW* II, 96.

55 pages on philosophy—an indication of the centre of his attention at that period.

His original assumption of the Resistance being waged on Chinese territory now became the basis of his theory on the protracted war. Japan, he observed, was a powerful imperialist country with well-organized military, economic, and political systems; the war she pursued was one of imperialist aggression; she was deficient in manpower, in military and financial strength, and in material resources, and so was unable to sustain a protracted war; her objectives in the war, being aggressive in nature, were incapable of commanding world sympathy. China, on the other hand, was a weak, semi-colonial, and semi-feudal country; her national liberation movement of the last hundred years had made her people more politically conscious than ever before; she was a big country with a vast territory, rich resources, an enormous population, and huge military forces capable of sustaining a prolonged war; her just cause in the war would help her to win international support. The war was a contest between these characteristics.[96] In the initial stages, Japan, being the stronger, would win battles and advance, but, as the war wore on and as long as China made no mistakes in strategy, the position would alter until a decisive point was reached when China's growing strength became enough to tip the balance. Her retreat would then stop and the advance would begin. The war would therefore be a long one, passing probably through three stages—'the enemy's strategic offensive and our strategic defensive, the enemy's strategic defensive and our preparation for the counter-offensive, and our strategic counter-offensive and the enemy's strategic [sic] retreat.'[97] These changing positions could be brought about only by the preservation of China's own strength and the annihilation of that of Japan.[98]

From the very beginning when Japan was on the offensive and China was on the defensive until the coming of the final counter-offensive, the war was fought with the Japanese on the exterior line and the Chinese on the interior line. Even so, Mao laid down, China must not resort to 'pure defence'[99]; instead, she should take

96. [46] II, 437–8 or *SW* II, 167–8.
97. [46] I, 185 and II, 451–2 or *SW* I, 197 and II, 182–4.
98. [46] II, 397 or *SW* II, 121–2.   99. [46] II, 366 or *SW* II, 92.

tactical offensives in a strategically defensive war, wage swift campaigns in a protracted war, and fight battles on the exterior line within the strategic interior line.[1] Consequently she needed both guerrillas and the regular army—in other words, supplementary and main forces. Their relationship was discussed in Mao's celebrated essay, *On the Protracted War*:

It is the main forces that, relying upon the big rear of the country, extend their front to the very line which marks off the enemy's occupied areas. It is the guerrilla detachments that, separated from our big rear, extend the front into the enemy's rear. But in each guerrilla area, there is still a small rear for the guerrilla force upon which the establishment of fluid operational lines depends. Distinguished from these are guerrilla detachments dispatched from each guerrilla area which is also the enemy's rear, to engage in temporary activities; such guerrilla detachments have neither a rear nor operational lines. 'Operations without a rear' are a peculiar feature of the revolutionary war waged in a new era under the conditions of a vast territory, a progressive people, an advanced political party and an advanced army! ...[2]

Thus a jig-saw pattern of complicated exterior and interior lines was formed and the main and guerrilla forces were fighting several kinds of encirclements and counter-encirclements.

Taking the war as a whole, we are no doubt in the midst of the strategic encirclement of the enemy, because he has adopted strategic offensive and exterior-line operations and we strategic defensive and interior-line operations. This is the first kind of encirclement the enemy imposes on us. As we have, with numerically preponderant forces, adopted a policy for exterior-line operation in campaigns and battles against the enemy forces advancing on us in separate columns from strategically exterior lines, we can place into our encirclement one or several of the separately advancing enemy columns. This is the first kind of counter-encirclement we impose on the enemy. ... Furthermore, considering the guerrilla base areas in the enemy's rear, each isolated base area is surrounded by the enemy either on three ... or on four sides. This is the second kind of encirclement the enemy imposes on us. But if we look at the interconnections of these base areas with the fronts of the regular forces, we shall see that we have in turn surrounded a great number of enemy units. ... This is the second kind of counter-encirclement we impose on the enemy.[3]

---

1. [46] I, 228 *et seq.* and II, 399 or *SW* I, 248 *et seq.* and II, 124.
2. [46] II, 461–2 or *SW* II, 194–5.   3. [46] II, 462 or *SW* II, 195.

The basic formula for fighting counter-encirclement battles was still that which Mao had developed in 1928:

Enemy advances, we retreat; enemy halts, we harass; enemy tires, we attack; enemy retreats, we pursue.[4]

Mao admitted that mobile warfare was the primary, and guerrilla warfare the secondary, form of fighting in the Resistance War,[5] but it would be wrong to understand this as a static rule-of-thumb. He wrote:

... in the first stage mobile warfare is the principal form and guerrilla warfare and positional warfare are supplementary forms. In the second stage guerrilla warfare will be raised to the principal position, supplemented by mobile warfare and positional warfare. In the third stage mobile warfare will again be raised to become the principal form, supplemented by positional warfare and guerrilla warfare. But mobile warfare in the third stage will not be undertaken entirely by the original guerrilla forces, who will by then have been raised from fighting guerrilla war to fighting mobile war.[6]

Guerrilla warfare therefore had three important aspects in addition to its normal function of attrition. Firstly, it must seek to create base areas in order to preserve the guerrilla forces (the base areas being co-ordinated among themselves, and should prepare itself for transformation into mobile warfare); secondly its scale, in a big country like China, was bound to be large; and thirdly it was fought independently on the exterior line. 'Because of all this, China's anti-Japanese guerrilla war steps out of the bounds of tactics and knocks at the door of strategy, demanding that problems of guerrilla warfare be considered from a strategic point of view.'[7] Questions such as strategic distinctions between defensive and offensive would arise; questions such as the preservation of initiative and the planning and the creation of bases would also have to be solved.

The basic principle running through Mao's strategy of both the offensive and defensive was 'to fight resolutely a decisive engagement in every campaign or battle when victory is certain; to avoid a decisive engagement in every campaign or battle when victory

4. [46] I, 199 or *SW* I, 212.
5. [46] I, 223 and II, 395 and 488 or *SW* I, 242 and II, 119 and 224.
6. [46] II, 488 or *SW* II, 224–5.　　　　7. [46] II, 396 or *SW* II, 120.

is uncertain; and to avoid absolutely a strategic decisive engagement which stakes the destiny of the nation'.[8] Aware of the enemy's superior military strength which gave him the strategic initiative, Mao aimed at making full use of the enemy's partial inferiority and passivity, by defeating one of his weak sections in detail in the first battle, and then turning on the rest of his forces and smashing them separately, thus transforming China's whole position into one of superiority and initiative.[9] The guerrillas' offensive should be conducted with the concentration of the biggest possible forces, with secrecy and swiftness,[10] and the aim should be the destruction of a single enemy column,[11] preferably when it was on the move.[12] When fighting a defensive battle, the commander of guerrillas should not be afraid of dispersing or shifting them and he should remember that:

The circumstances are often such as to make it necessary to 'run away', The ability to run away is precisely one of the characteristics of the guerrillas. Running away is the chief means of escaping from the passive state and regaining the initiative.[13]

The corollary to running away was to abandon territory,[14] but to exchange territory for a time could be a correct policy. Mao had no taste for such *desperadoism* as 'advance without retreat' or 'live or die with the city' or for such *flightism* as 'only backward movement without forward movement'.[15] The enemy's offensive against a guerrilla base or a detachment, according to him, often took the form of an encirclement, and consequently the guerrillas' defensive took the form of a counter-encirclement,[16] the success of which required the ability to launch a series of surprise attacks and ambushes, to prevent military information from reaching the enemy, and to create illusions for him.[17] On the strategic plane, the guerrillas should never forget co-ordination among themselves and with the regular forces, just as the regular forces should not neglect the guerrillas.[18]

8. [46] I, 215 and II, 495 or *SW* I, 233 and II, 233.
9. [46] II, 480 or *SW* 215–16.   10. [46] II, 400 or *SW* II, 124.
11. [46] II, 420 or *SW* II, 147.   12. [46] II, 475 or *SW* II, 209.
13. [46] I, 197 *et seq.* and II, 403 or *SW* I, 210 *et seq.* and II, 128.
14. [46] II, 496 or *SW* II, 234.   15. [46] II, 487 or *SW* II, 223.
16. [46] II, 419 or *SW* II, 146.
17. [46] II, 481 or *SW* II, 216.   18. [46] II, 424 or *SW* II, 152.

Mao insisted that guerrilla warfare should be carefully planned.

Questions of how to grasp the situation, to define the tasks, to dispose the forces, to carry out military and political training, to procure supplies, to make arrangements for equipment, to secure the help of the people, etc. should be carefully considered and thoroughly worked out by guerrilla leaders and the results should be checked. Without this there could be no initiative, flexibility or offensive.[19]

However, if too thorough or too rigid, planning would deprive the guerrilla corps of their initiative and flexibility. The optimum degree of planning, like so many other things in guerrilla warfare, was elusive, but Mao tried to define it in what he called 'a guerrilla war waged independently and on its own initiative under a unified strategy'.[20] In his view, apart from routine planning, the strategic operations should be commanded centrally by the general staff and the war zone commanders while the specific dispositions in a campaign should be left to the lower ranks in order to make adequate room for elasticity.[21] Another important point was the establishment of base areas which were necessary because 'in the present age of advanced communications and technology, it is more than ever an entirely groundless illusion to attempt to win victory after the fashion of the roving insurgents'.[22] In other words, for their own preservation and in order to turn the enemy's rear into his front so that he has to fight ceaselessly throughout the areas he occupies, guerrillas must have bases. In order to create a base, a guerrilla unit should have extensive knowledge of the locality in which it operates, the warmest support of the people, the ability to repulse the enemy in that area, and the skill to organize and arm the people for the consolidation and defence of the base.[23] Here strategy and tactics were fused into politics. 'The deepest source of the immense power of war,' said Mao, 'lies in the masses of people. . . . The army must be at one with the people and be regarded by the people as their own: then that army will be invincible throughout the world, and will find a single imperialist power like Japan rather small game.'[24]

19. [46] II, 405 and 485 or *SW* II, 131 and 221.
20. [46] II, 427 or *SW* II, 155.   21. [46] II, 426–7 or *SW* II, 154–5.
22. [46] II, 409 or *SW* II, 135.
23. [46] II, 414–15 or *SW* II, 140–1.   24. [46] 501 or *SW* II, 239.

Many people think that it is wrong methods that cause strained relations between officers and men and between the army and the people, but I have often said that it is rather a problem of basic attitude; which should be one of respect for the soldiers and for the people.[25]

This basic attitude was expounded in a number of principles in his interview with James Bertram:

First, the principle of unity between officers and men, i.e. eradicating feudal practices in the army, abolishing the practice of beating and bullying the men, building up a conscious discipline, and leading a life in which weal and woe are shared by all alike. . . . Secondly, the principle of unity between the army and the people, i.e. enforcing such discipline in dealing with the masses as forbids the army from violating even in the slightest degree the property rights of the people, carrying out propaganda among the masses and organizing and arming them, lightening the financial burden on the people, and dealing blows to the traitors and collaborators who undermine the army and the people. . . . Thirdly, the principle of disintegrating the enemy troops and giving lenient treatment to prisoners of war.[26]

As the war dragged on, the quality of the guerrilla units would improve both politically and organizationally along with their military capabilities, so as to make them ready for the task of mobile warfare. When the war of attrition was won and the strategic superiority of China established, these units would be reorganized into the regular army and take part in the final counteroffensive which would lead to the ultimate victory.[27]

Five important points seem to suggest themselves in the above summary of Mao's strategic thought. First, the elevation of guerrilla warfare from the plane of tactics to that of strategy must be reckoned as his original contribution to military thinking. Second, in his calculations, the KMT troops were to play an entirely subordinate role throughout the Resistance War. This showed his contempt for their fighting qualities and also tended to weaken, or even to invalidate, his argument about the final stage of the counteroffensive in the war, for their inefficiency would indefinitely postpone the arrival of that stage. Third, his thought evolved along a series of opposites, for example exterior and interior lines,

25. [46] II, 501 or SW, 240.   26. [46] II, 369 or SW II, 96.
27. [46] II, 423–5 or SW II, 145–8.

offensive and defensive, procrastination and swiftness, initiative and passivity, mobility and base areas, concentration and dispersal of troops, planning and flexibility, encirclement and counter-encirclement, and so on, and he tried to reconcile them by the application of Marxian dialectics. Fourth, he assumed that the political united front was to remain in force throughout the war and, at the same time, shunned the possibility of violent clashes happening between the KMT and CCP. Fifth, he referred to the army of the people being 'invincible throughout the world' and said:

Thus the protracted and extensive Anti-Japanese War is a war of jig-saw pattern in the military, political, economic and cultural aspects—a spectacle in the history of war, a splendid feat of the Chinese nation, a world-shaking achievement. This war will not only affect China and Japan, strongly impelling both to advance, but also affect the world, impelling all nations, first of all the oppressed nations like India, to march forward.[28]

He was deeply conscious of the international significance, not only of the war itself, but also of his strategic thought.

Undoubtedly his strategic ideas spring from his early experience in the civil war and his advocacy of encircling and cutting off the cities from the rural areas.[29] But it is of interest, too, to note that he had changed from complete reliance on the poor peasants in 1927 to the idea that political power grows out of the barrel of a gun.

Every Communist must grasp the truth: 'Political power grows out of the barrel of a gun.' Our principle is that the Party commands the gun, and the gun will never be allowed to command the Party. But it is also true that with guns at our disposal we can really build up the Party organisation, and the Eighth Route Army has built up a powerful Party organisation in North China. We can also rear cadres and create school, culture and mass movements. Everything in Yenan has been built up by means of the gun. Anything can grow out of the barrel of a gun.[30]

Although the support of the peasants was still deemed important, an independent military force under the sole control of the CCP

28. [46] II, 463 or *SW* II, 197.   29. [14] 92.
30. [46] II, 535 or *SW* II, 272.

was regarded, after ten years of civil war, as absolutely indispensable for the seizure of power. Small wonder then that Hu Ch'iao-mu praises the *Strategic Problems of China's Revolutionary War* as 'one of the most brilliant Marxist works of the world communist movement on military science', and goes on to say:

Comrade Mao Tse-tung has made outstanding contributions to Marxist-Leninist military theory by his works on the strategic problems of the Chinese revolutionary wars.[31]

General Liu Po-ch'eng, himself an accomplished strategist, pays this tribute to Mao's views on strategy:

Comrade Mao Tse-tung's thought on the strategy of the revolutionary wars in China, being itself a union of the well-tested Marxism-Leninism and the reality of China, is the only correct guiding thought of the Chinese revolution.[32]

Even Mao himself admitted in November 1938:

We can confidently say that in the struggle of the past seventeen years up to now the Chinese Communist Party has forged not only a firm Marxist political line but also a firm Marxist military line.[33]

While admitting the logical sequence from reliance on the poor peasants to that on a peasant military force, we must come to the inevitable conclusion that the essence of Maoism (Mao Tse-tung *ssu-hsiang*) lies in the man's theories on strategy which, instead of being 'a union of . . . Marxism-Leninism and the [mere] reality of China' is in fact that of Marxism-Leninism and the Chinese traditional pattern of peasant revolts. The Chinese were used to protracted revolutions which normally lasted years before success or failure came, the revolutions of the peasants spreading out from one or several base areas, such as the Red Eyebrows from A.D. 18 to 27 (9 years), the Wa-kang Army from 611 to 618 (7 or 8 years), the Manichaeans from 1353 to 1367 (14 years), Li Tzu-ch'eng's rebellion from 1630 to 1645 (15 years), Chang Hsien-chung's rebellion from 1630 to 1646 (16 years), and the T'aip'ing rebellion from 1850 to 1864 (14 years). All these revolts fell into a pattern similar to the communist revolution led by Mao Tse-tung from 1927 to 1949. By using Marxism-Leninism, relying on

31. [179] 40 and 92.
32. [249] 14.   33. [46] II, 536 or *SW* II, 274.

the peasants, and applying his political and military genius, Mao has not only forged 'a firm Marxist (or Maoist) military line' but also created a pattern of revolution new even to the most alert brains of the world of politics.

As early as 1936 the future of the Resistance or the revolutionary war in China was already mapped out by this original military brain, waiting for the unfolding of events to prove the power of its inspiration and farsightedness.

In the third century A.D. a minister and his secretary were confronted with a riddle. The former asked the latter: 'Do you see the answer?' The latter replied: 'Yes.' 'Well,' said the minister, 'don't tell me what it is, let me work it out for myself.' They rode on for ten miles before the minister also solved the riddle. Thereupon he remarked: 'I am slower than you by ten miles.'[34] How many miles were Mao's contemporaries slower than he?

Now we must turn to Mao's political blueprint of the united front as contained in his Ten-point National Salvation Programme[35] published on 25 August 1937, the main contents of which were:

(4) Reform the government structure.

Convoke a national assembly genuinely representative of the people to adopt a genuinely democratic constitution, to determine the policies of resistance and national salvation and to elect the national defence government.

The national defence government must draw in the revolutionary elements of all parties and groups and mass organisations and expel the pro-Japanese elements.

The national defence government shall adopt the system of democratic centralism which is at once democratic and centralised.

The national defence government shall carry out revolutionary policies for resisting Japan and saving the nation.

Carry into effect the principle of local autonomy, remove all corrupt officials, and establish a clean government.

(6) Wartime financial and economic policy.

Financial policy is to be based on the principle of letting those who have money give money and confiscating the property of the collaborators to defray the expenses of the war. The economic policy consists in overhauling and expanding defence production, developing rural economy, and assuring self-sufficiency in wartime supplies; encouraging the use of Chinese goods and improving home products; and completely

34. *Shih-shuo hsin-yü*, IIb, item 4.   35. [46] II, 341–4 or *SW* II, 70–2.

boycotting Japanese goods, suppressing unscrupulous merchants, and banning speculation and the manipulation of the market.

(7) Improvement of the people's living conditions.

Raise the pay of workers, office workers, teachers and soldiers fighting the Japanese.

Take good care of the families of the soldiers fighting the Japanese.

Abolish exorbitant assessments and miscellaneous taxes.

Reduce rent and interest.

Relieve the unemployed.

Regulate food supplies.

Give aid to victims of natural calamities.

A month later he again urged the KMT to adopt this Programme, together with Dr. Sun Yat-sen's Three Principles of the People, as the common programme of the united front[36]; and in October, when answering James Bertram, he said:

... first, the present government must be remoulded into a united front government in which the representatives of the people take part. Such a government should be at once democratic and centralised. It should carry out the necessary revolutionary policies. Secondly, the people should be granted freedom of speech, press, assembly, association and of making armed resistance against the enemy, so that the war will take on a mass character. Thirdly, the living conditions of the people must be improved through such assessments, reducing rent and interest, raising the pay of workers, officers at lower levels and soldiers, taking good care of the families of soldiers fighting the Japanese, and extending relief to the victims of natural calamities and of war refugees, etc. The government's finance must be based on the principle of a reasonable distribution of the economic burden, i.e. the principle that those who have money give money.[37]

These points, raised at a time when 'all the revolutionary bases were lost except the Shensi-Kansu border area, the Red Army was reduced from 300,000 to a few tens of thousands, the membership of the Chinese Communist Party was reduced also from 300,000 to a few tens of thousands, and the Party organizations in the Kuomintang areas were almost entirely wiped out',[38] represented the CCP's political demands. The request for the establishment of

36. [46] II, 356 or *SW* II, 83.
37. [46] II, 366 or *SW* II, 92–3.
38. [46] I, 181 or *SW* I, 193. The figures are correct; *cf.* [153] II, 380–1, [181] 103, 108, and 111, [185] 123, [189] 358, and [281] xxviii.

the national defence government, foreshadowing Mao's later proposal of a coalition government, received some response from the
KMT in the convocation of the People's Political Council in July
1938 and the participation of Chu Te and Chou En-lai in the
KMT Military Council in August 1937.[39] But his financial
and economic policies with perfectly justified objectives were difficult to put into practice in the initial stages of the war when the
Chinese armies were rapidly being driven back and economic dislocations were inevitable. It must also be borne in mind that the
civil service of the KMT Government was not efficient or honest
enough for the quantitative and direct controls Mao proposed and
that in the KMT China there was no well-organized financial or
taxation system to enable the war to be paid for by government
bonds or taxes. Consequently the KMT had to fall back on
financing the war by means of inflation. Impractical and made at a
time when the CCP was weak, these demands failed to command
much attention from the KMT or from the communist responsible
for the united front work, Wang Ming.

From what can be gathered of the charges laid against him,
Wang Ming seems to have made a series of 'mistakes'. On the
theoretical level, he did not believe that the CCP, weak as it was,
could actually lead the Resistance War. The leadership, in his
view, had to be conceded to the KMT in which he discovered many
talented and upright young people during his term of office in
Wuhan. Therefore he proposed a closer co-operation with the
KMT by integrating the communist armies into the KMT Army
in order to achieve unity in command, organization, equipment,
discipline, planning, and operations, and also by having every
decision approved by the united front before translating it into
action.[40] While in Wuhan, Wang Ming does not seem to have
obeyed the instructions given to him and published oral and written statements without having obtained the party's sanction beforehand. For all these 'mistakes' he was criticized first at the plenum
of the Politburo held at Loch'uan on 25 August and later at the

39. [153] II, 303–4 and [189] 357.
40. [18] 380–2, [179] 49–50, [185] 118–19 and 123–4. For Wang Ming's
(Ch'en Shao-yü) own view, see [255] and *Wan-chiu Shih-chü ti Kuan-chien*
(The key to saving the present situation), 1937, which, unfortunately, is not
available to me.

plenum of the Central Committee held at Yenan in October 1938.[41] The severe treatment he received suggested that he was by no means alone. Since his return to Moscow in 1931 Wang Ming had been the CCP representative at the Comintern and therefore his interpretation of the united front tactics may have commanded a considerable following in the party. His close friend, Ch'in Pang-hsien, was at this time the secretary of the Yangtze and the South China Bureaux and concurrently the head of the Organization Department,[42] but it is not clear whether he supported Wang Ming. Mao attacked Wang's interpretation of the united front policy as 'capitulationism'—not co-operation. Co-operation, according to him, meant the subordination of the class struggle to the anti-Japanese national struggle, sacrificing neither the independence nor the essential rights of the component parties and classes of the united front. Therefore Mao was against the advocacy that every action should have been sanctioned by the united front before it was taken; in particular he was opposed to the amalgamation of the communist forces with the KMT forces.[43] And as early as May 1937 he wrote:

It is a law proved in China's history that, because of its economic and political flabbiness, the Chinese bourgeoisie which can take part in fighting imperialism and feudalism in certain circumstances will vacillate and turn traitor in others. History has therefore decided that China's anti-imperialist and anti-feudal bourgeois-democratic revolution can be completed not under the leadership of the bourgeoisie, but only under the leadership of the proletariat.[44]

In other words, no matter how weak the CCP and its army were, they must not concede the leadership in the Resistance War to the KMT, even if it was only on paper, for they were, according to Mao, the only resolute fighters against the Japanese; nor must they repeat the mistake of the 'bloc within' policy of the first united front of 1924–7. The arms should never be buried or handed over.

The second united front differed from the first not only because it followed a policy of a 'bloc without', but also because it was directed against a foreign aggressor, Japan, instead of the war-

41. [18] 381–2, [179] 50, and also [46] II, 382 and 387 n.1 or *SW* II, 109 and 284 n.1.　　42. [280] 7.

43. [46] II, 525 *et seq.* or *SW* II, 262 *et seq.*

44. [46] I, 253 or *SW* I, 269.

lords and formed at a time when both the KMT and the CCP had their respective military forces and controlled areas. At the time of the first united front neither Mao nor Chiang Kai-shek was a figure of great importance, but now in 1936 one was the leader of the CCP and the other on his way to becoming the undisputed leader of the nation.

Indeed, in 1936 Chiang stood head and shoulders above all others in China; his erstwhile opponents, with very few exceptions, he had either defeated or had succeeded in reconciling to his views. The communist wanderings in 1935 and 1936 offered him excellent opportunities of penetrating into the provinces, e.g. Szechwan, Yunnan, and Shansi, hitherto dominated by warlords, thus achieving a measure of unity which China had not known for many long years and giving him a base from which he could resist Japan for seven years. His popularity was such that on his fiftieth birthday, 31 October 1936, the whole nation paid tribute to him by donating money for the purchase of military aeroplanes to strengthen China's defence against Japan's imminent invasion.[45] Success tends to inflate one's self-esteem and confidence. So, when Chiang met Chang Hsüeh-liang in Loyang on 3 December and heard from him that the Manchurian troops were restive in Shensi, he unhesitatingly accepted Chang's suggestion that he should fly to Sian to deal with the situation in person, quite oblivious of any possible danger to himself. He arrived at Sian on 4 December, announced another suppression campaign against the communists on the eleventh, and was kidnapped and imprisoned by Chang Hsüeh-liang and Yang Hu-ch'eng on the twelfth.[46]

Chiang himself and his official spokesmen denied that the Sian *Coup* had in any sense affected his Japanese policy,[47] but his biographer, Hollington Tong, reveals that in order to gain time for the unification and strengthening of China, Chiang was willing to pay the price of accepting the compromising T'angku Agreement of 31

45. [153] I, 188 and [254] 15. The city of Nanking alone presented 100 aeroplanes to him, but what mystifies the readers of Chiang's official biography is the fact that at the beginning of the Resistance War (autumn 1937) General Claire Chennault inspected the Chinese Air Force and found no more than 91 aeroplanes ([153] II, 274).

46. [20] 426 and [254] 123–30.   47. [153] II, 253 and 271 and [256].

May 1933.[48] He expressed his wish for a reasonable settlement and true co-operation between China and Japan in an article, 'Friends or Foes?', published under Hsü Tao-ling's name in the autumn of 1934, and intimated to Japan his peace plan through China's minister at Tokyo in 1935.[49] In his recent book, *Soviet Russia in China*, he has again denied that he entered into any political negotiation with the communists while interned in Sian,[50] but Ch'in Pang-hsien, Yeh Chien-ying, and the persuasive Chou En-lai did obtain from him the promise to round off the civil war and to form an anti-Japanese united front.[51] So far Mao has been reticent on this subject, except for his statement made in 1945:

As far back as the time when Japanese imperialism began to invade China, the Communist Party of China demanded an end to civil war and unity against foreign aggression. In 1936-37 the Party made tremendous efforts, forced Chiang Kai-shek to accept its proposal and so carried out the War of Resistance against Japan.[52]

The Sian *Coup* marked the beginning of the second united front, as Hollington Tong says:

President Chiang's attitude toward the 'communist party' remained unchanged after the Sian Incident. But in view of the unstable situation in the northwest, he felt that the gain would not justify the cost, if the Government was to spend all the resources at its disposal on another military operation against the so-called communist party. Being versatile in expedients, President Chiang began to consider whether it would be of national interest to come to an agreement with Mao Tse-tung and his followers in order to obtain their co-operation in case of a war with Japan.[53]

And the *Ta-kung Pao* editorial on the New Year's Day of 1937 spoke in a hopeful vein:

The foundation of China's reconstruction is now laid; the whole nation will henceforth stand on one front and no dissension can be tolerated.
From today China will have only the united front, and never again will there be internal hostility.[54]

48. The Agreement practically conceded Hopei to Japan. [153] II, 224.
49. [153] II, 225–7.   50. [169] 74–5.
51. [254] 150–2, 165–6 and 170 and [293] 79.
52. [46] IV, 1148 or *SW* IV (Peking), 42.
53. [153] II, 268–9.   54. [114] I, 231.

On 10 February, when the third plenum of the KMT Central Executive Committee was in session, the CCP proposed five policies and gave four pledges to the KMT. The policies were:

(1) end all civil wars and concentrate the nation's strength to cope unitedly with foreign aggression;
(2) guarantee the freedom of speech, assembly, and association and release all political prisoners;
(3) call a conference of representatives of all parties, all groups, all circles and all armies, and concentrate the nation's talents for a common endeavour to save the country;
(4) complete speedily all preparations for resisting Japan; and
(5) improve the living conditions of the people.[55]

'Since they contained no divergent views from those of the Central Government',[56] these proposed policies were accepted by Chiang.[57] The four pledges, as they were suggested, read:

(1) all over the country the policy of armed insurrection for overthrowing the National Government will be discontinued;
(2) the workers' and peasants' democratic government will be renamed as the government of the special region of the Republic of China, and the Red Army will be designated as a unit of the National Revolutionary Army, and will *accept guidance directly* from the Central Government in Nanking and its Military Council respectively;
(3) in the areas under the government of the special region, a thoroughly democratic system based on universal suffrage will be put into effect; and
(4) the policy of confiscating the land of the landlords will be discontinued and the common programme of the Anti-Japanese United Front resolutely carried out.[58]

After negotiations in Nanking and Lushan, the final agreed version was published on 22 September:

1. The Three People's Principles of Dr. Sun Yat-sen being what China needs today, our Party pledges itself to fight for their complete realisation;
2. The Communist Party will discontinue completely its policy of insurrections aimed at overthrowing the Kuomintang régime and its policy of forcible confiscation of the land of the landlords;

55. [46] I, 259 n. 7 or *SW* I, 373 n. 7.
56. [153] II, 269.   57. [46] III, 948 or *SW* IV, 145.
58. [46] I, 259 n.7 or *SW* I, 374 n. 7. (My italics.)

3. The present Red government will be reorganised as the democratic government of the special district to facilitate the unification of political power throughout the country;
4. The Red Army will change its name and designation, will be reorganised as the National Revolutionary Army and *placed under the command* of the Military Council of the National Government and will be ready for orders to march to the anti-Japanese front to carry out its duty.[59]

Of these four pledges, only two were important and also open to different interpretations. The 'placing of the communist troops under the command of the Military Council' was not nearly as straightforward as it sounded, as Mao qualified it in November 1938:

We have rejected the Kuomintang's request to appoint its members as cadres of the Eighth Route Army and have upheld the principle of the Communist Party's absolute leadership of the Eighth Route Army.[60]

In Mao's view, the communists should not break up the united front; nor should they be completely submissive to it. This point was to become the stumbling block in the formation of a coalition government and finally wrecked the united front. The other point of importance was a definition of the Three People's Principles. Mao explained:

The Three People's Principles in question are none other than the Three People's Principles as re-introduced by Dr. Sun Yat-sen in the Manifesto of the First National Congress of the Kuomintang. . . .
    The revolutionary Three People's Principles of the new period, the new or genuine Three People's Principles, contain the three cardinal policies of alliance with Russia, co-operation with the Communists, and assistance to the peasants and workers. Without these three cardinal policies, or minus any one of them, they become, in the new period, the false Three People's Principles or the incomplete Three People's Principles.[61]

But it must be remembered that the Manifesto was drafted not by Dr. Sun but by Borodin and that after its adoption in 1924 Dr. Sun gave a series of lectures which for the first time systematically expounded his Three Principles. The Manifesto and the lectures

59. [46] III, 946 or *SW* IV, 143. *Cf.* [4] 67 and [11] 524.   (My italics.)
60. [46] II, 383 or *SW* II, 111.
61. [46] II, 682-3 or *SW* III, 134-5.

should have been taken as equally representative of their author's point of view. To adopt the one and reject the other does not seem to be logically justifiable. It must also be remembered that the three cardinal policies as such are not to be found anywhere in Dr. Sun's writings.[62] It was natural that, as Mao perhaps expected, the Three Principles he insisted upon were widely at variance with those Chiang understood. Furthermore, the pledge to fight for their realization must not be comprehended as to 'tuck away communism'. Mao again explained:

Frankly, 'tuck it away' will not do; better let there be a contest. If anything else beats communism, we Communists will admit our own bad luck. But if not, then let all that stuff about 'one doctrine', which violates the Principle of Democracy, be 'tucked away' as soon as possible.[63]

With divergent views such as these still unreconciled, the marriage of the two major parties was hurriedly contracted under pressure of the popular demand of the time and the outbreak of the war between China and Japan, regardless of the possibility of 'each dreaming his own dreams while sleeping in the same bed'. The blame is not that the united front was formed too soon but that too little care was given to hammering out the initial agreement.

On 6 September 1937, two months after the outbreak of the eight years' Sino-Japanese War, the Shensi-Kansu soviet was renamed the Shensi-Kansu-Ninghsia Border Region and the Red Army reorganized into the Eighth Route Army with Chu Te as its commander and P'eng Te-huai its deputy commander. Its three divisions were the 115th under Lin Piao and Nieh Jung-chen, the 120th under Ho Lung and Hsiao K'e, and the 129th under Liu Po-ch'eng and Hsü Hsiang-ch'ien.[64] According to an agreement between the two parties, its strength was fixed at 45,000 officers and men and the National Government was to provide its pay and equipment.[65] A year later it was re-designated the 18th

62. [116].
63. [46] II, 680 or *SW* III, 132. The principle of democracy is the second of the Three Principles.
64. [181] 103, [185] 123, [189] 358, [282] 120, and [289] 6–7.
65. [11] 51.

Army Group and placed under the direct control of the commander-in-chief of the second war-zone, General Yen Hsi-shan. The other communist army, the New Fourth Army, was formed in January 1938 with General Yeh T'ing, who had come out from his long retirement in Hong Kong since the defeat of the Canton Uprising in December 1927, as its commander and Hsiang Ying as its deputy commander. There were four columns in this army—the first under Ch'en Yi, the second under Chang Ting-ch'eng, the third under Chang Yün-yi, and the fourth under Kao Chün-t'ing. As they had been the guerrilla units fighting in the vast areas of Kiangsi, Hunan, Fukien, Kwangtung, Chekiang, Anhwei, and Hupei since after the Long March, it took some time to assemble them together in the assigned areas in north and south Anhwei. It was not until October 1938 that the work of reorganization was completed and the Army's operations against the Japanese began.[66] Again under agreement, the strength of the New Fourth Army was limited to 15,000.[67]

Politically, the second united front was represented by the convocation of the People's Political Council on 6 July 1938.[68] Of its 200 members, 30 belonged to the CCP and other small parties and 20 were independents, the rest all being KMT representatives. At the inaugural meeting, Chiang Kai-shek defined the function of the Council as to assist the Government in prosecuting the war and rebuilding the nation and to lay the foundation for democracy in China. 'What is democracy?' he asked, and went on:

Democracy is liberty—a liberty which does not infringe on the liberty nor encroach on the rights of others; a liberty which maintains strict discipline, and makes law its guarantee and the basis of its exercise. This alone is true liberty; this alone can produce true democracy.[69]

At the same time Chou En-lai was appointed the deputy director of the Political Department of the Military Council and Kuo Mojo the head of its Propaganda Section.[70] The communist paper, *Hsin-hua Jih-pao*, began its publication in Wuhan in 1937.[71] The second united front was established in name and practice, but the

66. [153] II, 380–1, [181] 103, [189] 358, [234] 321, [274] 47 and 118, and [285] 3 and 4–5. 67. [153] 380–1 and [282] 120.
68. [20] 446. 69. [122] I, 73. 70. [11] 52 and [257] 19–22.
71. [11] 52.

strain between the two parties was always present. On 8 August 1938 both parties sent representatives to worship the Yellow Emperor. The communist deputy was none other than Chang Kuo-t'ao who, after the ceremony, went directly to Wuhan,[72] bringing with him the news that the CCP was [devoting 70 per cent. of its energy to territorial expansion, 20 per cent. to dealing with the KMT, and only 10 per cent. to resisting Japan.[73] Meanwhile the National Government's attempts to exercise direct command over the communist troops in the field and to direct their training were frustrated.[74] Therefore at the end of August General Ch'en Ch'eng suppressed three important mass organizations of the CCP in retaliation.[75] The honeymoon was definitely over and quarrels began. Charges and counter-charges of failure to abide by the promises of 1937 were made with increasing vehemence, leading to the issue of such secret documents as 'Methods of Dealing with the CCP', 'Methods for Guarding against Communist Activities in the Enemy Occupied Areas', and 'Methods of Restricting the Activities of the Other Party'[76] as well as to local clashes in 1939 and 1940.

Starting from the clash at Poshan in Shantung in April 1939, the KMT and the CCP guerrilla detachments fought each other in Shantung, Hopei, and Shansi intermittently until there was a pause in the spring of 1940,[77] resulting in the establishment of the communist supremacy behind the enemy lines and the surrender of Lü Cheng-ts'ao's Manchurian troops and Po I-po's Shansi New Army to the Eighth Route Army.[78] In the south, too, the KMT guerrillas clashed with the New Fourth Army, beginning with the so-called P'ingchiang Incident in Hunan on 12 June 1939[79] which was followed by other skirmishes in Hupei, Honan, and Kiangsu in the remaining months of the year and throughout the next.[80] The contact between General Ho Ying-ch'in and Ch'in Pang-

72. [257] 119.   73. [134] 206.
74. [11] 53.   75. [11] 52–3 and [257] 113.
76. [46] II, 714 n. 10 or SW III, 254 n. 10.
77. [46] 714 n.5 or SW III, 253–4 n. 5; [162] 240, [181] 107–8, and [279] 89.
78. [46] II, 713 ns. 3–4 or SW III, 253 ns. 3–4, [153] II, 382, [181] 108, and [279] 72.
79. [46] II, 568 n. 1 or SW III, 243–4 n. 1; [279] 99.
80. [46] II, 713 n. 2 and 714 n. 6 or SW III, 253 n. 2 and 254 n. 6, [153] II, 382, [169] 94–5, and [279] 99–100.

hsien early in 1940[81] failed to put an end to these. Meanwhile on 4 May Mao instructed the South-east Bureau of the CCP, whose secretary was Hsiang Ying:

When the anti-communist die-hards of the Kuomintang are obstinately carrying out their policy of guarding against, containing and opposing communism in preparation for capitulating to Japan, we must *stress struggle, not unity* . . .[82]

And on Christmas Day he issued this directive:

Military policy. We must expand the Eighth Route Army and the New Fourth Army in every possible way, because these are the Chinese people's most reliable armed forces in maintaining the national resistance to Japan. Towards the Kuomintang troops we must continue to adopt the policy of 'we will never attack unless attacked', and develop to the utmost the work of making friends with them.[83]

From the *Ta-kung Pao* jubilation of 'From today China will have only the united front, never again will there be internal hostility' on the New Year's Day of 1937 to 'we must stress struggle, not unity' and 'we will never attack unless attacked' on Christmas Day 1940, the second united front had dwindled to a nominal existence This was on the eve of the destruction of the New Fourth Army in the well-known South Anhwei Incident on 4 January 1941.

81. [11] 54.   82. [46] II, 750 or *SW* III, 205.
83. [46] II, 766 or *SW* III, 223.

Chapter XI

War and Soldiers

IT has been suggested that the *rapprochement* between Chiang and the communists and its resultant national unity in face of Japanese pressure hastened the outbreak of the Sino-Japanese war in July 1937[1]; it has also been suggested that the incident of the shooting at the Chinese garrison by the Japanese troops stationed near the Marco Polo Bridge on the outskirts of Peking which led to war, like the assassination of Marshal Chang Tso-lin in June 1928 and the Mukden Incident of 18 September 1931, was planned by Japanese officers on the spot.[2] Whatever Japan hoped to achieve by her action at the time was proved to be pure fantasy, for the Chinese, united to a man, spoke through Chiang Kai-shek:

Only a determination to sacrifice ourselves to the uttermost can bring us ultimate victory.

China was in no mood to be bullied any more and 'any settlement reached' between her and Japan 'must not infringe upon her territorial integrity and sovereign rights'.[3] The war was irrevocably on.

For Japan the strategy was *sokusen sokketsu*—blitzkrieg or lightning warfare[4]; for China it was the 'prolonged resistance' in Chiang's phraseology or the 'protracted war' in Mao's. Like Mao, Chiang also visualized that the war would go through three stages —the first, 'to trade space for time' while making the enemy pay as heavily as possible for every advance; the second, to tie down the enemy in a 'magnetic warfare' during which the front lines would

1. [153] II, 275 and [222] 202–3. 2. [222] 202.
3. [122] I, 22 and 24. 4. [134] 104.

be stabilized and the enemy subjected to flanking attacks and encirclements; and the third, to launch the general counter-offensive.[5] Unfortunately, owing to the weakness of the KMT troops, things did not work out according to plan. 'To trade space for time', as General Stilwell pointed out later, could easily become 'a very catchy way of saying he [Chiang] would never attack'.[6] Indeed, throughout the eight years of war the KMT army never undertook a single major offensive; even the famous battle of T'aierhchuang was chiefly defensive in nature.

Instead of the three stages predicted by Chiang and Mao, the war actually fell into two only. The first lasted from July 1937 to December 1938 and was characterized by Japan's swift advance and China's stubborn defence, resulting in the loss of the major cities along the coast as well as Wuhan; the second lasted from 1939 to August 1945 during which neither side launched any spectacular campaign except for the Japanese offensive in the summer of 1944. The general pattern of the war was therefore a short period of Japanese advance followed by a long stalemate.

In the first period, two fierce engagements were fought at Shanghai and Nanking with both sides suffering heavy losses, and after the battle of Nanking the Japanese Command instigated the most savage rape of a city known in history. Its calculations were that by annihilating the Chinese troops and committing atrocities against the Chinese people Japan might be able to break China's will to defend herself and bring down Chiang's Government. At the same time she offered peace terms to China through the German Ambassador, Dr. O. P. Trautmann. All this, however, came to nothing, apart from making China's resistance more resolute.[7] While peace was being offered, Japan halted her advance for three months, giving a chance for Chiang to settle in Wuhan and make arrangements for the transfer of the Government to Chungking. The pause has been adjudged unwise, for Japan lost valuable time in bringing the war to the heart of China.[8] But it would have been even more unwise for her to penetrate deeper without having dealt with the large army under General Li Tsung-jen at Hsüchow.

5. [4] 299.   6. [268] 293.
7. [114] II, 42, [153] II, 288, [222] 204, [263] 63 and 68, and [264] 35–6.
8. [134] 199–200 and [264] 36.

The battle of T'aierhchuang was later admitted by the Japanese themselves as delivering 'fatal blows against the Japanese forces, . . . [and constituting] an immortal page in Chinese military history',[9] but none the less the Japanese managed to dislodge General Li's troops and by October 1938 they were knocking at the gate of Wuhan. Although Wuhan fell into Japanese hands, large parts of Honan were saved by the bombardment of the dykes of the Yellow River by Chinese planes, causing the river to change its course and thus preventing the Japanese troops from invading that province.[10] Towards the end of 1938 Prince Konoye, the Japanese prime minister, offered new peace terms which, though firmly rejected by Chiang, lured Wang Ching-wei to Nanking to head a puppet government. Later puppet troops were organized, numbering over 780,000 by 1944,[11] to assist the Japanese in maintaining law and order in their occupied areas.[12]

From the end of 1938 to the end of the war in 1945 the KMT troops took no major initiative against the Japanese; in spite of this they still engaged 70 per cent. of all the Japanese forces in China. The front lines were stabilized and the officers and men on both sides conducted a thriving smuggling trade.[13] When in the summer of 1944 Japan launched her final offensive, the KMT soldiers were no longer the hardy fighters of 1938. Years of stalemate had corrupted and softened them, reducing them not only from field armies to garrison troops but also from warriors to men of clay. Therefore this period of inaction in the Resistance War had the gravest, almost a fatal, effect on the morale and fighting qualities of Chiang's troops.

Natural calamities also ensued, beginning with the two-year-long drought in Honan[14] which drove two to three million of the 30 million inhabitants to other provinces and killed off another two or three million.[15] The *Ta-kung Pao* published a report of it on 1 February 1943, and an editorial on the next day, drawing the attention of the Government and the public to it, but was promptly suspended from publication for three days.[16] Worse still, the more

9. [134] 200.   10. [153] II, 293 and [264] 57.
11. [153] II, 317–18; [221] 155; [296] 263.   12. [296] 263.
13. *Davies's Memorandum*, 9.3.1943, [10] 28, [263] 144–5, and [269] 74.
14. [153] II, 367.   15. [263] 169.
16. Gauss to Secretary of State, 15.2.1943, [10] 208–9 and [269] 159.

often 'face losing' things of this kind happened, the severer the repressive measures of the KMT became. The Honan drought, which weakened the Chinese defence, and the Allies' operations on the Pacific, which rendered the maritime communications between Japan and her possessions in south-east Asia precarious, together caused Japan to launch the Trans-continental Offensive— or, Operation *Ichi-gō*—in 1944.[17] General T'ang En-po, the 'iron man' who had so heroically defended the Nank'ou Pass in 1937,[18] was now scornfully referred to as 'the Other Sorrow of Honan'.[19] In three weeks he managed to lose the entire province while 50,000 of his troops were disarmed by the inhabitants.[20] On 17 June the Japanese took Ch'angsha and continued to drive south and west, taking Kweilin on 10 November and Liuchow on the next day, thus completing their task of linking up the railway system from Korea to Annam.[21] In seven months the KMT lost nearly 700,000 troops, 146 towns, 200,000 square kilometres of territory, 36 air-fields, and more than 60 million people.[22] How was this possible? Chiang himself explained:

... after seven years of war, the remaining forces were weary and ill-equipped.[23]

But Mao took a different view:

For five years and six months the Kuomintang has been standing by with folded arms, completely deprived of fighting capacity.[24]

Yet Operation *Ichi-gō* also showed clearly that the communists, too, were standing by with their arms folded, for the railway system actually ran through most of their base areas and they did not move a finger to stop or to slow down the Japanese advance.[25]

None the less, the corruption and ineptitude of the KMT party, administration, and army were fully exposed in 1944. Huang Shao-hsiung, a prominent member of the Kwangsi Clique, observed:

In 1944 when attending a conference in Chungking [the wartime capital], I heard everywhere, both inside and outside the party and the Government, complaints about the political situation.[26]

17. [153] II, 367 and [179] 58. See also [134] 219.   18. [261] 52.
19. 'Honan has two sorrows—the Yellow River and T'ang En-po.' [269] 170.
20. [269] 170.   21. [153] II, 370–1, [264] 83–4, and [269] 181–5.
22. [269] 188 and [279] 221.   23. [153] II, 370–1.
24. [46] III, 969 or *SW* IV, 167.   25. [22] 101.   26. [265] II, 429.

Huang meant by 'the political situation' the way the Government ruled the country. In *The United States Relations with China*, there are a great number of despatches critical of Chiang and his Government. For instance, J. S. Service reported:

Morale is low and discouragement widespread. There is a general feeling of hopelessness. . . .

The government and military structure is being permeated and demoralized from top to bottom by corruption, unprecedented in scale and openness.[27]

General Stilwell wrote:

Greed, corruption, favouritism, more taxes, a ruined currency, terrible waste of life, callous disregard of all the rights of men.[28]

Raymond Atkinson published this in the *New York Times* on 31 October 1944:

The Generalissimo's [Chiang's] régime, based on the support and subservience of General Ho Ying-ch'in, H. H. Kung, Minister of Finance, and Dr. [*sic*] Chen Li-fu, Minister of Education, has remained fundamentally unchanged over a long period of time and has become bureaucratic, inefficient, and corrupt.[29]

About Chiang personally, Atkinson went on:

Although he is the acknowledged leader of China, he has no record of personal military achievement and his basic ideas of political leadership are those of a war lord.

Davies, in a memorandum to Harry Hopkins, dated 31 December 1943, regarded Chiang as being:

incapable of reforming the Kuomintang and taking the lead in a genuine united front . . . not only personally incapable of this, he is hostage of the corrupt forces he manipulates.[30]

Chiang replied apologetically to his critics. Regarding his dictatorship, he said that the war had delayed the termination of the period of political tutelage and the inauguration of that of constitutional rule; regarding the welfare of peasants, he thought it a complex problem which the KMT should tackle according to

---

27. [11] 567. This is dated 20 June 1944.   28. [268] 293.

29. H. L. Boorman has informed me that Raymond Atkinson must be Brooks Atkinson, the paper's drama critic who was a war correspondent at Chunking in 1944.   30. [10] 399.

the Principle of Livelihood while it would pay due respect to the rights of landowners; regarding corruption, he blamed it on the warlords of the 1920s, arguing that it was also known on a comparable scale in other countries, including the United States. Chiang resented the unfavourable publicity he received in America, calling it 'unfair . . . biased'.[31]

But corrupt officers and officials, like so many millions of termites, had eaten away the two pillars of Chiang's political power— the efficiency of the army and the vitality of the economy.

The command system of the KMT army, elaborately formulated on paper, played no more than an advisory role. A decision was either taken, as it so often was, by Chiang himself without consulting others or worked out by negotiation with field commanders or their representatives in Chungking.[32] If the commander happened to be out of Chiang's favour, he would receive less or no supplies.[33] And among Chiang's high staff and commanding officers, personal rivalries, jealousies, and incompatibilities, sometimes mingled with disputes over matters of principle or policy, were notorious.[34] The ammunition production, as it was in 1944, amounted to 15,000,000 bullets per month, or 4 per man per month, in addition to a few thousand rounds of shells for guns and mortars.[35] As a result of this, the equipment deteriorated from 7,000 rifles, 100 light machine-guns, and 60 heavy machine-guns a division in 1937 to 2,500, 100, and 33 respectively.[36] After the close of the Yunnan–Burma Road the situation became even worse. Army lorries, for instance, were reduced from 15,000 to only 5,000 a year later and consequently officers preferred to keep vehicles and petroleum in store rather than use them.[37]

After the outbreak of the Pacific War there did not seem to be any coherent strategic plan at the headquarters of the General Chiefs-of-Staff in Chungking, except for preserving strength for the coming struggle for the control of China against the communists. All troops were therefore used for garrison purposes instead of as field and mobile units, and during the stalemate of five years, they had very little to do. The new levies had been recruited since

31. [153] II, 391–2.   32. *Davies's Memorandum*, 9.3.1943, [10] 27.
33. [263] 142.   34. [269] 104–5.   35. [269] 74.
36. [134] 203.   37. [269] 73 and 137.

1938 under conditions of great brutality and corruption.[38] When the conscripts were put into barracks they were treated like animals. Payrolls were nearly all 'padded'; some divisions had as few as 2,000 men only.[39] Lack of training and lack of medical attention were the rule rather than the exception. The soldiers in turn treated the people like animals.[40] Facing all these excesses and irregularities, Chiang had only one card to play when he lost his temper—summary execution.[41] T. H. White, having toured many battlefields and seen many soldiers, concluded:

The years of stalemate had made the Chinese Army a pulp, a tired, dispirited, unorganized mass, despised by the enemy, alien to its own people, neglected by its government, ridiculed by its allies. No one doubted the courage of the Chinese soldier, but the army had no mobility, no strength, no leadership.[42]

So much for the army; now we turn to the economy. It must be remembered that when the Resistance War broke out Chinese economy stood at the peak of its prosperity. The production of both agriculture and many key industries was high and the monetary unification of 1935 benefited the economy enormously.[43] But the loss of the coastal provinces meant financially the loss to the Government of two major taxes—the maritime customs and the salt gabelle. For the first time since 1860 the land tax regained its traditional importance in the Government's revenue from taxation.[44] The Government exploited the wartime patriotism by selling bonds, but of the 1,450 million *yuan* proffered in 1938 only 18·4 million was taken up and the record for 1939 showed no improvement.[45] The amount actually dwindled to a mere 8 million in 1940, and then rose to 127 million in 1941 while the deficits for those two years were 3,963 million and 8,693 million respectively.[46] The Government therefore had no other recourse than inflation as a means of paying for the war.

38. [10] 159, [263] 79–80, and 149–50, and [269] 128–9.
39. [153] III, 641 [263] 149, and [269] 135.
40. Gauss to Secretary of State, 5.11. 1943, quoting from the *Ta-kung Pao*, [10], 159; [261] 182.
41. [46] II, 506 n. 22 (or *SW* II, 292 n. 25 which is rather different from this) and [265] 39.
42. [269] 128.   43. [327] 1948.   44. [4] 187.
45. [260] 16.   46. [260] 38.

The question here is not whether the Government should have relied on inflation or not, but how it attempted to utilize it. To understand this question it is necessary to know Chiang's view of money. In his *Chinese Economic Theory*, he wrote:

The Great Learning states: 'Where there are men, there is land. Where there is land, there is money. Where there is money, there is use for it.' This simply means that manpower and land are the two important factors of production. If manpower is used to develop the land, there will be goods and money. . . . Money is not regarded as the essential factor of production in Chinese economic theory. Chinese economists regard goods as the products of manpower and the land, and money simply as a medium of exchange.[47]

Having thus completely ignored the part money played in encouraging or discouraging production, in facilitating or obstructing trade, and in widening or closing the gap between the rich and the poor, Chiang never admitted in public that inflation had been the cause of China's economic difficulties. He told the fifth session of the People's Political Council on 10 April 1940: '. . . if we exert ourselves to increase production there will be nothing else really worth worrying about.'[48] And he told the eighth plenum of the Central Executive and Supervisory Committees of the KMT on 24 March 1941: 'There are now sections of public opinion that entertain excessive anxiety over certain economic problems of the day. According to my own observation there is really no ground for such anxiety.'[49] Chiang and many of his economic advisers believed that inflation in itself would not result in an economic collapse in the near future because China was fundamentally an agricultural economy and the great majority of the population lived off the land.[50] Inflation therefore was not regarded as the chief malady of the time. For instance, the manifesto of the KMT plenum held in Chungking in May 1945 did not devote a single word to it.[51]

In fact, China, like other under-developed countries, was particularly susceptible to inflation. She had little unemployed productive capacity in terms of labour and capital, for her labour

47. [121] Philip Jaffe's translation, 245.   48. [122] I, 422.
49. [122] II, 581.
50. Gauss to Secretary of State, 30.11.1943, [10] 175. Mr. S. Adler held this opinion then; see *ibid.*, 176.   51. [4] 61–3.

lacked mobility and capital was scarce; supply would not increase in response to higher prices and prices would consequently rise at a great and accelerating rate. The businesses which had shorter periods of turn-over, such as commerce and notably speculation, would make more profit, and were therefore more attractive to investors, while agriculture and manufacturing industries would find capital for maintenance and expansion very hard to come by. Both the marginal and average propensities of the Chinese to consume were high, and inflation had the effect of making them even higher, so that capital became even scarcer. Higher rates of interest or profit, even if they could have compensated for the loss of the value of money, would not induce people to save and lend more. In addition to all this, the economy itself was loosely organized and control over inflation in order to check the speed or to achieve a measure of fairness in the distribution of income and wealth were bound to be less effective.[52]

Prices rose by 40–50 per cent. per annum in 1937–9, 160 per cent. per annum in 1939–41, and 300 per cent. per annum in 1942–5.[53] At the end of the Resistance War the general price index stood at 10,075 with its December 1941 level at 100.[54] As early as in 1943 the civil servant's average salary had already sunk to no more than 10 per cent. of its 1937 value, that of the teacher to 17 per cent., that of the serviceman to 57 per cent., and after a slump, to 10 per cent. in 1942, that of the rural worker to 58 per cent., and that of the labourer to 74 per cent. With the civil servants so poorly paid, it was difficult to check embezzlement and other irregularities. The middle class, whose support the KMT should have sought, were beggared, and the favourites of the time were speculators, smugglers, and manipulators of various kinds. No régime could be described as sound when it depended upon the support of such people.

Behind the Japanese lines, the Eighth Route Army, the New Fourth Army, and the base areas battled on and thrived. The Eighth Route Army triumphantly engaged the Japanese at P'inghsingkuan on 25 and 26 September 1937 in a *rencontre* which the

52. [11] 59–60 and [260] 59–60, 61–3, and 90–1.
53. [260] 12.
54. [260] 46.

Germans considered 'a classic piece of mobile warfare'.[55] In this battle, the Japanese lost over 3,000 men and the communists over a thousand. Despite the prestige the communists gained in it, it was for them a heavy loss in manpower for the Army was no more than 40,000 strong. So nothing on a comparable scale was attempted until 1940; instead, the communists turned their attention to the establishment of base areas and the expansion of their army. The Eighth Route Army grew from 30,000 in July 1937 to 156,000 in 1938[56] and to 400,000 in 1940,[57] while the New Fourth Army, beginning with some 10,000 men, reached 25,000 in 1938 and 100,000 in 1940.[58] This was possible because the Japanese were concentrating on attacking the KMT troops, and trying to force Chiang to surrender. They did not pay serious attention to the communists until after the fall of Wuhan and the establishment of Wang Ching-wei's régime in Nanking.[59]

Forestalling the Japanese campaigns against them, the communist troops mobilized 155 regiments in an all-out war of harassment in Shansi and south Hopei which lasted from August to December 1940. In over 1,800 engagements, most of them small, they inflicted 20,000 casualties on the Japanese and over 23,000 on the puppet troops, while they themselves sustained a loss of over 22,000 men.[60] The objectives of this operation were to destroy the Japanese communication system and the rapidly extending system of blockhouses.[61] The operation succeeded in destroying nearly 3,000 strong-points, 948 kilometres of railway, and 3,000 kilometres of roads,[62] but it also alarmed the Japanese and the KMT. Therefore in the following two years the KMT tightened its 'cordon sanitaire' round the Shensi-Kansu-Ninghsia Border Region and the Japanese launched a ruthless nibbling campaign against the base areas.

The Japanese divided the occupied territories into three categories—'orderly', 'semi-orderly', and 'disorderly'. In the 'orderly'

55. [134] 201. About the battle, see [261] 208–9, [264] 40, [265] II, 339, and [279] 17–18.

56. [185] 123.   57. [181] 108.   58. [185] 123.

59. Mao himself admitted that the Japanese did not take the communists seriously in 1938 and 1939. [46] III, 965 or SW IV, 161–2.

60. [279] 108–17.   61. [269] 189, [279] 108–17, and [282] 135.

62. [279] 116–17.

areas, they used the age-old system of collective responsibility known as the *pao-chia*—every 100 families were organized into a *chia* and every 1,000 families into a *pao* in which all members were made responsible for each other's actions. This was designed to enforce law and order there. Round the 'semi-orderly' areas, the Japanese created a no-man's-land and built blockhouses to strengthen the defence. In two years they had erected 7,700 such blockhouses and dug 11,860 kilometres of blockade trenches—six times the length of the Great Wall—in order to segregate these areas from communist infiltration and invasion. The 'disorderly' areas were where the battles were fought and the policy of scorched earth applied.[63] The communists also divided the enemy occupied areas into three categories—the 'liberated', the guerrilla, and the enemy occupied—roughly corresponding to the 'disorderly', 'semi-orderly', and 'orderly', and the war was to be fought in the guerrilla areas sandwiched between the other two.[64]

The Japanese campaign against the communists reduced their base areas by one-sixth and their population by one-third and killed 30,789 and wounded over 50,000.[65] The worst of all was the economic blockade simultaneously carried out by the KMT and the Japanese, creating the melancholy situation that Mao described at the end of 1942:

For a while we were reduced almost to the state of having no clothes to wear, no oil to cook with, no paper, no vegetables, no footwear for the soldiers and, in winter, no bedding for the civilian personnel.[66]

It was during this time that Mao initiated the tripartite system of political power in the united front in order to broaden the mass basis of the communist domination, the production drive in order to defeat the economic blockade, and the unification of leadership and the rectification campaigns (*cheng-feng*) in order to strengthen the CCP. By all these, he succeeded in maintaining the morale of his party, army, and people and in diverting their attention from the hardships of life to things more constructive and hopeful.[67]

The tripartite system meant that in the governments of the base areas one-third of the officials had to be members of the CCP, one-

63. [189] 336, [269] 69 and 194, [282] 220, and [279] 119.
64. [289] 122–7.   65. [189] 384, [234] 10, [269] 189, and [289] 122.
66. [46] III, 914 or *SW* IV, 106.   67. [46] III, 967 or *SW* IV, 163.

third progressive left-wing elements, and one-third independents. The main objects of this arrangement were to ensure the preponderance of the CCP leadership and to exclude right-wing elements from political power even if they were anti-Japanese.[68] The agrarian policy in the base areas was a moderate one which did not lay down the confiscation of land but guaranteed the reduction of rent and interest rates on the one hand and the collection of them on the other.[69] This was obviously designed to secure the support of both the poor and the middle peasants, so as to consolidate the administration and the economy of the base areas. The CCP also launched a stupendous production drive with all the able-bodied men and women, civilians and soldiers, the *élite* and the ordinary people taking part in it. As a result, the quantity of soldiers' rations which had gone down to 88 per cent. of the 1939 standard in 1940 and to 84·2 per cent. in 1941, showed signs of recovery in 1942 and became actually better than the 1939 standard in 1943. The rations of an average Eighth Route Army soldier consisted of 4 lb. 9 oz. of meat, 48 lb. of vegetables, and 60 lb. of millet per month with oil, seasonings, and fuel provided for them by the government.[70] Harrison Forman described the Red soldiers in 1943 as 'about the best nourished troops I had yet seen'; T. H. White described the people in Yenan as 'ruddier and healthier' than elsewhere in China; and R. P. Ludden's impression of them was 'a full belly, a warm back'.[71] According to Mao, the army achieved the tremendous feat of being economically self-sufficient in 1943.[72] The border region governments, too, were self-sufficient in 1944 when an independent observer visited Yenan and recorded this:

A civil servant was entitled to 20 oz. of rice and 1 lb. of vegetables per day and 2 lb. of pork and 1½ lb. of cooking oil per month. He was given one tunic suit for winter and another for summer, a shirt, a pair of trousers, a pair of winter shoes, and a pair of summer shoes each year. Medical care was free. . . .[73]

68. [46] II, 736 or *SW* III, 190 and [181] 118.
69. A Politburo decision on 28.10.1942. [162] 276–85, [275] 14, and [310] 64–8.
70. [282] 75.
71. [282] 42, [269] 213, and the *New York Times*, 23.3.1945 or [296] 290.
72. [46] III, 952 or *SW* IV, 149.   73. [288] 17. Also [273] 76.

There was little fighting to do and so the soldiers concentrated on production, expansion, and ideological rectification. This kept them busy, and all military commanders agree that a soldier should be fully occupied.

However, the most significant single event in the communist-controlled areas in this period was undoubtedly the rectification campaign. From May 1941 to May 1942 Mao had delivered five important speeches on the rectification of the styles of learning, working, and writing.[74] Of the style of learning he attacked what he called 'subjectivism' in either its doctrinaire or empirical sense, or both.[75] Doctrinairism sprang from 'crudity and perfunctoriness, boastfulness and satisfaction with scrappy knowledge',[76] from swallowing foreign things 'raw and whole' and being lacking in originality,[77] from studying 'theory for theory's sake' like shooting without a target,[78] and from a total dependence on books.[79] Empiricism, in Mao's view, was just the opposite, relying completely on experience instead of on both experience and study.[80] 'Thus,' Mao concluded, 'there are two kinds of incomplete knowledge: One is knowledge already contained in books and the other is knowledge which is usually perceptual and partial, and both are one-sided. Only through an integration of the two can real and comparatively complete knowledge emerge.'[81]

With regard to the party's method of working, Mao severely criticized the 'sectarianism', or, in other words, 'the assertion of independence', 'unduly emphasising the importance of [the] part of work which is in [one's] charge and wishing to subordinate the interests of the whole to those of the part', 'forgetting democratic centralism which subordinates the minority to the majority, the lower level to the higher level, the part to the whole and the whole Party to the Central Committee'. The individual must not come before the party; the cadres native to one locality and those from

74. The speeches are: 'Reform our Study', May 1941; 'Rectify the Party's Style in Work', February 1942; 'Oppose the Party "Eight-legged Essay" ', February 1942; and the introduction to and the conclusion of 'Talks at the Yenan Forum on Art and Literature', May 1942.

75. [46] III, 841 or *SW* IV, 35. See also [281].

76. [46] III, 817 or *SW* IV, 13.   77. [46] III, 818 or *SW* IV, 15.

78. [46] III, 819 or *SW* IV, 16.   79. [46] III, 840 or *SW* IV, 35.

80. [46] III, 840–1 or *SW* IV, 35–6.   81. [46] III, 840 or *SW* IV, 34.

the outside must unite; those who worked in the army must co-
operate with those who worked in the civilian departments;
different army units, different localities, and different departments
should assist each other, and then old and new cadres would get
on well.[82]

Art and literature, according to Mao, should be created with the
proletariat and the broad masses in mind, an audience composed
of workers, peasants, soldiers, and cadres. They should therefore
aim at praising the people's toil and struggle and educating them.
Political criteria should be placed before artistic criteria, since the
function of art and literature was to serve the revolutionary war.[83]

While the communists occupied themselves with the production
drive and rectification campaign and the KMT rotted, the Allied
forces gradually gained the upper hand in the Pacific theatre of
the War with the result that the Japanese were eventually compelled to relax their pressure on the Chinese communists. Hence
from 1943 to 1945 the Eighth Route Army entered into another
period of expansion, reaching 300,000 men in 1943 and 600,000
in 1945.[84] The New Fourth Army, on the other hand, had a more
chequered career.

Although a wing of the New Fourth Army penetrated into
Kiangsu and east Anhwei, the rest carried out guerrilla operations
on the periphery of the KMT controlled areas and enclaves, using
them as its rear.[85] The Army did not attempt to set up base areas of
its own in 1939 and 1940, nor did it carry out the communist
policy of reducing rates of interest and rent in the areas under its
influence. Hsiang Ying, for instance, did not refer to any such
efforts in his New Year's statement of 1939, and he had no plans
for reduction either.[86] Another example was Su Yü who, with his
column, was active in Chekiang but did not organize a base area
there. When the KMT governor of the province, Huang Shao-
hsiung, asked him to leave, Su duly did so and transferred his
troops to Kiangsu without making a gesture of defiance.[87] The

82. [46] III, 843–6 or *SW* IV, 38–41.
83. [46] III, 869 *et seq.* or *SW* IV, 63 *et seq.* See also [6] October–December
1960, 78.
84. [153] II, 393–4, [279] 219, and [296] 264.   85. [245] 1.
86. [46] II, 750 n. or *SW* III, 204 n., [179] 50, [279] 129, and [284] 33–4.
87. [265] II, 413–14.

Army as a whole was still weak; so when the supreme chief-of-staff, General Ho Ying-ch'in, ordered its units to evacuate the south of the Yangtze in October 1940, while the Eighth Route Army was ordered to move to the north of the Yellow River, the communists had to obey.[88]

The evacuation of the New Fourth Army began in December 1940, after consultations with the commander-in-chief of the third war-zone, General Ku Chu-t'ung, regarding the route the army was to take.[89] Here the communist sources differ. One of them says that General Ku agreed to the army crossing the Yangtze at a point in south Kiangsu.[90] Another source says that the original plan was to make the crossing at Fanch'ang and T'ungling in south Anhwei,[91] but the KMT broadcast the plan over the wireless and stuck farewell posters on the walls of the places of crossing, so as to make sure that the Japanese knew the communist movements and sealed off the river. The New Fourth Army was thus compelled to change its plan by endeavouring to cross the Yangtze somewhere in south Kiangsu.

Upon arriving at Hsint'an, a town in south Anhwei,[92] the New Fourth Army and the KMT troops clashed. Chiang says that the former attacked the KMT 40th Division which was ordered to take over the defence of the evacuated areas.[93] On this ground General Ku took disciplinary action by sending more government troops to the spot.[94] The communist version of the clash was that the KMT mobilized no less than seven divisions,[95] lying in wait and pouncing upon the New Fourth Army when it reached Maolin. There 10,000 officers and men of the New Fourth Army fought from 4 January to the tenth when their provisions became almost exhausted. On the thirteenth Yeh T'ing, the communist commander, contacted General Shang-kuan Yün-hsiang, offering to settle the question in person and it was at the latter's headquarters

88. [46] II, 775 n. 2 or *SW* III, 285 n. 2.
89. [279] 128.   90. [279] 128.   91. [247] II, 49.
92. [169] gives the place of Sanchih (95); [247], Hsint'an (II, 50); and [279], Maolin (128).
93. [153] II, 383 and [169] 95. See also [181] 109.   94. [153] II, 383.
95. The denominations were the 5th, 10th, 40th, 52nd, 79th, 108th, and 144th ([280] 249). [247] refers to the 52nd, 108th, 114th, and others with a total strength of 80,000 (II, 49–55).

that Yeh T'ing was arrested.[96] Thereafter the besieged New Fourth Army decided to break through on 14 January. Only 1,000 succeeded in this attempt; Hsiang Ying died in action.[97] Three days after this Chiang ordered the disbandment of the New Fourth Army.[98] But Mao, taking the matter into his own hands, appointed Ch'en Yi the acting commander and sent Hu Fu (Liu Shao-ch'i) as the political commissar to assist in regrouping and reorganizing the remnants of the New Fourth Army.[99] Liu and Ch'en organized them into seven divisions in their effort to turn them into regular troops and also ordered them to carry out the policies the Eighth Route Army had been applying in the north, namely the establishment of base areas, the formation of the 'united front' local governments, and the reduction of rent and interest.[1] Huang Shao-hsiung, the KMT governor of Chekiang, soon noticed the difference of Su Yü's methods of conducting the war when Su returned to set up a base on the Kiangsu-Chekiang border in 1941. This time Huang was unable to send him away.[2]

At a higher level, Chiang told the People's Political Council on 6 March 1941 that:

Provided unity can be preserved and resistance carried on to the end, the Government will be ready to follow your [the Council's] direction in the settlement of all outstanding questions.[3]

Mao, through the communist members at the Council, now proposed twelve conditions for a settlement, which were ignored by the KMT.[4] The united front was nevertheless preserved, at any rate in name. More important was the expansion of both the Eighth Route Army and the New Fourth Army, reaching, according to official statistics, the menacing totals of 321,000 and 154,000 in the summer of 1944 and 600,000 and 300,000 in 1945.[5]

The morale of these troops was excellent, for their commanding

96. [279] 129.
97. [181] 109, [247] II, 54–5, and [279] 129.
98. [46] II, 779 n. 2 or *SW* III, 285 n. 2, [153] II, 383, [269] 78, and [282] 161–2.
99. [46] II, 769 or *SW* III, 225 and [279] 131. See also [272] 12.
1. [279] 132–4, [289] 110–11, and Appendix B.
2. [265] II, 416–18.   3. [11] 54.
4. [46] II, 773–4 and 779 n. 4 or *SW* III, 230 and 259 n. 5.
5. [279] 219 and [296] 264.

officers and party workers paid close attention to it. Liu Po-ch'eng defined morale in these terms:

To us, war is an emotional struggle carried on through political consciousness. Morale is composed of hatred, love, revenge, and confidence in victory. It exists as a social phenomenon and does not lie in the strength of individuals, but in the strength of the society. It is decisive in combat and decisive in war.[6]

For keeping up morale, the communists closely watched three factors: leadership (or command), the education of the troops (or party propaganda), and the material welfare of the soldiers. Competent leadership required both sagacity in command and fairness in treatment, and the communists, in P'eng Te-huai's own words, allowed their commanding officers 'tremendous flexibility' in shaping their tactics.[7] After each campaign officers and men sat down for a frank discussion of their success or failure, during which soldiers could uninhibitedly criticize the mistakes and ineptitude of their officers.[8] The army was economically self-sufficient, burdening no one and receiving no pay as such. Each officer or soldier was given a piece of land to cultivate, which was looked after and cultivated by others when he was away fighting. There were no separate clubs, hospitals, or messes for officers and they wore the same uniforms as their men did.[9] The party naturally had an unrelenting grip on the army: 'Our principle is that the Party commands the gun, and the gun will never be allowed to command the Party.'[10] According to the Politburo resolution adopted in 1942, the political commissions in the army became a department in the party committees of corresponding grades. There was the military commission in the Politburo; likewise there was a military commission in the regional, district, or county party branch, and thus the party cells in the army were placed directly under the control of party branches of appropriate grades. The secretary of a branch was often concurrently the political commissar of the army unit stationed in his district.[11] Years of experience had taught the communists that the optimum ratio of party to non-party members in the army was one to three. For instance, in

6. [299] 344.   7. [293] 41.   8. [189] 240 and [296] 276.
9. [299] 332–4.   10. [46] II, 535 or *SW* II, 272.
11. [273] 233.

May 1946 the regular red army strength was 1,500,000, of whom nearly 400,000 were communists.[12]

Eyewitnesses spoke of the excellent discipline of the red army. Edgar Snow was impressed by their 'prompt obedience to orders'[13]; Robert Payne praised their careful way of dealing with village girls—'Because we wanted all the peasants on our side'[14]; Harrison Forman noticed that all their gun barrels, unlike those he had seen elsewhere in China, were spotlessly clean[15]; and Huang Shao-hsiung, a prominent KMT leader, paid tribute to the logistical swiftness and impeccable discipline of Liu Po-ch'eng's troops.[16] The officers and men were constantly reminded of the Three Main Rules of Discipline and the Eight Points for Attention.[17] In this way it was possible to rally the people round the army and to organize them into militia and guerrilla units to support it. The villagers became its ears and eyes, looked after the wounded, hid away grain when the enemy came, laid mines, dug tunnels, made wooden cannon, and destroyed enemy communications.[18]

With the regulars, guerrillas, and militia units, the communists succeeded in creating and expanding their base areas. A peasant told Forman: 'Under the KMT's rule we people had little to eat. Today even though our fields are in the very front lines of the war, we have more to eat than in the old days.'[19] And Davies reported to his government:

The communist governments and armies are the first governments and armies in modern Chinese history to have positive and widespread popular support. They have this support because the governments and armies are genuinely of the people.[20]

12. [46] I, 85 n.16 or *SW* I, 348 n.16 and Liu Shao-ch'i's interview with Mark Gayn, [326] 53.   13. [258] 171.   14. [293] 52.
15. [282] 223.   16. [265] II, 345.
17. [46] IV, 1241–2 or *SW* IV (Peking), 155–6. They are:
      The Three Main Rules: (1) Obey orders in all your actions. (2) Take not even a single needle or piece of thread from the masses. (3) Turn in everything captured.
      The Eight Points: (1) Speak politely. (2) Pay fairly for what you buy. (3) Return everything you borrow. (4) Pay for anything you damage. (5) Don't hit or swear at people. (6) Don't damage crops. (7) Don't take liberties with women. (8) Don't ill-treat captives.
18. [11] 567, *Davies's memorandum* dated 7.11.1944, [269] 196–8, [279] 224–30, [282] 123, 138–9, 141–2, 201–2, 207, 210, 217, 228, and 230–1, [289] 53, and [293] 51–2, 182–3 *et seq.*
19. [282] 204–5.   20. *Davies's memorandum*, 7.11.1944, [11] 567.

Here lies the key to the spectacular expansion from five base areas of a total area of 100,000 square kilometres and nearly two million people in 1937 to nineteen base areas of a total area of 1 million square kilometres and nearly 100 million people in 1945.[21] Though not yet joined into one mass of land, these areas and people, under the control of a party of nearly 1 million members and an army of equal strength, were in all senses another China which faced the China of the KMT at the end of the Resistance War. Even Mao's opponent, Chang Kuo-t'ao, had to admit that 'As far as Party interests were concerned, Mao's policy proved to be right.'[22]

21. [46] II, 428 ns. 2–6 or *SW* II, 289 ns.2–6, [181] 105–6 and 108, [279] 218–19, [289] 1–4, [275 and 276], and *News Chronicle* (London), 30.1.1945.
    22. [164] 4.

Chapter XII

Victory and Negotiations

O N 11 January 1943 China signed new treaties with both the United States and the United Kingdom, abrogating all the unequal treaties to which China had been subjected for a century, and a fortnight later, at the end of the Casablanca Conference, President Roosevelt and Mr. Churchill (as he was then) announced their decision to accept nothing short of the unconditional surrender of the enemy. It was at such a time of hope and jubilation that Chiang Kai-shek published his *China's Destiny* on 10 March 1943. He was, however, not the only one who tried to forecast the future of China; Mao did the same in two important writings—*On New Democracy* of January 1940 and *On Coalition Government* read at the seventh national congress of the CCP in April 1945. Here were two destinies for a united country envisaged by the two leaders of virtually two Chinas, a comparison of which may throw some light on the questions facing China before and after the end of the Resistance War.

In these writings, both Chiang and Mao blamed China's misfortunes on external causes—for Chiang, they were the results of the unequal treaties and for Mao, of imperialist oppression and the feudal traditions of Chinese society. Both authors found a remedy in democracy, a concept not explained by Chiang in his book but explained by Mao in his programme of New Democracy. 'The state system—joint dictatorship of all revolutionary classes. The political structure—democratic centralism. This is,' wrote Mao, 'new democratic government; this is a republic of New Democracy.'[1] In other words, he proposed to establish, after the

1. [46] II, 670 or *SW* III, 121.

defeat of Japan, 'a state of the united front or democratic alliance based on the overwhelming majority of the people under the leadership of the working class'.² And 'the state structure of New Democracy should be based on democratic centralism, with the people's congresses at various levels determining the major policies and electing the government'. How then to bring about the transition from the KMT political tutelage to Mao's New Democracy? Mao proposed two steps: 'In the first stage, to form a provisional coalition government by common agreement of the representatives of all parties and people without party affiliation; in the second stage, through free and unrestricted elections, to convene a national assembly which will form a proper coalition government.'³

What should be the political principles on which to build either Chiang's democratic or Mao's new-democratic China? The two parties agreed on Dr. Sun Yat-sen's Three Principles of the People, and yet differed in their interpretations of them. For Chiang, 'the Three Principles are rooted in the traditional moral philosophy of our nation. In simple terms, we may say that "altruism" constitutes the basic principle of the [National] Revolution, while "kindness and love" furnish the key to the salvation of the world'.⁴ Therefore the basis of the reconstruction of Chiang's new China was psychological and moral and of the moral principles he emphasized sincerity above all. 'Where there is selflessness,' he wrote, 'there is sincerity.'⁵ And 'with sincerity, a man concerns himself with public, not personal interests. With sincerity, a man works for a just cause in perfect self-possession, pushing steadily and calmly onwards, unheedful of difficulties and dangers, until he finally succeeds.'⁶ To the questions of how the people could be expected to obey such a moral code and what restrictions there were to be on the excesses of the scheming, the privileged, and the powerful, Chiang offered no answers. In fact, throughout his *China's Destiny*, he said very little about the law or the constitution and not a word on the adoption of a constitution for China. Mao's understanding of the Three Principles was very different, as he said:

2. [46] III, 1079 or *SW* IV, 271.
3. [46] III, 1079–80 and 1092 or *SW* IV, 271–2 and 285.
4. [121] 203.   5. [121] 149.   6. [121] 150. See also 153–4.

The revolutionary Three People's Principles of the new period, the new or genuine Three People's Principles, contain the three cardinal policies of alliance with Russia, co-operation with the Communists and assistance to the peasants and workers. Without these three cardinal policies or *minus* any one of them, they become, in the new period, the false Three People's Principles or the incomplete Three People's Principles.[7]

He remarked pointedly concerning Chiang's advocacy of 'the traditional moral philosophy':

There is also in China a semi-feudal culture which is a reflection of semi-feudal politics and economy and has as its representatives all those who, while opposing the new culture and new ideologies, advocate the worship of Confucius, the study of the Confucian canon, the old ethical code and the old ideologies. . . . This reactionary culture serves the imperialists and the feudal class, and must be swept away.[8]

In this new period, according to Mao, what China needed was *his* version of the Three Principles which he had pledged to put into practice. But he also made it clear that the Principles were only the *minimum* programme of the new-democratic revolution, upon whose completion the communists should strive to carry out their *maximum* programme of socialism and communism.[9] Mao's New Democracy and coalition government were therefore transitional so in his view were the Three Principles. In this respect Mao's New Democracy and coalition government differed from Chiang's *Destiny* which was a long-term programme.

Moreover, while Chiang stressed psychological and moral reconstruction as the key to the success of his programme, Mao hinged his whole idea on the formation of a coalition government[1] which he regarded as the only gateway to a peaceful China. In other words, Chiang relied on the spirit of self-discipline of both the privileged and the under-privileged, the Nationalists and communists, to maintain peace and order, so that the nation could proceed towards economic and social progress; Mao, on the other hand, insisted upon a common programme, as binding as a provisional constitution, to restrict the unscrupulous and depraved

7. [46] II, 682 or *SW* III, 134.   8. [46] II, 688 or *SW* III, 141.
9. [46] II, 680 and III, 1082, 1084 or *SW* III, 132 and IV, 274, 277.
10. [46] III, 1110 or *SW* IV, 304.

from breaking the peace. In these respects, Chiang was essentially a Confucian and Mao a legalist.

On such a basis, Chiang proposed to embark on an ambitious, planned economic reconstruction aiming at industrialization and the strengthening of the national defence.[11] Mao, however, did not think the time opportune for long-term projects. His new-democratic economic programme paid undivided attention to urgent relief and rehabilitation in the hope that the peasants might enjoy a measure of economic security. Industrialization, in Mao's view, though necessary, could come only after the major political questions had been settled.[12] Defence, too, weighed heavily on both authors' minds. Chiang was anxious to build a modern de-fence force, co-ordinated not only with China's economic strength but also with her cultural tradition.[13] With this aim Mao did not disagree, but he made it clear that such a force as well as other armed forces in the country should belong to the nation *ruled by a coalition government*, not by one party.[14]

Chiang's long-term approach coupled with his adherence to the Confucian tradition suggest that he omitted urgent problems from his *Destiny* perhaps because he deemed them unsuitable for open discussion. His party and government had tutelary authority which could be justified in terms of Confucian tradition and with which they could deal with short-term problems. Mao challenged this conviction. He demanded the end of such tutelage and doubted the KMT's authority as well as ability to solve those problems without consulting other parties. He wanted a new authority, namely the coalition government, which would be responsible for tackling such questions in the post-war period. This difference was to become the major bone of contention between the KMT and the CCP in their negotiations.

But as long as Japan remained undefeated, the legitimacy of the tutelary authority of the KMT was not openly denied by Mao. And even as late as October 1944, Chu Te could not yet see a way to drive the Japanese out of China. As he told Harrison Forman in an interview:

11. [121] 162–5.
12. [46] III, 671–2, 1081, 1100–1, and 1104 or *SW* IV, 122–3, 273, 294–5, and 298–9.   13. [121] 152.   14. [46] III, 1096–7 or *SW* IV, 289 *et seq.*

Lacking modern offensive weapons we can carry on a war of attrition only, and must depend on other factors for final victory.[15]

The 'other factors' Chu referred to turned out to be the Allied operations on land and sea in the Far East and the Pacific areas and particularly the atomic explosions on Hiroshima and Nagasaki. Japan announced her unconditional surrender over her radio on 10 August 1945.[16] What followed in China was a scramble for men, territory, property, and military equipment. The Supreme Chief-of-Staff, General Ho Ying-ch'in, sent memoranda to the Japanese commander-in-chief in China, General Yasuji Okamura, instructing him to surrender his 1,090,000 troops only to the Chinese commanders of the war zones, all of whom were KMT officers, thus depriving the communists of the right to accept the surrender of any Japanese units.[17] At the same time, Chiang telegraphed all units of the Eighth Route Army (or the 18th Army Group) 'to stay where they are, pending further orders', and forbade them to take over the enemy's arms.[18]

Mao ignored this order. Instead, his own orders to Ho Lung, Nieh Jung-chen, and others were 'to make all efforts to attack the enemy troops and be prepared to accept their surrender', and jointly with Chu Te, ordered them to advance swiftly to Inner Mongolia, Manchuria, and north and south Shansi.[19] He also ordered General Okamura to surrender his troops which had hitherto been fighting the communist units.[20] Faced with this open defiance, a spokesman of the National Government in Chungking stated at a press conference on 15 August: 'The orders of the Generalissimo must be obeyed. . . . Those who violate them are enemies of the people.' Mao at once rebutted this by saying that 'this shows that Chiang Kai-shek has declared civil war against the Chinese people'.[21]

Statements and orders could not stop the advancing communist units. Ho Lung's troops moved from their base in east Suiyuan to the western section of the Peking–Suiyuan railway and the middle

15. [282] 170.   16. [4] 317–18 and [153] III, 427.
17. [4] 319–22.   18. [46] IV, 1141 or *SW* IV (Peking), 33.
19. [46] IV, 1144 and 1139–40 n. 1 or *SW* IV (Peking), 36 and 30 n. 1.
20. [46] IV, 1144 or *SW* IV (Peking), 36.
21. [46] IV, 1147 or *SW* IV (Peking), 41.

section of the Lunghai railway, thus engulfing virtually the entire territories of both Suiyuan and Shansi. Nieh Jung-chen's units pushed on to the eastern section of the Peking–Suiyuan railway, the northern section of the Peking–Hankow railway, and the northern section of the Tientsin–Pukow railway, thus occupying Chahar and encircling the Peking-Tientsin-Paoting delta. Liu Po-ch'eng's troops dashed to the middle section of the Peking–Hankow and Lung-hai railways, taking large areas north of the Yellow River in Honan. Lo Jung-huan's troops went east to the middle section of the Tientsin–Pukow railway and to the Tsingtao–Chinan railway, seizing Shantung. Ch'en Yi's New Fourth Army advanced in several directions towards the Yangtze delta and the Huai River areas.[22] In two weeks after the victory, the communist-occupied areas expanded from 116 counties to 175[23] and this figure was increased to 313 counties in October 1945, covering 315,000 square kilometres in which 18,717,000 people lived.[24]

Of all the areas occupied by the communists after V-J Day the most important, and later bitterly disputed, was Manchuria. As early as in 1944 when Gunther Stein asked him whether the communists would take it, Mao answered: 'If we are strong enough when the time comes, we shall of course take up the task of driving the Japanese out of Manchuria as well as out of other parts of China. We hope that allied troops and ours will do it together.'[25] According to a KMT report, on 11 August 1945 Lin Piao led some 100,000 soldiers of Lü Cheng-ts'ao, Chang Hsüeh-shih, Wan Yi, and Li Yün-ch'ang on a forced march to Manchuria in at least four columns, and upon arrival, they acquired 300,000 rifles, 138,000 machine-guns, and 2,700 pieces of field artillery.[26] Not only was Lin Piao's army thus equipped; it also incorporated some 75,000 puppet troops into its ranks, swelling its strength to 200,000.[27]

22. R. B. Rigg, *Red China's Fighting Hordes*, N.Y., 1952, 252, quoted from [134] 228, [181] 131, and [279] 222.
23. [46] IV, 1151 or *SW* IV (Peking), 47.
24. [153] III, 461 and [279] 222.   25. [296] 367.
26. Dr. T. F. Tsiang's statement before the U.N. General Assembly, [5] 391. See also [302] 177–8 and [307] 4, both of which refer to the forced march, but do not say that the soldiers were unarmed.
27. [302] 178 and R. B. Rigg, *op. cit.*, 249 f.

Chiang was of course fully aware of the industrial and strategic importance of Manchuria in the unified China he visualized. But both his requests for permission to land troops at Dairen and for Russian co-operation in disbanding the communist guerrillas were rejected by the Soviet commander-in-chief in Manchuria, Marshal Malinovsky.[28] As a result, Chiang had to land his American-trained divisions at Yingkow and then take over the major cities along the railways in Manchuria.[29] The United States, on the other hand, helped Chiang by lifting half a million troops by air or by sea to the north and east.[30] The American forces in China, about 100,000 strong, also assisted the Chinese Government in protecting the Peking–Tientsin and Manchurian railways.[31]

As both the Government and the communist troops rushed to the north and east, a jig-saw pattern emerged. In the north and Manchuria the transport lines and major cities under the Government were surrounded by communist-held areas, while in central and east China communist enclaves were encircled by Government-controlled areas. To the Government this was not a satisfactory situation, but militarily the best it could hope for for the time being. The Government's influence in Manchuria, Inner Mongolia, and north China, though weak, was not beyond possibility of improvement. The victory itself had greatly strengthened the Government's economic position. An upsurge of the people's confidence in the Government currency brought down the wholesale price index at Chungking from 1,795·00 (January–June 1937 = 1) to 1,226·00 in September and 1,184·17 in October, while its U.S. dollar rate fell from 1,754 (January–June 1937 = 1) in August to 968·10 in September.[32] The Government's holding of U.S. dollars and gold on V-J Day stood at over U.S.$900 million, an unprecedented high level.[33] In addition to this, there was also the accession of enemy property, and of lend-lease and UNRRA and CNRRA material aid amounting to over U.S.$1,000 million. On top of this was an American bank loan of $62,550,000.[34] Yet, instead of making good use of these tremendous resources and the optimistic state of mind of the people to relieve and strengthen

28. [302] 163–6.   29. [302] 166.
30. [11] 311–12 and [269] 263.   31. [324] 338. See also [11] 268–9.
32. [271] 160 and 170.   33. [11] 129.   34. [153] III, 447–9.

the national economy, Chiang, persisting in his belief that inflation could never cause an economic collapse in China, kept these monetary and material assets in reserve for a possible civil war. In their taking over of the enemy occupied territories, Chiang's men made some fatal mistakes, alienating the people who had enjoyed better rule under the Japanese. The fixing of the official rate of exchange at 200 'puppet' currency to 1 *yuan* of Government currency was one of the major blunders, for it grossly undervalued the former. Equally unwise was the decision to put the soya beans of Manchuria under governmental control in the hope of earning more hard currency, since this only aggravated the serious food situation in Manchuria.[35] The KMT officials, going back to the enemy occupied areas to take over the administration, acted in a deplorable way.[36] The UNRRA and CNRRA relief material was either openly auctioned to the highest bidders or *sold* to those who needed it.[37] Soon the people in those areas began to regret the end of the Japanese and puppet régimes in China.[38]

Japan now having surrendered, the question of a post-war united front in China became an urgent problem. The principal parties—the KMT and the CCP—began a long series of negotiations in 1943 to this end, culminating in the talks between Chiang and Mao in 1945 and General George Marshall's mission in 1946 which ended fruitlessly in 1947. Since this was a matter not only of national but of international significance, the great Powers of the world were directly or indirectly involved in it. Stalin encouraged his Chinese comrades to reach a *modus vivendi* with the KMT, as he told Kardelj in 1948:

... after the war we invited the Chinese comrades to come to Moscow and we discussed the situation in China. We told them bluntly that we considered the development of the uprising in China had no prospects, that the Chinese comrades should seek a *modus vivendi* with Chiang Kai-shek, that they should join the Chiang Kai-shek government and dissolve their army. The Chinese comrades agreed here in Moscow with the views of the Soviet comrades, but went back to China and acted quite otherwise. They mustered their forces, organized their

35. [266] 116.   36. [302] 236.   37. [266] 4.
38. [11] 127–8 and [266] 2.

armies and now, as we see, they are beating Chiang Kai-shek's army. Now, in the case of China, we admit we were wrong.[39]

America, however, was deeply committed through giving financial and other assistance to the KMT Government as well as by stationing her troops in China. Her Ambassador, Patrick J. Hurley and later, President Truman's special envoy, General Marshall, were mediators and participants in many sessions of the KMT–CCP negotiations. By its act of generosity and friendliness, the United States hoped to strengthen its traditional ties with China and her people. Its position was reminiscent of Russia's in 1924–7. The Russian advisers in the 1920s did not observe the Chinese customs and etiquette and thus offended many Chinese.[40] Some American soldiers behaved much worse. 'The one abiding sentiment that almost all American enlisted personnel and most of the officers shared was contempt and dislike for China. . . . They believed that all Chinese were corrupt, inefficient, and unreliable.' They ill-treated their Chinese servants and called all Chinese 'slope-headed bastards' or simply 'slopies'.[41] Their misconduct culminated in the rape of a girl student of Peking University on 12 December 1946, which touched off a nation-wide protest against the arrogant GI's. Their misdemeanours went a long way to undermine what the American diplomats and other representatives had tried so hard to build up and also furnished the communists and malcontents with weapons of anti-Americanism. In time the Americans, like the Russians in the 1920s, got their fingers badly burnt in the 'China Tangle'.

Apart from America, there was a much weaker but nevertheless important political force in post-war China which had to be reckoned with. The Democratic League of small parties, with a combined membership of perhaps less than 100,000,[42] was formed in 1939 and adopted the name Democratic League in 1944.[43] Although its component parties had different views on a host of problems, they agreed on preventing the recrudescence of the civil war which had been left unfinished in 1936 and on bringing about a coalition government to replace the KMT tutelage.[44] Like the

39. [311] 331.   40. [193] 251.
41. [269] 154–8.   42. [296] 372.   43. [302] 114.
44. [11] 450 and [302] 114.

CCP, none of these parties had a legal status; unlike it, none of them had an army or a base area. The army, the members of the League thought, should properly belong to the State and the game of politics should be played according to democratic rules. In Chinese politics these unarmed parties had a 'Chinaman's chance' of success. But as long as there was no open breach between the two major parties, there was the hope, however faint, of a political settlement; as long as such a hope was alive, the League could play its role as a mediator.

Early in 1943 when the CCP had not yet recovered from the Japanese encirclement and suppression in the two previous years and when the KMT was in a position to reach a favourable settlement with the communists, Chiang treated Chou En-lai and Lin Piao, the communist negotiators, with disdain and refused either to grant legal status to the CCP or to expand the communist troops to four armies of twelve divisions.[45] However, speaking at the eleventh plenum of the fifth Central Executive Committee of the KMT, he said openly that the communist problem was a purely political one and should be solved by political means,[46] while his Chief-of-Staff, General Ho Ying-ch'in, attacked the CCP at the third People's Political Council in such harsh terms that Tung Pi-wu, the communist delegate, walked out in protest.[47] By the end of 1943 Chou En-lai left Chungking, and thus a golden opportunity for a *rapprochement* was lost.

In 1944 there were two rounds of negotiations, beginning unexpectedly, but not accidentally, in Sian where the communist representative, Lin Tsu-han, met with the Government representatives, Wang Shih-chieh and Chang Chih-chung.[48] It was on 4 May that Lin presented his conditions of the reorganization of the communist forces into twelve divisions under the same commanders as before and the recognition of the CCP and the Shensi-Kansu-Ninghsia Border Region, granting the latter a high degree of self-government.[49] Lin also raised the question of a constitutional coalition government which, Chang and Wang thought, should be

45. [11] 54, [46] III, 941 or *SW* IV, 136, and [169] 107.
46. [11] 54.
47. Gauss to Secretary of State, 20.9.1943, [10] 345.
48. [181] 124.   49. [4] 68.

postponed until they were in Chungking. Five talks in all were held in Sian, and according to Chang Chih-chung's report to the People's Political Council, Lin Tsu-han initialled the minutes of them.[50] Lin denied this.[51] The truth about the Sian talks is still not known; what is known is that another good opportunity was lost at the time because when Lin arrived at Chungking the military situation took a sharp turn against the KMT. The Japanese Operation *Ichi-gō* was in full swing and the KMT Government was on the verge of collapse; consequently the CCP's attitude stiffened. Not only was their demand for twelve divisions now raised to sixteen, but Lin also asked the KMT to recognize, in addition to the Shensi-Kansu-Ninghsia Border Region, all the other base areas in north, central, and south China.[52] Above all, Lin proposed the convocation of a National Affairs Conference to deliberate on the question of forming a coalition government. These changed terms made it impossible to reach an agreement and, moreover, destroyed the last shred of confidence between the parties, and Chiang disappointedly told Vice-President Henry Wallace that his concession of reorganizing the communist forces into twelve divisions had come to nought and Ambassador Gauss, too, was pessimistic over the prospects of the negotiations.[53]

But the negotiations dragged on, centring on the question of a coalition government. In November the United States decided to involve itself further in the China Tangle by sending its new Ambassador P. J. Hurley to Yenan. Full of enthusiasm though he was, Hurley was the wrong man for his task, and, at times, could not even pronounce the names of the Chinese with whom he had discussed matters of the utmost importance; nor could he understand the significance of a signature to a Chinese. However, he went to Yenan and met Mao there. According to the United States official assessment, he had impressed the communist leader by his initiative and cordiality; he also arrived at a five-point agreement with Mao.[54] Mao, in his capacity as the chairman of the Central Committee of the CCP, signed it; Hurley, too, signed *as a witness*. To the Chinese mind, however, the operative word here

50. [4] 81.   51. [4] 93.
52. [4] 68 and [302] 118.   53. [4] 68, [11] 64, and 559.
54. For details of the agreement see [11] 74–5 and [302] 127.

is 'signed' not 'as a witness', for later, when Chiang Kai-shek rejected the five points and the agreement became valueless, Hurley was accused by Mao of bad faith.[55] And the Chinese communist historians agree with Mao, as shown by the following quotations:

Ho Kan-chih—When Hurley returned to Chungking, he threw overboard the agreement reached in Yenan. . . .[56]

Hu Hua—But Hurley's sole purpose of going to Yenan was to gauge the communist position. Therefore when he went back to Chungking, he ate his own words.[57]

Liao Kai-lung—But the untrustworthy American envoy tore up the agreement bearing his own signature, as soon as he arrived back at Chungking from Yenan.[58]

Chou En-lai, however, wrote to Hurley politely: 'Chairman Mao Tse-tung has especially asked me to express his deep thanks and appreciation for your sympathy and energetic efforts on behalf of unity in China.[59]

Chiang did not explain in his book, *Soviet Russia in China*, why he rejected the points including the formation of a coalition government, but J. Service's memorandum to the State Department on 9 December 1944 had this to say:

The Generalissimo [Chiang] realizes that if he accedes to the communist terms for a coalition government, they will sooner or later dispossess him and his Kuomintang of power. He will therefore, unless driven to an extremity, not form a genuine coalition government. . . .

The Communists, on their part, have no interest in reaching an agreement with the Generalissimo short of a genuine coalition government. They realize that Chiang's position is crumbling. . . .[60]

Chiang, in turn, put forward a three-point counter-proposal, agreeing 'to incorporate, after reorganization, the Chinese Communist forces in the National Army which will then recieve equal treatment with the other units . . . and to give recognition to the Chinese Communist Party as a legal party', but saying not a word about the coalition government.[61] Chou En-lai received this counter-proposal on 12 November and went back to Yenan on 9

55. [46] III, 1139 or *SW* IV, 328.
56. [14] 421.   57. [18] 452.   58. [315] 43.
59. [11] 76. The letter was dated 6 December 1944.
60. [11] 572.
61. [4] 69, [11] 75, [46] III, 1096 or *SW* IV, 289, and [302] 128.

December. There followed a long spell of silence, despite Hurley's repeated requests for an answer to Chiang's conditions. On Christmas Eve, Mao said, in a reply to Hurley, that Chou was preoccupied with 'important conference preparations' which made his departure from Yenan difficult, and he also doubted whether the sincerity of the KMT warranted further negotiations on the basis of the five points agreed between him and Hurley.[62] Chou later replied too, naming the conditions of his return to Chungking: (1) the release of all political prisoners; (2) the withdrawal of KMT forces surrounding the border region and those attacking the New Fourth Army and the South China Anti-Communist Column; (3) the abolition of all oppressive regulations restricting the people's freedom; and (4) cessation of all secret service activity.[63] The gap was obviously too great to be bridged; so the talks ran aground for the time being.

In his New Year Message to the nation, Chiang pledged himself to end the political tutelage of the KMT by convening a National Assembly to draft a constitution,[64] while Ambassador Hurley kept up his contact with Mao, suggesting a visit to Yenan by T. V. Soong, Chang Chih-chung, and Wang Shih-chieh, which was to be followed perhaps by a visit of Mao himself and Chou En-lai to Chungking. In his reply, Mao welcomed the idea of sending KMT representatives to Yenan, but, at the same time, doubted its practical value. Once again Mao repeated the necessity of convening a National Affairs Conference including delegates from the KMT, the CCP, and the Democratic League. If this could be accepted, Mao went on, Chou En-lai would make a trip to Chungking. Hurley's message dated 20 January again urged Chou to come, and three days later Chou flew to Chungking.[65]

Though still insistent upon the formation of a coalition government as the prerequisite of transferring the armies from party to state control, Chou En-lai made the constitution of the National Affairs Conference the main task of this visit. The convocation of such a Conference was eventually accepted by both parties and Chou left for Yenan on 16 February.[66] A fortnight after Chou's departure, Chiang, in an attempt to remove the ground from

62. [11] 77.   63. [4] 70 and [11] 77.   64. [11] 80.
65. [11] 78.   66. [11] 79–82 and [302] 129.

under the feet of the proposed Conference, announced the Government's decision to call the National Assembly elected as far back as in 1936 to discuss and approve the 1936 Constitution. The date for the opening of the Assembly was fixed at 12 November 1945.[67] Chou was outraged by this, describing Chiang's announcement as 'deceitful' and as 'leaving no basis on which negotiations between the CCP and the other democratic parties and the KMT Government can be continued'.[68] Once again the talks broke down.

Before the talks could be resumed, both the KMT and the CCP convened their national congresses—the former took place in May and the latter from April to June.[69] It was to the seventh congress of the CCP that Mao read his well-known essay on coalition government. The congresses were followed by the fourth People's Political Council. Everyone was anticipating the coming of the victory over Japan which at last arrived on 10 August. As the leaders to victory, Chiang and the KMT stood then at the peak of their popularity and prestige, if not necessarily at the peak of their power.

With the traditional enemy, Japan, now vanquished, the KMT and the CCP faced each other in distrust and hostility. The situation demanded a further and greater effort to bring the two parties back to the conference table. Once again Ambassador Hurley flew to Yenan, asking Mao to come to Chungking in order to solve the urgent problems of co-operation, so that bloodshed could be avoided. Some people in Yenan (Professor Fan Wen-lan and his wife, for example) advised against Mao taking the trip,[70] but in view of the gravity of the issues at stake, Mao could hardly refuse Hurley's invitation on grounds of his personal safety.

This was to be a man-to-man talk between erstwhile colleagues and present enemies, for Mao and Chiang had worked for the same cause in Canton in 1925 and 1926 and now, after twenty years' enmity, were to work for the peace of China in Chungking. For Chiang, his uncompromising position was summarized in his V-J Day Message to the nation: 'The most important condition

67. [11] 73.
68. Chou to Hurley, 9.3.1945. See [11] 85 and also [4] 71.
69. [4] 53, [46] III, 1047 or *SW* IV, 241, [179] 60, and [162] 285 and 432.
70. [306] 6.

for national unity is the nationalization of all the armed forces in the country.'[71] But for Mao, his equally uncompromising position was revealed in his *On Coalition Government*:

'The army belongs to the state'—this is quite right. . . . But to what kind of state? . . . In China a new-democratic state only must be established and, on the basis of it, a new-democratic coalition government; and all the armed forces of China must belong to such a government of such a state so that they may safeguard the people's freedom and effectively fight foreign aggressors. As soon as a new-democratic coalition government appears in China, the armed forces of the Chinese liberated areas will be immediately handed over to it. And all the KMT troops must be handed over to it at the same time.[72]

These two principal figures of the negotiations formed a sharp contrast in personalities. Alert, energetic, quick witted and un-yielding on matters of their respective principles, both were being hailed as sagacious leaders by their respective followers, and therefore each had a popular image to live up to. Emotionally Chiang was quick-tempered while Mao was calm; morally Chiang was rigid and self-righteous while Mao was more flexible and less fastidious; politically Chiang was the less coherent while Mao was an un-adulterated Marxist. The meeting of these two enthralled the nation while it raised the hopes for peace.[73]

When, on 28 August 1945, the aeroplane touched down at Chungking airport and Mao stepped out of it, those who were waiting, including Shao Li-tzu, Lei Chen, Chou Chih-jou, Shen Chün-ju, and Kuo Mo-jo, saw a man slightly fuller and older than his photographs, wearing a new grey topee, a new tunic suit of greyish blue buttoned up to the neck, and a pair of new shoes. Chiang allotted him a car for his use in Chungking, and on the day of his arrival gave a dinner party in his honour.[74] On the next day Mao appeared at a press conference, wearing a dark brown tunic and black leather shoes, and correspondents noticed his habit of chain-smoking with deep inhalation and a slow exhalation.[75] On 1 September the Sino-Soviet Friendship Society gave a party in his honour, at which old friends like General Feng Yü-hsiang and T'an

71. Quoted from [134] 227.   72. [46] III, 1096–7 or *SW* IV, 290.
73. [302] 102, 104, 106–8, 234, and 238–9.
74. The *Ta-kung Pao*, 29.8.1945 and 30.8.1945.
75. *ibid.*, 30.8.1945.

P'ing-shan met him and talked nostalgically about the old days.[76] During his stay in Chungking, five young people went to see him and felt 'incomparable glory and happiness as well as excitement' while sitting beside 'the Chairman'. They had prepared what to say to him, but were tongue-tied in his presence. One of them, a young married woman by the name of Yeh Yüan, made a request at the end of the interview:

'Chairman Mao, I want to ask you something.'
'What is it?' the Chairman demanded.
Yeh Yüan blushed like a beetroot and entreated: 'To express to you the highest respect of Chinese youth, please let me kiss your hand.'
The Chairman looked at her smilingly but said nothing. Everyone was watching her who, before [the Chairman] had time to reply, bent her head down and impressed her youthful lips on the back of the warm hand of the giant, Chairman Mao. This was the respect the people had for their great leader; this was the gratitude Chinese youth expressed for their guide; this was the love and warmth a daughter had for her father; this was the lofty feeling the masses showed to their beloved leader![77]

On the eve of his departure, 10 October, Mao was entertained by Chiang to a performance of the classical opera.[78] Half way through it, a message was delivered to his *aides* that someone had fired at his car parked outside the theatre, killing one person in it. The message was passed on to Chou En-lai who, pale and agitated, went to have a word about it with the KMT negotiator, Chang Ch'ün. After the show, there was a farewell dinner at which Mao raised his glass and drank to the toast: 'Long live Mr. Chiang Kai-shek!'[79]

Behind this façade of cordiality hard bargaining went on between Chiang and Mao and between Chang Ch'ün, Wang Shih-chieh, Chang Chih-chung, and Shao Li-tzu representing the KMT, and Chou En-lai and Wang Jo-fei representing the CCP.[80] The points for negotiation were the coalition government and nationalization of armed forces, the communist base areas, and the distribution of the seats of the Government Council.[81] No agreement on any of

76. The *Hsin-hua Jih-pao* 2.9.1945.   77. [51] 21 and 23.
78. Mao is very fond of the classical opera.
79. [302] 140.   80. [153] III, 441.
81. [46] IV, 1155 or *SW* IV (Peking), 53.

them was reached, but Chiang and Mao decided to convene a National Affairs Conference, later known as the Political Consultative Conference, to deliberate on the formation of a coalition government, the convocation of the National Assembly, and the adoption of a constitution. Unless a genuine coalition government in one form or other were to be established, the CCP would not give up its armed forces. And regarding the armed forces, Mao raised his demand from the 16 divisions of 1944 to 48! Later he reduced this to 43, or in his own words, to one-seventh of the total strength of the KMT's 263 divisions, but insisted that the ratio of one to seven should be maintained if the KMT armed forces were to be reduced to 120 divisions. According to Mao's calculations, when the KMT forces were reduced to 120 divisions the communist forces should be reduced by the same proportion to 24 or 20 divisions. 'Does this mean that we [the CCP] are going to hand over our guns to the Kuomintang?' Mao answered: 'The arms of the people, every gun and every bullet, must all be kept, must not be handed over.'[82] Equally unyielding, Chiang regarded the divorce of the control in armed forces from the interests of individuals and the selfish ends of parties as the prerequisite for the lasting unity of the nation.[83]

Regarding the nineteen bases the communists admitted, Mao was willing to forsake eight, but, in return, wanted the KMT to recognize the existing authorities in the other eleven.[84] This attempt 'to legalise the communist control over such areas' was, in Chiang's view, detrimental to unity and democracy.[85] Subsequently Liu Shao-ch'i revealed at a Politburo meeting that Mao's concession in this respect aimed at the transfer of the isolated communist forces in the south to strengthen the defences of the party's possessions in the north.[86] As to the distribution of the seats in the Government Council, the KMT would have 20, the CCP 10, and other parties 6. Four crucial seats, Mao demanded, should be given to the Democratic League, and he also insisted on a two-

82. [46] IV, 1159 or *SW* IV (Peking), 57 and [153] III, 438.
83. [153] III, 437.
84. The eight were in Kwangtung, Chekiang, south Kiangsu, south Anhwei, central Anhwei, Hunan, Hupei, and Honan. See [46] IV, 1164 n. 5 or *SW* IV (Peking), 63 n. 7.   85. [153] III, 438–9.   86. [306] 7.

thirds majority for the Council on any major decision. Assuming that the Democratic League would on many issues vote with the communists, the CCP could then control 14 votes out of 40, thus constituting a *de facto* veto power which Chiang would not accept.[87]

But Chiang and Mao eventually signed an agreement on 10 October[88] promising to carry out the peaceful reconstruction of China and to call a Political Consultative Conference. Having thus laid the basis for further discussions, Ambassador Hurley left for America on 22 September and Mao for Yenan on 11 October.[89]

The Political Consultative Conference, which had no power to enforce its decisions, opened on 10 January 1946. There were eight representatives of the KMT, seven of the CCP, nine of the Democratic League, five of the Youth Party, and nine independents,[90] whose five decisions covered such problems as a programme for peaceful national reconstruction, a military settlement, and a political settlement. The KMT, for the first time, recognized the equal status of all the other parties which, in return, recognized Chiang as the leader of the nation. The question of the base areas was postponed until the reorganization of the National Government. The KMT undertook to revise the Organic Law of the National Government, making the Government Council the supreme organ in charge of national affairs, which was to have 40 members—20 from the KMT and the rest to be shared by other parties and independents. Here, once again, the discussion reached a deadlock, for the CCP demanded a share of 14—10 for itself and four for the Democratic League—while Chiang would promise no more than 12.[91] On military matters, the Conference decided on the reduction of both the KMT and the CCP armed forces to 50 or 60 divisions and on their nationalization. The Conference voted for the establishment of a committee of three to supervise the reorganization of the communist forces.[92]

Although the idea of the Political Consultative Conference was mooted during the Hurley period which ended with Hurley's resignation on 26 November 1945, it did not become a fact until

87. [153] III, 439–40.
88. [11] 105–7 and [46] IV, 1162–4 n. 1 or *SW* IV (Peking), 60–3 n. 1.
89. [11] 108–10 and [46] IV, 1167 or *SW* IV (Peking), 67.
90. [11] 111, [153] III, 451, and [302] 147.
91. [153] III, 471–2.   92. [11] 140.

after General Marshall's appointment as President Truman's special envoy on 27 November.[93] On 15 December, President Truman announced his China policy whose cornerstones were (1) the cessation of hostilities by negotiation; (2) no American intervention in the Chinese civil fighting; (3) the convocation of a national conference of the major Chinese political elements to bring about unification of the country on terms which would give all major political groups fair and effective representation in the Chinese Government; and (4) a promise of aid towards securing peace, unity, and economic reconstruction.[94]

In any case the Marshall mission could not be an easy one. Yet the earnestness of the American attitude and the authority and prestige General Marshall carried with him raised great hopes for peace and democracy not only in the minds of ordinary people but also in those of Chu Te and Chou En-lai.[95] General Marshall tackled his assignment in two ways: he called on the Political Consultative Conference to tackle the political issues and he set up a Committee of Three and an Executive Headquarters in Peking to find a military settlement. The Committee of Three, inaugurated on 7 January 1946, consisted of Chang Ch'ün (KMT), Chou En-lai (CCP), and Marshall himself as chairman,[96] and in Peking Generals Cheng Chieh-min and Yeh Chien-ying and the American chargé d'affaires, Walter S. Robertson, served on the three-member Executive Headquarters. Marshall's first success was to secure a cease-fire which Chiang and Mao ordered separately on 10 January.[97] And it was in such a tranquil atmosphere that Chou En-lai and Chang Chih-chung reached agreement on 25 February on the following points: (1) the parties agreed to a demobilization and organization plan under which their respective military forces were to be reduced to 90 divisions for the KMT and 18 divisions for the CCP within a year, and within the ensuing six months these forces were to be further reduced to 50 and 10 divisions respectively and to be distributed thus[98]:

93. [11] 111–12.
94. [11] 133 and Annex 62. See also Truman's directives to General Marshall, [324] 315, and Secretary of State, Byrnes's statement, [324] 316.
95. [293] 15 and [302] 156–7.   96. [11] 136.
97. [11] 136 and 930 and [302] 335.
98. [11] 140–1 and [153] III, 462.

Manchuria	KMT	14 divisions	CCP	1 division
North-west		9		–
North China		11		7
Central China		10		2
South China		6		–

(2) Chou En-lai promised to allow the movement of the KMT troops into Manchuria during the armistice.[99] With this agreement, hopes for a lasting peace rose even higher, and as Marshall himself commented:

I can only trust that its pages will not be soiled by a small group of irreconcilables who for a selfish purpose would defeat the Chinese people in their overwhelming desire for peace and prosperity.[1]

What General Marshall referred to as 'irreconcilables' were Ch'en Li-fu and his CC clique. Dr. J. Leighton Stuart recorded:

General Marshall had frequently referred to him [Ch'en Li-fu] as the leader of the reactionary forces which were blocking his efforts.[2]

Apart from Ch'en, the success or failure of this agreement depended upon two other factors—the sincerity of the two major parties and a solution to the Manchurian question, but the former was open to doubt and the latter hard to find. Under the agreement, both parties were required to submit within three weeks a list of the divisions to be retained and within six weeks a list of the units to be demobilized. The KMT duly sent a list of 90 divisions to the Committee of Three but the CCP never sent their list.[3] On the question of Manchuria, General Marshall twice proposed the dispatch of a field team thither by the Executive Headquarters and twice the KMT vetoed this, thus showing clearly that Chiang wanted to occupy this strategically important land by force. The field team was eventually sent on 11 March when General Marshall was on his way back to Washington for consultation, but was rendered impotent by the complicated restrictive conditions imposed on it.[4]

The departure of General Marshall marked the beginning of the end of serious negotiations, since in his absence incidents, skirmishes, and large-scale clashes occurred with increasing frequency,

99. [11] 137 and 140.   1. [11] 142.
2. [324] 164.   3. [11] 142.   4. [11] 146.

culminating in the capture of Ch'angch'un by the communists on 15 April.[5] Hurrying back to China, General Marshall blamed the KMT's foolishness in trying to wreck the armistice[6] and his strictures aroused a great deal of resentment from Chiang Kai-shek.[7] The loss of Ch'angch'un was interpreted by Chiang as a severe blow to his prestige and authority and therefore he was bent on recapturing it by force. General Marshall's and the Democratic League's efforts to persuade Chou En-lai to evacuate Ch'angch'un under certain compensatory conditions were rejected by Chiang outright, and Marshall was compelled to withdraw from his task of mediation for the time being.[8] Later, at the request of all concerned, General Marshall once more shouldered the thankless responsibilities of a mediator and with Chiang's return to Nanking on 1 May, the negotiations were revived. Through Marshall, Chiang named his cease-fire conditions: (1) the communists must make every effort to facilitate the restoration of communications; (2) in any agreement regarding the Manchurian issues, provisions must be made for carrying out the military demobilization and organization plan within specific dates; (3) when field teams or high staff groups reached an *impasse*, the final decision would be left to the American member. When handing these conditions to Chou En-lai, Marshall added his own, which were: (1) the communist evacuation of Ch'angch'un; (2) the dispatch of an advance section of the Executive Headquarters to Ch'angch'un; and (3) a halting of the advance of the National armies. Chou En-lai accepted all of Marshall's conditions and the second of Chiang's and showed willingness to discuss the first of Chiang's conditions with the KMT representative. But he reacted indignantly to Chiang's third condition on the ground that the question of a truce was a Chinese matter in which the final decision had to lie with the Chinese.[9]

In the meantime fierce battles were being fought in Manchuria: Ssup'ingchieh was taken by the National army on 22 May and Ch'angch'un the next day. The coming of June brought the negotiations into their most critical stage. Chiang agreed to install

5. [11] 146 and [266] 84–5.   6. [11] 151.
7. [153] III, 465.
8. [11] 153.   9. [11] 155–6 and [302] 176.

an advanced section of the Executive Headquarters in Ch'angch'un and to a general truce in Manchuria for ten days. He also proposed immediate discussion on the cessation of military activities in Manchuria, the restoration of communications and transport in north China, and detailed arrangements for military reorganization agreed upon on 25 February. Chou En-lai asked for an extension of the truce in Manchuria from ten days to a month and eventually accepted Chiang's compromise of fifteen days.[10] But, as the Government troops were advancing on all fronts, Chiang raised his price for an armistice a fortnight later by asking the communists to evacuate Jehol, Chahar, and Chefoo, Weihaiwei, and other areas in Shantung they had occupied since 7 June, to allow the reinforcement of the KMT garrison at Tsingtao and Tientsin and in Manchuria, and to transfer Harbin, Antung, Tunhua, Mutanchiang, and Paicheng to the KMT.[11] Although Chiang himself modified these conditions later, Chou En-lai found them 'too demanding to allow acceptance by the CCP'.[12]

At this stage Chiang insisted on a military settlement before a political one while the CCP regarded the formation of a coalition government as the crux of the entire question of peace. A corollary to the formation of such a government was the cancelling of the National Assembly scheduled to take place in November and this position was made clear to the visiting members of the People's Political Council by Mao Tse-tung.[13] The CCP objected to the convocation of the Assembly because 1,200 of its representatives were elected in 1936 and the constitution the Assembly was to approve was drafted in that year. True, Chiang promised to enlarge the membership of the Assembly by another 700, but of this the communists' share was a mere 190.[14] If no satisfactory formula could be found to secure communist co-operation, the convocation of the Assembly would ruin all the chances of a reconciliation between the KMT and the CCP.

The precarious truce arrangement of June disintegrated in July as hostilities spread. In particular, General Marshall protested

---

10. [11] 158.　　　11. [11] 160 and [302] 177.　　　12. [11] 160.
13. [288] 6 and 19.
14. I am not sure whether an assembly of 1,900 is a record. [153] III, 452–3 and [302] 196.

strenuously against Chiang's attack on Kalgan. Having failed to dissuade Chiang from the attack, Marshall ordered a suspension of all American aid to the KMT.[15] Yenan also put on pressure by staging an anti-American mass rally and the U.S. marines were attacked by communists in Hopei.[16] The KMT secret police were active too, assassinating prominent leaders of the Democratic League such as Li Kung-p'u and Professor Wen I-to.[17] Faced with this ominous situation, General Marshall recommended the appointment of a distinguished educationist, Dr. J. Leighton Stuart, as the U.S. Ambassador to China, to help him. Immediately after his appointment, Dr. Stuart flew to Kuling, where Chiang was spending the summer, to sound out Chiang's reaction to his suggestion of a committee of five, including two representatives from each of the two major parties with Dr. Stuart himself as the mediator.[18] Stuart's appointment was not what Chiang would have liked; he would have preferred General Wedemeyer. In Chiang's opinion, Dr. Stuart scarcely understood the power politics of the CCP and the appointment was interpreted by him as a communist success.[19] He countered Stuart's proposal of a committee of five by imposing elaborate pre-conditions which Chou En-lai could not accept. The idea of a committee of five was therefore still-born. Soon afterwards, Chou left Nanking for Shanghai—a gesture showing that the negotiations were no longer of much use— and the Marshall and Marshall–Stuart mediation to all intents and purposes ceased to have any meaning after September 1946. The Democratic League took up the mediation where Marshall had left off for a short period and its efforts also proved fruitless.[20]

On 10 October the KMT troops entered Kalgan and also took the important strategic point, Chihfeng in Jehol. At the same time the National Government ordered nation-wide conscription and the convocation of the National Assembly on 12 November 1946.[21] As a gesture for peace, Chiang unilaterally ordered a general cease-fire on 8 November to allow all other parties to nominate their representatives to the National Assembly.[22] Some parties of the

15. [153] III, 466.
16. [11] 171–12.   17. [11] 172 and [189] 440.
18. [11] 173–4, [153] III, 459–60, and [324] 167.   19. [153] III, 460.
20. [11] 174–5 and 675–6, [302] 179–80, and [324] 168.
21. [11] 196–7.   22. [302] 180.

Democratic League did send representatives to the Assembly, and thus on this issue the League was split asunder.

The recall of General Marshall on 6 January 1947 marked the beginning of a period when America had no active policy towards China. Chiang blamed Marshall's failure on the perfidy of the communists; in other words, he did not believe that General Marshall had really had a chance of success.[23] Chu Te attributed the failure to American policy[24]; Mao agreed with Chu by saying that the policy Marshall tried to put into practice was imperialistic, therefore bitterly opposed by the Chinese people.[25] He further explained what he meant by imperialistic policy:

Judging by the large amount of aid the United States is giving Chiang Kai-shek to enable him to wage civil war on an unprecedented scale, the policy of the U.S. Government is to use the so-called mediation as a smoke-screen for strengthening Chiang Kai-shek in every way and suppressing the democratic forces in China through Chiang Kai-shek's policy of slaughter so as to reduce China virtually to a U.S. colony.[26]

He, too, did not believe that Marshall had a chance of success. And General Marshall himself, summing up his mission, said:

The salvation of the situation, as I see it, would be the assumption of leadership by the liberals in the Government and the minority parties. . . . Successful action on their part under the leadership of Generalissimo Chiang Kai-shek would, I believe, lead to unity through good government.[27]

As his assumptions about the leadership of the liberals, their successful action, and a good government bore no relationship whatever to the realities of China at that time, General Marshall's wishes remained unfulfilled.

23. [153] III, 458.   24. [189] 441.
25. Interview with Mark Gayn, [326] 56.
26. Interview with A. T. Steele, [46] IV, 1199 or *SW* IV (Peking), 109.
27. Marshall's statement on January 7, 1947, [324] 333.

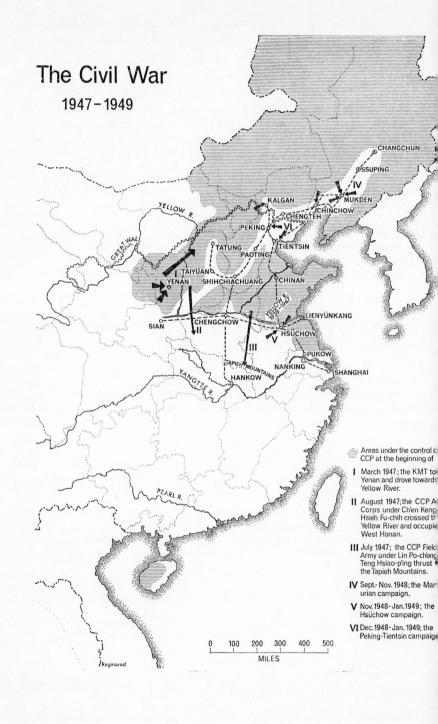

The Civil War

1947–1949

CHANGCHUN

SSUPING

IV

KALGAN

CHINCHOW

MUKDEN

CHENGTEH

YELLOW R.

PEKING

VI

GREAT WALL

TATUNG

TIENTSIN

PAOTING

TAIYUAN

SHIHCHIACHUANG

CHINAN

YENAN

YELLOW R. 1938-1947

LIENYÜNKANG

SIAN

CHENGCHOW

II

V

HSÜCHOW

III

PUKOW

TAPIEH MOUNTAINS

NANKING

HANKOW

SHANGHAI

YANGTZE R.

PEARL R.

Areas under the control o
CCP at the beginning of

I March 1947; the KMT to
Yenan and drove toward:
Yellow River.

II August 1947; the CCP A
Corps under Ch'en Keng
Hsieh Fu-chih crossed th
Yellow River and occupie
West Honan.

III July 1947; the CCP Field
Army under Lin Po-ch'eng
Teng Hsiao-p'ing thrust
the Tapieh Mountains.

IV Sept.- Nov. 1948; the Man
urian campaign.

V Nov.1948- Jan.1949; the
Hsüchow campaign.

VI Dec.1948- Jan. 1949; the
Peking-Tientsin campaig

0   100   200   300   400   500

MILES

Regmarad

Chapter XIII
The 'Coup de Grâce'

AFTER the eight-year resistance against Japan, the people of China, heartily sick of war, were dragged into an internecine conflict for another four years. At the outset everyone counselled against it—Stalin wanted the CCP to seek a *modus vivendi* with Chiang; General George Marshall and the American military representatives argued that, in spite of its military preponderance, the KMT could not destroy the communist movement by force and that the Chinese economy was unable to sustain another war and yet escape a total collapse[1]; the United Kingdom Trade Mission of 1946–7 regarded peace as the first economic need of China.[2] But Chiang believed that China, having an agrarian economy, did not have to fear an economic collapse in the foreseeable future[3] and that the KMT could efface communism from the country by force.[4] His Chief-of-Staff estimated that the KMT military strength was over eleven times as great as that of the CCP.[5] Mao characterized this kind of assessment in these words:

The enemy always underrates the energy of our army and overrates his own strength. . . .[6]

But Chiang held fast to his belief until March 1948,[7] for he, like the communists, regarded himself as a protagonist of a revolution whose triumph was pre-determined.[8]

The foundations on which Chiang based his confidence were,

1. [11] XI, XV, 173-4, and 212 and [324] 336.   2. [301] 14.
3. [11] 212 and [302] 238.   4. [11] XI.
5. Appendix E.   6. [46] IV, 1370 or *SW* IV (Peking), 292.
7. [11] 845.   8. [11] 919.

perhaps, the numerical superiority of his troops, his own immense popularity as the man who led his country to victory, and the steadfastness of United States' friendship and aid. The U.S. aid was of particular importance; without it the KMT's fate was sealed and because of it Mao and the CCP felt a certain hostility towards America and attacked her in tones so acrimonious that they recoiled on their users. What the CCP accused the Americans of was what Chiang was hoping for—their direct involvement in the war, but the Americans themselves, apart from giving substantial assistance, refused actual participation. The defeat of Thomas E. Dewey in the 1948 Presidential Election disappointed Chiang[9] whose subsequent urgent appeal to President Truman for military aid and the appointment of American officers to command the KMT troops was coldly received.[10] Even Madame Chiang's visit to the U.S. at the end of 1948, aiming at an alliance against the communists, resulted only in humiliation.[11]

As early as in June 1947 Dr. Leighton Stuart forecast the disappearance of Chiang from the scene,[12] but, reporting to the Secretary of State, General Marshall, he lamented the fact that in spite of Chiang's ineffective leadership 'no one can suggest anyone to take his place'.[13] The military reverses and the urgent need of peace to salvage the KMT, and the separatist movement in the ranks of the party, compelled Chiang to resign his seven-months-old Presidency.[14]

In contrast to the intemperate but sartorially immaculate Chiang Kai-shek, whose actual leadership Mao openly doubted for the first time in September 1946,[15] Mao Tse-tung remained informal in dress in spite of the personality cult that grew round him, but impressed his visitors as benign and calm.[16] The brown tunic he wore at the press conference in Chungking on 29 August 1945 he was still wearing when Robert Payne saw him in 1946 and when Yüan Hsüeh-k'ai met him on the eve of his departure from Yenan in March 1947.[17] Still free from mannerisms, he had changed

9. [299] 418.   10. [11] 889–90 and [153] III, 505.
11. [153] III, 505–6.   12. [11] 241.   13. 10.8.1948, [11] 886.
14. [46] IV, 1301 n. 3 and 1356 n. or SW IV (Peking), 226 n. 3 and 280 n., [153] III, 509, and [324] 205–6.
15. [46] IV, 1200 or SW IV (Peking), 110.   16. [50] 214 and [293] 89.
17. [50] 213 and [61] 86.

some of his old habits, eating less pepper, smoking fewer cigarettes, and going to bed earlier at night, with the result that he put on some weight.[18] His long, thick hair was still black, crowning his high and bronzed forehead.[19] Before leaving Yenan on 18 March 1947, he still lived in the same cave-like dwelling where he had received Gunther Stein and other visitors. The sofa with fiendish springs, the chair, and the rickety table were there, too. Prominent on the wall was a map bearing numerous pencil marks in blue and red.[20]

His food remained frugal, consisting normally of potatoes, turnips, and cabbage, some meat, and millet or steamed wheat buns.[21] But in the minds of his followers, a strong personality cult centring on this simple-living man had become deep-rooted, as Yüan Hsüeh-k'ai's description of a meeting with him bears out:

As I grasped the Chairman's hand in both of mine, a streak of warmth came up from them and spread all over my body, making my heart throb all the faster. A thousand things suddenly surged up in my mind, but I could not find a single word to express them.[22]

For strategic reasons which we shall presently explain (see p. 301), Mao, with his pretty wife, Chiang Ch'ing, and Chou En-lai, Jen Pi-shih, and others, left Yenan in March and played a game of hide-and-seek with the KMT troops under General Hu Tsung-nan until March 1948. He and the others went to Wangchiawan at the beginning of April and stayed there in a cave for two months. There were three compartments in this cave dwelling, with Mao and his wife sharing the inner and Chou En-lai and Lu Ting-yi sharing the outer chambers, both of which were at the time filled with vats of stinking pickles.[23] Before long Hu Tsung-nan's troops discovered where Mao was and dashed thither only to find that he had left.[24] At Hsiaoho in Yülin Mao called a military conference[25] which lasted until the beginning of July. During the night of 31 July Mao and his retinue left Yülin for Chiahsien, and on the way Chou En-lai was ill and had to be carried on a stretcher. It was

18. [293] 85 and 126.
19. [293] 85.   20. [61] 86.   21. [61] 89.   22. [61] 86.
23. [30] 334 and 342–3 and [58] I, 92–3.   24. [58] I, 104–5.
25. Attended by Chu Te, Chou En-lai, Jen Pi-shih, Lu Ting-yi, P'eng Te-huai, Ho Lung, Ch'en Yi, and Ch'en Keng.

then that the carriers saw how the soles of Chou's feet showed through the holes in his shoes. Mao was at times carried on a stretcher, too.[26] In Chiahsien Mao spent the Double Tenth of 1947 and announced his new land law.[27]

The wandering made Mao look thinner and older. His tunic and shoes were tattered, but he journeyed on until the news of the success of Liu Po-ch'eng and Teng Hsiao-p'ing in Tapieh Mountains reached him.[28] In December 1947 he called a meeting of the Politburo at Yangchiakou at which it was decided that there was no longer any need for Mao to remain in north Shensi, and so at the end of March 1948 he and the party centre moved into Shansi.[29] This ended the famous Yenan period.

During this period, Mao's wife—Chiang Ch'ing to the communists and Lan-p'ing to others—was with him; so were their daughters, Maomao and Lina, both of whom were at school in 1952.[30]

Under these two rival leaders—Chiang and Mao—were two rival parties. The KMT was corrupt and inefficient, a fact that the democratic façade of the National Assembly of 1946 and 1948, the multi-party Cabinet of 1947, and the Presidential Election of 1948 could not conceal.[31] General Wedemeyer in his report dated 19 September 1947 spoke of the KMT 'whose reactionary leadership, repression, and corruption have caused a loss of popular faith in the Government'.[32] Dr. Leighton Stuart, the U.S. Ambassador, regretted the fact that none of the innumerable reform plans adopted by the KMT was ever carried out. Stuart also commented on the incredible stupidity of the KMT propaganda and traced the origins of the weaknesses of the party:

And yet this party almost from the time it came into power had tolerated among its officials of all grades graft and greed, idleness and inefficiency, nepotism and factional rivalries—all the evils in short of the corrupt bureaucracy it had overthrown. These evils had become more pronounced after the V-J Day in the attempts to crush communism by a combination of military strength and secret police.[33]

26. [30] 353 and 357 and [58] II, 116–18.   27. [30] 360.
28. [30] 358 and [58] II, 126.   29. [30] 361.   30. [28] 47.
31. [153] III, 476.   32. [11] 769.
33. [324] 242.

Not only foreign observers were of this opinion; General Yen Hsi-shan told Gunther Stein in 1944:

... the reason why so many people are following them [the communists] is that our administration, the administration of the National Government, is bad.[34]

And in 1949, Dr. Sun Fo admitted:

The spread of communist influence today is a result of our failure to put into effect the principles we believe in. Our party's greatest mistake in the past was that certain members worshipped force too much and scrambled for power among themselves, thus giving the enemy opportunities to sow dissension in our ranks.[35]

When finally the KMT organ, the *Chung-yang Jih-pao*, exhorted the Government 'to lose no time in winning the people's confidence', and spoke out bluntly against the privileged classes and nepotism, it was already 4 November 1948[36] and the 'Mandate of Heaven' was changing hands. Nevertheless, General Yen Hsi-shan was still spending 300,000 U.S. dollars a day for the airlift to his native city, T'aiyüan, in Shansi, which, after the fall of Peking and Tientsin, was a city of no military or any other value to the KMT.[37]

The CCP fared differently in the civil war years. Its membership soared from 1,210,000 at the time of the seventh national congress in April 1945[38] to 2,500,000 in 1948, 3,000,000 in September 1948, and 4,500,000 at the time of its assumption of national power in 1949.[39] Thus in twelve years it had increased 112 times.[40] Most of the new recruits were peasants. At the seventh congress Mao was elected to the chairmanship not only of the Central Politburo but concurrently of the Central Secretariat, thus combining even greater powers in his hands.[41] The next step in the CCP development came in September 1948 when the Politburo held an enlarged session attended by the 7 regular members, 14 members and alternate members of the Central Committee, 10 high-ranking cadres of various regions, and military commanders, to make decisions on (1) the unification of the administrative

34. [296] 44.   35. [46] IV, 1421 or *SW* IV (Peking), 356.
36. [11] 880–2.   37. [324] 226.
38. [46] III, 1049 or *SW* IV, 242, [179] 60, [181] 113–14. About the congress, see [162] 285.
39. [46] IV, 1346 or *SW* IV (Peking), 270, [181] 111, and [281] xxviii.
40. [281] xxviii and [296] 146.   41. [162] 432.

system of the 'liberated areas', obviously as a preparatory step towards the establishment of a national government; (2) the training of 30 to 40 thousand cadres for working in urban districts, so that the party's power could be transferred from the countryside to the cities; and (3) the reorganization of the PLA in order to be able to fight positional warfare.[42]

In the spring of 1949 the centre of the party was at the important railway junction of Shihchiachuang in Hopei, but it was at P'ingshan that the Central Committee of the CCP met from 5 to 13 March to discuss the KMT's peace terms and the problems facing the party on the eve of final victory.[43] After these meetings, the party centre moved to Peking and engaged itself in the preparation for the foundation of the People's Republic.[44]

The armies of the parties were startlingly different. Chiang firmly believed that the CCP soldiers were ruthless savages,[45] and yet his methods of conscription and the way his soldiers were treated were anything but humane. The official news agency, the *Central News*, reported:

Hsü Cheng-k'un was accused of misappropriating military food supplies, causing the death of 105 recruits, the murder of company commander Wei Chao-jen, burying recruit Tai Chung-shan alive and sundry offences. ... Lieutenant Feng Tsun was accused of viciously beating up recruit Sun Chiu-hsün, torturing his relative, and extorting 10,000 *yuan*. Captain Li Po-chien was accused of misappropriating military food supplies, causing the death of Li Cheng-chin and other recruits by physical torture, extortion to the amount of 197,000 *yuan*, and maiming recruit Tseng Hsien-feng.[46]

And General Feng Yü-hsiang remarked:

Having been a soldier for 55 years from the time when I was 12 to my retirement from the Army in 1946, I have never known that an army recruited by kidnapping could fight and win.[47]

It was with such an army and some U.S. aid that the KMT managed to launch a general offensive against the PLA in 1946 and

42. [46] IV, 1345, 1348, and 1350 or *SW* IV (Peking), 269, 272, and 274.
43. [46] IV, 1426 and 1437 or *SW* IV (Peking), 362 and 371–2.
44. [46] IV, 1426 or *SW* IV (Peking), 362.
45. *N.Y. Herald Tribune*, 31.10.1948.   46. [269] 257.
47. [263] 228.

actually reduced the size of the communist areas. But the comparative military strengths of the CCP and the KMT changed from 1:4·3 in September 1945 to 1:1·9 in June 1947,[48] owing more to the losses suffered by the KMT than to the expansion of the PLA.[49] Towards the end of 1946 the KMT advance was slowed down and the lines held by the opposing sides became more stable. If this stability indicated anything at all, it was that the KMT had to have an army three times the size of the PLA in order to maintain a military stalemate, provided that there was no deterioration in its equipment and other conditions. Between July 1946 and spring 1947, this ratio of 1:3 had been roughly maintained, but the suspension of the U.S. aid for eight months together with corruption caused a deficiency in the equipment of the KMT troops and consequently the KMT gradually lost its military supremacy. The PLA, for its part, was able to launch limited offensives in various areas. The summer of 1948 was the turning-point, since heavy casualties and mass desertions brought the KMT army down to the numerical level of the PLA and, according to Mao, in November 1948 the PLA actually outnumbered the KMT troops. Soon afterwards the end of the civil war came.[50]

Apart from corruption and the brutal treatment the soldiers suffered, the defeat of Chiang Kai-shek could be attributed to the following military conditions: (1) The command system of the KMT army was exceedingly complicated, yet, in fact, all the major decisions were in the hands of Chiang alone. The best way to illustrate the cumbersomeness of the KMT military structure is to quote the beginning of Chiang's radio message on 1 July 1946:

Directors, Generalissimo's Field Headquarters, Directors, President's Field Headquarters, Directors, Pacification Bureaus, Commanding Generals, War Areas, Commanding Generals, Pacification Areas, Commanding Generals, Garrison Commands, the Commanding General, Nanking Garrison Command, Commanding Generals, Army Groups, Commanding Generals, Armies, Commanding Generals,

48. Appendix E.
49. Mao ordered a halt in army expansion at the end of 1945. [46] IV, 1172 or *SW* IV (Peking), 76.
50. Appendix E.

Reorganized Divisions, General Cheng Chieh-min, Commissioner, Executive Headquarters, Peiping. . . .[51]

The headquarters, bureaux, areas or zones were all duplicated. In contrast to this, Mao's military order began simply and concisely: 'To all Field Commanders . . .'[52]

(2) The commanding officers were selected by Chiang 'on the basis of personal reliability rather than military competence',[53] and the personal rivalries among them, particularly between the Whampoa Academy clique and the rest,[54] were such as often to render strategic or even tactical co-operation impossible. Chiang's policy of favouring the Whampoa officers by giving them lighter tasks, higher posts, more lucrative rewards, and more plentiful supplies,[55] merely served to rub salt into the wounds of the other officers. Had the Whampoa officers been really competent, their critics would have been silenced. Alas! they were corrupt and impotent.[56] They faltered and bungled and were not infrequently reprimanded or dismissed, but owing to the difficulty of finding replacements, the dismissed officers were given new commands shortly afterwards. In this way, reward and punishment in the KMT army meant scarcely more than cutting for partners in a game of bridge.[57]

It is difficult to generalize on Chiang's strategy in the civil war for it changed from year to year; one thing was, however, certain: the KMT for the sake of necessity and prestige paid more attention to the defence of a city or an area than to the preservation of its military strength. In Chiang's own words to A. T. Steele, 'the traditional ideal and conception of duty of the Chinese soldier decrees that it is imperative for him to die if the city falls or to live if he can hold it and that it is a disgrace for him to withdraw from or give up a city for this reason'.[58] Chiang also said that he had given up this ideal, but in fact his defence of Peking-Tientsin and of Hsüchow showed clearly that he had not done so. The Americans

51. [11] 647–8.   52. [11] 648. See also 760, 885, and [134] 232–3.
53. Stuart to Marshall, 10.8.1948, [11] 885.
54. [134] 244.   55. [11] 885 and [134] 245–6.
56. General Wedemeyer's comment, quoted in [302] 236, Paul Parker's conversation with Dr. Stuart, [324] 236, and also [266] 101.
57. [46] IV, 1260 n. 2 or SW IV (Peking), 174 n. 2.
58. N.Y. Herald Tribune, 31.10.1948, quoted from [11] 891.

called this strategy 'criminally inept and wasteful'[59] while Mao described such a strategy as 'desperadoism'.[60]

Another characteristic of Chiang's strategic planning was a costly lack of co-ordination. Many of his operation orders were conveyed neither to his Minister of Defence nor to his Supreme General Staff.[61] This, as well as the dishonesty, inefficiency, and corruption of the military personnel, resulted in an inaccurate assessment of the CCP's and the KMT's own military strength, which in turn led to many ludicrous blunders.[62]

The Government was known to have an absolute supremacy in the air; yet throughout the civil war the air force played only a negligible role.[63]

In the first year of the civil war the Government troops made considerable advances in Manchuria, north Kiangsu and south Anhwei, the Hupei-Honan border areas, and Inner Mongolia; thus their manpower was widely distributed and their lines greatly stretched and they themselves became garrisons, thereby losing a good deal of their offensive capacity.[64] In the second and third years of the war they were often ordered to hold on to a city or territory while supplies and reinforcements came all too slowly or simply did not reach them in time to save them. Seeing no future in holding on any longer, many of them surrendered to the communists.[65] After the battles of Manchuria, Peking-Tientsin, and Hsüchow, the Yangtze was laid bare to attack and Acting President Li Tsung-jen was of the opinion that the river had to be defended by using the vast areas in the south-west as the rear in the same manner as in the Resistance War. Chiang entertained this idea for a short time but eventually decided to leave for Formosa.[66]

The PLA grew from strength to strength as the war wore on. At the end of 1945 Mao ordered a halt in the expansion of the communist army in order to intensify training. Despite this, in July 1946 when China was irrevocably committed to civil war, he estimated the total strength of the PLA at 1,278,000, showing an

59. [11] 267.   60. [46] I, 200 or *SW* I, 214.
61. [11] 330, 334, and 337 and [324] 197.   62. [11] 809.
63. [11] 330 and 338.   64. [11] 336–7 and [181] 133.
65. [11] 283–4 and 885.
66. [134] 267 and [153] III, 526.

increase of over 400,000 from the end of the Resistance War.[67] This, however, is not as important as the reorganization of the PLA. The idea of organizing field armies was mooted by Mao as early as 1938 in his famous dissertation *On the Protracted War*[68] and the actual reorganization was prepared for in 1945 and carried out in November 1948 when the PLA occupied areas were divided into the north-west, the central, the east, and the north-east and placed under the control of four Field Armies—the 1st led by P'eng Te-huai and Ho Lung, the 2nd by Liu Po-ch'eng and Teng Hsiao-p'ing, the 3rd by Ch'en Yi and Su Yü, and the 4th by Lin Piao and Lo Jung-huan.[69] Soon after the reorganization Mao made his historic announcement that the PLA had achieved numerical superiority over the KMT army, and he went on to say:

This is a sign that the victory of the Chinese revolution and the realization of peace in China are at hand.[70]

The soldiers of the PLA were well-disciplined and well be-haved. Dr. Leighton Stuart praised their morale as being 'excellent', and in Nanking he found:

In painful contrast [to the KMT] the Communist Party was free from private graft, officers and men lived very much together, simply and identically. ... There was almost no maltreatment of the populace. They borrowed extensively but generally returned these articles or made restitutions.[71]

And O. B. van der Sprenkel obtained a similar impression in Tient-sin:

The soldiers looked fierce enough with their big fur caps and ear-flaps, their padded cotton uniforms draped around with cartridge bandoliers and hung with dangerous-looking home-made grenades. All were well armed, with Japanese rifles or automatic weapons of American make. In every group of half a dozen or so there would be one with a scrap of paper in his hand. These we discovered bore the addresses of the private houses on which the squads were to be billeted. Several times I saw a soldier approaching a knot of bystanders, average-looking '*lao-pai-hsing*' and, proffering his paper with a polite bow and a wide smile, ask for

67. [46] IV, 1172 and 1298 or *SW* IV (Peking), 76 and 224.
68. [46] II, 475 or *SW* II, 210.
69. [46] IV, 1342 n. 3 or *SW* IV (Peking), 266 n. 3.
70. [46] IV, 1363 or *SW* IV (Peking), 287.
71. [324] 242.

directions to the street and house number his group were seeking. These must have been some of the first occasions in Tientsin's history of uniformed soldiers using all the forms of Chinese courtesy to ordinary civilians. On the civilians, at first astounded, and in the end mightily pleased, the effect was enormous.

As the weeks passed, standard of politeness, modesty, honesty and high discipline showed no signs of falling off. There was no looting, no pilfering. . . .[72]

The exemplary role played by the CCP members among the soldiers, by reminding them of the Three Main Rules of Discipline and the Eight Points for Attention,[73] and the intensification of discipline at the beginning of 1948 when ordinary soldiers were encouraged to air their grievances against their officers and were thoroughly interrogated regarding their class background, work, and fighting spirit, were factors undoubtedly responsible for the soldiers' good conduct.[74]

The war of 1945–9, which was admittedly the continuation of the undecided contest of the 1930s, was waged under vastly different conditions, notably the enormously increased military strength of the CCP; but Mao at the beginning did not make any drastic change in his strategy. From his point of view, it was to be a protracted war of attrition in which,

It [our policy] should rest on our own strength, and that means regeneration through one's own efforts. . . . Relying on the forces we ourselves organize, we can defeat all Chinese and foreign reactionaries.[75]

In other words, the guiding principle of his strategy was still the preservation of the strength of the PLA rather than dogged disputes over the control of a piece of land or a city.[76] A corollary to this was the sapping and destruction of the KMT military strength by fighting, psychological warfare, interrupting the communications, and capturing equipment. In 1946 Mao expected to settle the quarrels between the parties in five years,[77] but according to

72. [323] 4–5 and 9.
73. [46] IV, 1241 and 1242 n. 1 or SW IV (Peking), 155 and 156 n. 1.
74. [46] IV, 1292 or SW IV (Peking), 214–15.
75. [46] IV, 1132 or SW IV (Peking), 20.
76. [46] IV, 1183–5 or SW (Peking), 89–92.
77. [46] IV, 1337–8 or SW IV (Peking), 261.

Robert Payne, he still had doubt in his mind as to their final outcome.[78] P'eng Te-huai, too, said: 'We cannot be defeated, but it is probably true that we cannot win.'[79]

Li Li-san, though believing in the final triumph of communism, saw many difficulties ahead:

We never sanguinely hope that the victory will one day fall into our laps. On the road of revolution we only know how to march forward, how to stand up after having tripped over. But we have faith in our victory, the inescapable victory.[80]

Yet from the end of 1946 the PLA did not seem to have lost, however temporarily, its military initiative.[81] Its command system from the Military Commission of the Party Centre, through the commanding officers, down to the regimental level, seemed to work smoothly and every responsible officer had enough latitude to make his independent decisions. The PLA's aim which persisted throughout the war was the annihilation of the KMT army at the planned rate of 100 brigades per annum.[82] For fulfilling this, the general strategy had a slightly different emphasis from that during the 1930s and the Resistance War, namely, instead of deploying the PLA units in a guerrilla or manoeuvre warfare, they were concentrated on annihilating the KMT armies one by one.[83] In this way they succeeded, according to the communist claims, in destroying 2,640,000 of the KMT troops and capturing 64,000 machine-guns and 14,100 artillery pieces between July 1946 and June 1948; by June 1950 they had destroyed all together 8,070,000 KMT troops and captured 319,000 machine-guns and 54,000 artillery pieces.[84]

All the time Mao conducted the war with caution until 18 January 1948 when he issued this instruction:

Oppose overestimation of the enemy's strength. For example: fear of U.S. imperialism; fear of carrying the battle into the KMT areas; fear of wiping out the comprador-feudal system, of distributing the land

78. [293] 89.   79. [293] 41.   80. [266] 106.
81. [11] 337.
82. [46] IV, 1204, 1229–30, 1232, 1299–1300, and 1337–8 or *SW* IV (Peking), 141–2, 144, 223–4, and 261–2.
83. [11] 511.
84. [46] IV, 1346 or *SW* (Peking), 269 and [11] 323 and [179] 75.

of the landlords and of confiscating bureaucrat-capital; fear of a long-drawn-out war; and so on.[85]

Although he had discarded the mainly defensive strategy early in 1947,[86] positional war was not adopted as the principal form of struggle until the Politburo meeting in September 1948[87] and a general frontal attack was not ordered until 21 April 1949,[88] when the KMT régime was obviously crumbling.

Throughout the civil war the National Government was haunted by the spectre of inflation, as ferocious as the one which haunted Central Europe in the 1920s. At the end of 1945 the Government's gold and dollar reserves stood at U.S.$835 million, but a year later this dwindled to $450 million and another six months later to some $300 million.[89] The main cause of this rapid decrease was the military expenditure which at the same time impelled the Government to issue bank-notes for astronomical figures. From 1946 to 1948 the deficit in the Government budget amounted to 70 per cent. of its revenue and was invariably met by issuing new notes.[90] It was by no means pure coincidence that this percentage was often the same as the percentage of the Government's military expenditure to its total expenditure.[91] The *Ta-kung Pao* ruefully commented:

In the light of recent experience, the budget figures announced at the beginning of each fiscal year were often the actual figures of revenue and expenditure of the last month of that year.[92]

But, believing that inflation would never lead to the collapse of the Chinese economy, Chiang made no gesture to curb such expenditure. In addition to budgeted expenses, those authorized by his personal orders amounted to 38·33 per cent. of the total expenditure of 1945, 16·81 per cent. of that of 1946, and 14·88 per cent. of that of 1947.[93] High officials in his Government did not have such absolute power, but they made use of their positions to their own benefit. For instance, in February 1946, when the official

85. [46] IV, 1267 or *SW* IV (Peking), 181.
86. [46] IV, 1204 or *SW* IV (Peking), 114.
87. [46] IV, 1349–50 or *SW* IV (Peking), 273.
88. [46] IV, 1452 n. or *SW* IV (Peking), 387–8 n.
89. [11] 210 and 783.   90. [11] 782, [260] 71–2, [271] 96, and [313] 78.
91. [260] 71–2 and [271] 96.   92. *Loc. cit.*, 30.1.1947.
93. [271] 153.

dollar rate of exchange was to be raised from 20 *yuan* to 2,020,[94] a documentary film company under the control of the CC clique bought $1,900,000 at the old rate, thus making a profit of 2,280 million *yuan*.[95]

The unrestrained issue of notes forced the price level to rise at an ever increasing rate. In June 1946 the wholesale price index of Shanghai was 378,217 (January–June 1937 = 100) and in August 1948 this became 558,900,000![96] In 1947 prices leapt up at two-month intervals and settled at a relatively stable level after every fluctuation. The intervals were shortened to one month at the beginning of 1948, then to a week, until finally the rise became continuous.[97] In the second half of 1947 prices increased by 30 per cent. a month and afterwards they doubled, trebled, and in the end quadrupled themselves.[98]

An ironic accompaniment to this hyper-inflation was the Government's announcement of a five-year plan of economic reconstruction in January 1947, with a total investment fixed at U.S.$700 million.[1] But for those who had lived through it, the inflation did not seem a light-hearted matter. The worst hit were the civil servants and teachers who, in 1946, found it impossible to provide a reasonable standard of living for their families out of their salaries.[2] By 1948 their monthly incomes were only enough to keep them for a few days.[3] Strikes and rice riots therefore took place and people began investing their capital abroad either to preserve its value or for the sake of more reliable investments.[4]

The Government's measures to combat the inflation were piecemeal, often ill-conceived and lacking in efficacy. One day at the end of 1946, the Government threw five tons of gold into the money market in an attempt to check it, but it was like throwing a pebble to check the rising tide of the sea.[5] There were also the grain tax in kind which caused a great deal of hardship to the people,[6] and the Stabilization Programme of February 1947 fixing ceiling prices and wages, which proved futile.[7]

94. [153] III, 445.   95. [314] 40.
96. [260] 79. Compare with [11] 783 and [271] 98.
97. [313] 81.   98. [313] 82.   1. [314] 43.
2. [301] 18.   3. [299] 410.
4. [11] 729, 781, and 841–2 and [299] 410. See also [314] 3.
5. [11] 33 and [314] 9.   6. [314] 1 and 11.   7. [11] 771 and [260] 72.

The cost of printing banknotes caught up with their face values[8]; the issue of *fa-pi* ceased to be an effective means of paying for the civil war and the functioning of the Government. The newly constituted multi-party Government had to tackle the question of inflation in earnest lest the economy collapse through the credit bankruptcy of the Government and the total loss of all the functions of the currency. The new Finance Minister, however, had peculiar ideas about balancing the budget in order to equilibrate the economy. He considered it impossible to reorganize the Government's finances unless economic stability was achieved, and he proposed to change the currency standard so that stability could be restored. Once this was done, he believed, a balanced budget would automatically follow.[9] It was therefore decided in May 1948 to issue the now infamous gold *yuan* notes. According to Chiang's statement at the National Assembly, the new currency had the backing of gold bullion, U.S. dollars, and government property amounting to U.S.$610 million. Each gold *yuan* equalled 3 million *fa-pi*, 0·2217 centigram of pure gold, or U.S.$0·25. The Government undertook not to exceed the prescribed maximum issue of 2,000 million gold *yuan*, and as a means of strengthening the confidence in what the premier called 'this last chance', a committee of Shanghai citizens was elected to assist in supervising the issue and was to publish a monthly statement of accounts.[10] The issue began in August and, at the same time, the Government froze all prices and wages and ordered the people to surrender the specie and foreign exchange in their private possession.[11]

Chiang also sent his son to Shanghai to enforce the new fiscal measures by means of police terror, and he fulfilled his duties so thoroughly that the pulse of the financial centre of China stopped. 'The disruption of all trade, the injustice and suffering, the evasions and threatening outbreaks became so serious that the Generalissimo [Chiang] finally called him off.'[12]

In October the gold *yuan* in circulation had already exceeded the

---

8. [153] III, 501–2. Theoretically this is impossible, but convenience always puts a limit to the size of the face value.   9. [260] 79.

10. [11] 914, [153] III, 501–2, [260] 79–80, and [324] 194.

11. [153] III, 502, and [260] 80.

12. [324] 197. See also [11] 278 and [260] 80.

prescribed maximum by ten times[13] while prices rocketed eleven times in one week.[14] Seeing the absurdity of the prescribed maximum, the Government abolished it on 12 November[15] and in April 1949 the total issue went up to 9,487 times the originally planned 2,000 million,[16] which could have been bought up by U.S.$20 million.[17] Prices rose by 3·6 times in January 1949, 7 times in February, and 4·5 times in March; the rate of increase was slowed down only by the shortage of printed notes.[18] The bullion and dollar reserves, once used to back the gold *yuan,* were now shipped to Formosa[19] at a time when the Government's revenue was enough to cover only 5 per cent. of its expenses. In a desperate move to keep the Government financially afloat, Acting President Li Tsung-jen went back to the silver standard by issuing both the old silver coins in the treasury and silver dollar notes,[20] but the collapse of the Government economy was now complete and no effort could have saved it at such a late hour.[21]

The story of the simpler economy of the 'liberated areas' is itself simpler. Prices were much more stable, rising, for instance, by about 68 per cent. from January to June 1948 while in the KMT areas they rose by 19·7 times.[22] Each of the 'liberated areas' had its own currency, well managed and circulating only in that area.[23] The unified currency, *jen-min p'iao,* was not introduced until the end of 1948 but showed a remarkable stability in value throughout 1949.[24] The more notable aspect of the communist economy was the change in the land policy. In November 1945 Mao reaffirmed his policy of reducing land rent, organizing mutual-aid teams, and giving loans to peasants but refraining from confiscating land.[25] The first sign of breaking away from this moderate policy appeared in December 1946 when the Draft Land Law empowered the government of the Shensi-Kansu-Ninghsia Border Region to purchase compulsorily landlords' excess land. But the cautious approach of the Draft Law made clear the government's fear of driving the landlords and wealthy peasants away from the CCP

13. [153] III, 504 and [260] 81.   14. [260] 82.
15. The *Ta-kung Pao,* Shanghai, 12.11.1948.
16. [271] 122.   17. [324] 225.   18. [260] 85.
19. [260] 84.   20. The *Ta-kung Pao,* Hong Kong, 3 and 7.5.1949.
21. [260] 84.   22. [260] 79 and [299] 107.   23. [313] 103–4.
24. [323] 37–8.   25. [46] IV, 1169–70 or *SW* IV (Peking), 71–2.

while the outcome of the civil war was still uncertain. Ten months later, as the prospect became much brighter for the communists, the party's land policy became more radical—the land conference, held at P'ingshan in Hopei in Mao's absence, passed the Outline Land Law of China on 13 September, promulgated by Mao on 10 October. The Law terminated the ownership of all landlords (Article 2) and of temples, schools, and other organizations (Article 3) and abolished all the loans contracted before the date of promulgation (Article 4). It stipulated that all peasant bodies were to elect representatives to a committee which would be responsible for carrying out land reform (Article 5). All land in the 'liberated areas' was to be redistributed among the peasants on an egalitarian basis (Article 5).[26] The political significance of this return to a policy advocated by the Comintern as early as 1927[27] was to win more enthusiastic support from the poor peasants, thereby consolidating the communist ranks in preparation for the eventual establishment of a new régime. In the processes of the reform, according to Jen Pi-shih,

the depraved and abject leading counter-revolutionaries and the big bullies, whose execution is demanded by everyone, should be tried and sentenced to death by people's courts and the sentences should be carried out and the charges against them should be announced by the authorities. This is an absolutely necessary step without which a revolutionary social order cannot be introduced.

Jen went on to say:

The communists must not forbid or prevent the masses from getting even with those who have oppressed them and whom they hate. Instead, they should sympathise with them or they will be cut off from them.[28]

With official blessings such as this, the poor peasants and communists cadres committed leftist mistakes by labelling some who had not engaged in 'feudal exploitation' as landlords or rich peasants, by encroaching upon the industrial and commercial enterprises of landlords and rich peasants, and by beating and killing without discrimination.[29] Therefore the first instruction

26. [310] 15–16.
27. *Vide supra*, p. 111.   28. [320] 56–7.
29. [46] IV, 1305 or *SW* IV (Peking), 228–9.

Mao issued upon his arrival at the Shansi-Suiyüan Border Region from north Shensi was to stop such excesses. His admonition against encroachment on industrial and commercial enterprises in urban areas was of special importance, for by then the communists were in control of some large cities, for instance, Shihchiachuang and Kaifeng, and a correct attitude towards urban properties was urgently needed lest city dwellers should harden their opposition to the communists. Hence on 1 September 1948 the editorial of the *Tung-pei Jih-pao* (Northeast Daily) exhorted the communist cadres to protect industrial plants and business organizations because they were 'assets of the nation' and 'the crystallisation of the blood and sweat of the labouring people of China'.[30] Jen Pi-shih, Ch'en Yün, and Ch'en Po-ta either made speeches or published articles in official organs to the same effect.[31] Mao himself telegraphed his troops in Loyang, ordering them to:

set a clear line of demarcation in defining bureaucratic-capital; do not designate as bureaucratic-capital and do not confiscate all the industrial and commercial enterprises run by Kuomintang members. The principle should be laid down that the democratic government should take over and operate all industrial and commercial enterprises which are definitely verified as having been run by the Kuomintang's central, provincial, county or municipal governments, that is, enterprises operated wholly by official bodies. But if, for the time being, the democratic government is not yet ready to take them over or is unable to do so, the individuals previously in charge should be temporarily entrusted with the responsibility of management so that these enterprises can function as usual until the democratic government appoints people to take over. The workers and technicians in these industrial and commercial enterprises should be organized to participate in management, and their competence should be trusted. . . . Enterprises run by notorious big bureaucrats of the Kuomintang should be dealt with in conformity with the principles and measures stated above. Industrial and commercial enterprises run by small bureaucrats or by landlords, however, are not subject to confiscation. Encroachment on any enterprise run by national bourgeoisie is strictly prohibited.[32]

In March 1949 he made the following historic statement:

From 1927 to the present the centre of gravity of our work has been in the villages—gathering strength in the villages, using the villages in

30. [319] 34.   31. [319] *passim*.
32. [46] IV, 1323-4 or *SW* IV (Peking), 247-8.

order to surround the cities and then taking the cities. The period for this method of work has now ended. The period of 'from the city to the village' and of the city leading the village has now begun.[33]

Having compared the two opposing leaders, the parties, their military strength, their strategies, and their economies, we now come to the civil war itself. The fight for the control over China is in effect a fight for the control over the 'A' formed by the three major railways—the Tientsin–Pukow, Peking–Hankow, and Lunghai—and the cities along them. A threat to any corner of the 'A' is a real threat to the security of the Central Government and the occupation of it offers a good chance of success to an insurgent. For either the attack or defence of the 'A' it is important to take or maintain its periphery—Honan, Shansi, Inner Mongolia, and Manchuria, especially Manchuria because of its agricultural and industrial potentials and its proximity to Russia and Japan. It was precisely on the periphery that the civil war of 1946 and 1947 was fought. When that stage was over, the 'A' was exposed to attack from north and west and in two decisive campaigns—the Peking–Tientsin and the Hsüchow—it fell into the hands of the communists. Thereafter the communist domination of China as a whole was merely a matter of time.

In the second half of 1945 and the first half of 1946 Manchuria was under Russian occupation, consequently no clashes occurred there between the KMT and the PLA. But elsewhere there were skirmishes.[34] The biggest battle of this period took place at Shang-tang in Shansi at a time when Mao was discussing peace in Chung-king.[35] On the whole, through the efforts of General George Marshall and the minor parties, peace was maintained, however precariously. With the expiry of the second truce at the end of June 1946, war flared up and therefore Chinese historians generally regard July 1946 as the beginning of the civil war. From July to September the KMT deployed no less than 196 brigades which advanced on all fronts[36]; by the end of the year its troops had

33. [46] IV, 1428 or *SW* IV (Peking), 363.
34. [46] IV, 1127, 1135 n. 6, 1156, 1164 n. 2, and 1168 n. 5 or *SW* IV (Peking), 15, 24 n. 12, 53–4, 63 n.2, 66, and 69 n. 5. See also [11] 313 and [181] 132.
35. [46] IV, 1164 n. 2 or *SW* IV (Peking), 63 n. 2.
36. [46] IV, 1184 n. or *SW* IV (Peking), 90 n,

taken 174,000 square kilometres from the communists including 165 towns, large and small.[37] However, the territorial expansion and the consequent extension of lines of communications compelled the KMT to diffuse its strength,[38] thereby slowing its advance. From November 1946 to February 1947 its gain of 87 towns was offset by its loss of 87 others.[39] However, at the end of June 1947 the 'liberated areas' were reduced in size by 191,000 square kilometres, and in population by 18,000,000.[40]

Early in 1947 Chiang planned the next stage of his strategy which Teng Hsiao-p'ing picturesquely called 'Operation Dumb-bell'. Instead of an offensive along the entire front as in 1946, Chiang chose to attempt to destroy Ch'en Yi's army in Shantung, to re-open the Tientsin–Pukow railway and to take Yenan and drive the communists to the east of the Yellow River into Shansi. This done, he hoped, the country south of the river would be free from communist harassment. An essential part of this plan was to re-direct the river from its 1938 course through east Honan and north Kiangsu back to its old course through north Shantung. By doing this he would not only separate Liu Po-ch'eng's army in central China from Ch'en Yi's in the east, but also channel the river through the districts where the communist troops concentrated.[41] The work on the dykes of the river at Huayüank'ou in Honan began on 1 March and in the wake of it the battles of south Shantung and north Shensi were started. It was also a time of important meetings—the Central Executive Committee of the KMT sat on 15 March and the foreign ministers of the Big Four conferred at Moscow.[42] The news of the capture of Yenan on 19 March served as a great fillip to the members of the Central Executive Committee. But before long the mistakes of Operation Dumb-bell were fully exposed.

In May Ch'en Yi's army crushed the American trained and equipped 74th Army Corps at Mengliangku in south Shantung, thus removing one end of the 'Dumb-bell'.[43] On the north-west

37. Chou En-lai's statement on 10.1.1947, [11] 708. Compare with [18] 513.
38. [18] 513.
39. [18] 531.   40. [315] 80.
41. [153] III, 481–3 and [299] 354–5.
42. [20] 565, [46] IV, 1219 n. 2 or *SW* IV (Peking), 132 n. 2, and [299] 358.
43. [18] 516, [134] 252, and [181] 134–5.

battlefield, fully aware of the meaning of his continued stay in north Shensi, Mao began to play a game of hide-and-seek with Hu Tsung-nan's troops who were thus bogged down in an area of little strategic value. Meanwhile Mao ordered Liu Po-ch'eng's army to drive south-east to the Tapieh Mountains and Ch'en Keng's army to thrust into west Honan. 'The unexpected movements of the communist troops in Honan,' Chiang ruefully recalls, 'cut the railway communications of the 400,000 National troops in north Shensi and immobilised them in the area west of the T'ungkuan Pass.'[44] The Government had no choice but to dispatch other units to deal with Liu Po-ch'eng.

Liu Po-ch'eng's army did not move south in one close column, but in several small bands, appearing to be engaged in a desperate flight to avoid the raging river and the KMT troops who came after them. Taken in by this feint and relying on the six or seven rivers lying ahead of Liu Po-ch'eng, Chiang did not send troops to block Liu's 'escape route'. Not until 23 August did he realize his misjudgement and hurriedly dispatched the 15th and 85th Divisions to defend the south bank of the Ju River. But it was too late and on 28 August Liu crossed the Huai River and established a base on the Tapieh Mountains which towered above the central and eastern plains, to pose a threat to the Huai districts and the entire area north of the Yangtze.[45]

In concert with Liu, Ch'en Yi attacked east Honan from Shantung and Ch'en Keng pushed towards west Honan from south Shansi.[46] Chiang, fearing that the PLA would take Loyang, Sian, and the Lunghai railway, concentrated his troops for their defence, consequently leaving wide gaps for Ch'en Keng to slip through and effect a junction with Ch'en Yi's army.[47] The 'Dumb-bell' had now lost a ball and the bar and the remaining ball weighed heavily on Chiang's mind.

The gain of Honan and north Hupei marked the beginning of the PLA's fighting on exterior lines. The stalemate was turned into a communist offensive, compelling Chiang to send more troops to defend central China, which would otherwise have been deployed

44. [153] III, 483–4.   45. [153] III, 483 and [308] 41 and 46–8.
46. [308] 41.
47. Ch'en Keng's recollection, [305] 74–82 and [306] 152–3.

in Manchuria to strengthen the garrison. In this sense the battle of the central plain weakened the KMT position in the north-east and also gave Lin Piao's army a chance to consolidate and prepare for the next assault.[48]

Before Christmas 1947 when the PLA launched its winter offensive in Manchuria, the morale of the 500,000 KMT troops was already very low and their commanders were hopelessly divided.[49] In ninety days Lin Piao took no less than nineteen towns including the strategic point Ssup'ingchieh, destroyed some 150,000 of the troops, and compressed the KMT holdings to three small enclaves around Mukden, Ch'angch'un, and Chinchow, a mere 1 per cent. of the total area of Manchuria.[50] As soon as this was over, Lin embarked on the preparation for the next stage of the conquest.[51] On 7 September 1948 Mao, in the name of the Military Commission of the CCP, telegraphed to Lin Piao and Lo Jung-huan:

If in the two months of September and October, or a little longer, you can wipe out the enemy along the line from Chinchow to Tangshan and take Chinchow, Shanhaikuan and Tangshan, you will have achieved the task of wiping out some 18 enemy brigades. In order to wipe them out, you must now prepare to employ your main force on this line, leaving the enemy forces at Changchun and Shenyang [Mukden] alone.[52]

Mao's decision to open the Manchurian campaign at Chinchow was undoubtedly correct, for it was there that the communists could have had a stranglehold on the KMT supply line and retreat route.[53] The battle was joined on 12 September with the PLA nibbling away point after point around Chinchow. Chiang ordered General Wei Li-huang's troops in Mukden to rescue the eight divisions now besieged in Chinchow, but, on 9 October instead of 25 September as ordered by Chiang, Wei made a half-hearted move and was thrown back.[54] Chiang at once flew to the north-east to direct the campaign himself while Mao telegraphed to Lin Piao:

48. [46] IV, 1205 or *SW* IV (Peking), 115.
49. [11] 315–16 and 733 and [134] 256–7.
50. [46] IV, 1293 n. 2 or *SW* IV (Peking), 216 n. 5.　　　　51. [308] 67.
52. [46] IV, 1338 or *SW* IV (Peking), 262.
53. [11] 320 and [153] III, 497.
54. [11] 320–1 and [153] III, 497–8.

You must centre your attention on the operations in Chinchow and strive to capture this city as quickly as possible. Even if none of the other objectives is attained and Chinchow alone is captured, you will have won the initiative, which in itself will be a great victory.[55]

On 14 October Lin launched his final assault on Chinchow and thirty-one hours later the commanding officer in Chinchow was captured and his 100,000 troops destroyed.[56] Four days later the beleaguered city of Ch'angch'un surrendered and on 2 November Mukden followed.[57] Chiang attributed the defeat in Manchuria to Wei Li-huang's disobeying his orders,[58] but to President Truman he explained:

I need hardly point out that, but for persistent Soviet aid, the Chinese Communists would not have been able to occupy Manchuria and develop into such a menace.[59]

Nevertheless there were more fundamental reasons for this defeat as we have already analysed. The causes of the defeat are perhaps less important than its effects. The gain of Manchuria gave the PLA 'a strategically secure rear area with a fair industrial base'[60]; the destruction of 470,000 (Chiang admitted 300,000) of the cream of Chiang's troops not only tipped the military balance but also swelled the ranks of Lin Piao's army from 360,000 to nearly 800,000 and freed them from Manchuria to move against the KMT's north flank, thus virtually sealing the fate of the 10 per cent. of the territories north of the Yellow River still under the KMT; the airlift to the untenable city of Ch'angch'un for two months and four days exhausted the Government defence budget for the 1948–9 fiscal year; it was unwise of Chiang to take personal command of a hopeless campaign and the defeat greatly injured his prestige. Therefore Major-General David Barr remarked that the campaign 'spelled the beginning of the end'.[61]

In the thick of the Manchurian campaign, on 26 September, Ch'en Yi took the KMT's last bastion in Shantung, Chinan. On

55. [46] IV, 1340 or *SW* IV (Peking), 265.
56. [11] 321 and [46] IV, 1341 or *SW* IV (Peking), 265 n. 1.
57. [46] IV, 1375 n. 2 or *SW* IV (Peking), 297 n. 2.
58. [153] III, 499.   59. [11] 888.
60. [46] IV, 1338 n. or *SW* IV (Peking), 262 n., and [153] III, 499.
61. [11] 334–5, [46] IV, 1338 n. or *SW* IV (Peking), 262 n., [134] 257, and [324] 196.

the right leg of the 'A' shape—the Tientsin–Pukow railway—only Tientsin and Hsüchow remained to be conquered by the communists, before the PLA marched on Nanking, Peking, and Hankow. Giving no respite to Chiang's army, Mao ordered the rested armies of Liu Po-ch'eng and Ch'en Yi to advance in a pincer movement to Hsüchow and its adjacent areas. Mao's telegram, dated 11 October and addressed to Teng Hsiao-p'ing, the secretary of the Front Committee, and Liu Po-ch'eng, Ch'en Yi, Su Yü, and T'an Chen-lin, outlined the three stages of the campaign:

In the first stage of this campaign, the central task is to concentrate forces to wipe out Huang Po-t'ao's army. . . . You must strive to conclude the first stage two to three weeks after the start of the campaign.

In the second stage, use about five columns to attack and wipe out the enemy in Haichow, Hsinpu, Lienyunkang and Kuanyun and capture these towns. . . . You must strive to conclude this stage also in two or three weeks.

In the third stage, it may be assumed that the battle will be fought around Huaiyin and Huaian. . . . This stage will also take about two to three weeks.[62]

For this campaign, the PLA deployed 550,000 troops[63] while Chiang used 400,000 equipped with tanks, heavy artillery, and other modern weapons.[64] The terrain was flat, ideal for a war of manoeuvre but disastrous for a static war of garrisoning; yet garrisoning was exactly the strategy Chiang adopted. American observers considered the troops 'far inferior to the former Mukden garrison and their commanders . . . already resigned to defeat', they found 'no reason to believe in their will or ability to resist an offensive' and considered that when they were gone, Nanking would have no defences worthy of the name.[65]

Hsüchow itself was defended by the 2nd, 13th, and 16th Army Groups with the 7th on its east flank and the 6th on its south. These were Chiang's last 'mechanized' units and each was supported by some less well-equipped units. In the first stage, Ch'en Yi's field army, supported by Liu Po-ch'eng's on its west, attacked

62. [46] IV, 1355–6 or SW IV (Peking), 279–80.
63. [5] 261 and [153] III, 501. See also [324] 201.
64. [302] 240.   65. [11] 919 and [299] 420.

the 7th Army Group under Huang Po-t'ao on 6 November. Two divisions of the less well-equipped troops, almost as soon as the battle was joined, went over to Ch'en Yi with the result that the 7th Army Group had to withdraw towards Hsüchow. At the same time the headquarters in Hsüchow sent out a column to make contact with the retreating army, only to find that its way was blocked by the communists. The 7th Army Group thereupon decided to turn back to where it had started and was at once encircled by the main force of Ch'en Yi. From 11 to 22 November the 100,000 strong 7th Army Group fought in a pocket of three by two miles and was completely wiped out.[66]

In haste Chiang dispatched the 12th Army Group under Huang Wei, about 120,000 strong, to rescue Hsüchow, but, hampered by snow and rain and misled by bad intelligence work, they walked into a trap laid for them by Liu Po-ch'eng. The second stage of the Huai-hai campaign thus began.

Taken by surprise, the 12th Army Group turned to retreat southward and it was then that its 110th Division, about 50,000 strong, surrendered to Liu Po-ch'eng. Seeing that his rescuing troops were now in danger, Chiang ordered the south flank to move northward to Hsüchow, but this movement, too, was intercepted and delayed. On 6 December Liu Po-ch'eng launched a fierce attack on the panicky 12th Army Group, which, nine days later, ended in its complete annihilation.[67]

At this juncture, Mao suddenly decided to postpone the *coup de grâce*:

In order not to prompt Chiang Kai-shek quickly to decide to ship his troops in the Peiping-Tientsin area south by sea, we are going to order Liu Po-ch'eng, Teng Hsiao-p'ing, Ch'en Yi and Su Yü, after they have wiped out Huang Wei's army, to spare the remainder of Tu Yü-ming's[68] armies under Ch'iu Ch'ing-ch'üan, Li Mi and Sun Yüan-liang (about half of which have already been destroyed) and for two weeks to make no dispositions for their annihilations.[69]

This shrewd decision lured Chiang into believing that the PLA in Hsüchow area was in need of consolidation and regrouping before

66. [181] 136, [299] 421, and [306] 243–5.
67. [181] 136–7, [299] 421–2, and [306] 246–7.
68. The C.-in-C. of the KMT troops in this campaign.
69. [46] IV, 1396 or *SW* IV (Peking), 291.

it could become a serious menace again. It did indeed give the PLA a chance to rest while the KMT troops were starved, frozen and demoralized, for the latter, in an attempt to break through the communist encirclement, had abandoned most of their supplies and heavy equipment.[70] Mao also wrote to General Tu Yü-ming:

You are now at the end of your rope. Huang Wei's army was completely wiped out on the night of the 15th, Li Yen-nien's army has taken to its heels and fled south, and it is hopeless for you to think of joining them. ... For more than ten days, you have been surrounded ring upon ring and received blow upon blow, and your position has shrunk greatly. ... You should ... immediately order all your troops to lay down their arms and cease resistance. ... This is your only way out. Think it over! If you feel this is right, then do it. If you still want to fight another round, you can have it, but you will be finished off anyway.[71]

Meanwhile Lin Piao's field army, now said to be 800,000 strong, and Nieh Jung-chen's North China Army Group were ordered to close in to Peking and Tientsin. Mao's directives to them said:

Our real aim is not to encircle Peiping first but rather to encircle Tientsin, Tangku, Lutai, and Tangshan first.

In the two weeks beginning from today (December 11–25), the basic principle is to encircle without attacking (in the case of Changchiakou [Kalgan] and Hsinpaoan) and, in some cases, to cut off without encircling (in the case of Peiping, Tientsin and Tungchow, to make only a strategic encirclement and cut the links between the enemy forces, but not to make a tactical encirclement) in order to wait for the completion of our dispositions and then wipe out the enemy forces one by one. In particular you must not wipe out all the enemy forces at Changchiakou [Kalgan], Hsinpaoan and Nankow because that would compel the enemy east of Nankow to make a quick decision to bolt. Please make sure you understand this point.

The main or the only concern is that the enemy might flee by sea. Therefore, in the coming two weeks the general method should be to encircle without attacking or to cut off without encircling.

This plan is beyond the enemy's range of expectation, and it will be very difficult for him to discern it before you complete your final disposition. At present, the enemy is calculating that you will attack Peiping.

The sequence of attacks will be roughly the following: first, the

70. [308] 247–9.   71. [46] IV, 1373–4 or SW IV (Peking), 295–6.

Tangku-Lutai sector; second, Hsinpaoan; third, the Tangshan sector; fourth, the Tientsin and Changchiakou [Kalgan] sector; and, lastly, the Peiping sector.[72]

There were all together about half a million KMT troops in the Peking-Tientsin-Kalgan enclave under the command of General Fu Tso-yi,[73] a tenacious soldier with a remarkable record, but no Whampoa man. Although the supplies and equipment of his army were plentiful, replenishment and reinforcement were out of the question. In their customary fashion, Lin Piao and Nieh Jung-chen began by nibbling away at the towns around Peking and Tientsin. Kalgan fell on Christmas Eve 1948; Tientsin on 14 January 1949; and after a lull in the fighting during which negotiations were conducted, Fu Tso-yi surrendered with Peking and some 200,000 troops at the end of January.[74]

Having sealed off all the escape routes of the KMT troops in Peking and Tientsin, Mao ordered the third stage of the Huai-hai campaign to begin on 6 January. Four days later it was all over: Tu Yü-ming was captured and his armies were all destroyed.[75] From September 1948 to January 1949, the Government had lost no less than one and a half million troops.

Before the Manchurian campaign started, Mao estimated that five years from July 1946 would be required for the overthrow of the KMT régime[76]; at the beginning of the Huai-hai campaign, he forecast the PLA's crossing of the Yangtze in the autumn of 1949[77]; but half-way through the Huai-hai campaign, on 14 November, he made the announcement that the PLA had achieved its numerical superiority to the KMT army and said confidently:

Accordingly, the war will be much shorter than we originally estimated. The original estimate was that the reactionary KMT government could be completely overthrown in about five years, beginning from July 1946. As we now see it, only another year or so may be needed to overthrow it completely.[78]

72. [46] IV, 1367–70 or *SW* IV (Peking), 289–92.
73. Now the Minister of Water Conservancy and Electric Power.
74. [46] IV, 1370–1 n.1 or *SW* IV (Peking), 292 n.1, [153] III, 499–500, and [308] 90–100.   75. [306] 247–9.
76. [46] IV, 1337 or *SW* IV (Peking), 261.
77. [46] IV, 1356 or *SW* IV (Peking), 281.
78. [46] IV, 1363–4 or *SW* IV (Peking), 289–90.

On the question of founding a government of his own, Mao, however, did not change his original decision of 20 March 1948:

We do not contemplate setting up the Central People's Government this year, because the time is not yet ripe. . . . After the capture of one or two of the country's largest cities, and after northeastern China, north China, Shantung, northern Kiangsu, Honan, Hupeh, and Anhwei are all linked together in one contiguous area, it will be entirely necessary to establish the Central People's Government.[79]

But some time before that, in October 1947, he began to call Chiang and other leaders of the KMT 'the civil war criminals'.[80] His reply to Chiang's appeal for peace, dated 5 January, was entitled 'On a War Criminal's Suing for Peace',[81] which was a scathing and merciless attack on Chiang and his policies. Chiang in his New Year Message laid down his peace terms:

If the communists are sincerely desirous of peace, and clearly give such indication, the Government will be only too glad to discuss with them the means to end the war.

If a negotiated peace is not detrimental to the national independence and sovereignty, but will contribute to the welfare of the people; if the Constitution is not violated and constitutionism preserved, the democratic form of government maintained, the entity of the armed forces safeguarded; and if the people's free mode of life and their minimum living standard are protected, then I shall be satisfied.[82]

And Chiang went on to strengthen his case by saying:

It must be understood that today the strength of the government in the military, political, economic or any other field is several times or even tens of times greater than that of the Communist Party.[83]

Mao, having rebutted every point Chiang raised, mocked sardonically:

Oh! Ho! How can people not be scared to death by such immense strength? Leaving political and economic strength aside and taking only military strength, one sees that the People's Liberation Army now has over three million men, that two times 'greater' than this number is over six million and that ten times 'greater' is over thirty million.

79. [46] IV, 1297 or *SW* IV (Peking), 221.
80. [46] IV, 1237 or *SW* IV (Peking), 150.
81. [46] IV, 1387 *et seq.* or *SW* IV (Peking), 309 *et seq.*
82. [11] 921 and [46] IV, 1387 or *SW* IV (Peking), 309.
83. [46] IV, 1389 or *SW* IV (Peking), 312.

And how many will 'tens of times' be? All right, let's take twenty times, which gives over sixty million men; no wonder President Chiang says he has 'full confidence in winning the decisive battle'. Why then should he beg for peace? . . .

As we said long ago, Chiang Kai-shek has lost his soul, is merely a corpse, and no one believes him any more.[84]

This rejection drove a wedge between the war and peace factions of the KMT, the latter of which, represented by Generals Li Tsung-jen and Pai Ch'ung-hsi, regarded Chiang as the only stumbling-block to a political settlement. Chiang, on his part, tried to persuade Britain, the United States, France, and Russia to mediate between him and Mao, but the Powers showed no interest.[85] The awkward position of the KMT was best described by the party's Information Department:

If we cannot fight, we cannot make peace.[86]

This is reminiscent of the position of the Manchu Government after the Anglo-French Expedition in 1860:

Before the defeat at Taku, we had the choice of either fighting against the foreigners or making peace with them; and after it we can only appease them. At a time when foreign troops occupy the Imperial Capital, we are certainly not in a position to fight, not even for our own defence. Both fighting and appeasing are to our disadvantage.[87]

But, as a continuation in fighting could only lead to the total effacement of the KMT on the mainland, the peace faction won the day and on 21 January 1949 Chiang handed the authority of the President to General Li Tsung-jen.[88]

A week before Chiang's retirement, Mao announced his peace terms:

(1) Punish the war criminals; (2) Abolish the bogus constitution; (3) Abolish the bogus 'constituted authority'; (4) Reorganize all reactionary troops on democratic principles; (5) Confiscate bureaucrat-capital; (6) Reform the land system; (7) Abrogate treasonable treaties; (8) Convene a political consultative conference without the participation of reactionary elements, and form a democratic coalition government

84. [46] IV, 1389–90 or *SW* IV (Peking), 312–13.
85. [11] 290–1, 897, 900.
86. [46] IV, 1412 or *SW* IV (Peking), 342.   87. [84] 244.
88. [153] III, 513.

M.C.R.—21

to take over all the powers of the reactionary Nanking Kuomintang government and of its subordinate governments at all levels.[89]

Li Tsung-jen was prepared to conduct negotiations with the communists on the basis of these terms, but his premier, Dr. Sun Fo, objected.[90] At that time Li was in Nanking, Sun in Canton, and their Ministry of Defence nowhere to be found. 'Thus,' Mao, quoting from the 14th-century poet, Sadul, described, 'all that is left for Li Tung-jen to see from the ramparts of the "Stone City" [Nanking] is,

> *The sky brooding low over the land of Wu and Ch'u*
> *With nothing between to meet the eye.'*[91]

Yet on 22 January Li announced the appointment of his peace delegation, including Shao Li-tzu, Chang Chih-chung, Huang Shao-hsiung, P'eng Shao-hsien, and Chung T'ien-hsin; the CCP, however, objected to the inclusion of P'eng on the ground that he was a prominent member of the CC clique.[92] In the end P'eng and Chung were replaced by Chang Shih-chao, Li Cheng, and Liu Fei[93] and the delegation went to Peking on 1 April to discuss with Chou En-lai, Lin Tsu-han, Li Wei-han, Lin Piao, and Nieh Jung-chen.[94] A fortnight later the delegations reached an agreement which was brought back by Huang Shao-hsiung for Li's approval while the other KMT negotiators stayed behind.[95] Under the agreement, the CCP promised, on condition of the KMT's acceptance of its eight terms, to refrain from attacking the troops of the Kwangsi clique and other peace factions and from reorganizing them for a year, to allow the Nanking Government to be represented both at the forthcoming people's political consultative conference and in the coalition government, and to protect certain interests of the capitalists in the south.[96] Li Tsung-jen and Pai Chung-hsi found these conditions unacceptable and informed the Ambassadors of the United States, Britain, and Aus-

89. [46] IV, 1394 or *SW* IV (Peking), 318.
90. [153] III, 515.   91. [46] IV, 1412 or *SW* IV (Peking), 343.
92. [153] III, 514 and [46] IV, 1401–2 ns.1 and 2 or *SW* IV (Peking), 330 ns.1 and 2.   93. [153] III, 516–17.
94. [46] IV, 1440 n. 2 or *SW* IV (Peking), 375 n. 3.
95. [153] III, 517.   96. [46] IV, 1437 or *SW* IV (Peking), 371–2.

tralia of their decision and of the communist terms.[97] This was at
Easter 1949. Thereafter Chiang resumed his control and war
began again.[98]

On 21 April Mao issued his order to the PLA for the country-
wide advance.[99] The 2nd and 3rd Field Armies under Liu Po-
ch'eng and Ch'en Yi crossed the Yangtze at three points[1] while
the KMT 'grandiose plans for defence crumbled amid political
bickering, desertions or betrayals, disorderly retreats.'[2] Nanking
fell on 24 April and a month later Shanghai followed.[3] Thence-
forth the collapse gained speed. The 1st Field Army of the PLA
mopped up the north-west and south-west from 1949 to February
1950, destroying Hu Tsung-nan's army in the process[4]; the 2nd
Field Army, having taken Chekiang, drove into Kiangsi and
Hunan and then swept across Kwangtung to Szechwan[5]; the 3rd
Field Army, after the battles of Nanking and Shanghai, moved
along the sea coast to Chekiang and Fukien[6]; and the 4th Field
Army defeated General Pai Ch'ung-hsi first at Wuhan on 16 May,
then at Hengyang on 11 October, and finally in Kwangsi in
December.[7] In the eleven months since the Manchurian campaign
the PLA had advanced 2,000 miles to end the war on the mainland
at the close of 1949.

Amid these triumphant military activities, the new Political
Consultative Conference took place in Peking on 9 September.
Addressing its preparatory committee on 15 June, Mao had said
that only by proclaiming the foundation of the People's Republic
of China and electing a democratic coalition government to represent it could 'our great mother land free herself from a semi-
colonial and semi-feudal fate and take the road of independence,
freedom, peace, unity, strength, and prosperity'[8]; now at the opening session of the Conference he said:

---

97. [153] III, 517; [324] 231.   98. [153] III, 517.
99. [46] IV, 1451 or *SW* IV (Peking), 387.
  1. [187] 96, [306] 311–13 and 316–17.   2. [11] 305 and [324] 242.
3. [316] 323–5 and [312] ch. 6.
4. P'eng Te-huai's part in the civil war was surprisingly small. [134] 269 and
[187] 99. See also [322] A.62.
5. [187] 100 and [322] A.63–4.   6. [187] 100 and [322] A.64–5.
7. [153] III, 527–53, [134] 270, [187] 100, and [322] A.65–6.
8. [46] IV, 1467–8 or *SW* IV (Peking), 405–6.

We have now entered into the community of peace-loving and freedom-loving nations of the world. We shall work with courage and industry to create our own civilisation and happiness and, at the same time, to promote world peace and freedom.[9]

And on 1 October 1949 Mao, the newly elected Chairman of the People's Republic of China, proclaimed the foundation of the republic for which he had incessantly fought for twenty-two years.

9. [309] 5.

Part Two

*Thirty-seven Poems by
Mao Tse-tung*

translated from the Chinese by
MICHAEL BULLOCK and JEROME CH'ÊN

Introduction to Mao's Poems

THERE is something peculiarly Chinese about a revolutionary leader who, at the same time, achieves fame as a poet, as Mao Tse-tung has done. The West offers few parallels to such a dual achievement as artist and man of action. No doubt Mao's status as a poet has been enhanced by his eminence as a political figure; nevertheless his poetic abilities, although they are uneven, are of no mean order and would have secured him a place in contemporary Chinese literature independent of his pre-eminent position in the political sphere.

Curiously enough, Mao Tse-tung's poems are classical in construction, though their themes are drawn almost entirely from his experiences and hopes as a militant communist. This apparent dichotomy becomes less surprising when we know something about his life and background, and the detailed study which precedes the poems will perhaps provide an explanation. But here we must say a few words about the poetic legacy which Mao inherited.

The anthologies of Chinese classical poems—*shih* as well as *tz'u*—often contain works expressing a feeling of unrestraint more in idea than form and these are frequently the products of men of similar dual attainment to Mao's. The Martial Emperor of Wei (155–220), from whose works Mao quotes, wrote this, for instance:

> Crouching in its stable, an old steed
> Aspires to run another thousand leagues.
> In his last years, a hero
> Still kindles the flame of his ambition.

And the most widely read poem of his has these lines:

> Sing, whenever there is wine,
> For life is as ephemeral
> As dew in the morning,
> With the days to come numbered.
> Mind must be generous,
> But seldom is it free from sorrow
> That dissolves
> Only in a cup of wine.

Another great poet and political personality, Su Tung-p'o (1036–1101), dedicated a well-known piece to his brother, which began thus:

> How is the moon, so round and clear!
>   With cup in hand, I ask the blue sky,
> 'I do not know in the celestial sphere
>   What name this festive night goes by?'
> I want to fly home, riding the air,
> But fear the ethereal cold up there,
>   The jade and crystal mansions are so high!
> Dancing to my shadows,
>   I feel no longer the mortal tie.
>   (Lin Yutang, *Gay Genius*, 155)

He also wrote:

> The Great River flows east;
> Its waves have washed away
>   All the princely men of the past.

The spirit of which is echoed in the concluding lines of Mao's *Snow*:

> All are past and gone!
> For men of vision
> We must seek among the present generation.

But for an even closer parallel we must refer to Hsin Ch'i-chi (1140–1207), a patriot, a military commander, and needless to say, a celebrated poet. While fighting against the invading Tartars Hsin wrote:

I clip the wick
   And examine my sword with drunken eyes.
The bugle notes
   Rising from rows of tents recall me from my dreams.
In the eight hundred leagues
   Under my standard
   Men are sharing out the roast,
While fifty strings
   Vibrate to tribal melodies.
I call the roll
   On this autumn battlefield.

Mine is a fine steed
   Swift as a bird flying;
My bow thunders
   When suddenly its string is released.
Having done my duty
   On behalf of my liege
And made a name
   In my life and after my death,
My sorry hair is greying!

How similar is this to Mao's *Chingkang Mountain*! The pathos may not be present in Mao, but the imagery is the same.

For all these men as well as for Mao, the landscape possesses a singular charm, quite different from that which it holds for the eyes of an artist or a man of letters. Hsin Ch'i-chi sought for its associations with heroes of the past, and Mao wrote,

     Such is the beauty of these mountains and rivers
     That has been admired by unnumbered heroes —.

For Mao, the months and years have been turbulent, marquisates are valued as dust, or mountains are like a thousand stallions rearing and plunging in the thick of battle.

Like other Chinese poets, these men of action love landscape but incline to conquer it; unlike other Chinese poets, they eschew sentiments too delicate or too tenuous. So Mao advises his poet friend:

     Beware of breaking your heart with too much sadness.

Women and love play no part in Mao's poems, except in *The Immortals*. Since his youth, Mao has always been interested in 'the nature of men, of human society, of China, the world, and the universe'.[1] He first showed literary promise when he was still a schoolboy,[2] but he himself seems to take greater pride in his prose. In 1946 when Mr. Robert Payne saw him in Yenan and asked him about his poem *Snow*, Mao replied:

I gave it to my friend [Liu Ya-tzu], urging him not to let anyone see it, but he published it without my permission.[3]

And in 1957 he wrote to the editor of his poems:

Up to now I have never wanted to make these things known in any formal way, because they are written in the old style. I was afraid this might encourage a wrong trend and exercise a bad influence on young people. Besides, they are not up to much as poetry, and there is nothing outstanding about them.[4]

His choice of the old style is due to his early classical training and his lack of knowledge of modern poetry.[5]

In prose Mao is an entirely different man—cool-headed and logical, almost devoid of deep feelings. Yet there is something common to both his prose and poetry—a rugged beauty and rustic directness both of which, alas, are lost in the highly urbane translations of his *Selected Works*. Take, for instance, his famous speech on the *New Democracy*. In its first edition, he referred to Wang Ching-wei, another man of action as well as an accomplished poet, as *k'ai-tai* (a Cantonese swear word) which provoked loud laughter among his audience. This, however, appears neither in his *Hsüan-chi* nor in his *Selected Works*.[6]

Certain of these poems have already appeared in other English versions and in these cases our translations do not offer radically

----

1. [258] 145.   2. [43] 29.   3. [293] 87.   4. [48] 7.

5. Mao's knowledge of modern literature seems to be confined to Lu Hsün and one or two Russian novels. He has referred to no other modern literary works in his *Selected Works*.

6. Siao Yu tends to belittle Mao's literary attainment. He also says at several places in his book ([54] 54, 67, and 114) that Mao's handwriting 'was always very poor'. This is a small point, but is contradicted by a post-card reproduced in Li Jui's book, which clearly shows that in his youth Mao studied Emperor Hui-tsung's (reigned 1101–26) calligraphical style with considerable success. Unfortunately he only scribbles now.

new and different interpretations. They do, however, differ in one rather important respect. Previous translations have made the poems appear smooth, almost gentle, in rhythm; whereas in fact the originals are characterized by precisely that vigorous, almost violent, and distinctly staccato quality which one would expect from such a forceful, combative personality as Mao's. This quality we have endeavoured to retain in the translations—so far as the differences of the language allows—by using short, stabbing lines and as few polysyllables as possible. The few exceptions to this general rule include the first poem to Liu Ya-tzu which is elegiac in mood and slower and more languid in tempo and the *Long March* which, in our view, is rather prosaic.

Like all Chinese poetry, these poems, by no means the only ones Mao has written, contain a wealth of allusions—some referring to classical literature, others to local topography, and yet others to ancient and modern historical events—and these allusions, without which the reader's understanding of the poems would be incomplete, are elucidated in the notes.

We offer these poems to the reader both for their intrinsic interest as literature and for the light they cast upon the mind of the man whose life and times are dealt with in the first part of this book.

M. B. and J. C.

Ch'angsha

to the melody of *Shen Yüan Ch'un*   1926

Alone in the autumn cold
I scan the river
   that flows northward
Past the Orange Islet
And the mountains crimson
With the red leaves of the woods.
On this broad stream
   of rich green water
A hundred boats
   race with the currents.
Eagles dart
   across the wide sky,
Fish swim
   in the shallows—
All display their freedom
   in the frosty air.
Bewildered by the immensity,
I ask the vast grey earth:
'Who decides men's destinies?'

I brought hither
   hundreds of companions
In those turbulent
   months and years.
We were fellow students
Then in our lissom youth.
In the true manner of scholars
We accused without fear or favour,
Pointed at these rivers and ranges,
And wrote vibrant words,
Valuing marquisates
   as dust.

Do you not remember
How in mid-stream
   our boats struck currents
And were slowed down by torrents?

The city is on the east bank of the River Hsiang which flows northward into Lake Tungt'ing. The Orange Islet lies to its west, and farther west a range of mountains. The melancholy this poem expresses is unique among Mao's verse. The landscape depicted in the first stanza and the treasured memories in the second are beautiful and vivid, touched here and there with a tinge of sorrow. It is written with consummate skill.

The 1964 edition of Mao's poems published in Peking dates this poem in 1925, but as shown in the chronology on pp. 379-80, this is impossible, for Mao did not spend the autumn of that year in Ch'angsha.

Yellow Crane Tower

to the melody of *P'u Sa Man*   Summer 1927

Broad, broad
   through the country
   flow the nine tributaries.
Deep, deep
   from north to south
   cuts a line.
Blurred in the blue haze
   of the rain and mist
The Snake and Tortoise Hills
   tower above the water.

The yellow crane
   has departed.
   Who knows where it has gone?
Only this resting-place
   for travellers remains.
In wine I drink
   a pledge to the surging torrent.
The tide of my heart
   rises as high as the waves.

The tower is on the western outskirts of Wuch'ang on the Yangtze, made famous by earlier poems dedicated to it. Mao visited the tower in the summer of 1927 when the fifth national congress of the CCP was held and he was re-elected to the Central Committee of the party. It was a time when the waves of revolution rose high (*vide supra*, pp. 115-16). Of the two stanzas of this poem, the first is unquestionably the better.

Chingkang Mountain

to the melody of *Hsi Chiang Yüeh*   Summer 1928

At the foot of the mountain
  waved our banners.
Upon its peak
  sounded our bugles and drums.
A myriad foes
  were all around us.
But we stood fast
  and gave no ground.

Our defence was strong
  as a mighty wall.
Our wills united
  to form a fortress.
From Huangyangchieh
  came the thunder of guns.
And the army of our foes
  had fled into the night!

Chu Te and his troops arrived at Chingkang Mountain in April 1928 and soon afterwards the combined forces of Mao and Chu defeated the first KMT attack at Huangyangchieh. This was probably written after the first but before the second KMT assault in July 1928.

New Year's Day 1929

to the melody of *Ju Meng Ling*

Ninghua! Ch'ingliu! Kweihua!
Narrow the path, deep the woods
    and the moss slippery.
Where are we bound today?
Straight to the foot of Wuyi Mountain.
The foot of the mountain,
    the foot of the mountain,
There the wind will unfurl,
    like a scroll,
      our scarlet banner.

Mao and Chu led their troops east to Fukien to open up a base area there. The places whose names form the first line are situated in the province of Fukien.

Huich'ang

to the melody of *Ch'ing P'ing Lo*   January 1929

In the east
   the dawn will soon be breaking,
But do not say
   we are marching early.
Though we have travelled
   all over these green hills
   we are not yet old
And on this side
   the landscape is strangely charming.

Straight from the walls of Huich'ang
   lofty peaks
Extend range upon range
   to the eastern ocean.
Our soldiers point and gaze
   south towards Kwangtung,
So green and luxuriant
   in the distance.

The town lies on the border between Kiangsi and Fukien.
Written on the same expedition as the previous one, this poem
chirps blithely, producing a melodious sound similar to that
heard when walking alone on mountains on a fine morning.

Advance to Fukien

to the melody of *Ch'ing P'ing Lo*

September or October 1929

A sudden wind gathers clouds
As warlords renew their clashes
And a pillow of dreams of fortune,
Only to spread hatred among men.

Over the Ting River
And straight to Lungyen and Shanghang
Are carried the crimson banners.
A part of the realm has been recovered
And the land is being actively redistributed.

Against the background of fighting between Chiang Kai-shek and the military leaders of Kwangsi, Mao and Chu Te accomplished their plan to set up a base in north Fukien, hence the references to such places as the Ting River, Lungyen, and Shanghang.

'The dream of fortune' is an allusion to a story from the T'ang dynasty (618–907) in which a poor scholar enjoys evanescent good fortune in a dream while his Taoist friend is cooking millet for him.

The Double Ninth Day, 1929

to the melody of *Ts'ai Sang Tzu*

11 October 1929

Man, not heaven, ages easily
As the Double Ninth Festival
  passes by year after year.
Once more the Festival returns.
On the battlefield
  yellow flowers are singularly fragrant.

Once every year
  the autumn wind smites hard
To paint a scene unlike the spring.
Even better than the spring
Is a myriad leagues of frosty sky and waters.

The ninth day of the ninth month, the Double Ninth Day, is a day on which both the sun and the moon are *yang*. It is a day of feasting in celebration of this fact.

March on Chian

to the melody of *Chien Tzu Mu Lan Hua*
February 1930

Seeing under the sky only white,
   no green of cypress,
The troops march in the snow.
Peaks tower above them.
The wind unfurls the red flags,
As they climb over the mountain pass.

Where are they going?
To the Kan River where wind sweeps up snow.
The order of yesterday
To a lac of workers and peasants
   was to take Chian.

According to Kuo Mo-jo (the *People's Daily*, 12.5.1962), the communists attacked Chian in Kiangsi no less than nine times in 1930. The first attack was in February; the second at the beginning of April; the third at the end of April; the fourth in May; the fifth and the sixth in June; the seventh in July; the eighth at the end of August; and the ninth in September and October. The march in snow dates this poem precisely at February 1930.

Attack on Nanch'ang

to the melody of *Tieh Lien Hua*

after June 1930

June: the peerless troops attack
   the corrupt and villainous,
Seeking to bind the cockatrice
   with a rope a myriad ells in length.
On the far side of the Kan River
   a patch of ground has turned red,
Thanks to the wing
   under the command of Huang Kung-lüeh.

The million elated workers and peasants
Roll up Kiangsi like a mat
   and thrust straight on to Liang Hu.
The heartening *Internationale*,
   like a hurricane,
Whirls down on me from heaven.

Kuo Mo-jo thinks that this was written after the attack; however, the second stanza tends to invalidate his theory, for the attack ended in a defeat for Mao.

The attempt to capture Nanch'ang was a part of Li Li-san's plan of nation-wide uprisings (*vide supra*, pp. 157-58), a disastrous scheme for the communists. Huang Kung-lüeh (1898–1931) took part in the P'ingchiang Uprising in the summer of 1928 and then served as commissar of the 2nd Regiment of the 14th Division of the 5th Red Army under P'eng Te-huai. He remained in P'ingchiang during the winter of 1928 when P'eng and his troops went to Chingkang Mountain. Upon their return to P'ingchiang in the autumn of 1929 Huang was appointed deputy commander of a division and at the end of 1929 he took command of the 3rd Army which formed a part of the 1st Army Corps. He was killed in action in Chian in October 1931.

The First Encirclement

to the melody of *Yü Chia Ao*   January 1931

The red of a myriad trees
  glitters under the frosty sky
To which rises the indignation of the matchless troops.
The Dragon Creek is dimmed by fog.
A cry with one voice:
'Chang Hui-tsan has been captured at the front!'

Entering Kiangsi is another army of two lacs;
Down from the sky come whirling wind and dust.
We call on millions of workers and peasants
To fight with one heart.
At the foot of the Puchow Mountain
  the red banners are spreading out.

Chang Hui-tsan was a Hunan warlord, served under T'an Yen-kai, and finally joined forces with Chiang Kai-shek's expeditionary troops shortly before 1926. The capture of Chang is described on pp. 166-67 above.

The last line refers to an ancient myth. In his note to this poem Mao quotes the following sources for it:

'"A Discourse on Astronomy", *Huai-nan-tzu*: "In ancient times Kung-kung and Chuan-hsü fought for supremacy. In a rage Kung-kung knocked his head against the Puchow Mountain, thus breaking the pillar that supported the sky and lifted up the earth. The sky consequently slanted to the northwest and the sun, the moon, and stars also moved in that direction; the earth became lower in the southeast and waters and dust flowed towards the southeast."

"Chou-yü", *Kuo Yü*: "In the past, Kung-kung acted against this law by seeking excessive pleasure and losing his integrity. He wanted to block all the rivers and flatten the mountains in order to fill up hollows, with the intention to do harm to the world. Heaven ceased to bless him; the people ceased to support him; the disasters and unrests that followed eventually destroyed him." (The commentary by Wei

Chao of the Wu of the Three Kingdoms: "The King's Chancellor, Chia K'uei, says that Kung-kung was a baron, a descendant of the King of Fire whose family name was Chiang. At a time when the fortunes of Chuan-hsü were in decline, Kung-kung invaded the territory of other barons and struggled for hegemony against the Kao-hsin family.")

Ssu-ma Chen, "The Supplementary Annals of the Three Primeval Kings" attached to *The Chronicles* by Ssu-ma Ch'ien: "In her (Nü-kua's) last years, Kung-kung, a baron, grew in strength by relying on the intelligent use of punishment. He was the hegemon, but did not assume the title of a king. He overcame water with wood and fought against Chu-jung who defeated him. In a rage, he knocked his head against the Puchow Mountain whose collapse removed the pillar that supported the sky and lifted up the earth."

Mao adds his own note: 'These versions differ from each other and I prefer the *Huai-nan-tzu* version which describes Kung-kung as a victorious hero. One sees [in the *Huai-nan-tzu*], "In a rage Kung-kung knocked his head against the Puchow Mountain, thus breaking the pillar that supported the sky and lifted up the earth. The sky consequently slanted to the northwest and the sun, the moon, and stars also moved in that direction; the earth became lower in the southeast and waters and dust flowed towards the southeast." Did he die? This is not explicitly stated. Kung-kung actually won.'

There are other versions of the Kung-kung story, such as Ssu-ma Chi'ien's in *The Chronicles*, to which neither Mao nor Kuo Mo-jo has paid any attention. Even the name Kung-kung (*lit.* 'work in unison' or perhaps used as a pun here to mean 'communist workers') is still open to different interpretations. Some say that it was the name of a man; others maintain that it was the title of a government post, equivalent to the modern Minister of Works. Mao's note on the text is far from being flawless.

The last character of the last line, *luan*, means 'disorderly, chaotic, or confused'. If we accept Mao's interpretation of Kung-kung and regard him as the symbol of the workers' army led by Mao, we are still at a loss as to the true meaning of the character *luan*. If the workers' army was victorious, why should the red banners be 'disorderly, chaotic, or confused'? Or is this simply a case of doggerel rhyming? Out of this confused imagery, our rendering of the line cannot be more than tentative.

The Second Encirclement

to the melody of *Yü Chia Ao*   May 1931

On the White Cloud Mountain
  clouds are about to rise;
Below the White Cloud Mountain
  there are quickened cries.
Dry wood and hollow trees
  are joining in the battle.
A forest of rifles press forward.
The flying generals descend
  as if from heaven.

The army has covered
  two hundred miles in fifteen days
Along the grey Kan River and the green Fukien mountains,
To sweep away thousands of troops like rolling up a mat.
Someone is weeping
Belatedly regretting the strategy of slow advance.

Three points here require a word of explanation. the 'dry
wood and hollow trees', according to Kuo Mo-jo (the *People's
Daily*, 8 June 1962), refer to the enemy troops; the 'two hundred miles in fifteen days' agrees with Mao's account of the
battle in his *Selected Works* (the Chinese version, I, 213); and
'the strategy of slow advance' was adopted by General Ho
Ying-ch'in, the commander-in-chief of the second encirclement campaign.

Tapoti

to the melody of *P'u Sa Man*
written after the Fourth Encirclement in February 1933

Red, orange, yellow
  green, blue, indigo, violet—
Who is dancing in the sky,
  whirling this ribbon of colour?
After the rain
  the sun has returned to set,
And the pass and the lines of hills
  are blue.

A desperate battle
  raged here once.
Bullet holes
  pit the walls of the village.
They are an embellishment
And today the hills
  seem yet more fair.

Loushan Pass

to the melody of *Yi Ch'in O*   January 1935

Cold blows the west wind,
Far off in the frosty air
  the wild geese call
  in the morning moonlight.
In the morning moonlight
Horses' hoofs ring out sharply
And the bugle's note
  is muted.

Do not say
  that the pass is defended with iron.
This very day
  at one step
  we shall cross over it.
We shall cross over it.
The hills are blue like the sea,
And the dying sun is like blood.

Written shortly after the Tsunyi Conference in January 1935
at which Mao was elected to the chairmanship of the Politburo
of the CCP for the first time. The pass is to the north of
Tsunyi in Kweichow.

Three Short Poems

to the melody of *Shih Liu Tzu Ling*

March or April 1935

Mountains!
Faster I spur
    my coursing horse,
    never leaving the saddle.
I start as I raise my head,
For the sky is three foot three above me!

Mountains!
Like surging, heaving seas
    with rolling billows,
Like a thousand stallions,
    rearing and plunging
In the thick of battle.

Mountains!
Piercing the blue of the sky,
    their peaks unblunted!
The heavens would fall
If their strength did not support them.

Mao's note: A folk song runs—

'Skull Mountain stands high above;
Treasure Mountain lies down below.
The sky is only three foot three away.
On crossing, you must bend your head
Or dismount from your horse.'

This was probably written in southern Kweichow in March or
April 1935.

The Long March

Lü-shih   September 1935

The Red Army fears not the trials of the Long March
And thinks nothing of a thousand mountains and rivers.
The Wuling Ridges spread out like ripples;
The Wumeng Ranges roll like balls of clay.
Warmly are the cliffs wrapped in clouds
    and washed by the Gold Sand;
Chilly are the iron chains lying across
    the width of the Great Ferry.
A thousand acres of snow on the Min Mountains delight
My troops who have just left them behind.

Having crossed the Gold Sand River, the Tatu (Great Ferry) River, the Grassland, and the Min Mountains, and having successfully dealt with Chang Kuo-t'ao at Maoerhkai, Mao was now in Kansu and the junction of his troops with those from north Shensi base was in sight. This is one of his less distinguished poems.

Mount Liup'an

to the melody of *Ch'ing P'ing Lo*　October 1935

Lofty the sky
　and pale the clouds—
We watch the wild geese
　fly south till they vanish.
We count the thousand
　leagues already travelled.
If we do not reach
　the Great Wall we are not true men.

High on the crest
　of Liup'an Mountain
Our banners billow
　in the west wind.
Today we hold
　the long rope in our hands.
When shall we put bonds
　upon the grey dragon?

The 1st Front Army under Mao captured the Liup'an Mountains on 7 October 1935.

K'unlun

to the melody of *Nien Nu Chiao*   October 1935

Towering aloft
  above the earth,
Great K'unlun,
  you have witnessed
  all that was fairest
  in the human world.
As they fly across the sky
  the three million dragons
  of white jade
Freeze you with piercing cold.
In the days of summer
  your melting torrents
Fill streams and rivers
  till they overflow,
Changing men
  into fish and turtles.
What man can pass judgement
  on all the good and evil
You have done
  these thousand autumns?

But today
  I say to you, K'unlun,
You don't need your great height,
  you don't need all that snow!
If I could lean on the sky
  I would draw my sword
And cut you in three pieces.
One I would send to Europe,
One to America,
And one we would keep in China.

Thus would a great peace
  reign through the world,
For all the world
  would share your warmth and cold.

Both the Min and Liup'an Mountains are branches of the
Karakoram (K'unlun) Range. Mao wrote this dedication just
before his arrival at north Shensi on 20 October 1935.

Snow

to the melody of *Shen Yüan Ch'un*

Winter 1944–5?

The northern scene:
A thousand leagues locked in ice,
A myriad leagues of fluttering snow.
On either side of the Great Wall
Only one vastness to be seen.
Up and down this broad river
Torrents flatten and stiffen.
The mountains are dancing silver serpents
And hills, like waxen elephants, plod on the plain,
Challenging heaven with their heights.
A sunny day is needed
For seeing them, with added elegance,
In red and white.

Such is the beauty of these mountains and rivers
That has been admired by unnumbered heroes—
The great emperors of Ch'in and Han
Lacking literary brilliance,
Those of T'ang and Sung
Having but few romantic inclinations,
And the prodigious Gengis Khan
Knowing only how to bend his bow
    and shoot at vultures.
All are past and gone!
For men of vision
We must seek among the present generation.

Mao's note: 'The highlands are those of Shensi and Shansi.'

In August 1945, while in Chungking discussing peace and unity with Chiang Kai-shek, Mao met his old friend Liu Ya-tzu, whom Mao might describe as '*il miglior fabbro*', and he gave this poem to Liu at Liu's request. This is undoubtedly Mao's best known piece in China and abroad.

The snow scene suggests that the poem was actually composed before their meeting in August 1945, most likely in the winter of 1944–5. But the 1964 edition of Mao's poems dates it 1936. However, its tenor and images do not seem to support such a dating.

It would be of interest to compare the poet's ambition in this poem with his youthful visions in the first. After an interval of eighteen years since *Ch'angsha* was composed, Mao could see that his adolescent dreams had become a reality. It was a poetic situation and with Mao's craftsmanship this is an outstanding poem.

We have taken the liberty of rendering the names of the great emperors in this simplified form in an attempt to ease the readers' task in memorizing strange names.

The Occupation of Nanking
by the PLA

Lü-shih   April 1949

A tumult rises with wind and rain from Mount Chung
As a million matchless troops cross the Great River.
The mountain is a recoiling dragon, the city a seated tiger,
  both more regal than ever.
The sky is inverted, the earth turned upside down,
  and our spirits are soaring.
We should whip up our courage and pursue the routed bandits;
We must not imitate Pa Wang in vainly seeking a reputation for
  charity.
Had heaven feelings it would long since have grown old!
People are beginning to talk of a sea turning into mulberry fields.

> Mount Chung, lying to the east of Nanking, stretches out like
> a dragon, whereas the city of Nanking resembles a seated tiger.
> So said Chu-ke Liang (181–234). Pa Wang, or Hsiang Chi
> (233–202 B.C.), referred to in line six, was a hegemon with a
> charitable heart who, after defeating his rival, Liu Pang,
> allowed him to occupy the western part of the Empire, whence
> Liu eventually advanced to engulf the whole country and
> destroy Hsiang.
>
> In the *People's Daily* of 4 January 1964, Kuo Mo-jo has
> written a lengthy appreciation of this poem, analysing each
> line and each allusion in great detail.

To Liu Ya-tzu

Lü-shih   April 1949

I can never forget the tea we took in Canton
And the poem you asked for in Chungking
  as the leaves were turning yellow.
Thirty-one years have passed
  and I am back in this ancient capital;
At the season of falling flowers
  I am reading your beautiful verses.
Beware of breaking your heart with too much sadness;
Always take a farsighted view of world events.
Do not say that the waters of Lake K'unming are too shallow;
For watching fish they are better than Fuch'un River.

Liu came to Peking for the New Political Consultative Conference discussing the foundation of the People's Republic of
China and during his stay he wrote a poem expressing his wish
to go back to Wuchiang in Kiangsu, his native town. Mao here
puts his exhortations in verse. We do not have Liu's original
poem, but we would like to quote the first line of a poem he
wrote on 1 October 1950 as a footnote to his feelings: 'As a
poor scholar, I have served under two reigns.' The two reigns
were the Ch'ing and the Republic of China. Was Liu troubled
by the thought of serving under yet another reign?

Mao's first line alludes to his meeting with Liu in 1924, the
second to Liu's request for *Snow*, and the third to Mao's first
visit to Peking in 1918. The lake mentioned in the tenth line
is in the grounds of the Summer Palace in Peking and the
Fuch'un River is in Chekiang where Yen Kuang of the Later
Han dynasty (25–220), having refused to remain in the
Imperial Court, fished and farmed.

Liu Ya-tzu, who had never been a communist, died in 1958.

Reply to Liu Ya-tzu

to the melody of *Wan Hsi Sha*   2 October 1950

The night was long and the crimson dawn cracked slowly;
For hundreds of years demons and monsters danced frantically;
Our five hundred million people were disunited.

Once the cock has crowed and all beneath the sky is bright,
Music rises from Khotan and a thousand places
To fill the poet with unparagoned inspiration.

> Mao's note: 'While watching the performances [of Uighur dances] on the first anniversary of the founding of the People's Republic (1 October 1950), Mr. Liu Ya-tzu composed an impromptu poem to the melody of *Wan Hsi Sha* and I replied with another using the same rhymes.'

> This reply was composed on the next day.

Peitaiho

to the melody of *Lang T'ao Sha*   1954

A storm of rain
  falls on this northern land,
White breakers leap to the sky.
Of all the fishing boats
  from Ch'inhuangtao
There is not one to be seen on the ocean.
Where have they gone?

More than a thousand years ago
The Martial Emperor of Wei
  cracked his whip.
'Eastwards to Chiehshih', his poem remains.
'The autumn wind' still 'sighs' today—
Yet the world has changed!

This town is in the north-east of Hopei near Ch'inhuangtao, a
holiday resort. The Martial Emperor of Wei, Ts'ao Ts'ao (A.D.
220–280), marched north-east against the Wuhuan Tartars,
passing Chiehshih near Peitaiho, and wrote a poem which
opened with this line: 'Eastwards to Chiehshih.' 'The autumn
wind sighs' is another line in the same poem.

Swimming

to the melody of *Shui Tiao Ko T'ou*   May 1956

Just then a drink of water in the south,
Now a taste of fish in the north.
A swim cuts across the Long River;
A glance gauges the sky's width.
Let the wind blow and waves strike,
This surpasses an aimless stroll in the court.
Today's leisure is well spent.
Standing at a ford, the Master once said:
'Thus life flows into the past!'

Breeze shakes the masts
While Tortoise and Snake Hills are motionless,
A grand project is being conceived—
A bridge will fly across
And turn a barrier into a path.
To the west, new cliffs will arise;
Mount Wu's clouds and rains will be kept from the countryside.
Calm lakes will spring up in the gorges.
Were the goddess still alive
She would be amazed by the changes on this earth.

In May 1956 the author, at the age of sixty-three, swam across
the Yangtze from Wuch'ang to Hankow. That summer he swam
it a second and a third time from Hanyang to Wuch'ang.

The opening lines are a paraphrase of a folk song of the
Three Kingdoms period (220–264):

'We would rather drink the waters of Chienyeh
Than eat the fish of Wuch'ang.'

The people of the State of Wu were against the transfer of the
capital from Chienyeh (present-day Nanking) to Wuch'ang
which was a part of the ancient state of Ch'u. The last line of
the first stanza is a quotation from *The Analects*. The Tortoise
and the Snake Hills are in Hanyang and Wuch'ang respectively,
facing each other across the Yangtze.

The Immortals

to the melody of *Tieh Lien Hua*   11 May 1957

My proud poplar is lost to me,
   and to you your willow;
Poplar and willow
   soar to the highest heaven.
When they asked Wu Kang
   what he had to give them
He presented them
   with cassia wine.

The lonely goddess
   who dwells in the moon
Spreads her wide sleeves
   to dance for these good souls
   in the boundless sky.
Suddenly word comes
   of the Tiger's defeat on earth,
And they break into tears
   that fall as torrential rain.

This poem is dedicated to Li Shu-yi, Liu Chih-hsün's widow. Liu, an old friend of Mao, served in the Hunan branch of the CCP since 1923, took part in the Nanch'ang Uprising in August 1927, and fell in the battle of Hunghu in September 1933. An essay by Liu is quoted on p. 120 above.

The name Liu means 'willow' and the name Yang, 'poplar'. Yang was the maiden name of Mao's second wife, Yang K'ai-hui, killed by General Ho Chien when the Red Army withdrew from Ch'angsha in 1930 (*vide supra*, p. 157).

Legend has it that Wu Kang, because of the crime he had committed during his search for immortality, was condemned to cut down the cassia tree in the moon, which became whole again each time he raised his axe. According to tradition, Ch'ang O stole the elixir of immortality and fled to the moon to become the goddess there. Mao perhaps intends the elixir to allude to the communist truth and the Tiger to Chiang Kai-shek.

This and *Ch'angsha* and *To Liu Ya-tzu* have a thread of melancholy running through them and are very elegant poems.

Farewell to the God of Plagues

Lü-shih

Mao's note: 'The news of the extinction of leeches in Yüchiang in the *People's Daily* of 30 June [1958] excited me so much that I was unable to sleep that night. When the next morning came, the breeze rose, and the sun shone upon my windows, I was still gazing at the southern sky and happily writing these lines.'

The waters and hills displayed their green in vain
When the ablest physicians were baffled by these pests.
A thousand villages were overrun by brambles and men were
    feeble;
Ghosts sang their ballads in a myriad desolate houses.
Now, in a day, we have leapt round the earth
And inspected a thousand Milky Ways.
If the Cowherd asks about the god of plagues,
Tell him that with joy and sorrow he has been washed away by the
    tide.

Thousands of willow branches sway in the spring wind;
The six hundred million on this great land are all saintly.
As they wished, the peach blossoms have turned into waves
And the green mountain ranges into bridges.
On lofty Wuling rise and fall silver hoes.
Iron arms shake the earth and tame the broad rivers.
'Where are you bound, God of Plagues?
For your farewell we'll burn candles and paper boats.'

    The Cowherd is a constellation including some stars in Aquila.

Return to Shaoshan

Lü-shih   June 1959

On 25 June 1959 I returned to Shaoshan, after an absence
of thirty-two years.

I curse the time that has flowed past
    Since the dimly-remembered dream of my departure
From home, thirty-two years ago.
With red pennons, the peasants lifted their lances;
In their black hands, the rulers held up their whips.
Lofty emotions were expressed in self-sacrifice:
So the sun and moon were asked to give a new face to heaven.
In delight I watch a thousand waves of growing rice and beans,
And heroes everywhere going home in the smoky sunset.

Shaoshan is Mao's native village, where he had led the peasants
to form associations and fight for better living conditions from
their landlords, before he was forced to flee in the summer of
1927.

Lushan

Lü-shih   1 July 1959

Beside the Great River the mountain rises majestically.
I ascend four hundred spirals to reach its verdant peaks.
Coldly I scan the world towards the sea;
Warmly the wind carries rain to this riverside.
Clouds hang above the nine tributaries flowing by the tower of the
    Yellow Crane;
Waves race down to the ancient state of Wu, giving off white mist.
Who knows where Magistrate T'ao has gone?
Could he be farming in the Land of Peach Blossoms?

> Mount Lu (Lushan) stands on the west bank of Lake Poyang
> in Kiangsi. It is a summer resort. The ancient state of Wu is
> present-day Kiangsu. Magistrate T'ao was T'ao Ch'ien (372–
> 427) of P'engtse in north Kiangsi, a great poet and famous
> recluse, among whose works was the *T'ao-hua-yuan-chi* (The
> Land of Peach Blossoms), describing the author's longing for
> a land of peace and happiness in a turbulent age.

Inscription on a Photograph of Women Militia

Ch'i-chüeh　　　　　　　　　　February 1961

These well-groomed heroines carry five-foot rifles,
On this parade ground in the first rays of the sun.
Daughters of China have uncommon aspirations,
Preferring battle-tunics to red dresses.

Reply to a Friend

Lü-shih 1961

Clouds fly over Mount Chiu-yi
As gods, riding the wind, descend from heaven.
A myriad teardrops created the spots on bamboos;
A thousand pieces of rosy cloud form the garments of the gods.
The white breakers in Lake Tung-t'ing, like snow, rise to the sky;
The songs of the people of Long Islet make the earth vibrate.
I want to dream of the immensity
Of this country of hibiscuses upon which the morning sun always
    shines.

    The scene is again Hunan, where the mountain, lake, and islet
are to be found. Legend has it that when the saintly Emperor
Shun died, his consorts' tears fell on bamboos, which ever
afterwards bore the marks. This species of spotted bamboo
grows in Hunan and Kiangsi.

Inscription on a Photograph of the Cave of the Immortals, Lushan, taken by Comrade Li Chin

Ch'i-chüeh　　　　9 September 1961

The sinewy pines are seen in the dimness of twilight,
Unperturbed by the fleecy clouds that hurry by.
The Cave of the Immortals is a work of nature.
Much charm resides in these craggy peaks.

Watching the Opera 'The Monkey King Thrice Fights the Skeleton Spirit'

a reply to Kuo Mo-jo (*Lü-shih*)

17 September 1961

KUO:

Confused are men and slaves; so are right and wrong.
Kindness is bestowed upon foes and meanness upon friends.
The Golden Hoop Spell is heard ten thousand times
As the Skeleton Spirit thrice escapes.
Hsüan-tsang's flesh should have been cut with a thousand knives.
But to pull out a hair does no harm to the Monkey King.
Education in time deserves praise
For making the Pig more intelligent than men.

MAO:

Since the thunderstorm has broken out over this earth
A spirit has emerged from a heap of skeletons.
The Monk, though stupid, is capable of correction,
But the evil spirit will bring disasters.
The Monkey King raises his mighty staff
To disperse the spectral dust that fills the world.
Let us hail him today,
For the noxious fog is returning once again.

The story of the opera comes from Chapter 27 of Wu Ch'eng-en's *Hsi-yu Chi* ('Monkey', translated by Arthur Waley) and runs as follows: Hsüan-tsang, on his way to India with the Monkey, the Pig, and the Monk, encountered the Skeleton Spirit, who believed that a piece of Hsüan-tsang's flesh would enable him to live for ever. In order to acquire a piece, the Spirit changed himself into a beautiful woman and approached the travellers. His disguise was seen through by the Monkey, who killed him for the first time. The Spirit came back to life and approached them again, this time in the guise of an old woman, and was once more killed by the Monkey. At his third approach the Spirit assumed the appearance of an old man, but with the help of mountain gods the Monkey finally destroyed him. Instead of being grateful to the Monkey, Hsüan-tsang, influenced by the slanderous talk of the Pig, blamed the Monkey for wantonly killing two defenceless women and an old man and punished him by reciting the Golden Hoop Spell. The Golden Hoop enclosed the Monkey's head and shrank each time Hsüan-tsang recited the spell, giving the Monkey an unbearable headache. After the Monkey had killed the Spirit for the third and final time, Hsüan-tsang was so angry that he sent him away.

We suggest that these two poems should be read in the context of the Sino-Soviet dispute, with the Monkey symbolizing Marxism–Leninism, the Skeleton Spirit modern revisionism, Hsüan-tsang Mr. Khrushchev, and the Pig Moscow's satellites.

Plum Tree

to the melody of *P'u Suan Tzu*   December 1962

This poem follows that of Lu Yu (1125–1210) on the same
theme, while reversing its meaning.

LU:

Beside the broken bridge, outside the courier station,
Alone, it blooms for no one.
The dusk is sad enough,
But now wind and rain are added.

It does not intend to display itself in the spring,
Or to arouse other flowers' envy.
Once its blossoms have fallen and been trampled to dust
Only its fragrance remains.

MAO:

Wind and rain bid farewell to the spring
As fluttering snow welcomed it in.
The inaccessible cliff is covered in a hundred ells of ice
Yet ornamented by its blossoming branches.

It does not display its charm in the spring,
But only to herald spring's approach.
When the mountain flowers are glowing like brocade
It smiles among them benignly.

This poem, which betrays a feeling of isolation and loneliness, was, according to Kuo Mo-jo (the *Kuang-ming Jih-pao*,
17.3.1964), first circulated among the leaders of the CCP, in
order to heighten their morale in the Sino-Soviet dispute. The
plum tree is the traditional symbol of integrity, used here
perhaps to allude to the poet himself.

Winter Clouds

Lü-shih   26 December 1962

Fluttering snow weighs down the winter clouds.
All flowers have wilted.
Up in the sky cold currents flow;
On the ground warmth still breathes.
Alone, a hero drives away tigers and leopards.
The brave have no fear of bears.
The plum tree welcomes a snowy sky,
Caring nothing for the flies frozen to death.

Composed on his 69th birthday, Mao felt the coldness of
the Sino-Soviet dispute and resolved to drive away tigers and
leopards, and to have no fear of bears.

Reply to Kuo Mo-jo

to the melody of *Man Chiang Hung*

9 January 1963

KUO:

Only among the cross-currents of this vast sea
Does the greatness of man become manifest.
The six hundred million,
Having consolidated their unity,
Hold fast to their tenets.
When the sky falls, raise it;
When the world goes wrong, right it.
Listen to the cockcrow
As dawn breaks in the east.

The sun comes out
And ice drips on the mountains.
But pure gold
Is never consumed by flames.
The four majestic volumes
Set a standard for the people.
It is absurd that a rogue's dogs should bark at a saint,
And there should be no news of the clay oxen that went overseas.
Unfurl the red flags into the east wind
To turn the world scarlet.

Since this was also written at the height of the Sino-Soviet dispute,
the references to cross-currents, raising the fallen sky, righting
the world gone wrong, cockcrow, pure gold, the four majestic
volumes of Mao's works, the dogs of Chieh (the rascally king
of the Hsia period), and Yao (the legendary saintly king) are to
be understood in that context. It is not clear, however, whether
the 'clay oxen' (the allusion comes from *Ch'uan Teng Lu*,
relating the fight between two clay oxen) refers to Chiang Kai-
shek and his supporters or to the disputes between Russia and
the United States.

MAO:

In this small world
A few flies knock against walls.
The noise they make
Is sometimes spine-chilling
And sometimes like sobbing.
Ants climbing up an ash tree brag about a great country,
But it is easy to say that beetles can shake the roots of a stout tree.
In Ch'angan, when leaves were falling in the west wind,
The signal was given.

There have always been
Many things that were urgent.
Although the world spins on
Time is short.
Millennia are too long:
Let us dispute about mornings and evenings.
The four seas are tempestuous as clouds and waters show their
    wrath;
The five continents are shaken as gales and thunder rage.
Pests should be stamped out
So that we may become invincible.

In the same context as Kuo Mo-jo's, this poem shows Mao's
indignation, determination, and fearlessness. He compares
his enemies to flies, beetles, and pests, his country and
Russia to great trees, and the dispute between them to tempestuous seas and gales and thunder. The author's impatience
is also clearly expressed in the lines stating that time is short
and millennia are too long.

The last two lines of the first stanza remain a mystery. They
seem to imply that Mao, while in Sian (Ch'angan) one autumn,
gave the signal for the dispute to begin.

Founder Members of the CCP, 1921

A TENTATIVE LIST

1. Chang Kuo-t'ao
2. Chang Mei-hsien
3. Chang Shen-fu
4. Chao Shih-yen
5. Ch'en Ch'iao-nien
6. Ch'en Kung-po
7. Ch'en T'an-ch'iu
8. Ch'en Tu-hsiu
9. Ch'en Wang-tao
10. Ch'en Yen-nien
11. Chou En-lai
12. Chou Fo-hai
13. Ch'ü Ch'iu-pai
14. Chu Te
15. Ho Shu-heng
16. Hsiang Ching-yü (Miss)
17. Hsü Pei-hao
18. Hsü T'e-li
19. Jen Cho-hsüan
20. Kan Nai-kuang
21. Kao Chung-yu (or Tsung-yü)
22. Kao Yü-han
23. Li Fu-ch'un
24. Li Han-chün
25. Li Li-san
26. Li Sen
27. Li Ta
28. Li Ta-chao
29. Li Wei-han (Lo Mai)
30. Lin Tsu-han
31. Liu Jen-ching
32. Lo Chang-lung
33. Mao Tse-tung
34. Nieh Jung-chen
35. Pao Hui-sheng
36. P'eng Pai
37. Shang Cheng-yü (?)
38. Shao Li-tzu
39. Shih Hsiang
40. Shih Ts'un-t'ung
41. Shen Ting-i
42. Ssu Yang (?)
43. Tai Chi-t'ao
44. Teng Chung-hsia
45. Teng En-ming
46. Ts'ai Ch'ang (Miss)
47. Ts'ai Ho-sen
48. Tung Pi-wu
49. Wang Ching-mei
50. Wang Jo-fei
51. Yü Hsiu-sung
52. Yüan Hsiao-hsien

Both Ho Kan-chih ([14] 44) and Hu Hua ([18] 53) say that there were 57 founder members at the time of the first national congress of the CCP. The 12 representatives at the congress were:

Hunan—Mao Tse-tung, Ho Shu-heng
Hupei—Tung Pi-wu, Ch'en T'an-ch'iu
Shantung—Wang Ching-mei
            Teng En-ming
Shanghai—Li Ta, Li Han-chün
Peking—Chang Kuo-t'ao
         Liu Jen-ching
Canton—Ch'en Kung-po
Tokyo—Chou Fo-hai

Sources: [39] 107–8, [96] 248, [130] XVI, 54–5 and XVIII, 132–4, [163] 87–8 and 144–5, [181] 5–7, [190] 39–41, [193] 48–51, [210] 54–6, and [258] 154–5. See also [18] 37 and Wu Yü-chang, 'Yi Chao Shih-yen lieh-shih' (In memoriam of Chao Shih-yen), the People's Daily, 19.7.1962. Tung Pi-wu admits that the documents of the first congress were lost ([8], 1961, nos. 13–14, 11).

Appendix B

The Growth of the Red Army directly under Mao and Chu, 1927–1945

SANWAN, YUNGHSIN, KIANGSI, September–October 1927:
the 1st Regiment, the 1st Division, the 1st Workers' and Peasants' Revolutionary Army—about 1,000 men under Mao

CHINGKANGSHAN

October 1927: the 31st Regiment under Mao
the 32nd Regiment under Yüan Wen-ts'ai and Wang Tso

April 1928: the 28th Regiment under Chu Te
the 31st Regiment under Mao
the 32nd Regiment under Yüan and Wang

August 1928: The 4th Red Army—about 10,000 men
Commander, Chu Te; Political Commissar, Mao
the 10th Division   Chu Te
  the 28th Regiment
  the 29th Regiment
the 11th Division   Mao
  the 30th Regiment
  the 31st Regiment
the 12th Division   Ch'en Yi
  the 32nd Regiment   Yüan Wen-ts'ai and Ho Ch'ang-kung
  the 33rd Regiment

November 1928:
the 4th Red Army
the 5th Red Army   P'eng Te-huai   about 1,000 men

End of 1929:
  the 1st Army Corps   Chu Te and Mao Tse-tung
    the 3rd Army   Huang Kung-lüeh
    the 4th Army   Lin Piao
    the 12th Army   Lo Ping-hui
  the 3rd Army Corps   P'eng Te-huai and T'eng Tai-yüan
    the 5th Army   P'eng Te-huai
    the 7th Army   Chang Yüng-yi and Teng Hsiao-p'ing
    the 20th Army   Liu Te-ch'ao and Li Wen-lin

THE CENTRAL SOVIET

December 1931:
  the 1st Front Army   Chu Te
    the 1st Army Corps   Lin Piao   Lo Jung-huan
    the 3rd Army Corps   P'eng Te-huai   T'eng Tai-yüan
    the 5th Army Corps   Chi Chen-tung   Hsiao Ching-kuang
      the 13th Army   Chao Po-sheng
      the 14th Army   Tung Chen-t'ang
    the 6th Army Corps   Hsiao K'e   Jen Pi-shih (Chingkangshan)
    the 7th Army Corps   Hsün Huai-chou (Fukien)
      the 10th Army   Fang Chih-min   Shao Shih-p'ing
July 1934:
  the 10th Army broke through the encirclement, to be destroyed in
  January 1935

August 1934:
  the 6th Army Corps broke through the encirclement to join forces
  with the 2nd Front Army under Ho Lung

October 1934:
  the 1st Front Army   Chu Te   Mao Tse-tung   Liu Po-ch'eng
    the 1st Army Corps   Lin Piao   Nieh Jung-chen
    the 3rd Army Corps   P'eng Te-huai   T'eng Tai-yüan
    the 5th Army Corps   Tung Chen-t'ang
    the 9th Army Corps   Lo Ping-hui

                                        total strength 100,000 men

MAOERHKAI

August 1935:
  the east column   Mao Tse-tung
    the 1st and 3rd Army Corps
    the 4th and 30th Armies of the 4th Front Army
  the west column   Chu Te   Chang Kuo-t'ao
    the 5th and 9th Army Corps
    the 31st and 32nd Armies of the 4th Front Army

NORTH SHENSI

October 1935:
  the east column Mao Tse-tung about 7,000 men
  the 15th Army Corps Hsü Hai-tung Liu Chih-tan
                                    about 7,000 men

October 1936:
  the east column and the 15th Army Corps
  the 2nd Front Army led to Shensi by Chu Te and Ho Lung
                        total strength about 30,000

May 1937:
  the remnants of the west column led to Kansu and Sinkiang,
  originally about 1,500 men, but now only a few hundred left, went
  back to North Shensi under the command of Hsü Hsiang-ch'ien

September 1937:
  the Eighth Route Army Chu Te P'eng Te-huai
    the 115th Division Lin Piao Nieh Jung-chen
    the 120th Division Ho Lung Hsiao K'e
    the 129th Division Liu Po-ch'eng Hsü Hsiang-ch'ien
                        total strength about 40,000

January 1938:
  the Eighth Route Army (later designated the 18th Army Group)
  the New Fourth Army Yeh T'ing Hsiang Ying
    the 1st Column Ch'en Yi
    the 2nd Column Chang Ting-ch'eng
    the 3rd Column Chang Yün-yi
    the 4th Column Kao Chün-t'ing
                total strength of the New Fourth Army, 10,000

NORTH AND EAST CHINA

The Expansion of the Eighth Route Army and the New Fourth Army:

	the 8th Route Army	the 4th Army
1938	156,000	25,000
1939	270,000	50,000
1940	400,000	100,000
1941	305,000	destroyed
1942	300,000	110,960
1943	200,000	125,892
1944	321,000	154,000
1945	600,000	260,000

The New Fourth Army after January 1941:
  Commander   Ch'en Yi
  Deputy Commander   Chang Yün-yi
  Political Commissar   Liu Shao-ch'i (Hu Fu)
  Head of Political Department   Teng Tzu-hui
  Chief-of-Staff   Lai Ch'uan-chu
the 1st Division   Su Yü   north Kiangsu
the 2nd Division   Lo Ping-hui   east Anhwei
the 3rd Division   Huang K'e-ch'eng   north Kiangsu
the 4th Division   P'eng Hsüeh-feng   north of the Huai River
the 5th Division   Li Hsien-nien   Hupei-Honan
the 6th Division   T'an Chen-lin   south Kiangsu
the 7th Division   Chang Ting-ch'eng   central Anhwei
                   (later T'an Hsi-lin)
a guerrilla detachment under Ho K'e-hsi   east Chekiang

Appendix C

The Itineraries of 1934–1936

1934

16 October	Kiangsi	evacuation from Juichin, Ninghua, Ch'angting, and Yütu
24 October		Hsinfeng
3 November	Hunan	Juch'eng
7 November	Kwangtung	Jenhua
13 November	Hunan	Ichang
		Chianghua
22 November		Yungming
24 November	Kwangsi	Wenshih
29 November		crossing the upper course of the Hsiang River
	Hunan	T'ungtao
14 December	Kweichow	Lip'ing conference
21 December		Chienho
		T'aikung
26 December		Shihping
		Chenyüan
		Shihch'ien

1935

1 January		crossing the Wu River
7 January		Meit'an
8 January		Tsunyi conference
14 January		Loushankuan
		T'ungtzu
17 January		Sungk'an
		Hsishui
24 January		T'uch'eng

367

27 January		crossing the Ch'ihshui River
	Szechwan	
	Kweichow	
19 February		second crossing of the Ch'ihshui River
		T'ungtzu
25 February		Tsunyi (while the 3rd Army Corps pushed on to Weihsin in Yunnan on 6 February and then turned back to T'ungtzu)
		Jenhuai
17 March		Maot'ai
	Szechwan	
	Kweichow	
27 March		third crossing of the Ch'ihshui River
31 March		crossing the Wu River near Kweiyang (while the 9th Army Corps remained north of the River and drove to Tating in April)
		Lungli
		Tingfan (now Huishui)
		Ch'angshun
		Kwangshun
14 April		Tzuyün
17 April		crossing the Peip'an River
		Chenfeng
26 April		Anlung
		Hsingjen
		Hsingyi
	Yunnan	Chanyi (while the 9th Army Corps cut through Chihchin and Maoch'ang, crossed the Peip'an River, and reached Hsüanwei in Yunnan)
		Malung
end of April		Sungming
		Hsüntien
1–8 May		crossing the Chinsha River near Huitse (while the 9th Army Corps fought rearguard action near Huitse and Ch'iaochia)
	Sikang	Huili
		Hsich'ang
21 May		Luku
23 May		Mienning

27 May		Anshunch'ang (the 1st Regiment crossed the Tatu River at this point)
30 May		the Luting Bridge
		crossing the Tatu River
		T'iench'üan
		Lushan
		Paohsing
		crossing the Great Snow Mountain
12 June	Szechwan	Moukung (the 1st and 4th Front Armies met)
26 June		Lianghok'ou conference
29 July–23 August		Maoerhkai conference (while waiting for the dry season to begin)
		Panyu
29 August		Pahsi
2 September		Ahsi
		Paotso
18 September	Kansu	Latzuk'ou
		cutting through Minhsien and Hsiku
		cutting through Changhsien and Wushan
2 October		T'ungwei
7 October		crossing the Liup'an Mountains
		Huat'ing
		Huanhsien
20 October	Shensi	Wuch'ichen (the 1st Front Army met with the 15th Army Corps)

(Panyu, Pahsi, Ahsi, Paotso) } crossing the Grassland

B. THE 2ND FRONT ARMY UNDER HO LUNG AND JEN PI-SHIH

1935

19 November	Northwest Hunan	evacuation from Sangchih
		occupation of Hsinhua
		Hsik'uangshan
		Lant'ien
		Hsüp'u
		Ch'enhsi
		P'uk'ou

1936

1 January		Chihchiang
2 January		Huanghsien
7 January	East Kweichow	Shihch'ien Wengan

7 January	East	Niuch'ang
	Kweichow	Lungli
		Chatso
		Hsiuwen
		Yach'ihho
		crossing the Wu River
9 February		Tating
		Pichieh
		Ch'ihsingkuan
		P'ingshanpao
		Yehmashan
		Maku
7 March	Northeast Yunnan	Chenhsiung
16 March	Kweichow	Weining
23 March	Yunnan	Hsüanwei
end of March		P'ingyi
	Kweichow	P'anhsien
1 April	Yunnan	Hsinchieh
28 April		crossing the Chinsha River
May		Chütien and Chungtien
Mid-May	Sikang	Taoch'eng
		Lihua
		Kantzu (the 2nd and 4th Front Armies met)
June		crossing the Grassland (forty days)
August	Kansu	Lint'an
		Wushan
		Hsiho
		Ch'enghsien and K'anghsien
		Huihsien
		Liangtang
		T'ungwei
20 October		Huining (the 2nd Front Army and the others made a junction)

C. THE 4TH FRONT ARMY UNDER HSÜ HSIANG-CH'IEN AND CHANG KUO-T'AO

1935

February	North Szechwan	evacuation from Nanchiang, T'ung-chiang, and Pachung
		crossing the Chialing River at Ts'anghsi

February		Chienko
		Chaohua
		Tzut'ung
		Changming and Chiangyu
2 June (or before)		Moukung (the 4th and 1st Front Army met)
July–August		Maoerhkai
		Chok'echi
		crossing the Grassland
		Apa and Panyu
September		back to Maoerhkai with Chu Te
		Moukung
	Sikang	Paohsing
		T'iench'üan and Lushan
		Yaan
1936		
March		Patan
		Taofu
		Luho
May		Kantzu (the 4th and 2nd Front Armies met)
		Tungku
June		crossing the Grassland
		Apa and Paotso
August	Kansu	Lint'an
		Weiyüan
8 October		Huining (the 4th Front Army and a contingent of the 1st Front Army met)
25 October		crossing the Yellow River at Chingyüan
		Kulang
		Kaot'aich'eng
		Liyüank'ou
		Ch'ilien Mountain Ranges
1937		
April		Paituntzu
1 May	Sinkiang	Hsinghsinghsia (the remnant, about 700 men, of the 4th Front Army met the party representatives, Ch'en Yün and T'eng Tai-yüan)

Appendix D

The Economic Conditions of the Shensi-Kansu-Ninghsia Border Region

Year	Cultivated Land (*mou*—total arable land estimated at 40 mil. *mou*)	Grain Output (picul)	Cotton Plantation (*mou*)
1935–6	8,431,006		
1937	8,626,006	1,100,000	
1938	8,994,483	1,300,000	
1939			3,767
1940			
1941		1,630,000	
1942	12,486,937	1,680,000	94,405
1945	15,205,553	1,840,000	350,000

Year	Cattle and Asses	Sheep	Export of Salt (load = 150 catties)
1935–6	100,000	400,000	
1937	an increase of 300,000		
1938			70,000
1939	257,827	1,171,066	190,000
1940			230,000
1941			299,068
1942	364,702	1,802,097	200,000
1943	403,920	1,954,756	300,000

CO-OPERATIVE MOVEMENT

a. Consumers' Co-operatives

	No of Societies	Membership	Capital	Consumption
1937	131	57,847	55,525 *yuan*	261,189 *yuan*
1941	155	140,218	693,071	6,008,000

b. Producers' Co-operatives

1939	10		11,130	60,000
1942	50		2,491,600	2,300,000

Grain Tax (picul)

1936	16,000		1941	200,000
1937	14,000		1942	160,000
1938	10,000		1943	180,000
1939	50,000		1944	160,000
1940	90,000		1945	120,000

Sources: [282] 83, [289] 15–17, [319] 9, 33, 57–9, and 202–3. Also [273] 186 and 197–8.

Appendix E

The Relative Strengths of the PLA and the KMT Army 1945–1949

	PLA	KMT	*Ratio*
Ho Ying-ch'in's estimates ([134] 254)			
Sept. 1945	320,000	3,700,000	1:11·6
June 1948	2,600,000	2,180,000	1:0·84
Russian estimates ([134] 254)			
July 1946	1,200,000	4,300,000	1:3·58
June 1947	1,950,000	3,730,000	1:1·9
June 1948	2,800,000	3,650,000	1:1·3
American estimates ([11] 313–14, 317, and 322)			
July 1946	1,000,000	3,000,000	1:3
End 1946	1,100,000	2,600,000	1:2·36
June 1947	1,150,000	2,700,000	1:2·35
Beginning 1948	1,150,000	2,723,000	1:2·37
Feb. 1949	1,622,000	1,500,000	1:0·92
CCP estimates (Mao, *Selected Works*, IV (Peking), 223, 269, 272, 287, and 406; [187] 72; [279] 219; and NCNA 16.7.1949)			
Sept. 1945	860,000	3,700,000	1:4·3
July 1946	1,278,000	4,300,000	1:3·36
June 1947	1,950,000	3,730,000	1:1·9
June 1948	2,800,000	3,650,000	1:1·3
Nov. 1948	3,000,000	2,900,000	1:0·96
June 1949	4,000,000	1,500,000	1:0·37

I am grateful to Mr. J. Gittings of Chatham House for his generous assistance in the compilation of this table.

Chronology

1893 **Mao is born on 26 December.**

1895 Japan defeats China. Dr. Sun Yat-sen organizes the China Revival Society in Hawaii and Hong Kong.

1898 **Mao learns to read and write under a tutor.**
The Hundred Days Reform ends in failure and T'an Ssu-t'ung, the Hunanese reformer, is executed.

1900 Peking is occupied by the allied troops as a result of the Boxer Uprising.

1904 Huang Hsing's plan for an uprising in Hunan fails.

1905 Li Hsieh-ho's plan for an uprising in Hunan is foiled. Dr. Sun Yat-sen forms the Alliance Society in Tokyo.

1906 **Mao works full time on his father's farm.**
Floods in Hunan.

1907 **Mao marries a girl four years older than himself.**
Chang Chih-tung, the viceroy of Hupei and Hunan, is recalled.

1908 Prince Ch'un's regency is proclaimed after the deaths of the Emperor and the Dowager Empress.

1910 **Mao goes to the Tungshan Primary School in Hsiang-hsiang.**
Drought in Hunan.

1911 **Mao passes the entrance examination to the Hsiang-hsiang Middle School in Ch'angsha, leaves for Ch'angsha in summer, embraces republicanism, and joins the revolutionary army in October.**
Revolution breaks out in Ch'angsha on 22 October. T'an Yen-k'ai takes office as the governor of Hunan in November.

1912 **Mao is demobilized in February, admitted into a school of commerce and then into the Hunan First Middle School. Towards the end of the year he reads books by west European scholars at the Provincial Library.**
The Ch'ing dynasty comes to an end with the abdication of the

last Emperor and Yuan Shih-k'ai succeeds Dr. Sun Yat-sen as
the Provisional President of China.

1913 **Mao enters the Fourth Teachers' Training School which
is merged into the First Teachers' Training School in
autumn.**
The assassination of Sung Chiao-jen and the Reorganization
Loan lead to the 'Second Revolution'. The KMT is outlawed.
T'ang Hsiang-ming is appointed the governor of Hunan.

1914 **Mao reads F. Paulsen's *A System of Ethics* and his
radicalism begins to develop.**

1915 **Mao takes part in a campaign against the School col-
lecting extra fees from the students and is elected the
secretary of the Students Society.**
Yuan Shih-k'ai's monarchical movement in full swing.

1916 **Mao distributes anti-Yuan leaflets in the School. He
goes on a long hike with Siao Yu in summer.**
In May T'ang Hsiang-ming declares independence from Yuan
Shih-k'ai who dies in June. Li Yüan-hung becomes the President and T'an Yen-k'ai the governor of Hunan.

1917 **Mao is selected a model student and the chairman of
the Students Society. He meets Li Li-san in summer
and disarms a band of Fu Liang-tso's soldiers in
autumn.**
Chang Hsün attempts to restore the Ch'ing dynasty. Feng Kuo-
chang succeeds Li Yüan-hung as the President and Dr. Sun
Yat-sen is elected the generalissimo of the headquarters at
Canton. Fu Liang-tso's appointment to the governorship of
Hunan leads to war in that province. T'an Yen-k'ai again the
governor of Hunan. The Work-study Scheme for students to
go to France is announced.

1918 Apr. **Mao and his friends found the New Citizens
Society. Mao teaches at an evening class for workers
and shop-assistants and graduates from the First
Teachers' School.**

Sept. **He goes to Peking, working at Peking University
library as an assistant, where he meets Li Ta-
chao, Ch'en Tu-hsiu, and Chang Kuo-t'ao and
reads anarchist books.**
War in Hunan continues and Chang Ching-yao is appointed the governor of Hunan. Hsü Shih-ch'ang is in-
stalled as the President in October.
Li Ta-chao and Ch'en Tu-hsiu found a society for the
study of Marxism.

1919 Feb. **Mao visits Shanghai via Shantung.**
Ts'ai Ho-sen and others sail for France.

Mar. **Mao teaches at the Hsiu-yeh Primary School in Ch'angsha. His mother dies either in March or later in the year.**
Comintern 1st Congress.

May The May 4th Movement. Chou En-lai, Yün Tai-ying, and others found socialist groups at various places.

July– **Mao edits the *Hsiang River Review* and writes**
Aug. **'The Great Union of the People' and later he edits the *Hsin Hunan*. Both papers are ordered to stop publication by Chang Ching-yao. Mao organizes the Problem Discussion Group.**

Dec. **Mao leaves for Peking.**

1920 Jan. **Mao is initiated to Marxist books and agitates against Chang Ching-yao among the Hunanese in Peking.**

Feb. Voitinsky arrives at Peking.

Mar. A Chinese communist youth group comes into existence in Paris.

Apr. **Mao visits Shanghai again and meets Ch'en Tu-hsiu there. He is now a convinced Marxist.**

May General Wu P'ei-fu's troops leave Hunan and war breaks out there.

June T'an Yen-k'ai again the governor of Hunan.

July **Mao returns to Ch'angsha to become the director of the Primary School Section of the First Teachers' Training School. He founds a Russian Affairs Study Group.**
The Chihli-Anhwei War breaks out and Hunan demands provincial autonomy.
Comintern 2nd Congress.

Aug. The Socialist youth corps is founded in Shanghai.

Sept. **Mao publishes articles advocating provincial autonomy and organizes Marxist and communist groups in Ch'angsha.**
Communist Party Monthly begins issue and communist groups come into existence in Shanghai, Peking, and other places.
The question of founding the CCP is discussed.

Nov. The Ch'angsha branch of the socialist youth corps is formed and a communist group comes into being in Canton.

1921 May Ch'en Tu-hsiu disbands all branches of the socialist youth
          group in order to reorganize them.
     July **Mao attends the CCP 1st Congress in Shanghai.**
          The All-China Labour League is formed in Shanghai and
          Chang Kuo-t'ao becomes its secretary.
          Comintern 3rd Congress.
     Aug. **Mao establishes the Self-education College.**
     Oct. **Mao becomes the secretary of the Hunan Com-
          mittee of the CCP and marries Yang K'ai-hui.**
     Nov. Ch'en Tu-hsiu reorganizes the socialist youth corps.
     Dec. **Mao organizes the Hunan branch of the socialist
          youth corps and a party cell among the miners of
          Anyüan.**
          Maring sees Dr. Sun Yat-sen at Kweilin.
1922 Jan. The Hunan Provincial Constitution is promulgated.
          Chang Kuo-t'ao attends the Far-Eastern Toilers' Con-
          ference in Moscow.
     May **Mao opens the Anyüan Workmen's Club whose
          director is Li Li-san.**
          The Chihli-Fengtien War breaks out.
     June A plenum of the Central Committee of the CCP discusses
          the question of alliance with the KMT.
     July **Mao misses the CCP 2nd Congress.**
          Chao Heng-t'i advocates a confederation of provinces.
          Dr. Sun Yat-sen is driven out of Canton by Ch'en Chiung-
          ming.
     Aug. The CCP decides to co-operate with the KMT. A. Joffe
          arrives at Peking.
     Sept. **Mao and Liu Shao-ch'i direct the strike of the
          Anyüan miners.**
     Nov. **Mao resigns the directorship of the Primary
          School Section of the First Teachers' Training
          School and is elected to the chairmanship of the
          Association of Trade Unions of Hunan.**
          Comintern 4th Congress.
     Dec. **Mao discusses Hunan problems with Chao Heng-t'i.**
          Dr. Sun Yat-sen discusses co-operation with Joffe.
1923 Jan. Sun-Joffe Entente is announced.
     Feb. Dr. Sun returns to Canton.
     Apr. **Chao Heng-t'i orders Mao's arrest and Mao leaves
          Hunan.**
          The Self-education College publishes its monthly, *Hsin
          Shih-tai*.

May   **Mao works at the CCP centre in Shanghai.**

June   **Mao takes part in the CCP 3rd Congress in Canton.**

July   **Mao returns to Shanghai and is given charge of co-ordinating the measures of the CCP and the KMT.**

Sept. Borodin arrives at Canton and Chiang Kai-shek at Moscow.

Oct.   Ts'ao K'un is 'elected' the President.

Nov.   The Self-education College is closed down on Chao Heng-t'i's orders, but it re-emerges as the Hsiang-chiang Middle School.

Dec.   **Mao sails for Canton to attend the KMT 1st Congress.**

1924 Jan.   **Mao is elected an alternate member of the Central Executive Committee of the KMT.**

The KMT 1st Congress is held.

Apr.   The KMT right wing tables a motion of censure against the CCP members in the KMT.

May   Chiang Kai-shek is appointed the head of the Whampoa Academy.

June   The Sino-Soviet diplomatic relations are formally established.

Comintern 5th Congress.

Sept. The Chihli-Fengtien War breaks out.

Oct.   Chao Heng-t'i promulgates the provincial constitution of Hunan and Feng Yü-hsiang organizes his *Kuomin* Army.

Nov.   **Mao is ill and goes back to Hunan.**

Tuan Ch'i-jui becomes the provisional head of the Peking Government and invites Dr. Sun Yat-sen to Peking.

1925 Jan.   **Mao is voted out of the CCP Politburo.**

The CCP 4th Congress is held in Shanghai.

Feb.   Dr. Sun Yat-sen's will is signed.

Mar.   Dr. Sun dies in Peking.

May   The 2nd congress of the All-China Labour League is held in Canton with Liu Shao-ch'i in the chair. The May 30th Movement takes place and the year-long Canton-Hong Kong trade boycott begins.

The Sun Yat-sen University is founded in Moscow.

June   **Mao takes a deep interest in the peasant movement in Hunan.**

July   **Mao leaves Hunan for Canton.**

Aug.   **Mao takes charge of a training college of organ-**

izers for the peasant movement in Canton. Later he becomes the secretary of the Propaganda Department of the KMT and concurrently the editor of the *Political Weekly*. Still later he is appointed the deputy head of the Department.

Liao Chung-k'ai is assassinated.

Nov. The Western Hill Group confers in Peking.

Dec. **Mao goes to Shanghai to agitate against Chao Heng-t'i.**

Chao Heng-t'i orders his troops to open fire against the Anyüan miners on strike.

Chiang Kai-shek unifies the province of Kwangtung. Kuo Sung-ling rebels against Chang Tso-lin. The war against the *Kuomin* Army begins.

1926 Jan. **Mao is again elected an alternate member of the KMT.**

The KMT 2nd Congress is held in Canton.

Feb. **Mao returns to Canton.**

Mar. **Mao leaves Canton for Shanghai where he heads the Peasant Department of the CCP. He writes 'An Analysis of the Classes in Chinese Society'.**

The Canton *Coup* takes place.

May The 3rd Congress of the All-China Labour League is held in Canton.

June The Standing Committee of the KMT decides to launch the Northern Expedition.

July Chiang Kai-shek orders the mobilization of his troops.

Aug. **Mao goes back to Hunan to lead the peasant movement.**

Sept. **Mao's poem on Ch'angsha is composed.**

The Peasants' Association of Hunan becomes an open organization.

Oct. The KMT army takes Wuhan.

Dec. The Conference of the peasants' delegates is held in Ch'angsha and confiscation of land begins in Hunan.

The Nationalist Government is transferred to Wuhan.

Roy arrives at Wuhan.

1927 Jan. **Mao inspects the peasant movement in Hunan.**

Mar. **Mao publishes his report on the peasant movement in Hunan.**

The KMT troops take Shanghai and Nanking. Anticommunist campaign begins in Hunan and Kiangsi.

Apr. T'ang Sheng-chih orders the arrest of Mao Tse-tung, who leaves for Wuhan to attend the CCP 5th Congress.

Russian official buildings in Peking are searched and Li Ta-chao is executed. The Shanghai *Coup* takes place and Chiang Kai-shek is 'expelled' from the KMT.

May **Mao is elected the chairman of the All-China Peasants' Union.**

The 4th Congress of the All-China Labour League takes place.

The May 21 Massacre is followed by persecution of the communists in Hunan.

July The KMT orders the arrests of Mao and other communists.

The KMT-CCP co-operation breaks up and Nanking and Wuhan patch up their differences. Chou En-lai and other communists assemble at Nanch'ang.

Roy resigns his post as the Comintern representative and is replaced by Lominadze.

Aug. **Mao leads the Autumn Harvest Uprising as the secretary of the Front Committee of the CCP.**

The Nanch'ang Uprising takes place. The 7 August emergency meeting is convened at Kiukiang. The Red Army comes into existence.

Chiang Kai-shek resigns his post as the commander-in-chief of the KMT Army.

Sept. **Mao is detained and escapes.**

The Ch'aochow-Swatow Uprising takes place.

Oct. **Mao establishes a base on the Chingkangshan.**

Chiang Kai-shek sails for Japan.

Nov. The CCP Politburo holds a meeting at Shanghai and **dismisses Mao from the Politburo.**

P'eng Pai organizes a revolutionary régime in the East River region.

Dec. The Canton Uprising fails.

1928 Jan. **Mao defeats a regiment of Wu Shang's 8th Army at Ningkang.**

Chu Te and Lin Piao, with the remnant of their troops, reach Chenchow in Hunan.

Chiang Kai-shek resumes the command of the KMT Army.

Mar. **The Front Committee of the CCP is abolished and Mao is appointed the secretary of the Special Committee of the Chingkangshan base area.**

Other base areas are established on the borders of Hupei-Honan-Anhwei and Chekiang-Fukien, at the Lake Hung area, and in Kwangsi.

1928 Apr. **Chu Te joins Mao on the Chingkangshan.**
The 4th Red Army comes into existence.

May First attack on the Chingkangshan base is attempted and **Mao calls the Maop'ing Conference.**
Japanese troops open fire on the Chinese in Chinan.

June The CCP 6th Congress is held in Moscow.
The Northern Expedition is brought to a successful end.

July **Mao is replaced by Yang K'ai-ming as the secretary of the Special Committee.**
P'eng Te-huai stages the P'ingchiang Uprising.
Second attack on the Chingkangshan base begins.

Aug. **Mao leads a contingent to Chu Te's rescue in Kweitung.**

Sept. **Mao and Chu return to the Chingkangshan base and Mao is once more the secretary of the Special Committee.**

Nov. P'eng Te-huai joins Mao on the Chingkangshan.

Dec. Third attack on the Chingkangshan base begins and fails.
(Mao marries Ho Tzu-chen either in this year or in 1930.)

1929 Jan. **Mao's troops invade southern Kiangsi.**
The Demobilization Conference at Nanking ends in failure.

Feb. **Mao's troops invade western Fukien.**
P'eng Te-huai is driven out of the Chingkangshan by the KMT troops.

Mar. **Mao and Chu take Tingchow.**
The KMT 3rd Congress is convened.

Apr. **Mao and Li Li-san disagree on strategic problems. Mao's troops take Kanchow.**

May Nanking and Kwangsi are at war.

June **Mao and Chu harass the Kiangsi-Fukien border.**
P'eng Te-huai reoccupies Chingkangshan.

July K'uang Ch'i-hsün and Yün Tai-ying set up a soviet at Hsich'ung and Hoch'uan in Szechwan.

Aug. **Mao and Chu are active in western Fukien.**
K'uang Ch'i-hsün is defeated.

Sept. **Mao suffers from malaria.**
Chang Fa-k'uei's troops mutiny at Ich'ang.
Chiang and Feng Yü-hsiang are at war.

Oct. The Comintern message calls for transfer of peasant struggles to urban insurrections.

Nov. **Mao takes Shanghang.**
Ch'en Tu-hsiu is expelled from the CCP.

Dec. **Mao makes his report on the Rectification of Incorrect Ideas in the Party at the Kut'ien Conference.**

The insurrections of T'ang Sheng-chih, Chang Fe-k'uei, and the Kwangsi Clique are all quelled.

1930 Jan. **Mao writes a letter to 'a comrade'—'A Single Spark Can Start a Prairie Fire'.**

Feb. Mao is appointed the Political Commissar of the 1st Front Army. The south-west Kiangsi soviet government is set up. The CCP orders the reorganization of the Red Army.

Mar. **Mao's troops attack Kanchow.**

Li Li-san urges the establishment of a revolutionary régime in one or more provinces.

Chang Hui-tsan is appointed the commander-in-chief of the army fighting the communists.

Apr. **Mao is urged to attend a projected conference of delegates of soviet areas in Shanghai.**

The 1st Front Army attack Nanhsiung.

Feng Yü-hsiang, Yen Hsi-shan, and the Kwangsi generals form an anti-Chiang united front.

May National conference of delegates from Soviet areas meets in Shanghai and urges the formation of a national soviet government.

The authorities of Kwangtung, Fukien, and Kiangsi discuss the suppression of the communists led by Mao and Chu.

June Pavel Mif and his students (Ch'en Shao-yü and others) arrive in China. The Li Li-san line is adopted by the CCP.

Chang Fa-k'uei's troops pass through Ch'angsha.

July **Yang K'ai-hui and Mao Tse-hung are executed and Mao An-ying, Mao's son, is missing.**

Ch'angsha falls to P'eng Te-huai's troops.

Aug. **Mao and Chu attack Nanch'ang.**

The Central Action Committee of the CCP is formed.

Ho Ying-ch'in orders a general attack on the communists in Hunan and Kiangsi.

Sept. The second attack on Ch'angsha fails. Ch'ü Ch'iu-pai calls the 3rd plenum of the CCP Central Committee at Lushan.

Chiang and Feng Yü-hsiang and Yen Hsi-san patch up their differences. Wang Ching-wei calls the Peking Conference of the Reorganization Clique.

1930 Oct. **Mao takes Chian and creates the Kiangsi Provincial Soviet Government.**
Li Li-san leaves for Moscow.

Dec. The Fut'ien Incident occurs.
The 1st Encirclement begins.

1931 Jan. The 4th plenum of the CCP Central Committee liquidates the Li Li-san line and inaugurates the Wang Ming-Ch'in Pang-hsien line.
The Central Bureau of the Soviet Areas is set up with Chou En-lai, Hsiang Ying, Mao Tse-tung, Chu Te, and others as members.
General Chang Hui-tsan is captured by Chu Te.

Feb. The 2nd Encirclement begins.
Hu Han-min is interned in Nanking.

Apr. The 3rd Encirclement begins. Ku Shun-chang is arrested.

May Chiang is elected the President by the National Convention.

June Hsiang Chung-fa, the CCP secretary, is executed.
Chiang supervises the anti-communist campaign in person.
An anti-Chiang government is set up in Canton.

Aug. Great floods devastate the Yangtze valley.

Sept. The Provisional Centre of the CCP under Ch'in Pang-hsien begins its power struggle with Mao.
The Mukden Incident occurs.

Oct. Representatives of Nanking and Canton meet in Shanghai.

Nov. The 1st National Soviet Congress opens at Juichin.
The KMT 4th Congress is held. Chiang retires.

Dec. **Mao assumes duty as the chairman of the National Soviet Government, with Hsiang Ying and Chang Kuo-t'ao as his vice-chairmen.**
P'eng Te-huai attacks Kanchow.
The brigades under Tung Cheng-t'ang and Chi Chen-tung surrender to the communists.

1932 Jan. The Politburo adopts a resolution on winning preliminary successes in one or more provinces.
Chiang and Wang Ching-wei co-operation begins. Lin Sen is elected the President. Japan attacks Shanghai.

Feb. Chiang is appointed generalissimo of the Military Council.

Apr. The National Soviet Government declares war on Japan.

May Chiang calls a conference at Lushan to deliberate on the next anti-communist campaign and sets up a headquarters at Wuhan.

June The nine-month 4th Encirclement starts.

Aug. **The Ningtu conference marks the beginning of Mao's waning influence in the red army. He is ill after the conference.**

Oct. Ch'en Tu-hsiu is arrested in Shanghai.

Nov. Chang Kuo-t'ao and Hsü Hsiang-ch'ien move from Hupei-Honan-Anhwei border to north Szechwan and Ho Lung moves from the Lake Hung area to west Hunan.

1933 Jan. The CCP centre moves to Juichin.

Chiang sets up his headquarters at Nanch'ang.

Feb. Attack on the Lo Ming line in full swing.

Mar. Chang Kuo-t'ao sets up a soviet in north Szechwan.

The 4th Encirclement is called off. Japanese and Chinese troops fight at Kupeik'ou.

Apr. Chou En-lai is appointed general political commissar of the red army, and concurrently of the 1st Front Army.

Ch'en Tu-hsiu is sentenced to thirteen years' imprisonment.

May Szechwan is at war. China and Japan sign the T'angku agreement.

Oct. The 5th Encirclement begins. A military alliance is concluded between the CCP and the prospective People's Government in Fukien.

Nov. A ring of blockhouses is built around the central soviet area.

The People's Government in Fukien is proclaimed.

1934 Jan. The People's Government in Fukien is destroyed by Chiang.

Feb. **The 2nd National Soviet Congress, held in Juichin, elects Mao the chairman of the National Soviet Government.**

Apr. General Ch'en Ch'eng defeats the communists at Kwangch'ang.

June The 'anti-Japanese vanguards' led by Fang Chih-min break through the encirclement.

July **Mao organizes a special corps to run the KMT blockade.**

Aug. Hsiao K'e's army breaks through the encirclement to join forces with Ho Lung in west Hunan.

Sept. **Mao has fever.**

Oct. The Long March of the 1st Front Army begins.

Nov. The KMT army takes Juichin.

Dec. The 1st Front Army suffers a crippling blow in the battle of the Hsiang River. The Lip'ing Conference is called.

1935 Jan. **At the Tsunyi Conference Mao is elected the chairman of the Politburo.**
The 1st Front Army is reorganized. Fang Chih-min is captured.

Feb. Chang Kuo-t'ao's 4th Front Army begins its Long March.

May Ch'ü Ch'iu-pai is arrested and Mao Tse-t'an killed by KMT troops.

June The 1st and 4th Front Armies meet at Moukung and the Lianghok'ou Conference takes place.

July–
Aug. The Maoerhkai Conference is held.

Oct. **The 1st Front Army under Mao makes a junction with Hsü Hai-tung's 15th Army Corps at Wuch'i-chen, thereby ending the Long March for Mao.**
Chang Kuo-t'ao sets up a régime in Sikang.
Chang Hsüeh-liang is appointed the commander-in-chief of the anti-communist operations in the north-west.

Dec. The KMT 5th Congress is convened and an attempt is made on Wang Ching-wei's life.

1936 May The 2nd Front Army, which began its Long March in November 1935, and the 4th Front Army meet at Kantzu.

June Kwangtung and Kwangsi rebel against Chiang.

July **Mao is interviewed by E. Snow in north Shensi.**
Chiang quells the insurrection in Kwangtung and Kwangsi.

Oct. **Mao orders the communist troops to stop fighting the Manchurian troops under Chang Hsüeh-liang.**
All three front armies meet at Huining. Chang Kuo-t'ao leads his troops to Kansu and Sinkiang.

Dec. **Mao writes the 'Strategic Problems of China's Revolutionary War'. The red capital is moved to Yenan.**
The Sian *Coup* takes place.

1937 Jan. Chang Kuo-t'ao is tried for his disobedience.

Feb. The KMT Central Executive Committee holds its 3rd plenum to discuss the question of the KMT-CCP co-operation.
The Manchurian troops attack the soviet area in north Shensi.

Apr. The Yenan Conference of the Politburo discusses Chang Kuo-t'ao's mistakes.

May The remnants of Chang Kuo-t'ao's troops are brought back to Yenan.

July The Sino-Japanese War begins.

Aug. The Loch'uan Conference of the Politburo is held. Chu Te and Chou En-lai join the KMT Military Commission.

Sept. The 8th Army Route is organized and the north Shensi soviet is renamed the Shensi-Kansu-Ninghsia border region.

Oct. The 8th Route Army wins the battle of P'inghsingkuan. **James Bertram interviews Mao.**

Nov. Shanghai falls to the Japanese and the National Government decides to move to Chungking.

Dec. Japan takes Nanking.

1938 Jan. The New Fourth Army is formed.

Mar. **Mao writes 'On the Protracted War'.**

Apr. General Li Tsung-jen directs the battle of T'aierhchuang.

May **Mao publishes his essays on the Strategic Problems of the Anti-Japanese War and the Protracted War.** The Yellow River changes its course.

July The 1st People's Political Council opens. The *San-min-chu-i* Youth Corps is organized.

Oct. Wuhan falls to the Japanese.

Nov. **Mao writes 'Problems of War and Strategy'.** Konoye announces his policy of a new order for the Far East.

Dec. Wang Ching-wei calls for peace negotiations between China and Japan. **(Ho Tzu-chen visits Russia in 1938.)**

1939 Apr. KMT and CCP guerrillas clash at Poshan in Shantung. An attempt on Wang Ching-wei's life is made in Hanoi.

May Wang Ching-wei leaves for Shanghai.

June KMT troops and the New Fourth Army clash near P'ingchiang. Wang Ching-wei visits Japan. **(Mao marries Lan-p'ing, also known as Chiang Ch'ing, in this year.)**

1940 Jan. **Mao writes his essay on New Democracy.**

Mar. The Wang Ching-wei régime is set up in Nanking.

Aug. The 8th Route Army launches the Hundred Regiment Campaign.

Oct. More clashes occur between the KMT troops and the New Fourth Army in north Kiangsu. General Ho Ying-ch'in orders the transfer of the 8th Route Army and the New Fourth Army.

1940 Dec. The New Fourth Army plans to cross the Yangtze and move northwards.

1941 Jan. **Mao appoints Ch'en Yi, Chang Yün-i, and Liu Shao-ch'i to reorganize the New Fourth Army.**
The South Anhwei Incident takes place.

Mar. The CCP boycotts the 2nd People's Political Council.

Apr. The Rectification (*Cheng-feng*) Campaign begins.

Dec. The Pacific War breaks out.

1942 Jan. General Stilwell is appointed the chief-of-staff of the China theatre.

Sept. Mao Tse-min is arrested in Sinkiang.

1943 Jan. China signs new, equal treaties with the U.S. and the U.K.

Feb. The KMT and CCP have their first discussion on the problems of the United Front.

Mar. Chiang's *China's Destiny* is published.

Nov. The Cairo Conference takes place.

1944 May Chang Chih-chung and Wang Shih-chieh, representing the KMT, and Lin Tsu-han, representing the CCP, hold their discussions in Sian.

June Japan launches the Trans-Continental Drive. Vice-President Wallace visits China.

Sept. General Stilwell recalled.

Nov. **Mao meets Ambassador Hurley in Yenan,** who brings Chou En-lai to Chungking for further discussions with the KMT.

Dec. Chou En-lai returns to Yenan.

1945 Jan. Chou flies to Chungking again.

Feb. After discussions with Chung Chih-chung and Wang Shih-chieh, Chou returns to Yenan.
Yalta Conference is held.

May **Mao announces his views on a coalition government.**
The CCP 7th Congress and the KMT 6th Congress take place.

July **Mao comments on Hurley's policy towards China.**

Aug. **Mao visits Chungking and discusses questions of peace and unity with Chiang.**
Russian troops march into Manchuria. Japan surrenders.

Oct. **Mao and Chiang sign the October 10th Agreement.**
The national conference of the Democratic League is held.

Nov. Ambassador Hurley resigns. General George Marshall is sent to China as President Truman's special envoy.

1946 Jan. The Political Consultative Conference is convened. The Committee of Three and the Peking Headquarters are set up.

Mar. General Marshall is recalled for consultation.
Russian troops begin to leave Manchuria.

Apr. Communist troops take Ch'angch'un.
General Marshall returns to China.

May The National Government moves back to Nanking. KMT troops take Ssup'ingchieh and Ch'angch'un.
Russian evacuation from Manchuria is completed.

June General Marshall arranges the second truce.

July Chiang announces his decision to convene the National Assembly in November, which is opposed by the CCP.
Dr. Leighton Stuart is appointed the American Ambassador to China.

Aug. Mao is seen by G. Stein and A. L. Strong.
Ambassador Stuart suggests the formation of a committee of five.

Sept. Chou En-lai leaves Nanking for Shanghai.

Oct. KMT troops take Kalgan and Ch'ihfeng.
General Marshall sees Chou En-lai in Shanghai.

Nov. The National Assembly is held in Nanking and Chiang unilaterally announces a truce in fighting.
Chou En-lai flies to Yenan, thus ending the KMT-CCP negotiations.

Dec. The National Assembly approves the Constitution.

1947 Jan. General Marshall is recalled; the Peking Headquarters cease functioning. The Constitution is promulgated.

Mar. **Mao departs from Yenan.**
KMT troops take Yenan. The work of rebuilding the dykes of the Yellow River at Huayüank'ou begins.

Apr. **Mao is at Wangchiawan.**

May Ch'en Yi wins the battle of Mengliangku in Shantung.
The Yellow River is channelled back to its old course.

June **The Supreme Court orders the arrest of Mao Tse-tung.**
Ch'en Keng's and Liu Po-ch'eng's armies move south to invade Honan and Tapieh Mountains.

July **Mao leaves Yülin.**
The Nationalist Government orders a general mobilization.
General Wedemeyer visits China.

Aug. Chiang flies to Yenan on a tour of inspection. Wedemeyer leaves China.

1947 Sept. The Wedemeyer report is submitted to President Truman.

Oct. **Mao announces the new land law at Chiahsien.**

Dec. **Mao makes the statement on the current situation and the tasks of the CCP at the Yangchiakou Conference of the Politburo.**

The communist troops take Shihchiachuang. The battle of Manchuria is in full swing.

1948 Jan. The Democratic League holds its meeting in Hong Kong.

Mar. **Mao leaves north Shensi for Shansi.**

Ssup'ingchieh falls to the communists.

Apr. Chiang is elected the President and Li Tsung-jen the Vice-President by the National Assembly.

May **Mao calls for a political consultative conference.**

Chiang is sworn in as the President and Weng Wen-hao as the premier.

Aug. The gold *yüan* notes begin issue.

Sept. The PLA launches the Manchurian Campaign. Ch'en Yi occupies the entire province of Shantung.

Nov. **Mao announces the numerical superiority of the PLA to the KMT troops.**

The PLA is organized into four field armies. The Manchurian Campaign ends in a complete victory for the PLA. The Hsü-chow Campaign begins.

The CCP issues the order for the punishment of the war criminals.

Madame Chiang Kai-shek visits the U.S.

Dec. The Peking-Tientsin Campaign begins.

1949 Jan. **Mao refutes Chiang's peace terms and announces his own.**

The PLA victoriously concludes both the Peking-Tientsin and the Hsüchow Campaigns.

President Chiang resigns.

Feb. The CCP centre moves to Shihchiachuang; the National Government moves to Canton.

The KMT-CCP peace negotiations begin.

Mar. The P'ingshan Conference of the Politburo discusses the KMT peace terms and later the party centre moves to Peking.

Apr. **Mao pronounces the beginning of the period of 'the city leading the village'.**

The KMT-CCP peace negotiations fail. Ch'en Yi's and Liu Po-ch'eng's armies cross the Yangtze.

Chiang resumes his duties as the leader of the KMT.

The PLA takes Nanking.

May Lin Piao's troops cross the Yangtze.

The PLA takes Shanghai and Wuhan.

June **Mao addresses the preparatory meeting of the Political Consultative Conference.**

July **Mao makes his statement of the people's democratic dictatorship and on the policy of 'leaning to one side'.**

Aug. **Mao comments on the U.S.** *White Paper.*

General Ch'eng Ch'ien surrenders to the communists and thus Hunan falls into the communists' hands.

Sept. **Mao addresses the opening session of the Political Consultative Conference in Peking, which approves the Common Programme.**

Vice-President Li Tsung-jen issues the order for Mao's arrest.

Oct. **Mao proclaims the founding of the People's Republic of China.**

The PLA occupies Hengyang and Canton.

Selected Bibliography

(* indicates an important reference for this study)

GENERAL

[1] Chang Ch'i-yün, *Chung-hua-min-kuo shih-kang* (An outline history of the Republic of China), 4 vols., Taipei, 1954 onwards. (The first two volumes are the verbatim reproductions of the author's *Tang-shih kai-yao*)

[2] *Cheng-fu kung-pao* (The Government Gazette, 1913–1928)

[3] *Chin-tai-shih tzu-liao* (Source materials of the modern history of China), a bi-monthly, Peking

*[4] *China Handbook 1937–1945*, N.Y., 1947

[5] *China Handbook 1951–1953*, Taipei, 1953

[6] *China Quarterly, The*, London, 1960 onwards.

*[7] *China Year Books*, ed. H. G. W. Woodhead, Tientsin and Shanghai, 1912–1939

[8] *Chung-kuo ch'ing-nien* (The Chinese youth), a fortnightly, Peking

[9] *Chung-kuo hsien-tai-shih-liao ts'ung-k'an* (Source materials of the contemporary history of China), ed. Wu Hsiang-hsiang, Taipei

*[10] Department of State, The U.S., *The United States Diplomatic Papers 1943—China*, Washington, 1957

*[11] —— *The United States Relations with China*, Washington, 1949

*[12] Fairbank, J. K., *The United States and China*, Cambridge, Mass., revised ed. 1958

[13] Fu Jun-hua, *Chung-kuo tang-tai ming-jen-chuan* (Who's who in China), Shanghai, 1948

[14] Ho Kan-chih, *A History of the Modern Chinese Revolution*, Peking, 1960

[15] Hsiao Pai-fan, *Chung-kuo chin-pai-nien ke-ming-shih* (A history of the Chinese revolutions in the past hundred years), Hong Kong, 1951

[16] *Hsien-tai shih-liao* (Source materials of the contemporary history of China), 3 vols., Shanghai, 1934 (microfilm)

[17] Hu Hua, *Chung-kuo hsin-min-chu-chu-i ke-ming-shih* (A history of the Chinese new democratic revolution), Peking, 1950

[18] —— *Chung-kuo ke-ming-shih chiang-i* (Lectures on the history of the Chinese revolution), Peking, 1959

[19] Hua Kang, *Chung-kuo min-tsu chieh-fang yün-tung-shih* (A history of the Chinese national liberation movement), 2 vols., Shanghai, 1947

*[20] Kao Yin-tsu, *Chung-hua min-kuo ta-shih-chi* (A chronology of the Republic of China), Taipei, 1957

[21] MacMurray, J. V. A., *Treaties and Agreements with and concerning China, 1894–1919*, 2 vols., Washington, 1921

[22] Purcell, V., *China*, London, 1962

[23] Shih Chün, *Chung-kuo chin-tai ssu-hsiang-shih tzu-liao chien-pien* (Selected source materials of the history of modern Chinese thought), Peking, 1957

[24] Su Chi-ch'ang, *Tang-tai jen-wu* (Contemporary personalities), Chungking, 1947

[25] *Times, The*, London

[26] *Tung-fang tsa-chih* (Eastern miscellany), a periodical, Shanghai, 1912–39

[27] *Who's Who in China*, ed. China Weekly Review, Shanghai, 1925 and 1931

MAO

*[28] Chai Tso-chün, *Tsai Mao-chu-hsi shen-pien* (With Chairman Mao), Wuhan, 1959. (The author was Mao's bodyguard from 1937 to 1939)

[29] Ch'en Shu-nung and Chia-shih, 'Mao-chu-hsi ku-shih shih-ling' (Anecdotes about Chairman Mao), the *Hsin Hunan Pao*, 1 July, 1950

[30] Chiang Ch'in-feng, 'Tsai Mao-chu-hsi chou-wei' (With Chairman Mao), *Hung-ch'i p'iao-p'iao*, III, 332–61. (The author was with Mao in 1947)

[31] Chou Shih-chao, 'Ti-i-shih-fan shih-tai ti Mao-chu-hsi' (Chairman Mao at the First Teachers' Training School), the *Hsin Kuan Ch'a*, II, no. 2

[32] —— 'Wo so jen-shih ti Mao-chu-hsi' (The Chairman Mao I knew), the *Hsin Hunan Pao*, 1 July 1950 (being an account of Mao's youth)

[33] Epstein, Israel, *et al.*, *Mao Tse-tung tsai Chungking* (Mao Tse-

tung at Chungking), Shanghai, 1946. (Also including articles by H. Forman, G. Stein, and Emil Hsiao)

[34] Fang Hui, 'Chi hsin-fa-hsien ti *Hsiang-chiang P'ing-lun*' (An account of the newly discovered *Hsiang River Review*), *Li-shih Yen-chiu*, 1954, II, 30

*[35] Fu Lien-chang (Nelson Fu), 'Mao-chu-hsi tsai Yütu' (Chairman Mao at Yütu), *Hung-ch'i p'iao-p'iao*, X, 3–12. (Accounts of Mao in 1934 are very rare, and so this is rather precious. The author was Mao's doctor)

*[36] —— 'Chung-yang hung-se i-yüan ti chien-li' (The founding of the Central Red Hospital in 1932), *ibid.*, XI, 3–18

[37] Griffith, S. B., *et al.*, *Mao Tse-tung and Che Guevara on Guerrilla Warfare*, with a foreword by Capt. B. H. Liddell Hart, London, 1962

[38] Hsia Chia, 'Peiching Ta-hsüeh ti Mao-chu-hsi ho Li Ta-chao T'ung-chih chi-nien-shih' (The Chairman Mao and Comrade Li Ta-chao Room in Peking National University), the *Ch'ang-chiang Jih-pao*, 29 June 1951

*[39] Hsiao San (Emil Hsiao), *Mao Tse-tung t'ung-chih ti ch'ing-shao-nien shih-tai* (Comrade Mao's boyhood and youth), Peking, 1949

[40] Hsieh Chüeh-tsai, 'Ti-i-tz'u hui-chien Mao-chu-hsi' (My first meeting with Chairman Mao), the *Hsin Kuan-ch'a*, 1952, no. 11. (Being an impression of Mao as a young man. The author has been Mao's friend for many years and is an alternate member of the Central Committee of the CCP)

[41] Kan Yu-lan, *Mao-Tse-tung chi ch'i ch-it'uan* (Mao Tse-tung and his clique), Hong Kong, 1954

[42] Kuo Mo-jo, 'Hsi-tu Mao-chu-hsi ti tz'u liu-shou' (My pleasure in reading Chairman Mao's six poems), the *People's Daily*, 12 May 1962

*[43] Li Jui, *Mao Tse-tung t'ung-chih ti ch'u-ch'i ke-ming huo-tung* (Comrade Mao's early revolutionary activities), Peking, 1957. (Being the only serious study of Mao in Chinese, this covers the period from Mao's childhood to the beginning of the Northern Expedition. Well-documented and extremely important)

[44] Liu Liu-wen, 'Wo so chih-tao ti Mao Tse-tung hsien-sheng erh-san shih' (A few things I know about Mr. Mao), the *Hsin Hua Jih-pao*, 8 September 1945. (Written during Mao's visit to Chungking, this is an account of Mao's youth)

[45] Lu Ch'ang, *Chingkangshan shang ti 'Ying-hsiung'* ('Heroes' on the Chingkangshan), Hong Kong, 1951. (The title is misleading as the book actually deals with Mao's activities from 1920s to

1940s. It is violently anti-communist and based largely on hear-say)

*[46] Mao Tse-tung, *Mao Tse-tung hsüan-chi* (Selected Works), 4 vols. (5 in English), Peking, 1960–1 reprint

*[47] —— *Mao Tse-tung tzu-chuan* (Autobiography), tr. from the English (E. Snow, *Red Star over China*, part 4) by Fang Lin, Hong Kong, 1948

*[48] —— *Shih-tz'u shih-chiu-shou* (Nineteen poems), with notes by Chou Chen-fu and an appreciation by Tsang K'e-chia, Peking, 1958. (The Chinese originals of these poems can be found in *Shih-hüan*, Peking, 1957)

[49] Paulsen, F., *A System of Ethics*, 1899, Chinese translation by Ts'ai Yüan-p'ei, Shanghai, 1913

[50] Payne, R., *Mao Tse-tung, Ruler of Red China*, London, 1950. (The revised edition of this book is entitled *Portrait of a Revolutionary: Mao Tse-tung*, N.Y., 1961)

[51] P'u Kung-ying, 'Ch'ing-nien ti yin-lu-jen' (The leader of the youth), *Hung-ch'i p'iao-p'iao*, X, 12–24. (Written under a pseudonym, this is an account of the author's interview with Mao in Chungking, 1945)

*[52] Schwartz, B., *Chinese Communism and the Rise of Mao*, Harvard, 1951. (This scholarly work is of great importance and can be even better if its *terminus ad quem* were at January 1935)

[53] —— The legend of the 'Legend of "Maoism"', *The China Quarterly*, London, II

[54] Siao Yu, *Mao Tse-tung and I were Beggars*, London, 1961

[55] Snow, E., *The Autobiography of Mao Tse-tung, as told to the writer*, Hong Kong, 1949. (Emil Hsiao says that there are mistakes in this pioneer work)

[56] Wang Wei-lien, 'Mao Tse-tung', *Hsien-tai shih-liao*, Shanghai, 1934, I, part 2

[57] Wittfogel, K. A., 'The Legend of "Maoism",' *The China Quarterly*, London, I and II

[58] Yen Ch'ang-lin, 'Hsiung-chung tzu-yu hsiung-ping pai-wan' (A million crack troops in his strategic thought), *Chung-kuo kung-jen*, 1960, no. 12. (The author was Mao's cook in 1947)

[59] —— 'Wei-ta ti chuan-che-tien' (The momentous turning-point), *ibid.*, 1960, nos. 17 and 18. (This also describes Mao in 1947)

[60] Yü-ming, 'Mao Tse-tung tsai chung-hsüan-pu' (Mao Tse-tung at the Central Propaganda Department), *Hsien-tai shih-liao*, 1934, IV, part 3, 341 *et seq.*

[61] Yüan Hsüeh-k'ai, 'Ying-ming ti yü-chien' (Brilliant foresight),

Ch'ien-fang-chün wen-i, 1960, no. 10. (This account of Mao's prediction of the final victory before leaving Yenan in 1947 and the items [57] and [58] can also be found in *Chieh-fang-chan-cheng hui-i-lu*, see [306])

HISTORICAL BACKGROUND

[62] Ch'ai Te-keng, *et al.*, *Hsin-hai ke-ming* (The 1911 Revolution), 8 vols., Peking, 1957

[63] Ch'en, Jerome, 'A footnote on the Chinese army in 1911–1912', *T'oung-pao*, Leiden, 4–5, 1960

[64] —— 'The nature and characteristics of the Boxer Movement— a morphological study', *Bulletin of the School of Oriental and African Studies*, vol. XXIII, part 2, 1960

[65] Cheng T'ien-t'ing, *et al.*, *Ming-mo nung-min ch'i-i shih-liao* (Historical documents concerning the peasant uprisings at the end of the Ming dynasty), Peking, 1952

[66] Ch'i Hsia, *Sui-mo nung-min ch'i-i* (The peasant uprisings at the end of the Sui dynasty), Shanghai, 1954

[67] Ch'ien Shih-fu, *Ch'ing-chi chung-yao chih-kuan nien-piao* (Chronological tables of important officials at the end of the Ch'ing dynasty), Shanghai, 1959

[68] *Chung-kuo chin-tai-shih lun-ts'ung* (Selected source materials of the modern history of China), Taipei, 1959

[69] Chung-kuo shih-hsüeh-hui, *Wu-hsü pien-fa* (The 1898 Reform), 4 vols., Shanghai, 1953

[70] Feng Tzu-yu, *Chung-kuo ke-ming yün-tung erh-shih-nien tsu-chih-shih* (A history of the organization of the revolutionary movement in China for the past twenty years)

[71] Hsüeh Chün-tu, *Huang Hsing and the Chinese Revolution*, Stanford, 1961

[72] Johnston, R. F., *Twilight in the Forbidden City*, London, 1934

[73] Liang Ch'i-ch'ao, *Yin-ping-shih ho-chi* (Collected works of the Yin-ping Studio), Shanghai, 1926

[74] Liu Chin-tsao, *Hsü Ch'ing-ch'ao wen-hsien t'ung-k'ao* (A sequel to the collected official documents of the Ch'ing dynasty), 4 vols., Shanghai, 1937

[75] Liu Yen, *Chung-kuo chin-tai wai-chiao-shih* (A diplomatic history of modern China), Shanghai, 1921

[76] Purcell, V., *The Boxer Uprising, a background study*, Cambridge, 1962

[77] Ssu-ma Kuang, *Tzu-chih t'ung-chien* (A general history for the Rulers), 10 vols., Peking 1956 ed. (This 11th century work is the main source of Mao's historical knowledge)

[78] Sun Tso-min, *Chung-kuo nung-min chan-cheng wen-t'i t'an-so* (An inquiry into the problems of Chinese peasant wars), Shanghai, 1956

[79] Sun Yao, *Chung-hua min-kuo shih-liao* (Historical documents of the Republic of China), Shanghai, 1929

[80] Wang Tan-ts'en, *Chung-kuo nung-min ke-ming shih-hua* (A history of the Chinese peasant revolts), Shanghai, 1952

[81] Yang Yu-chiung, *Chin-tai chung-kuo li-fa-shih* (A legislative history of modern China), Shanghai, 1936

WARLORDS

[82] *Ch'en Ching-ts'un hsien-sheng nien-p'u* (A chronological biography of General Ch'en Chiung-ming), place and date of publication unspecified

*[83] Ch'en Han-sheng, 'Chung-kuo nung-min fu-tan ti fu-shui' (The tax burden of the Chinese peasants), [26], 10 October 1928, 9–28

[84] Ch'en, Jerome, *Yüan Shih-k'ai, Brutus assumes the purple*, London, 1961

[85] —— *Tables of Chinese Military Leaders* (unpublished)

*[86] Feng Yü-hsiang, *Wo-ti sheng-huo* (Autobiography), 2 vols., Chungking, 1949

*[87] Hsieh Sheng-chih, *Ch'en Chiung-ming p'an-kuo-shih* (The treacheries of Ch'en Chiung-ming), Canton (?), 1922

*[88] Li Chien-nung, *Tsui-chin san-shih-nien chung-kuo cheng-chih-shih* (A political history of China of the past thirty years), Shanghai, 1930

[89] Liang Shih-i, *San-shui Liang Yen-sun hsien-sheng nien-p'u* (A chronological biography of Liang Shih-i) compiled by Liang's disciples of the Feng-kang College, Feng-kang, 1939

[90] T'ao Chü-yin, *Pei-yang chün-fa t'ung-chih shih-ch'i shih-hua* (A history of the rule of the northern warlords), 6 vols., 1957–61

[91] —— *Tu-chün-t'uan chuan* (Chronicles of the military governors' conferences), Shanghai, 1948

[92] —— *Wu P'ei-fu chuan* (A biography of General Wu P'ei-fu), Taipei, 1957 reprint

*[93] Wu P'ei-fu, *Wu P'ei-fu hsien-sheng chi* (Collected works), Taipei, 1950. (This book contains a very useful chronological biography of Wu)

THE MAY FOURTH MOVEMENT

*[94] Ch'en Tu-hsiu, *Tu-hsiu wen-ts'un* (Collected works), 4 vols., Shanghai, 1922

[95] Chiang Monlin, *Tides from the West*, Yale, 1947

*[96] Chow Tse-tsung, *The May Fourth Movement*, Harvard, 1960

[97] Ch'ü Ch'iu-pai, 'Hsien-tai wen-ming ti wen-t'i yü she-hui-chu-i' (Problems of modern civilization and socialism), [26], 1923, 21st anniversary issue

*[98] Chung-kuo K'e-hsüeh-yüan Li-shih Yen-chiu-so, *Wu-ssu ai-kuo yün-tung tzu-liao* (Source materials of the patriotic May 4th Movement), Peking, 1959

*[99] *Hsin ch'ing-nien (La Jeunesse)*, Shanghai, 1917–25

*[100] Hu Shih, *Hu Shih wen-ts'un* (Collected works), 3 series, Shanghai, 1931

[101] I-ch'ün, 'Wu-ssu wen-hsüeh ke-ming ti kuang-hui ch'uan-t'ung', *Wen-i yüeh-pao*, V, 116 *et seq.*

[102] Li Tao-chao, *Li Ta-chao hsüan-chi* (Selected works), Peking, 1959

[103] —— *Shou-ch'ang wen-chi* (Collected works), Shanghai, 1950 reprint

*[104] Lu Hsün, *Lu Hsün ch'üan-chi* (Complete works), 20 vols., Peking, 1956 reprint

[105] Pien Hsiao-hsüan, 'Liu-Fa ch'in-kung-chien-hsüeh tzu-liao' (Source materials of the work-study students in France), *Chin-tai-shih tzu-liao* [3], 1955, no. 2

[106] Russell, B., *The Problem of China*, London, 1922

[107] Shu Hsin-ch'eng, *Chin-tai Chung-kuo chiao-yü-shih* (A history of modern education in China), 4 vols., Shanghai, 1928

[108] Ts'ai Hsiao-chou and Yang Ching-kung, 'Wu-ssu' (The May 4th), [3], 1955, no. 2

[109] 'Wu-ssu ai-kuo yün-tung Peiching tzu-liao hsüan-chi' (Selected source materials of the patriotic May 4th Movement in Peking), [3], 1955, no. 2

THE KMT

[110] Buck, J. L., *Chinese Farm Economy*, Shanghai, 1930

[111] —— *Land Utilization in China*, Shanghai, 1937

[112] Carlson, E. F., *The Chinese Army, its organization and military efficiency*, N.Y., 1940

[113] Chang Chi, *Chang P'u-ch'üan hsien-sheng ch'üan-chi* (Complete works), Taipei, 1951

[114] Chang Chi-luan, *Chi-luan wen-ts'un* (Collected works), 2 vols., Tientsin, 1947

[115] Chang Ch'i-yün, *Tang-shih kai-yao* (A brief history of the KMT), 2 vols., Taipei, 1951 reprint (see [1])

[116] Ch'en, Jerome, 'The Left Wing Kuomintang', *Bulletin of the School of Oriental and African Studies*, October 1962

[117] Ch'en Po-ta, *Jen-min kung-ti Chiang Chieh-shih* (Chiang Kai-shek, public enemy of the people), Peking, 1954 reprint

[118] Ch'en T'ien-hsi, *Tai Chi-t'ao hsien-sheng pien-nien chuan-chi* (A chronological biography of Mr. Tai Chi-t'ao), Taipei, 1958

*[119] Chiang Kai-shek, *Chiang Tsung-t'ung yen-lun hui-pien* (Speeches and messages by President Chiang), Taipei, 1956

*[120] —— *Chiang Wei-yüan-chang ch'üan-chi* (Complete works of Generalissimo Chiang), ed. Shen Feng-kang, Shanghai, 1937

*[121] —— *Chung-kuo chih ming-yün* (China's Destiny), Chungking, 1943. (There are two English translations, one authorized and the other containing his *Chinese Economic Theory* and Philip Jaffe's notes and commentary, London, 1947. Unless otherwise specified, the authorized translation is used in this book)

*[122] —— *The Collected Wartime Messages of Generalissimo Chiang Kai-shek*, 2 vols., N.Y., 1946

*[123] Ch'ien Tuan-sheng, *The Government and Politics of China*, Harvard, 1950

[124] Chung-kuo K'e-hsüeh-yüan Ching-chi Yen-chiu-so, *Chung-kuo chin-tai nung-yeh-shih tzu-liao* (Source materials of the history of modern Chinese agriculture), 3 vols., Peking, 1957

[125] Chung-yang Tang-shih Shih-liao Pien-tsuan wei-yüan-hui, *Huang-p'u chien-chün kai-shu* (A brief description of army training at the Whampoa Academy during the past thirty years), Taipei, 1954

[126] Feng Yü-hsiang, *Wo so jen-shih ti Chiang Chieh-shih* (The Chiang Kai-shek I know), Hong Kong, 2nd ed., 1949

[127] Ho Hsiang-ning (Madame Liao Chung-k'ai), *Hui-i Liao Chung-k'ai* (My memories of Liao Chung-k'ai), *Hung-ch'i p'iao-p'iao*, I, 75–87

[128] Hu Han-min, *Hu Han-min hsüan-chi* (Selected works), ed. Wu Chün-man, Taipei, 1959

[129] Hua Lin-i, *Chung-kuo Kuomintang shih* (A history of the KMT), Shanghai, 1928

*[130] *Ke-ming wen-hsien* (Documents of the revolution), 7 vols., Taipei, 1954

*[131] Li Tsung-huang, *Chung-kuo Kuomintang tang-shih* (A history of the KMT), Nanking, 1935

[132] Liang Yü-kao (ed.), *Wang Ching-wei tsui-chin yen-lun-chi* (Wang Ching-wei's recent speeches and essays), Penang, 1928

[133] Linebarger, P. M., *The China of Chiang Kai-shek*, Boston, 1941

[134] Liu F. F., *A Military History of Modern China, 1924–1949*, Princeton, 1956

[135] Mao Ssu-ch'eng, *Min-kuo shih-wu-nien i-ch'ien chih Chiang*

Chieh-shih hsien-sheng, (Mr. Chiang Kai-shek before 1926), 20 vols., Shanghai, 1936

[136] Martin, B., *Strange Vigour*, London, 1944

*[137] North, R. C., *Kuomintang and Chinese Communist Elites*, Stanford, 1952

[138] Sun Yat-sen, *Fundamentals of National Reconstruction*, 1924, Taipei, 1953 reprint

*[139] —— *Sun Chung-shan hsüan-chi* (Selected works), 2 vols., Peking, 1956

*[140] —— *The Principle of Democracy*, 1927, Taipei, 1953 reprint

*[141] —— *The Principle of Nationalism*, 1927, Taipei, 1953 reprint

*[142] —— *Tsung-li ch'üan-chi* (Complete works), 3 vols., Shanghai, 1930

[143] Tai Chi-t'ao, *Tai Chi-t'ao wen-ts'un* (Collected works), 4 vols., ed. Ch'en T'ien-hsi, Taipei, 1959

[144] Tang Leang-li, *Wang Ching-wei, a political biography*, Tientsin, preface date 1931 (substantially the same as the author's *Inner History*)

[145] Tawney, R. H., *Land and Labour in China*, London, 1932

[146] Teng Yen-ta, *Teng Yen-ta hsien-sheng i-chu* (Collected works, a posthumous publication), Hong Kong, preface date 1949

[147] Ts'ai T'ing-k'ai, *Ts'ai T'ing-k'ai tzu-chuan* (autobiography), place of publication unspecified, 1946

[148] Tso Shun-sheng, *Chin san-shih-nien chien-wen tsa-chi* (An eye-witness account of the events in the past thirty years), Hong Kong, 1952

[149] Tsou Lu, *Chung-kuo Kuomintang shih-kao* (A draft history of the KMT), 2 vols., Shanghai, 1947

[150] —— *Hui-ku lu* (Recollections), Shanghai, 1943

[151] —— *Tsou Lu wen-ts'un* (Collected works), Peking, 1930

*[152] Ts'ui Shu-ch'in, *Sun Chung-shan yü kung-ch'an-chu-i* (Sun Yat-sen and communism), Hong Kong, 1954

[153] Tung Hsien-kuang (Hollington K. Tong), *Chiang Tsung-t'ung chuan* (A biography of President Chiang Kai-shek), 3 vols., Taipei, 1954 reprint. (This is the Chinese translation of the author's *Chiang Kai-shek*, 1937, and is also brought up to date. But the Chinese is difficult to understand)

*[154] Wang Ching-wei, *Wang Ching-wei chi* (Collected works), 4 vols., Shanghai, 1929

[155] Wang Ching-wei, Li Tsung-jen, Sun Fo, and others, *T'ao Chiang yen-lun-chi* (Anti-Chiang Kai-shek messages), Canton, 1931

[156] Wang Ching-wei, Wu Chih-hui, and others, *Fen-kung i-hou ti*

lun-wen-chi (Essays after the dissolution of the KMT-CCP alliance), Shanghai, 1928

[157] Wang Po-ling, Ho Ying-ch'in, Ch'en Chi-ch'eng, and others, *Huang-p'u chien-chün shih-hua* (A history of the organization of the Chinese army at the Whampoa Academy), Chungking, 1943

[158] Wang Yün-sheng, *Yün-sheng wen-ts'un* (Collected works), Shanghai, 1937

[159] Woo, T. C., *The Kuomintang and the Future of the Chinese Revolution*, London, 1928

[160] Yao Yü-hsiang, *Hu Han-min hsien-sheng chuan* (A biography of Mr. Hu Han-min), Taipei, 1954

THE CCP AND COMMUNISM

*[161] Brandt, C., *Stalin's Failure in China 1924–1927*, Harvard and London, 1958

*[162] Brandt, C., Schwartz, B., and Fairbank, J. K., *A Documentary History of Chinese Communism*, Harvard, 1952

[163] Chang Hsi-man, *Li-shih hui-i* (Recollections of some historical events), Shanghai, 1949

[164] Chang Kuo-t'ao, *An interview with R. C. North*, 3 November 1950 (microfilm)

[165] Ch'en Kung-po, *The Communist Movement in China 1924*, ed. and with an introduction by C. Martin Wilbur, Columbia, 1960

*[166] Ch'en Tu-hsiu, *Chung-kuo ke-ming wen-t'i lun-wen-chi* (Essays on the problems of the Chinese revolution), I (microfilm)

*[167] —— *Kao ch'üan-tang t'ung-chih shu* (A letter to all the comrades), 10 December 1929 (microfilm)

[168] Ch'eng Shih, *Kung-chün nei-mo chieh-p'ou* (An inner story of the communist army), Kowloon, 1951

[169] Chiang Kai-shek, *Soviet Russia in China*, London, 1957

[170] Chin Ta-k'ai and Chang Ta-chün, *Chung-kung chün-shih p'ou-shih* (An analysis of the Chinese communist army), Kowloon, 1954

[171] Chinese Communist Party, *Ti-liu-tz'u ta-hui hou Chung-kuo kung-ch'an-tang ti cheng-chih kung-tso* (The political work of the CCP after the 6th congress), I (microfilm)

[172] —— *Resolutions and Telegrams of the Sixth Plenum of the Central Committee of the Chinese Communist Party*, 6 November 1938, Hong Kong, 1938

*[173] Degras, J., *The Communist International 1919–1943 Documents*, 2 vols., London, 1956 and 1960

*[174] —— *Soviet Documents on Foreign Policy*, 3 vols., London, 1951–3

[175] Elegant, R. S., *China's Red Masters*, N.Y., 1951

[176] Fischer, L., *The Soviets in World Affairs*, 2 vols., London, 1930

[177] Ho Meng-hsiung, *Ho Meng-hsiung i-chien-shu* (Three statements by Ho Meng-hsiung), 1930 (microfilm)

[178] Hua Ying-shen, *Chung-kuo kung-ch'an-tang lieh-shih-chuan* (Martyrs of the CCP), Hong Kong, 1951

*[179] Hu Ch'iao-mu, *Chung-kuo kung-ch'an-tang ti san shih-nien* (Thirty years of the Chinese Communist Party), Peking, 1951, and English translation, London, 1951. (Unless specified, references are made to the English translation)

[180] Kennedy, M. D., *A Short History of Communism in Asia*, London, 1957

*[181] Ku Kuan-chiao, *San-shih-nien lai ti Chung-kung* (Thirty years of the CCP), Hong Kong, 1955. (A rebuttal of [179])

[182] Li Ang, *Hung-se wu-t'ai* (The red stage), Peking, 1946

[183] Li Li-san, *Kung-ch'an kuo-chi tui Chung-kuo ke-ming chüeh-i-an* (Resolutions on the Chinese revolution by the Third International), with an introduction by Li. (microfilm)

[184] Mif, P., *Heroic China*, N.Y., 1937

[185] Miu Ch'u-huang, *Chung-kuo kung-ch'an-tang chien-yao li-shih* (A brief history of the CCP), Peking, 1956

[186] 'Peiching Ta-hsüeh Ma-k'e-ssu hsüeh-shuo yen-chiu-hui' (The Marxism study group at Peking National University), [3], 1955, no. 2

*[187] Sheng Li-yü, *Chung-kuo jen-min-chieh-fang-chün san-shih-nien-shih-hua* (A history of the PLA during the past thirty years), Tientsin, 1959

[188] Shih Ch'eng-chih, *Lun Chung-kung ti chün-shih fa-chan* (The development of the Chinese communist army), Hong Kong, 1952

[189] Smedley, A., *The Great Road, the life and times of Chu Teh*, London, 1958

[190] Wales, N., *Red Dust*, N.Y., 1952, with an introduction by R. C. North

[191] Wang I-shih, *K'ang-chan i-ch'ien ti Chung-kuo kung-ch'an-tang*, (The CCP before the Resistance War), Chungking, 1942

[192] Wei, H., *China and Soviet Russia*, Princeton, 1956

*[193] Wilbur, C. Martin, and How, J. L. Y., *Documents on Communism, Nationalism, and Soviet Advisers in China 1918–1927*, Columbia, 1956. (Being the translations of the papers seized in the 1927 raid of the Russian official buildings in Peking, with commentaries and notes by the translators)

THE NORTHERN EXPEDITION

[194] Besedovsky, G., *Revelations of a Soviet Diplomat*, London, 1931
[195] Borg, D., *American Policy and the Chinese Revolution 1925–1928*, N.Y., 1947
*[196] Chang Tzu-sheng, 'Kuo-ming ke-ming-chün pei-fa chan-cheng chih ching-kuo' (Chronicles of the northern expedition of the National Revolutionary Army), [26], 10 and 25 August and 10 September 1928
[197] Chapman, H. O., *The Chinese Revolution 1926–1927*, London, 1928
[198] Ch'ü Ch'iu-pai, *Chung-kuo ke-ming chih cheng-lun wen-t'i* (Disputed problems of the Chinese revolution), Shanghai, 1927 (microfilm)
[199] —— *Chung-kuo ke-ming yü Chung-kuo kung-ch'an-tang* (Chinese revolution and the CCP), 1928 (microfilm)
*[200] Chung-kuo Hsien-tai-shih Tzu-liao Ts'ung-k'an, *Ti-i-tz'u Kuo-nei ke-ming chan-cheng shih-ch'i ti kung-jen yun-tung* (The labour movement in the first revolutionary war), Peking, 1954
*[201] —— *Ti-i-tz'u kuo-nei ke-ming chan-cheng shih-ch'i ti nung-min yün-tung* (The peasant movement in the first revolutionary war), Peking, 1953. (This and [200] are collections of source materials of great importance)
[202] Dallin, D. J., *The Rise of Russia in Asia*, London, 1950
[203] Hsü K'e-hsiang, *Ma-jih ch'uan-kung hui-i-lu* (A recollection of the attack on the communists on 21 May 1927), Taipei, 1956. (Col. Hsü led the attack on that day)
[204] Hua Kang, *Chung-kuo ta-ke-ming shih* (A history of the great revolution of China), Shanghai, 1932
[205] Isaacs, H., *The Tragedy of the Chinese Revolution*, Calif., 1951
[206] Kuo Liang, *Hunan kung-jen yün-tung ti kuo-ch'ü yü hsien-tsai* (The past and present of Hunan labour movement), Ch'angsha, 1927 (microfilm)
*[207] Kuo Mo-jo, *Mo-jo wen-chi* (Collected works), Peking, 1958
[208] Lai Hsin-hsia and Wei Hung-yüan (ed.), *Ti-i-tz'u kuo-nei ke-ming chan-cheng-shih lun-chi* (Collected essays on the first revolutionary war), Wuhan, 1957
[209] Liu Ya-ch'iu, *Ti-i-tz'u kuo-nei ke-ming chan-cheng ch'ien-hou Shuik'oushan ti kung-jen yun-tung* (The labour movement at Shuik'oushan before and during the first revolutionary war), the *Hsin Hunan Pao*, 1 May 1952
*[210] North, R. C., *Moscow and Chinese Communists*, Stanford, 1953
[211] P'eng Chiang-liu, 'Tsai Mao-chu-hsi ling-tao hsia ch'ien Anyüan mei-k'uang ti kung-jen yün-tung (The Anyüan coal-miners'

struggles under the leadership of Chairman Mao), the *Kiangsi Jih-pao*, 1 July 1951

[212] Roy, M. N., *Revolution and Counter-revolution in China*, Calcutta, 1946

[213] Strong, A. L., *China's Millions*, N.Y., 1928, and London, 1936

[214] Tang Leang-li, *The Inner History of the Chinese Revolution*, London, 1930

[215] Trotsky, L., *Problems of the Chinese Revolution*, N.Y., 1932

[216] Tseng Min-chih, *Lu Hsün tsai Kuangchow ti Jih-tzu* (Lu Hsün's sojourn in Canton), Canton, 1956

[217] Yeh Hu-sheng and Lo Yang-shen, *Ti-i-tz'u kuo-nei ke-ming chan-cheng chien-shih* (A brief history of the first revolutionary war), Shanghai, 1957

JAPAN

[218] *Documents on British Foreign Policy 1919–1939*, China Question, second series, vol. VIII, London, 1960

[219] James, D. H., *The Rise and Fall of the Japanese Empire*, London, 1951

[220] North China Daily News and Herald, *The Sino-Japanese War in Shanghai*, 1932

*[221] Shigemitsu, Mamoru, *Japan and Her Destiny*, tr. O White, London, 1958

*[222] Storry, R., *A History of Modern Japan*, London, 1960

*[223] —— *The Double Patriots, a study of Japanese nationalism*, London, 1957

*[224] Wang Yün-sheng, *Liu-shih-nien lai Chung-kuo yü Jih-pen* (Sino-Japanese relations in the past sixty years), 7 vols., Shanghai, 1932–4

THE SOVIETS

[225] Ch'en Hsiao-pai, *Hai-lu-feng ch'ih-huo chi* (The red scourge at Haifeng and Lufeng), Canton, 1932

[226] Ch'en Po-ta, *Kuan-yü shih-nien nei-chan* (On the ten-years civil war), written in 1944, Peking, 1953

[227] Ch'en Shao-yü (Wang Ming), *Wu-chuang pao-tung* (Armed uprisings), Shanghai, 1929 (microfilm)

[228] Ch'en Shao-yü and K'ang Sheng, *Revolutionary China Today*, Moscow, 1934 (microfilm)

[229] Chou En-lai, *Mu-ch'ien kung-ch'an-tang ti tsu-chih wen-t'i* (Problems of the organization of the CCP at the present), Shanghai, 1929 (microfilm)

[230] —— *Shao-shan pao-kao* (A report on the third plenum of the central committee of the CCP), no. 9, 3 January 1931 (microfilm)

[231] *Chung-kuo Chi-nan Tsung-hui, Chi-nien Kuangchow ta-ts'an-sha* (Commemorating the Canton Massacre), Canton, 1928

[232] *Chung-kuo kung-ch'an-tang chung-yang wei-yüan-hui k'uo-ta ti ti-ssu-tz'u ch'üan-t'i-hui-ti i-chüeh-an* (Resolutions of the 4th enlarged plenum of the Central Committee of the CCP), Shanghai, 1931 (microfilm)

[233] *Chung-kuo kung-ch'an-tang ling-tao Hunan jen-min ying-yung fen-tou san-shih-nien* (The struggles of the Hunan people in the past thirty years under the leadership of the CCP), Ch'angsha, 1951

*[234] *Chung-kuo kung-ch'an-tang tsai Kiangsi ti-ch'ü ling-tao ke-ming tou-cheng ti li-shih tzu-liao* (Historical documents concerning the revolutionary struggles under the leadership of the CCP in Kiangsi), Kiangsi Jen-min Ch'u-pan-she, vol. I, 1958

[235] Chung I-mou, *Hai-lu-feng nung-min ti pa-nien chan-tou* (The eight-years' struggle of the peasants in Haifeng and Lufeng), [3], 1955, no. 1

[236] *Fundamental Laws of the Chinese Soviet Republic*, N.Y., 1934

*[237] Hsiao Tso-liang, *Power Relations within the Chinese Communist Movement 1930–1934*, Seattle, 1961. (Summaries of and commentaries on communist documents of this period)

[238] Hsieh Fu-min, 'Chuang-tsu jen-min yu-hsiu ti erh-tzu Wei Pa-ch'ün' (A worthy son of the Chuang people, Wei Pa-ch'ün), *Hung-ch'i p'iao-p'iao*, V, 54–61

[239] Hsü Kuang-ta, Wang Chen, and Wang Shang-jung, 'Hsiang-o-hsi ho Hsiang-o-ch'uan-ch'ien ti wu-chuang tou-cheng' (Armed struggles in west Hupei-Hunan and Hupei-Hunan-Szechwan-Kweichow), the *People's Daily*, 1 February 1962

[240] Kung Ch'u, *Wo yü hung-chün* (The red army and I), Hong Kong, 1954

[241] Li Wei, *Chingkangshan*, Shanghai, 1956

[242] 'Nanch'ang ta-shih-chi' (Important events at Nanch'ang), [3], 1957, no. 4

[243] Shih-hsüeh Shuang-chou-k'an (ed.), *Ti-erh-tz'u kuo-nei ke-ming chan-cheng shih-ch'i shih-shih lun-ts'ung* (Collected essays on the historical events of the second revolutionary war), Peking, 1956

[244] Tang Leang-li, *Suppressing Communist Bandits in China*, Shanghai, 1934. (Based on police records)

THE LONG MARCH

[245] Chang Ai-p'ing, *Ts'ung Tsunyi tao Tatuho* (From Tsunyi to the Tatuho), Hong Kong, 1960

[246] Hsü Hai-tung, *Shan-pei Hui-shih* (Junction in north Shensi), *Hung-ch'i p'iao-p'iao*, III, 168–80

[247] *Hung-ch'i p'iao-p'iao*, 16 vols., Peking, 1957 onwards (a rich collection of *memoirs*)

*[248] Li T'ien-huan, *Ch'i-chuang shan-ho* (The spirit as magnificent as the mountains and rivers), [247], X, 73–111. (An account of Chang Kuo-t'ao's unsuccessful expedition into Sinkiang)

*[249] Liu Po-ch'eng, *et al.*, *Hsing-huo liao-yüan* (A spark that sets the prairie ablaze), Hong Kong, 1960

*[250] Miu Ch'u-huang, 'Chung-kuo kung-nung hung-chün ch'ang-cheng kai-shu' (A brief account of the Long March of the Workers' and Peasants' Army of China), *Li-shih yen-chiu*, 1954, II, 85–96

[251] Shih Fen, *Lo Ping-hui chiang-chün sheng-p'ing* (The life of General Lo Ping-hui), *Hung-ch'i p'iao-p'iao*, V, 180–224

*[252] *Chung-kuo kung-nung hung-chün ti-i fang-mien-chün ch'ang-cheng chi*, Russian translation, *Veliki pokhod*, Moskva, 1959. (The Chinese original was first published in 1958, being an account of the First Front Army on the Long March. The Russian edition, perhaps the Chinese edition too, has an excellent itinerary, giving the day-by-day journey of the Army)

[253] Wang Ch'ün, *Ch'ang-cheng t'u-chung ti Mao Tse-min t'ung-chi* (Comrade Mao Tse-min on the Long March), [247], V, 152–5

THE ANTI-JAPANESE UNITED FRONT

*[254] Bertram, J. M., *Crisis in China, the story of the Sian Mutiny*, London, 1937

[255] Ch'en Shao-yü, *Old Intrigues in New Clothing*, Chungking, 1939. (New China Information Committee, Bulletin, no. 7, microfilm)

*[256] Chiang Mayling Soong, *Sian, a coup d'état*, Shanghai, 1937

[257] Kuo Mo-jo, *Hung-po ch'ü* (A song of the magnificent waves), Tientsin, 1959

*[258] Snow, E., *Red Star over China*, London, 1937

[259] Wang Chia-hsiang, Ch'en Po-ta, and Lo Fu, *Communists and the Three Principles*, Chungking, 1940 (New China Information Committee, Bulletin, no. 16, microfilm)

THE RESISTANCE WAR

*[260] Chang Chia-ao (Kia-ngau), *The Inflation Spiral, the experience of China 1939–1950*, N.Y., 1958

*[261] Fan Ch'ang-chiang, *Hsi-hsien feng-yün* (Wind and clouds on the western front), Shanghai, 1937

[262] —— *Hsi-pei hsien* (The north-west front), Hankow, 1938

[263] Feng Yü-hsiang, *Hui-i-lu* (Memoirs), Shanghai, 1949

[264] Hsü Sung-ling, *K'ang Jih ta-chan-chi* (Major campaigns in the Anti-Japanese war), Canton, 1947

[265] Huang Shao-hsiung, *Wu-shih hui-i* (Fifty years of my life), 2 vols., Shanghai, 1945

[266] P'an Yu-hsin, *Hsien-shih ti ya-yü* (The irony of the reality), Canton, 1948

[267] Rosinger, L. K., *China's Wartime Policies, 1937–1944*, Princeton, 1945

[268] Stilwell, J. W., *The Stilwell Papers*, ed. by T. H. White, London, 1949

[269] White, T. H. and Jacoby, A., *Thunder out of China*, London, 1947

[270] Woodhead, H. G. W., *A British Editor in China, 1902–1942* (unpublished, being the revision of the author's *Adventures in Far Eastern Journalism*, Tokyo, 1935)

[271] Wu Kang, *Chiu-chung-kuo t'ung-kuo p'eng-chang shih-liao* (Historical documents of the inflation in the old China), Shanghai, 1958

THE ANTI-JAPANESE BASES

[272] Boorman, H. L., 'Liu Shao-ch'i, a political profile', [6], April–June 1962

[273] Chao Ch'ao-kuo, *Yenan i-yüeh* (A month in Yenan), Nanking, 1946

[274] Ch'en Chün, *Hsin-ssu-chün man-chi* (About the New Fourth Army), Shanghai, revised ed. 1939. (Chapters 1 and 2 of this book are taken from J. Beldon and there is also an account of the activities of the Army by Hsiang Ying)

[275] Ch'en K'e-han, *The Shansi-Hopei-Chahar Border Region 1937–1938*, Chungking, 1940 (New China Information Committee, Bulletin, no. 8, microfilm)

[276] —— *The Shansi-Hopei-Honan Border Region, report for 1937–1939*, Chungking, 1940 (New China Information Committee, Bulletin, no. 15, microfilm)

[277] Chin Tung-p'ing, *Yenan Chien-wen-lu* (An eyewitness account of Yenan), Chungking, 1945

[278] Chou En-lai, Yeh Chien-ying, and others, *China's Resistance 1937–1939*, Chungking, 1940 (New China Information Committee, Bulletin, no. 12, microfilm)

*[279] Chung-kuo Hsien-tai Shih-liao Ts'ung-k'an, *K'ang-jih-chan-cheng shih-ch'i ti Chung-kuo jen-min chieh-fang-chün* (The Chinese PLA during the anti-Japanese war), Peking, 1953

[280] Chung-kuo Kung-ch'an-tang Tai-piao-t'uan, *Ssu-pa lieh-shih*

pei-nan chi-nien-ts'e (In memory of the martyrs who died in the accident of 8 April 1946), Chungking (?), 1946

[281] Compton, B., *Mao's China: Party Reform Documents, 1942–44*, Seattle, 1952

[282] Forman, H., *Report from Red China*, N.Y., 1945

[283] *Friction Aids Japan* (documents concerning instances of friction, 1939–40, New China Information Committee, Bulletin, no. 14, microfilm)

[284] Hsiang Ying, *I-nien-lai ti Hsin-ssu-chün* (The New Fourth Army during the past year), 1939

[285] Hsiang Ying, Yeh T'ing, and others, *The Eighth Route and New Fourth Armies*, Chungking, 1939 (New China Information Committee, Bulletin, no. 10, microfilm)

[286] *Ti-ssu-chün chi-shih*, Canton, 1949. (This in fact deals with the 4th Army of 1926–8)

[287] Hsü Yung-ying, *A Survey of Shensi-Kansu-Ninghsia Border Region*, N.Y., 1945

[288] Huang Yen-p'ei, *Yenan kuei-lai* (Returning from Yenan), Chungking, 1945

*[289] *K'ang-jih-chan-cheng shih-ch'i chieh-fang-ch'ü kai-k'uang* (The liberated areas during the anti-Japanese war), Peking, 1953

[290] Li T'ien-yu, *Shou chan P'inghsingkuan* (The first engagement at P'inghsingkuan), [247], III, 263–75

[291] Lin Tsu-han, *Annual Report of the Shensi-Kansu-Ninghsia Border Region Government for the year 1943*, Yenan, 1944

[292] Liu Po-ch'eng, 'Wo-men tsai T'aihangshan shang' (We are on the T'aihangshan), the *People's Daily*, 21 June 1962

[293] Payne, R., *Journey to Red China*, London, 1947

[294] P'eng Te-huai, *Unity and the Defence of North China*, Chungking, 1940 (New China Information Committee, Bulletin, no. 13, microfilm)

[295] Smedley, A., *Battle Hymn of China*, N.Y., 1943

[296] Stein, G., *The Challenge of Red China*, London, 1943

[297] Supreme National Defence Council, *Documents on the Problem of the Communist Party* (presented at the People's Political Council March 1941 and at the 4th Plenum of the Central Executive Committee of the Kuomintang, October 1943, Chungking, 1944, microfilm)

[298] Wales, N., *Inside Red China*, N.Y., 1939

NEGOTIATIONS AND CIVIL WAR

[299] Beldon, J., *China Shakes the World*, London, 1950

[300] Bodde, D., *Peking Diary*, a year of revolution, N.Y., 1949

[301] British Board of Trade, *Report of the United Kingdom Trade Mission to China, October–December 1946*, London, 1948

[302] Chang, Carsun, *The Third Force in China*, N.Y., 1952

*[303] Chang Chün-ying, *Ke-ming yü fan ke-ming ti chüeh-chan* (The decisive battles between the revolutionary and the counter-revolutionary), Peking, 1961

[304] Ch'en Po-ta, *Chung-kuo ching-chi ti kai-tsao* (Chinese economic reform), Hong Kong, 1949

[305] Ch'eng Yüeh-ch'ang, *Ch'ien-li yüeh-chin tu Juho* (Advance a thousand *li* and cross the Ju River), Hong Kong, 1961

*[306] *Chieh-fang chan-cheng hui-i-lu* (Recollections of the liberation war), ed. Hung-ch'i p'iao-p'iao she, Peking, 1961

[307] Chieh-fang Jih-pao (ed.) *Po Chiang Chieh-shih chi ch'i-t'a* (Refuting Chiang Kai-shek and other essays), Yenan, 1947 (?)

[308] Chung Hsi-tung, *Hu-k'ou pa-ya* (Pulling out the tiger's teeth), Hong Kong, 1961. (Being recollections of the civil war in 1946–49)

[309] *Chung-hua Jen-min Kung-ho-kuo k'ai-kuo wen-hsien* (Documents concerning the founding of the People's Republic of China), Hong Kong, 1949

[310] *Chung-kuo Kung-ch'an-tang yü t'u-ti ke-ming* (The CCP and land reform), Hong Kong, 1948 (?)

[311] Dedijer, V., *Tito Speaks*, London, 1953

[312] Forman, H., *Blunder in Asia*, N.Y., 1950

[313] Hsü Ti-hsin, *Chung-kuo ching-chi ti tao-lu* (The outlook of Chinese economy), Hong Kong, 1949

[314] —— *Lun Chung-kuo ching-chi ti pen-k'uei* (The collapse of the Chinese national economy), Hong Kong, 1947

*[315] Liao Kai-lung, *Hsin-chung-kuo shih tsen-yang tan-sheng ti* (How was new China born?), Shanghai, revised ed. 1952

[316] Liu Chien-hua and others, *Wuling Feng-yün* (The gathering clouds on the Wuling Mountains), Hong Kong, 1961

[317] Liu Chin, *Ch'uan-Kang i-shou ch'ien-hou* (The Szechwan-Sikang situation before and after the communist occupation), Hong Kong, 1956

*[318] Mao Tse-tung, *Ching-chi wen-t'i yü ts'ai-cheng wen-t'i* (Economic and financial problems), written in 1942, Hong Kong, 1949

[319] Mao Tse-tung and Jen Pi-shih, *Lun kung-shang-yeh cheng-ts'e* (On industrial and commercial policies), Hong Kong, 1949

[320] Mao Tse-tung and Liu Shao-ch'i, *T'u-kai cheng-tang tien-hsing ching-yen* (Instructive experiences of land and party reform), Hong Kong, 1948

[321] Pao Chih-hsien and others, *Hsiung-shih tu Ch'angchiang* (The Yangtze crossing), Hong Kong, 1961

[322] Shen Sung-fang, *1950 jen-min nien-chien* (People's yearbook 1950), Hong Kong, 1950

[323] Sprenkel, O. B. van der, Guillain, R., and Lindsay, M., *New China, three views*, London, 1950

*[324] Stuart, J. Leighton, *Fifty Years in China*, N.Y., 1954

[325] *Ti-san-tz'u kuo-nei ke-ming-chan-cheng ta-shih yüeh-piao* (A chronology of the third revolutionary civil war, from July 1945 to October 1949), Peking, 1961

[326] *T'ung-i-chan-hsien chu wen-t'i* (Problems of a united front), Hong Kong, 1948

[327] United Nations, Economic Commission for Asia and the Far East, *Economic Surveys of Asia and the Far East*, 1948 and 1949

Index